POLITICAL CORRECTNESS

DOES MORE

HARM

THAN GOOD

HOW TO
IDENTIFY, DEBUNK, AND DISMANTLE
DANGEROUS IDEAS

POLITICAL CORRECTNESS
DOES MORE
HARM
THAN GOOD

DOUGLAS KRUGER

Ambassador International
GREENVILLE, SOUTH CAROLINA & BELFAST, NORTHERN IRELAND
www.ambassador-international.com

"In a room where
people unanimously maintain
a conspiracy of silence,
one word of truth
sounds like a pistol shot."

—Czesław Miłosz

Why is it that among the far Left,

which has traditionally promoted itself as

the only true champion of civility, tolerance and fair play,

that we find those habits least practiced,

and even denounced?

—Stephen Hicks

We have replaced the divine right of kings

with the divine right of self-righteous groups.

—Newt Gingrich

One thing that everybody has begun to at least sense in recent years is that a
set of trip-wires have been laid across the culture.

—Douglas Murray

Envy was once considered to be one of the seven deadly sins before it became
one of the most admired virtues under its new name, "social justice."

—Thomas Sowell

Open your mouth for the speechless.

—Proverbs 31:8

Facts don't care about your feelings.

—Ben Shapiro

Political Correctness Does More Harm Than Good

How to Identify, Debunk, and Dismantle Dangerous Ideas
©2020 by Douglas Kruger
All rights reserved

ISBN: 978-1-64960-081-3
eISBN: 978-1-64960-092-9

AMBASSADOR INTERNATIONAL
Emerald House
411 University Ridge, Suite B14
Greenville, SC 29601, USA
www.ambassador-international.com

AMBASSADOR BOOKS
The Mount
2 Woodstock Link
Belfast, BT6 8DD, Northern Ireland, UK
www.ambassadormedia.co.uk

The colophon is a trademark of Ambassador, a Christian publishing company.

For the child who stands alone against the class,

resisting enticement to group-think:

You can fight giants and win, and it matters that you do.

Keep standing.

CONTENTS

PART I

HOW TO IDENTIFY POLITICALLY CORRECT IDEAS 15

PART II

HOW TO DISMANTLE AND DEBUNK POLITICALLY CORRECT IDEAS 135

CHAPTER 1

WALK TOWARD THE FIRE. 137

CHAPTER 2

KNOW THE HISTORY OF THEIR IDEAS: ROUSSEAU, KINSEY, ADORNO, PIKETTY, AND MARCUSE. 147

CHAPTER 3

BE ABLE TO DEFEND YOUR CULTURE. 167

The conservative looks about and finds things to love and preserve.

The progressive looks about and finds things to detest and change.

In the irony of the century, the progressive then accuses the conservative of being hateful.

—DK

PART I
HOW TO IDENTIFY POLITICALLY CORRECT IDEAS

YOU CAN HAVE POLITICAL CORRECT-NESS, OR YOU CAN HAVE TRUTH,

BUT YOU CAN'T HAVE BOTH.

The warriors of political correctness think of themselves in the category of the struggle between David and Goliath. Nothing can be further from the truth. They belong to the mainstream, having all instruments of power at their disposal. On their side are the courts, both national and international, the UN and its agencies, the European Union with all its institutions, countless media, universities, and public opinion. The illusion they cherish of being a brave minority heroically facing the whole world, false as it is, gives them nevertheless a strange sense of comfort: they feel absolutely safe, being equipped with the most powerful political tools in today's world but at the same time priding themselves on their courage and decency, which are more formidable the more awesome the image of the enemy becomes.–**Ryszard Legutko, *The Demon in Democracy***[1]

---

1   Ryszard Legutko, *The Demon in Democracy* (New York: Encounter Books, 2016).

IN THE BEGINNING, THERE WAS a bad idea. Sadly, no one squashed it.

It invariably begins with a liberal professor in the university's department of sociology. Next, you hear it on the news. Politicians repeat it because it sounds "inclusive," and before long, it has become the new normal. It is a "politically correct" idea, a new notion of "social justice," and it is one of the deadliest forms of thinking known to humanity. Its premises are always skewed; its thinking is consistently emotional; and its outcomes are invariably disastrous.

Still, that's not enough to stop it from spreading like wildfire. Soon enough, it seems as though everybody believes it. This is actually not true. The true believers, the zealots, are merely a very vocal minority, who aggressively regulate public thinking. Nevertheless, they hit a critical mass, and groupthink kicks in. Fearful people thought-police the herd's new guiding mantra.

Then it begins to gather elements of violence. Actual mobs of young men and women, masked and shouting, shut down debate through force, destroying first the college campuses and then the city streets. Astonishingly, the rule of law is suspended for them. Liberal mayors instruct their police forces to fall back and permit the rioting, for their cause is considered just by the progressive intelligentsia. They assault civilians, without consequence.

That is when the idea begins to collide with us: *with you and me.* Mothers, fathers, families, business owners—going about our lives. The new wave of ideology crashes over our unsuspecting worlds. Fail to tow the line, or even applaud the new cause right alongside the mob, and you will be labeled a bigot. They may even attempt to destroy your career. Yet something about it seems *off* to you.

From its smaller incarnations—such as when a biological male pretending to be a female enters a woman's wrestling match and cracks the skull of his competitor—to the large-scale manifestations, in which nations like Venezuela plunge from first-world prosperity to extreme poverty, all while chanting epithets about kindness and "the greater good"—the reasoning is clearly flawed.

The truth is an early casualty of political correctness. Did you know that Venezuela has made it illegal to report a baby starving to death in a state hospital on the grounds that it makes socialism look bad?

Pedophilia gets re-labeled "man-boy love." Nations protecting their own borders from invasion are called "oppressors." People who don't want their wealth stolen are termed "greedy" by the very people trying to steal it. All of this is presented as "enlightened," "progressive," and "liberated."

You're not quite certain how to articulate it, but there's a definite dishonesty to the new idea, an insidious dogma that seems, somehow, ugly.

Why, for starters, would a good idea need violent goons to enforce it? And why are we seemingly not allowed to debate the idea? Isn't debate at the very heart of the scientific method? And of democracy? And free speech? Don't we believe in science and democracy anymore? Did we actually agree to give up free speech? And when did the merit of this new idea become "settled," and by whom exactly?

There's more. The longer you mull over the concept itself, the more you can see that it is not universalizable: If everybody took it seriously and if it were taken to its logical end, the world would be much worse for it.

The idea might help one group. Actually, it generally *privileges* one group. But in doing so, it punishes another, and the PC police don't seem to know or care about that. Point it out, and they will argue that the disadvantaged group somehow "deserves" its comeuppance.

All the same, they insist that this new orthodoxy is the only way forward, and will demand your assent. Indeed, your assent alone is insufficient. They are not just asking for tolerance. That was the ruse by which they opened the door to public dialogue. Now they are demanding enthusiastic endorsement or, in its absence, accusing you of hate, of thought-crimes. You may speak out against the new orthodoxy only at your great peril.

Still, after their violent and all-too-personal hailstorms have passed, this much remains: It's plainly a bad idea.

So, now what?

If an idea is fundamentally wrong, then it *can* be challenged. And if you care for human welfare and if you respect truthfulness, then you *should* challenge it. And if enough of us stand up and challenge bad ideas, society discards them. This book shows you how to do that.

You will need three things:

1. Knowledge about what is precisely wrong with the idea and the ability to articulate it clearly,

2. Courage to speak up, at which point you will find that you were not alone in your reservations about the bad idea after all,

3. Understanding about what you are fighting *for*. It is not sufficient enough just to be opposed to bad ideas. You must be able to argue for their replacement with *better* ideas and also actively champion such replacement.

Losing arguments is not trivial. It can cost nations and lives.

In 1953, Polish writer, poet, and Nobel laureate Czesław Miłosz wrote a book called *The Captive Mind*. He was living in Poland, under the relentless tyranny of Communist Russia, and he wrote the book in secrecy and at great personal risk. He described one of his laments about his fellow intellectuals in the face of tyranny. They were, he said, completely unable to respond to the arguments put forward by tyrants.

As part of their efforts to conquer and culturally colonize eastern European nations for the Communist empire, Moscow would send representatives to a series of what we might call "town hall" meetings. This party representative would be highly trained in dialectic materialism, the philosophy underpinning Communism. Basically, he knew how to speak political correctness in Polish.

Milosz points out that no one, himself included, was able to counter their arguments. The town hall meetings invariably ended with the highly trained Russian agent dismantling every objection against Communism, one by one, and leaving the people baffled as to why they shouldn't simply submit to the "obviously superior" new system. The party representative explained that all this was simple science and merely the inevitable next step in history.

Both claims were patently untrue. But the people present could not articulate *why* they were not true.

Imagine not being able to adequately debate why Communism was a bad idea! And look at the outcome.

Yet that is precisely what happened. And although these nations were ultimately overpowered by military force (or "liberated" by military force, if you prefer Soviet terminology), the job of the conquerors was made infinitely easier when an entire culture could offer no valid objections to the new ideology. *By all means, conquer us. We see no reason why you shouldn't.*

Pause for Reflection. Can you currently defend your own culture? If a usurping force were aggressively fighting to dismantle it (which I will demonstrate to you is the case right now) would you know what values, practices, beliefs, and norms might require protecting? And could you successfully argue for the superiority of these things over an alternative? It is concerning to reflect on the thought that if most of us were in that town hall today, we might fare no better.

We *must* be able to argue against tyranny. When your thoughts, norms, morals, and behaviors are being imposed upon you by political correctness, that is tyranny. And in our modern case, just as in Poland, our submission does create power structures for those whose interests it serves.

It is equally possible today to surrender an entire culture—say, to the new norms of Islam. Political correctness aids Islam in this regard and aggressively attacks Western culture on its behalf.

We must also be able to explain why we *value* the things that such tyranny is attempting to replace. If we can't, tyranny wins. Cultures surrender and die. That's how history works.

And so, I intend to show you how the new ideological tyranny of political correctness, which has strong elements of the Marxism and dialectic materialism of Soviet Russia, presents itself in modern debates.

Objection: This all sounds very grand. But in reality, it's usually just about a transgender man who wants to become a woman. So what? How does that hurt *you*?

Response: The beneficiaries of political correctness are outliers in the sense that they are statistical minorities. Yet they are used as the means by which to destroy and replace institutions that apply to the majority. A few unusual cases become the norm by which majorities must live; and important laws, structures, and ideals must be destroyed in order to achieve this accommodation. My task will be to make it clear which important institutions are targeted for destruction and how badly things go wrong when they are successfully destroyed. This is not about merely "live and let live" for a small and vulnerable group. Instead, it is about destroying an entire society on behalf of a few violent agitators.

Political correctness is Marxism by stealth.

I will show you what the primary arguments are and where the shortfalls, errors in logic, fallacies of reasoning, and, sometimes, outright lies are to be found. Point them out, and you can easily win the argument. The community needn't leave the town hall baffled as to why it should even resist.

But more than just that, I intend to arm you for the *human* part of this debate. I contend that advocates of political correctness do not fight fairly. They will use emotional manipulation, fabrication, accusations of bigotry, mob justice, and mistruth. They will twist logic into forms even its own mother wouldn't recognize. They will blur words, and they will use a bait-and-switch technique with ideas. Above all, they will bully.

I want you to be prepared for that. If you are unprepared, it will work on you, and you will lose. If you are prepared, it will have no effect on you, and you will laugh it off, then go on to win the debate. More than just understanding their techniques, you must understand where they are coming from emotionally.

Finally, and perhaps most fascinatingly, I will argue that *who you are* is at least as important as the logical arguments that you employ. The identity of the champion of ideas is a surprisingly efficacious part of the battle for hearts and minds. A person with a good sense of humor, for example, will always be held to be more reasonable than a brittle and humorless radical.

Okay, but why bother? Can't we all just get along?

Let's begin by answering the simple question: What exactly is so very problematic about political correctness? Can we not afford to sit out this fight and just hope to get along with everyone we meet? Why wage war against it? Is it really so bad? The answer to that last question is *yes*.

I will demonstrate that in every instance where political correctness purports to help a demographic group—be it women, black people, transgenders, the poor—it invariably ends up harming this very group through its policies. It *always* does more harm than good. It promises peaceful pluralism but delivers rape gangs. It promises kindness toward the homeless or the drug-addicted but ends up vastly swelling their number. It hurts its own interest groups, *and* it hurts its host societies.

When carried out as prescribed, political correctness transforms entire nations. It does profound societal damage. History reveals that it can even be murderous.

Still, surely, "live and let live"?

That is a laudable idea. The problem, which is one of the chief failings of political correctness, is that it does not work both ways. That which is deemed a politically protected minority group always (and we shall demonstrate this claim, group by group) begins by asking for special protection from bullying, then ends up as the bully, begins by asking for respect for its own beliefs, then ends up disrespecting the beliefs of others.

Take the example of what might easily be viewed as the most peace-loving, protective, humanitarian group imaginable: vegans. The point of veganism is ideological. Vegetarianism by itself aims for health. Veganism shares that aim but also adds in the desire for nonviolence against all living things.

However, on January 30, 2018, *Sky News* ran a feature on the new, violent vegan activists. Newspaper reviewer and businesswoman Michelle Dewberry displayed a newspaper headline reading, "Farmers get death threats from 'violent' vegan activists" and said:

> Farmers are speaking to anti-terrorism police and asking, how do they manage this rising threat from these vegan activists . . . I don't mind vegans' food choices, that's your choice, you eat what you want, but when you start forcing your belief system on to somebody else, I think it's absolutely wrong. By all means campaign or focus on the treatment of the animals in the food chain by these farmers, that's not a problem, but for me, when you start resorting to violence, you've just lost the argument, I'm sorry.

This level of violence made headlines on an international news channel, and it proceeds from arguably the least violent, politically correct interest group. How much worse when the group is inherently proselytizing and believes that God has given them the mandate to crush competing ideas, using violence if necessary? Qur'an 8:39 says, "And fight them until there is no Fitnah (disbelief and polytheism: i.e. worshipping others besides Allah) and (until) the religion, all of it, is for Allah."[2]

---

2   Qur'an, Sahih International, Verse 8:39, English Translation, http://corpus.quran.com/translation.jsp?chapter=8&verse=39.

THE KINDLIEST KILLER AROUND

As we set the scene for our battle, let me ask you a question. It is a bit of a bleak one, but it is also important. Which single idea has led to more human death than any other in all of human history? As a species, what is our most murderous concept? What would you currently guess?

Did you say *religion*? That's a popular reflex answer. But it's also wrong—by a very large margin. Nevertheless, if that was your answer, you would be in good company. Secular thinkers like Richard Dawkins and Sam Harris have written bestselling books arguing this case. Harris called religion "the most potent source of human conflict, past and present."[3]

And yet, Planned Parenthood, an organization that performs abortions in the United States, has ended more human lives in the past six days alone than the entire Spanish Inquisition managed in 350 years. This puts religious violence into some degree of perspective.

In *Stealing from God*, Frank Turek points out that over a period of five hundred years, the Crusades, the Inquisition, and witch burnings all taken together were responsible for about two hundred thousand deaths.[4] Yet in a period of less than fifty years (one-tenth of that time), abortion has killed over sixty million in America alone since *Roe v. Wade*.[5]

Still, abortion is also not our deadliest idea. It, too, lags behind our greatest killer.

If we combine all deaths directly caused by religion from the founding of Christianity—including the Roman slaughter of Christians, the spread of Islam, the Aztec sacrifices, the Crusades, the Salem witch trials, and so on—and pooled them all together, the estimated total comes to between ten to twenty-five million.[6]

3   Sam Harris, *The End of Faith* (New York: W. W. Norton & Company, 2004).
4   Frank Turek, *Stealing From God* (Colorado Springs, NavPress Publishing Group, 2015).
5   "Americans Oppose Cloning Human Embryos for Research," National Right to Life. org, July 26, 2001, https://nrlc.org/uploads/factsheets/FS01AbortionintheUS.pdf.
6   Warren Kramer, "How many people have died because of religion?" Quora.com, November 26, 2016, https://www.quora.com/How-many-people-have-died-because-of-religion.

The international question-and-answer website Quora points out that higher estimates make the error of trying to include into this number wars that have been about resources, power, or political and border disputes. This error is perhaps understandable, as all through history, such wars have been waged by people who were "religious," which in the pre-Darwinian error was everyone. It further points out that only about seven percent of all wars in history were waged for religious reasons, accounting for some two percent of history's war deaths. Of those, half were Islamic.[7]

The one idea that outstrips religion as the greatest killer of human beings has a total death toll of over one hundred million. And this was accomplished in just the past one hundred years. In two thousand years, all religions combined killed only a fraction of this figure.

So, what is this deadly idea?

The answer, surprisingly and counter-intuitively, is "equality." Equality is the idea at the heart of political correctness. It is also the deadliest notion we have ever had. And the political Left continues to hold this idea as its highest value, and that is where it goes wrong on every issue.

Here is how it played out: Atheism began to become a prominent idea among intellectuals following Darwin's publication of *On the Origin of the Species* in 1859. Philosophers like Friederich Nietzsche were quick to point out an obvious problem with the so-called "death of God." The problem was how do we construct morals? How can we even tell what is right and wrong? This was a serious difficulty.

Under the Judeo-Christian tradition, right and wrong were obvious and absolute. There was a God, the Maker of all things, and He said that humans were made in His image. He directed, "Assuredly, I say to you, inasmuch as you did it to one of the least of these my brethren, you did it to Me" (Matt. 25:40). This was the beginning of the notion of intrinsic worth. A human is *like God* and, therefore, inherently valuable. Also *inviolable.*

---

7   Ibid.

Coupled with this was the directive, "Whatever you want men to do to you, do also to them" (Matt. 7:12). As a result of these pronouncements, violating a human being was self-evidently morally wrong. This kernel evolved over time into our modern, Western notion of human rights, which forms the foundation of our present-day judicial systems. It is the value system I defend and which I hope to equip you to defend.

But if there were no God, how could any moral or judicial system be constructed? Relative to what? *God?* They didn't believe there was one. The importance of man? Well, why is man important? Shouldn't we prioritize the planet over our mere species? Aren't we just a virus—a plague—after all? Where do we even begin to assign value?

Many Enlightenment thinkers—and, indeed, many scientists today— glibly believe that the answers to these riddles were self-evident and that human rights would have evolved logically and organically, absent Christian values. It is so obviously wrong to harm others that anyone would eventually arrive at a system similar to Judeo-Christian justice and mercy. It was the only inevitable conclusion.

But other thinkers—and, indeed, many more honest scientists and philosophers—point out that there is nothing whatsoever obvious or self-evident about these values. Indeed, in a universe with no God, it would seem much more self-evident that the natural laws of survival should apply, not moral notions of self-restraint.

For instance, if my family might survive and prosper as a result of killing your family, then wouldn't that be the logically "correct" thing to do? If not, why not? You're not intrinsically valuable, after all. You are merely a meaningless carbon-based obstacle to my good. Survival of the fittest—that was the first principle to be induced from godlessness. Moreover, it is noteworthy that human rights took root in the Judeo-Christian West alone and not in any other place or culture throughout all of human history.

No, justice and mercy are not self-evident societal values. Absent God, all things are relative, and everything is up for grabs. There is no "obvious" way of organizing a society. Karl Marx and his successors, like Lenin, attempted to solve this conundrum.

In a world without God, the only sensible foundation on which to build a society was proposed to be state-managed "equality." *If everyone is equal,* the reasoning essentially went, *then we could all just get along. Get rid of class differences. Get rid of wealth differences. Get rid of property differences.* In fact, get rid of all concepts of "difference." (Later, we will see how ideas of "difference" and "category" are profoundly important to the Judeo-Christian deity and, therefore, to the society that proceeded from this worldview). The state becomes the arbiter of right and wrong, which is viewed through the lens of conformity-to-sameness, and it enforces the realization of this status quo between its subjects.

Can you already see the problem?

It's the same problem that we will encounter in political correctness. The problem is this: If the ideal is for everybody to be the same, then everybody must be *made* to be the same. This requires a leveling of the population. Anyone who is not level—or the same—is an affront to the new morality and must either be leveled or disposed of. If you have more, it must be taken from you. If you are more, you must be reduced.

Disposing of such problematic subjects is not considered immoral. After all, there is no God to determine a moral right or wrong. The state determines right and wrong, which is premised on equality. And they assert that those who are different are in the wrong and must go, by execution if necessary, for there is no inherent worth in them.

In *The Communist Manifesto,* violent revolution was openly preached as the means to achieve this goal. Bloodshed was prescribed as necessary.

Historian of science Loren Graham points out that staunch Darwinians often describe Darwinian evolution and revolutionary political thought as being so intimately connected that they amount to the same thing.[8] It is note-worthy that Karl Marx himself corresponded with Charles Darwin, excited by how Darwin's theory seemed to lend credibility to his own.

Darwin's theory seemingly dismissed the spiritual and instead re-placed it with a universe that was "material only." Marx's theory attempted to do the same, replacing all morals, values, spirituality, and ideas of right and wrong with purely materialistic theories.[9] This change led unhesi-tatingly to state-mandated murder. Large groups of the population were problematic. They practiced "wrong-think," believing in ideas like God and the possibility of moral values. They believed in laws and rights. They had to go.

And then there was the material problem. Some people had more mate-rial gains than others, and they did not want to give their possessions to the state police. This, too, would have to be rectified.

Side Note: Do scientists today unanimously agree that evo-lution has disproven the existence of God? The answer is no. In fact, in studying DNA, evolutionary biologist Dr. Stephen C. Meyer became a professed theist, convinced that the evi-dence from encoded language and information systems within human cells argued for the presence of a God and could not possibly have arisen blindly.[10]

His research caused a number of leading scientists and phi-losophers to publicly renounce their atheism, too. Meyer's book *Signature in the Cell—DNA and the Evidence for Intelligent Design* explains the science and the seismic ruptures it created throughout the scientific community and even in the main-stream media in great detail.

---

8   D'Souza Dinesh, *The Big Lie: Exposing the Nazi Roots of the American Left* (Avon: Simon & Schuster, 2017).
9   Stephen C. Meyer, *Signature in the Cell* (San Francisco: HarperOne, 2009).
10   Meyer, Ibid.

Even *Scientific American* magazine published an article in 2019 titled "Atheism is Inconsistent with the Scientific Method, Prizewinning Physicist Says," in which theoretical physicist Marcelo Gleiser points out that atheism is not the correct scientific response for skeptics. Instead, agnosticism—the admission that we don't know—is a more honest and scientifically grounded response to the question of God.[11] This, too, was widely met with outrage. It was deemed politically incorrect. Nevertheless, this book does not attempt to proselytize. It is sufficient for our purposes to point out that the matter is not settled and that the validity of the ensuing belief systems emanating from the so-called "death of God" faces profound challenges from science. For now, back to the project of equality . . .

Who, precisely, might require leveling?

The list was substantial. For starters, anyone who practiced wrong-think. Political correctness was the measure of correct thinking, and anyone who opposed it was either re-educated, or, failing that, executed. Historically, the groups varied, but not by much.

First on the hit list, for obvious reasons, tends to be capitalists. This means anyone who owns or runs a business and anyone who is financially successful. They are arguably Enemy Number One. Their assets must be confiscated and redistributed among the masses. In this, do you hear echoes of modern movements targeting the wealthy? Occupy Wall Street and antagonistic talk about one percenters?

To justify this dislike of capitalists, it often proved useful to vilify them in racial terms. In Communist Russia (and in Nazi Germany), the bankers and moneylenders were often Jewish. Thus, it was easy to create a narrative

---

11   Lee Billings, "Atheism is Inconsistent with the Scientific Method, Prizewinning Physicist Says," Scientific American, March 2019.

about the "greedy Jew" and the "Jewish capitalist pigs," who were "stealing from the rest of us." Racial slurs against entrepreneurs helped to isolate and vilify them in these autocratic nations.

Similar tactics are used in nations like Britain and the United States today, when wealthy capitalists are classified as "racist, old, white men." The United States, in particular, has incredibly varied racial representation among its wealthy. We might mention its wealthiest television personality, Oprah, and its wealthiest female pop star, Rihanna, just in passing. And in my book, *Is Your Thinking Keeping You Poor?*, I demonstrate that the wealthiest people in nations like America actually out-give everyone else on a scale of charity that is extraordinary. Yet you would never know this if you listened to the PC narrative.

Authors like Thomas Piketty—with his highly flawed, yet, unfortunately, very successful book, *Capital in the Twenty-First Century*—have painted a dystopian picture of the evil and oppressive wealthy that makes for excellent sound bytes on the news and inspires fanatical hatred of the rich. We will explore just seven of his egregious errors when we look at how you can respond to charges leveled against free-market capitalism.

Next come free thinkers. If your goal is to create an easy-to-regulate sameness in which all humans are equal, then people with strong ideas pose a major obstacle. They become the "wrong kind of people," and they must be re-educated or disposed of. This includes writers, who might point out problems with the new ideal of equality; scientists, who can provide logically sound observations on why the new system will not work; Christians, whose belief systems are premised on moral right and wrong, rather than on equality and who are often doubly dangerous insofar as they might be willing to die for their ideals; and any form of non-compliant teacher, politician, or notoriety. For this reason, intellectuals are labeled "dissidents," and they are often the first group to face the firing squad when totalitarian regimes assume power.

In communist societies, the next under the hatchet would be anyone who didn't "work correctly"—farmers who refused to become part of collectives, people who hoarded their goods, those who wouldn't concede their intellectual property to the state.

Perhaps our final group is the nuclear family. We like to flatter ourselves into believing that ours is the first generation to espouse the "enlightened" idea that the traditional family represents a form of outdated male tyranny, or patriarchal oppression, and that we are now intellectual pioneers, operating in the service of a new and more liberated humanity when we go about dismantling this outdated ideal: "Dismantle the patriarchy!"

The Russian communists got there first. They knew that the definitive vehicle for transmission of values and ideals—ideals that might have proved strong enough to oppose their new worldview—was the family.

One of the first things Vladimir Lenin instituted after 1917 was de facto *no fault* divorce in order to facilitate the break-up of families. This was intentional. The strategic goal was to destroy the family as a unit of "the old order." *The* technique for progressive revolution is family break-up. (By contrast, *the* unit of the Western Judeo-Christian tradition is the strong and united family).

The family is the primary source of strength, nurturing, growth, education, and dissemination of values for each generation. We will see later how important family is in the transmission of good values and how much damage we do when we dismantle the institution. (By contrast, I view the gang as the unit of dissemination for criminality and destructive values).

The Russian communist regime actively targeted the nuclear family in order to weaken, and then re-form, society. Today, we in the West are volunteering ourselves for the same project, even though we have extensive research regarding how much harm we do to ourselves in the process.

The modern liberal playbook, like communism, follows the exact same formula. The following is from Saul Alinsky's modern progressive bible, *Rules for Radicals*, of which past-president Barack Obama and Hillary Clinton were self-professed fans:

The first step in community organization is community disorganization. The disruption of the present organization is the first step toward community organization. Present arrangements must be disorganized if they are to be displaced by new patterns that provide the opportunities and means for citizen participation. All change means disorganization of the old and organization of the new.[12]

In this manner, the Soviet Union put to death, or killed via repressive policies, no fewer than twenty million people.[13] That is not counting the millions who died of starvation in the ensuing struggle to force the idea of communism to work. The Chinese communist regime murdered an additional three million people, and killed a further forty-five million via starvation.[14] Other communist nations managed to push the ideology's total death toll over the one hundred million mark. As historian and author David Satter observes in the *Wall Street Journal*, "That makes communism the greatest catastrophe in human history."[15]

These staggering numbers represent real human individuals murdered in the service of a kindly ideal: equality. This system of equality openly labeled itself as socialism.

Side Note: The word *socialism* appears in *all* of the major murderous ideologies of the twentieth century, and not merely the communist ones.

---

12   Jeff Hedgpeth, *Rules for Radicals Defeated* (CreateSpace Independent Publishing Platform, 2012).
13   David Satter, "100 Years of Communism—and 100 Million Dead," WSJ.com, November 6, 2017, https://www.wsj.com/articles/100-years-of-communismand-100-million-dead-1510011810.
14   Ilya Somin, "Remembering the Biggest Mass Murder in the History of the World," Washington Post.com, August 3, 2016, https://www.washingtonpost.com/news/volokh-conspiracy/wp/2016/08/03/giving-historys-greatest-mass-murderer-his-due.
15   Satter, Ibid.

Many people are taken aback to learn that the word *Nazi* translates into "National Socialist." Nazism was a different flavor of socialism, preferencing racial theories of group-over-individual, rather than economic theories of group-over-individual. But it was socialism nonetheless. It did the same thing: denying the sanctity of the individual, elevating the importance of the group. This is *always* the recipe for genocide.

Author and former policy analyst in the Reagan White House Dinesh D'Souza asserts, "All the religions of the world put together have in three thousand years not managed to kill anywhere near the number of people killed in the name of atheism in the past few decades."[16] Atheism achieved this through communism, which was based on equality.

A COMPASSIONATE AND INCLUSIVE CANCER

From the beginning to the end of these state murder sprees, the citizenry were taught politically correct ideas about how all of this was in the service of the greater good. *Negate yourself. Act for the collective.* They were policed in their thought and speech and made to conform in every way. And the policy to which they were to conform was presented as kindness, inclusivity, and even as science. It was all so very progressive.

In many cases, both the citizens and the government officials genuinely believed that they were on the side of the public good and on the side of science. This is critically important to understand, as we face off against modern political correctness, which pulls the same trick.

These people used and disseminated politically correct ideas and shut down those who opposed those ideas in the firm belief that they were helping, not harming. They did not believe to be operating in the service of evil. Yet through them, great evil was accomplished. Political correctness was the mechanism that enabled the murder. *The greater good* was the rallying cry. The same applies today.

---

16   Mark A. Smith, *Secular Faith: How Culture Has Trumped Religion in American Politics* (Chicago: University of Chicago Press, 2015).

So, collectivist systems view individuals as means, as tools, and most importantly, as expendable for the cause. By contrast, we will argue for a view of the individual as an end in himself. We view the individual as having inalienable rights from birth. Collectivists consider an individual to be born *into* society, and society, therefore, to be their arbiter and the provider of their rights. By this latter measure, collectivist governments award themselves unlimited power. Our interest is in the sanctity and sovereignty of the individual and the limiting of state power.

Objection: You're just trying to turn political correctness and communism into the same thing. You're blurring categories to make modern political correctness look more evil.

Response: All collectivist systems (including communism and liberal democratic socialism) employ political correctness and always have.

We can clearly equate political correctness with communism because that is where it originated. In a scholarly analysis of the roots of political correctness, published in *The Journal of Social, Political, and Economic Studies*, Frank Ellis states: "But long before Marcuse and Derrida, and a host of other New Left and postmodernist writers were required reading on the campus, we find political correctness established as an ideological criterion of Marxism-Leninism. Official Soviet sources clearly show that the term was in use as early as 1921."[17]

The very term itself is a Soviet communist creation. To be politically correct is, by definition, to live up to a mode proposed by communist Russia. Moreover, the same precise points are made by Polish author Ryszard Legutko, who lived under communist tyranny and sees their techniques rising again in modern political correctness.

---

17   Frank Ellis, "Political Correctness and the Ideological Struggle: From Lenin and Mao to Marcuse and Foucault," *The Journal of Social, Political, and Economic Studies, Vol. 27 [4] Winter 2002*, https://search.proquest.com/openview/2b06da1bbc242863798d3772b f132cdd/1?pq-origsite=gscholar&cbl=22044.

Ryszard Legutko details the correlations in his book, *The Demon in Democracy: Totalitarian Temptations in Free Societies*, which opens with the following lines:

> This book is about the similarities between communism and liberal democracy. The idea that such similarities exist started germinating timidly in my mind back in the Seventies of the last century, when, for the first time I managed to get out of Communist Poland to travel to the so-called West. To my unpleasant surprise, I discovered that many of my friends who consciously classified themselves as devoted supporters of liberal democracy . . . displayed extraordinary meekness and empathy toward communism. I was unpleasantly surprised because it seemed to me that every liberal democrat's natural and almost visceral response to communism should be that of forthright condemnation. . . . A hypothesis came to my mind, that both attitudes—the communist and the liberal democratic, are linked by something more profound, some common principles and ideals.[18]

SWOT-ANALYSIS FOR A SPECIES

Business leaders conduct this exercise regularly. If the entire human race were to perform a SWOT-analysis, in order to discover our own **S**trengths, **W**eaknesses, **O**pportunities, and **T**hreats, we would determine two things under the Threats column:

- The single most dangerous living organism for our species is the mosquito. It kills around one million of us each year.
- The single most dangerous word for us is *equality*. It is an idea that is utterly deadly to us. It is the most dangerous word there is for human beings. Whenever you hear high-sounding talk of society first and the individual second, of "the greater good," at the expense of "just a few," you are dealing with the seeds of mass murder.

---

18 Ryszard Legutko, *The Demon in Democracy: Totalitarian Temptations in Free Societies* (New York City: Encounter Books, 2016).

And yet in spite of its appalling track record, the concept of equality nevertheless requires some explaining. We think of it as inherently good. Surely, "equal" remains a laudable ideal. What is the alternative? *Un*equal? Surely that would be bad!

DIFFERENT TYPES OF EQUALITY

Using the word *equality* is a slippery slope, and we must pay close attention to how it is used in debate. Context is everything. In one sense, equality is very important. In the alternative sense, it is a killer. When arguing with the politically correct, you must be able to point out the difference between desirable equality and murderous equality. If you don't know the difference, it will be possible to trip you up in a debate using bait-and-switch.

The first kind of equality is Equality Before the Law.

This is the idea that regardless of your skin color, background, parentage, history, ethnicity, or affiliations, you should be treated equally by the legal system. You have rights, just as every other person has rights. This idea proceeds from the Judeo-Christian notion of inherent human value, coupled with the Greek tradition of democracy. Over time, these two schools of thought have been refined in the West, giving rise to our modern democratic and judicial systems. This type of equality is good, important, and necessary, and it has an excellent track record of success. Humans flourish where it is present.

The second kind of equality is Equality of Outcomes.

The second form of equality is popularly called "social justice." Social justice is incompatible with legal equality and with legal justice. You can have one, or you can have the other, but you can't have both. Equality of outcomes is the idea that everyone should live equally and have the same.

In its simplest incarnation, it is the kiddy's race in which everybody wins. In its worst incarnation, it is the communist autocracy in which everyone shares equally in the yields.

Calling for the right to live equally only makes sense in nations where some citizens do not enjoy equal *legal* rights. For instance, in certain Islamic states and some African nations, women still do not have the right to vote. In such places, a call for social justice actually makes sense, insofar as it is a call for equal legal rights for a certain group. Efforts of this nature warrant our support.

In a nation where all citizens already enjoy equal legal rights, however, social justice must necessarily fight for something else. That something else is the right to live equally. To *live* equally, people must all *have* equally. To *have* equally, the population must be leveled, precisely as it was in socialist/communist nations.

It is the same as saying: If ten people compete in a race, *everybody* must win. The fact that some may do more preparation, or work harder on the day, or learn more technique through study is irrelevant. Their outcome must be the same, or, per the philosophy of the social justice warrior, an "injustice" has occurred.

As such, social justice is actually a call for injustice. It is a call for leveling. Leveling always requires theft, murder, hindrance, redistribution, unfair assignment, or displacement of some form. At the very least, it requires nullification of merit. It is a direct cheat against those who work harder, or make greater sacrifices, or invest more.

Consider: If one man has more and one man has less, then social justice demands one of a few options:

- A part of what the first man has must be confiscated and given to the second man. This is theft, and it violates the first man's legal rights. Social justice advocates would say that this is fair because they think societally, rather than in terms of inviolable individual rights. They advocate the good of the masses at the expense of a few. Through this loophole, great evil re-enters society;
- The first man must face punitive measures when he succeeds in order to slow him down, so that the second man may catch up. This, again,

infringes on the first man's rights. It is, nevertheless, done quite regularly under Left-leaning governments. Its inevitable result is to disincentivize the successful, who often leave for the greener pastures of meritocratic societies, taking their capacities to generate and to innovate along with them.

- The second man is given a sort of "hand-up" in the form of government assistance. This option is the least problematic and can even be a laudable idea, if done correctly. There is little downside to the state assisting, say, new business owners. The potential for injustice reappears, however, when the state does this *at the expense* of the first man, for instance, by forcing him to give away a part of his business. Once again, this transgresses the first man's rights and constitutes legal gangsterism. Nevertheless, it is also fairly common in Left-leaning nations, where it is positioned as "the kindly thing to do." We must point out that it is not kindness when it is done by force of law and transgresses the sovereignty of the individual.

The best book on this topic: *Equal Is Unfair: America's Misguided Fight Against Income Inequality* by Don Watkins and Yaron Brook.

GROUP FIRST, NOT INDIVIDUAL FIRST

So, we see that political correctness is thinking on a societal level, on a group level, at the expense of the rights and sanctity of the individual. Equality *before the law* equals real justice. Equality *of outcome* necessarily leads to legal injustice. When debating with advocates of political correctness, make sure that you clearly define *justice* and *equality*. These words sound self-evidently good, but there are good and bad versions of them.

Debate Tip: Use this same technique against the progressive. Ask: "Do you believe in justice?" In so doing, lay the groundwork for agreement with your premises. Then properly define justice as being vested in the rights of the individual.

UNDERSTANDING SOME OF THE TERMINOLOGY: LIBERALS AND CLASSICAL LIBERALS

Objection: But even they call themselves *liberals*. Liberal means *free*. It means the opposite of tyranny, the opposite of ideas like communism. How could you possibly say that such people, or their language or ideas, are working in the service of tyranny?

Response: There is a difference between a classical liberal and the progressive liberal of today. The classical liberal was defined by the guiding mantra: "I may not agree with what you say, but I will fight to the death for your right to say it." The modern progressive liberal generally no longer defends this idea. By contrast, the guiding mantra might more accurately be phrased as: "That's offensive, and you're not allowed to say it." These two ideas are diametrically opposed.

If you define yourself as a classical liberal, you have my deep respect. But the term has been hijacked by a new guard, and it is not what we are dealing with here. Today, the self-identified liberal is a different animal.

There is a difference between liberalism and democracy. Liberalism and democracy actually make terrible bedfellows.

The bottom line is, liberalism takes a fairly simplistic view of history. It is anti-tyranny. In and of itself, that sounds like a good thing, and sometimes it is. However, for the same reasons, it is also anti-democratic. What if we, as a majority, democratically opt to live by Christian ideals, under our liberal freedom? Initially, liberalism will argue that you can do so privately, but not as a state. And then, having gained power and asserted itself as the state, it will ultimately move to say that you can no longer live so privately, insofar as your values are not in the interests of the greater good. This is the end result of extreme and simplistic anti-tyrannical, liberal policies. In various forms, this argument is put forward in *Why Liberalism Failed* and *The Demon in Democracy*.

A note for the Christian: Liberalism and Christianity also make terrible bedfellows. Both are ostensibly concerned with freedom, but each defines freedom in diametrically opposite terms.

Liberalism defines freedom as "the ability to indulge in anything you want without consequence." Christianity defines freedom as "the release from evil, from sin, from error, and from their terrible consequences for yourself and for humanity."

We might represent this as Christianity championing freedom *from* darkness, while liberalism champions freedom *to* darkness. Same open door, different direction of travel.

If Fascism ever comes to America, it will come in the name of liberalism.—Ronald Reagan

Where are we now?

Let us sum up what we have learned about political correctness so far. It begins with atheism. This creates a crisis of control for governments and authorities and a crisis of meaning for people. To establish control, authorities must assert a new system of values, so as to create legitimacy for themselves. To have people comply with their laws, they must teach the population to speak, think, and believe in certain ways. They must also discredit and depose the *old* ways. This is the genesis of political correctness, which is the acceptable way of speaking that aids a powerful state.

In terms of lived experience, political correctness starts out as a nice set of social rules seemingly aimed at helping everyone to get along. It ends in totalitarian tyranny. It starts with the guiding assertion: "To be part of an inclusive and peaceful society, you must diminish your individual importance and think about the group as a whole. Just obey this little rule. After all, it's for the greater good, and aren't you a decent enough person to care about the greater good?" It then progresses to prescribing to you what you may and may not say, then what you may and may not think or believe. It ends with governments getting rid of "the wrong kind of people," who believe all the "wrong kinds of things," all in the service of this greater good.

Tyrannies need political correctness in order to create their versions of peaceful, harmonious societies. These societies are defined by the absence of resistance. They are pointedly not defined by moral excellence. Moral excellence is, in fact, a hindrance to a society based on equality. So, the goal is to create conformity and sameness and to have the populations themselves police these ideas among their own.

Objection: Hang on. It sounds like the problem with these totalitarian regimes is a desire for sameness. But politically correct people like diversity.

Response: The diversity that politically correct advocates talk about generally has to do with skin color or disability. These are the most superficial kinds of diversity imaginable. The kind of diversity that actually matters is diversity of thought. Political correctness does not tolerate this. In fact, political correctness is about squashing diversity of thought in favor of conformity to the current trend.

Try this test: If diversity were genuinely welcomed among the politically correct, then a black woman who is a traditional, conservative Christian, and who does not believe that she is a victim, and who speaks positively about capitalism and personal accountability should be welcomed among their ranks.

Test this idea for yourself in the real world. You will quickly see that such a woman is marginalized and called a traitor to her race and to the cause. She will not be welcomed because she is the wrong kind of diverse.

We saw this in practice in the real world in 2018, when conservative women were informed that they should not join in the U.S. Women's March because of their pro-life beliefs. It was a women's march. Were they not women? Actually, they were the "wrong kind of women." How can anyone be a *wrong kind of woman* in a diverse and inclusive society?

True diversity should be able to incorporate different thinking; but under political correctness, it cannot. No, among the politically correct, diversity is merely a ruse-word.

Debate Tip: Advocates of socialism consistently use a simple trick when proposing their worldview. They put forward the *textbook* version of socialism, not the real-world version, then compare their kindly-sounding theory to the *real-world* version of capitalism. Defuse this dishonesty by pointing out you must compare *like* with *like*. There are many historically documented cases of socialism implemented as a system. All have led to catastrophic real-world failure. You do not get to hold up textbook socialism as representative.

Debate Tip: Karl Marx called his socialist system *science*. Yet every one of his predictions failed. Cite this fact. Marx predicted the failure and collapse of capitalist societies. He predicted mass starvation under capitalism. He predicted worldwide revolutions by the proletariat. He predicted that socialist governments would initially have to be tyrannical, but would then dissipate over time, as people learned to manage themselves, ultimately fading away. By contrast, every socialist system on earth has tended to greater control and tyranny over time. The science of socialism fails in every one of its predictions. It is, therefore, not science. Moreover, it is not in any other sense true.

FROM "THE DEATH OF GOD" TO TODAY

Political correctness has taken many guises over the past two centuries. It has constantly morphed and changed. Yet its core essence has remained unaltered, right from its genesis. Political correctness is just the language of progressive politics.

It begins with atheism and the search for a new kind of meaning, outside of the old paradigm, in which humanity tried to live up to the ideals of God. It then morphs into the social propaganda used to try and shape societies in a post-God era. That's all political correctness is. It is the prevailing and trendy language, and the prevailing and trendy ideas, derived from academia and then spread to the rest of us, in the service of the latest progressive fad. And there have been many fads, each more disastrous than the last.

Let us take a quick tour of the main ones.

FADS AND TRENDS IN PROGRESSIVE THINKING

U.S. PROGRESSIVES, SLAVERY, EUGENICS, AND NAZISM

Hot on the heels of Darwinism and the subsequent crisis of faith, genetics became the great and leading hope for progressive thinkers of the late twentieth and early twenty-first century. Perhaps meaningfulness might now be found within the DNA. And maybe some people were better than other people on demonstrable, scientific grounds, based on their genetic inheritance. Perhaps we could form a ruling elite, an oligarchy of benevolent experts, who would then guide humanity toward utopia!

It is no accident that the two great ideological catastrophes of the previous century, Nazism and communism—together responsible for a total death toll running into nine figures—arose at more or less the same point in history. This is not coincidental. It is because both proceed from the same crisis of meaning following the "death of God."

One school of thought believed that egalitarian social philosophy might solve the problem. It evolved into communism. The other believed that science would provide the answers. It evolved into theories of race. These theories led first to eugenics in the United States, and then later, to Nazism in Germany.

The liberal Democratic party of the United States, which today still identifies itself as the "progressive" party, has a history that few are aware of. Given how vitriolically they denounce racism today, one might assume that the human-rights crimes of slavery and eugenics were Republican, conservative crimes. They were not. They were squarely liberal-progressive crimes.

In a tour-de-force of facts, names, dates, and places, political and historical commentator Dinesh D'Souza shows how the Republican party—primarily conservative and Christian in its make-up—fought tooth-and-nail against both slavery and eugenics and, as a result, against the progressive Democrats.

In *The Big Lie—Exposing the Nazi Roots of the American Left,* D'Souza points out some fascinating and under-appreciated facts about the differences between conservative Republicans and liberal-progressive Democrats concerning slavery and eugenics, both of which were justified on progressive theories of racial superiority.

Here are some key observations:

> At the time of the Emancipation Proclamation, which legally freed predominantly black slaves in the United States, not a single Republican leader owned a slave. Not even *one.*

> In 1860, the year before the Civil War, all four million slaves were owned by Democrats. Every one of them. This fact caused outrage on the Left when D'Souza's book was published. Since then, despite spirited attempts, detractors have not found a single counter-example. The facts stand uncontested. One is inclined to say that we could actually stop there, having made our key point that progressivism was overwhelmingly responsible for deplorable human rights violations, while the conservative Christian community was not.

> In his own writings, Adolf Hitler referenced the U.S. Democratic party's eugenics program with great admiration. The program was designed to achieve the displacement, removal, and eradication of Native American Indians (and led to the infamous "Trail of Tears" in America).

> Hitler adopted and implemented this policy in his own campaigns, using it on Russians, Poles, and Slavs. Today, it is surprising to hear the U.S. Democratic party talking about potential reparations for descendants of black slaves. It is surprising because their own party has never taken accountability for their crimes and even goes so far as to blame the opposition for their own evils,

speaking as though "everyone knows" that these crimes were committed by conservative Christian Republicans. They were not.

The Nazi Nuremberg laws were directly modeled on the segregation and anti-miscegenation laws implemented in the Democratic South. Nazi eugenicists openly wrote about their adoption of these policies from U.S. Democrats.

Eugenics and social Darwinism were more prevalent in progressive America in the early twentieth century than they were in Germany. D'Souza observes, "Margaret Sanger (the founder of Planned Parenthood) and her fellow progressive eugenicists didn't get their ideas about killing off genetic undesirables, or preventing their births, from the German Nazis. The Nazis got them from the American progressives."[19]

D'Souza goes on from his observations about slavery and eugenics to link progressive thought squarely with the advent and uprise of fascism and Nazism.

Here are some of the key points which emerge from his detailing of the history:

- Benito Mussolini and Adolf Hitler admired the Democratic party, and the fascists and National Socialists identified themselves, by their own words and founding documents, with the progressive Left.
- Leftist philosophers have intentionally (if covertly) promoted and justified Nazi tactics and the fascist ideal of the all-powerful centralized state.
- The anti-free speech, anti-capitalist, anti-religious liberty, pro-violence, pro-abortion Democratic party is a national socialist (Nazi) party in everything but name.

D'Souza comes to the conclusion that the progressives in the U.S. have committed one of the biggest acts of malicious transference—the act of blaming the victim for the crime—in human history.

---

19   Dinesh, Ibid.

Today, they portray themselves as the party of emancipation, equality, and civil rights. When in fact, they were the party of slavery, eugenics, Jim Crow, and the Ku Klux Klan (the domestic terrorist arm of the Democratic party). They vehemently opposed the Civil Rights movement, but now they take credit for it. The brazenness of this lie, once you examine the history, is breathtaking.

Another good book on this topic is: *Liberal Fascism: The Secret History of the American Left, From Mussolini to the Politics of Change* by Jonah Goldberg.

Debate Tip: Modern talk of restitution? Perhaps it's not a bad idea. The Democratic party *should*, indeed, take accountability for its racial crimes. The same does not apply to their opposition, who paid with the lives of their sons to end slavery.

Objection: If America is so good, why didn't the founding fathers just ban slavery from the outset? For that matter, why doesn't God just ban slavery in the Bible? The fact that neither does so in their foundational documents shows them both to be deeply racist.

Response: Actually, both the founding fathers and the Bible *did* ban slavery. They both faced the same formidable problem; they both solved it in the same ingenious way; and both are to be lauded for their success.

Let's begin with the Bible. Consider the problem from God's perspective. You select a group of people to be Your chosen representatives. They are responsible for spreading ethical monotheism. But they live in ancient Mesopotamia, where slavery is the norm. If You simply and unilaterally tell them, "Here's your new religion and all its rules. It explicitly states that you may not have slaves," these people will utterly reject the religion right from the start. Your rules prohibiting slavery will never have the chance to take effect. Nevertheless, the Bible cleverly introduces the *conditions* by which slavery is ultimately rendered impossible for anyone who follows biblical teachings.

As far back as the Noahide laws in Genesis, which pre-date even the Ten Commandments, God provides the instruction that no one is permitted to take, or to steal, another person. The penalty for taking another against their will is death. This already precludes the possibility of obtaining slaves.

Next, it was mandated that existing slaves also celebrate Sabbath and be permitted to rest on that day. Why is that significant? Because the entire Sabbath tradition follows this line of thinking:

God made the universe.

On the seventh day, God rested.

You are made in the image of God.

To acknowledge this fact, *you, too,* will rest on the seventh day.

And by the way, so will your slaves.

What is the logical inference? It is this: Your slaves are *also* made in the image of God.

You can almost picture two ancient Jews haggling over this troublesome Torah assertion: "But if they, too, are made in the image of God, then we are enslaving someone who bears God's image. That's a problem." Yes. Yes, it was.

And the problem was later compounded by the teachings of Jesus, who not only further embedded the "made in the image of God" narrative, but added anti-slavery sentiments in the form of utterances like, "He has anointed Me . . . To proclaim liberty to *the* captives" (Luke 4:18), followed by behavioral prompts about how we should be like Him.

What a brilliant way of ensuring that a group of people accepts the new religion, while simultaneously making it untenable to continue to practice slavery. Taken cumulatively, this is why Judeo-Christianity has been the number one opponent of organized slavery throughout history.

The American founding fathers faced a similar dilemma, and they solved it in the same way. Recall that they had just concluded an eight-year-long bloody war with the mightiest empire on Earth. They had won, but they were significantly battered; and their founding documents were written even as they attempted to rebuild.

The founding fathers succeeded in having all thirteen original states agree to joining the Union (much like getting the Jews to accept ethical monotheism). Had they forbade slavery right at the outset and attempted to enshrine this prohibition in their founding documents, many of the states would simply never have joined. Result? Cause lost.

Instead, they wisely permitted all states to join the Union, regardless of their slavery-status, *and also* inserted some clauses that would ultimately make slavery untenable, such as:

> We hold these truths to be self-evident, that all men are created equal, that they are endowed by their creator with certain un-alienable rights, that among these are life, liberty and the pursuit of happiness. That to secure these rights, Governments are insti-tuted among men, deriving their just powers from the consent of the governed.

Read those words carefully. They cannot accommodate slavery, and they cannot tolerate its continuity. They ultimately must—and, indeed, they ulti-mately did—lead to abolition.

So, both the Bible and the U.S. founding fathers faced the same dynamic concerning slavery. Both solved it in the same sneaky, brilliant, and, ulti-mately, effective way.

The average person's reaction to these ideas? "I'd never thought of it that way." And that represents a failure of the West to teach its own values to its children. Perhaps that is what happens when political correctness insists on removing dead, white males from its curriculum, in order to teach third world, feminist, or homosexual history and literature instead.

THE FRANKFURT SCHOOL—FATHER OF MODERN POLITICAL CORRECTNESS

Our next development took place on U.S. soil, too. As economic Marxism proved itself to be a complete and embarrassing failure in every country in which it was tried, radical Marxists pulled a new trick. They transformed the basic theory from one pertaining to economic theory alone ("All history is the history of class struggle.") into one more broadly about cultural theory ("All history is the history of *demographic* struggle.").

It is the same thing, just repackaged to focus less overtly on systems of work and money and more on systems of human interaction. Replace "evil capitalists" with "evil power structures," and keep fighting for revolution.

The leading proponent of this switch in tracks for Marxism was the Frankfurt School. This group of radical German intellectuals has much to answer for. When Karl Marx originally described his vision of the masses rising up, overthrowing their oppressors, and establishing global communism, he genuinely believed that his theory was inevitable—that it was simply the next logical progression of events. To him, it was a *prediction*.

By contrast, the Frankfurt School was different. They saw that Marx's prediction was not coming to fruition and decided to force it to happen. They opted to actively and aggressively change Western U.S. culture in order to impose the Marxism that they wanted. Their goal, in fact, was to destroy Western culture from within, in order to create the necessary vacuum that is the precondition for a communist utopia.

So, while the "far distant" origins of political correctness are the teaming up of atheism and Marxism, we can say that the most immediate cause of our modern-day version of political correctness—its founding father in the West—is the Frankfurt School. They were responsible for transforming classical Marxism into a social movement and then setting it loose in the West. They are the creators and originators of the brand of toxic political correctness that we know today.

The essential mission of the Frankfurt School was to create the following dynamic. See if any of this looks familiar to you:

- Polarize people along tribal lines
- Teach different groups that Western civilization is oppressive
- Encourage awareness of oppression to create alienation among these new groups
- See that alliances are made among groups united by their grievances
- Encourage alienation to turn into anger and violence toward "the system"
- Tear down Western civilization
- Replace Western civilization in a socialist revolution.

In the simplest possible terms, political correctness, as conceived by the Frankfurt School, had one overarching goal: break society. Replace it with Marxism. Everything it did, and everything it still does, is geared toward that end. And so, this is what we are fighting today.

English Philosopher Sir Roger Scruton observed, "That is a dangerous attitude . . . Surely that is part of what erupts in all these strange academic disciplines like Gender Studies, which simply have as their goal the undermining of the existing order, without anything positive to put in its place. . . . Those academic studies recruit people all the time from this fund of isolation."[20]

Jordan Peterson responds to Scruton's observation by adding, "That's the cult-like element of them, because they do, I would say, to some degree, prey on people whose interpersonal relationships have been irreparably damaged."[21]

---

20   Jordan B. Peterson, "Sir Roger Scruton / Dr. Jordan Peterson: Apprehending the Transcendent," YouTube video, 1:32:35, December 14, 2018, https://www.youtube.com/watch?v=XvbtKAYdcZY.

21   Ibid.

What currently holds up Western society? Broadly, the answers are standards, morals, science, democracy, and truth. We might also add beauty to the list if we concede that post-modern art appears to be based on ugliness, shock, and provocation, in contrast to aesthetic classical Western art, which reverences the sacred.

The Frankfurt School introduced the tools of destruction for all of these Western standards. It introduced critical theory to academia. Misleadingly labeled, this is not an actual theory. The theory is just to criticize. In other words, critical theory's job is to continually attack everything until it breaks. And with that, welcome to modern political correctness: To achieve Marxism, criticize everything until it falls down. If your first line of attack doesn't work, you don't apologize and back away. You simply switch to a different line of attack. And keep right on attacking.

Progressives used this technique in academia, and they use this technique in their politics. Here is an example: Early Marxists judged the success of societies based on whether or not they meet the *needs* of their citizens. "Needs met" was the criterion. They forecast, based on what they called "science," that communist societies would meet these needs, while capitalist societies would not. When the opposite happened, they had a problem. How can you attack capitalism when it is meeting, and exceeding, the conditions for success that you set yourself?

So, they changed the conditions. "Needs met" had to go. In its place, they now substituted inequality. Sure, the needs of the people in the West are being met, but they are being met *unequally.* And based on this revised new standard, they renewed their attack and have kept it up ever since.

Once again, this is why it is important not only to be able to unravel the specific arguments in response to political correctness, but also to proactively champion our own culture and values. Their arguments change and morph, but their attack doesn't. Proactively promoting our values is the way to prevail.

Force them to defend the untenable.

Herein, however, lies one very interesting weakness of political correctness. It doesn't propose a coherent alternative. Because it merely aims to destroy, it renders itself inconsistent and, therefore, vulnerable. This creates the conditions for our response, which might play out like this:

"Capitalism is evil!"

> Response: Compared to what? Your non-existent utopian daydream, which *is* perfect, insofar as it doesn't exist? Explain your superior alternative to me, and show me where it has worked better than capitalism.

In another example, they might say, "You are Islamophobic!" (Notice that this statement does not support what they are *for*. Instead, as all critical theory does, it only asserts what they are *against*. This is useful to know.) The solution is to force them to be *for* something, which they will generally find indefensible. Don't allow them to simply call you Islamophobic. Instead, make them defend Islam, which they are already doing, but underhandedly and dishonestly.

It plays out like this:

"You are Islamophobic!"

> Response: Okay, so you are stating that you are an advocate for Islam. You're on its side. You approve of its tenets, practices, and beliefs. You are willing and prepared to champion and defend its doctrines as good ideas.
>
> If their response is no, then ask them why not and charge them with Islamophobia. If their response is yes, progress to: "I have some questions for you regarding the beliefs you are defending."

Critical theory is most effective for the social justice warrior, and against you, when you respond to it on its own terms. Don't. Instead, force the attacker to openly and honestly defend what he is already dishonestly and only tacitly defending.

And so, if the entire project of political correctness might be summarized in one paragraph, this is it, defined in light of the goals of the Frankfurt School:

If it is Judeo-Christian, if it is traditional, if it is Western, it must be labeled as oppressive and it must be destroyed. If it is beautiful, if it is true, if it has standards, it must be abolished, all in the service of Marxist ideals, all at the hands of the so-called disenfranchised, all of whom are taught to be angry at what they are persuaded is their "oppression." Push until it breaks, at any cost, using any tactic.

Here is a practical example: In 2019, U.S. liberal Democratic politician Saira Rao tweeted, "America hates poor people, Black people, brown people, gay people, trans people, Muslim people, Jewish people, disabled people. There are too many to count."[22]

The formula is disgusting, yet so simple. She's saying that monolithic America is a unified place of hate. Hence, it is the villain. If you are on the victims list, America hates *you*. *You* are the victim. And I've made my list as big as possible for recruiting purposes. We should all band together to overthrow it. If you're not on the victims list, you are an evil oppressor. The best you can do to escape this conundrum is to become a self-flagellating, America-hating social justice warrior who betrays his own and fights "on our side."

That is how modern political correctness carries out the Frankfurt School technique, in service of turning Western societies into Marxist ones. America is a particular target, given its global effect on culture.

Let's select just one demographic out of Rao's grouping: America hates *disabled people.* Seriously?! How utterly absurd. But remember, truth is not the point here. Victimization and attacking the Old Order—*that* is the point.

---

22 Saira Rao, Twitter Post, August 9, 2019, 7:58 PM, https://twitter.com/sairasameer-arao/status/1159977167847075847.

Again, we see why it is important not only to point out what is factually incorrect about politically correct arguments, but also to fight proactively *for* that which it attempts to pull down. One could successfully nitpick holes in every politically correct argument yet still lose an entire culture, such as America, to its relentlessly critiquing force. Finding the flaws in their arguments is only half the job. Defending and propagating a valuable civilization is the balance.

Premised on the goals of the Frankfurt School, there have been many additional contributors to the radical project of breaking Western society. Saul Alinsky is notable for his seminal work, *Rules for Radicals,* which never openly identifies itself as a communist handbook, but very clearly is. Notably, Hillary Clinton based her thesis on this work, and Barack Obama was a devotee of his teachings—a point he makes clear in his autobiographical *Dreams From My Father.*

POSTMODERNISM

If there exists a philosophy of the Left, it would have to be postmodernism. The postmodernist school of thought began to develop two centuries ago, ushered in by the work of Immanuel Kant, who wasn't actually aiming to achieve this end. He was trying to save faith from the attack of reason but ended up ostensibly proving that there was no connection between reason and the objective world.

The gist of postmodernism, which gained great sway in academic circles after World War II, was this: No interpretation should be privileged above any other. There are no subjective facts, no "true" science, no universal principles of any order, and certainly, no transcendent notions of morals or beauty. Only opinions, perspectives, and subjective experiences exist. Every idea is not true in itself; it is just a mask for the idea lying beneath it, and the masks all serve to hide power interests. Hence, all things are inherently ugly and selfish at their base. Understanding this viewpoint is key to understanding political correctness.

Postmodernism is contra-science and contra-rationality. It is *feelings*-based. It is also *identity*-based. It is about tribal narratives over objective truth. It, therefore, divides people into their "felt identities." And then it freezes and isolates them within those identities, as though it were impossible for each identity to ever relate to, or communicate with, any other identity, or for anyone to ever become anything more than merely a representative of their demographic grouping: *You are a victimized black; you are an oppressive white,* and so forth.

Interestingly, great art and profound literature are a terrible threat to this view. Take the example of a moving novel. It places the reader in the viewpoints of a diverse set of characters—good, evil, and indifferent—bridging gaps and helping us to better know one another. Postmodernism can't have this. It *wants* isolated individuals. It *wants* warring tribes. When art and beauty elevate humanity to the transcendent, this poses a significant threat to postmodernism's bid to hold us in meaningless debasement. That is why it matters to teach our children to appreciate beauty.

My own father, for example, introduced me to the music from the soundtrack to *Ben-Hur* when I was very young. That one act may have done more for my own sense of morality than any other act of parenting. It caused me to yearn for something higher, and that is a good path on which to set ensuing generations.

The philosophical school of postmodernism, by contrast, is both ugly by intention and self-professedly radical in nature. It is less interested in answering questions about truth or logic than it is in social agitation. It has no interest in beauty or transcendence. It is a thug and a street fighter, and it spits on romance.

In the world of art, it plumbs the depths by, for example, inviting viewers to place a goldfish in a blender and turn the blender on, in the name of exploring the meaninglessness of life.[23] More recently, it has

---

23   Clemens Bomsdorf, "Goldfish in a Blender? Marco Evaristti Calls it Art," *WSJ.com,* *August 28, 2013,* https://blogs.wsj.com/speakeasy/2013/08/28/marco-evaristti-and-his-goldfish-are-still-making-waves.

started to incorporate themes of children and sex, which I will not dignify by detailing.

In philosophy, it is relativistic, but every bit as ugly. A representative argument made by a modern postmodernist might look like this:

- Science does not give us truth. It's just another tool in the hands of privileged white males, being used to uphold their capitalist interests and repress black people.
- The law is not fair. It is a biased construct, a tool of manipulation used by the ruling Plutocrats to protect and uphold their interests at the expensive of the poor and disenfranchised, who it oppresses and holds down in perpetuity.
- Marriage is a fundamentally oppressive institution. It represents a purely parasitic and predatory relationship, in which the female is exploited by the male in perpetuity and by enforceable contract. Dissolution of the patriarchy begins with the dissolution of this archaic moral anchor to our species.

If the language of postmodernism sounds vaguely soviet, that's because it is. It shares the common traditions of meaninglessness, Marxism, and mass-movements, privileged over scientific certainty, rationalism, and individuality. It is the language of breaking down, not the language of building up. It is destruction-oriented, not life-oriented.

Notice also that there is zero concept of personal accountability represented here. An individual who falls afoul of, say, the law, is blindly presumed to be innocent, targeted only because of class warfare, and not because they made a conscious choice to walk into a convenience store and point a gun in another person's face. Marriage, too, is a crime with a victim, and never a negotiated path traveled jointly.

To the postmodernist, all things are subjective and ultimately devolve into games of power based on identity. Ultimately, all things are ugly and meaningless. Postmodernism is, in the most fundamental sense, anti-life.

This leads to three important outcomes:

1. Total relativism

My truth, your truth, his truth, her truth. But no *objective* truth. Everything is merely a construct, to be negotiated or broken, including law, science, mathematics, literature, tradition, religion—everything. They are all perceived as mere "masks for power."

One interesting real-world outcome of this is the progressive idea that the U.S. Constitution should be a living (read *negotiable*) document. It should be noted that a contract that is negotiable after the fact is fairly meaningless. If a party can change the terms and conditions at will, the contract never held any weight to begin with. It is precisely the upholding of agreed-upon principles that give a contract its rigidity and veracity. An eternally negotiable contract may as well not even exist. That, I believe, is rather the point in their efforts toward this end.

2. Group and class interests over individuality

Once again, we see a philosophy that prioritizes the group, or the society, over the individual. If there is no truth, then we are all just warring interest groups, tribes at clash, and so we must band together and fight the others! Once again, we have the necessary conditions for a toxic society at best, but serious injustice and tyranny at worst.

3. The celebration of ugliness and degeneracy

There is no such thing as love. Only masks. Behind every mask is self-serving greed. Idealism, self-sacrifice, transcendent truth, objective beauty—all are lies. Our only recourse is to admit our lies and then wallow in our debasement with honesty and authenticity. In reality, though, even a single, small light in the darkness defeats this argument. A poem that touches the soul is enough to destroy it.

How to Argue Against Post-Modernism

Much of the rest of this book constitutes responses to specific postmodern arguments expressed in politically correct language, as we attempt to wrest meaning, logic, and the potential for progress back from the clutches of their gaping, nihilistic void. Nevertheless, for the philosophically-minded, here are four brief responses to postmodernism itself:

1. Characterize the entire movement for what it is, then dismiss it wholesale on the grounds of its own absurdity: "So your school of thought spent two centuries coming to the conclusion that we can't know anything? You're fired."

2. Postmodern theory rests on the philosophy of Immanuel Kant, whose work effectively detached truth from objectivity with a complex set of arguments. Key to these arguments is the idea that our senses represent subjective reasoning machines. Kant essentially concludes that because we cannot access the external thing in itself, but rather, only an internal representation of it in our own minds that we, therefore, cannot know objective reality. Under Kant, reason and the real world have nothing in common and cannot know one another.[24] [25]

The perversity of this idea is that it blames the very apparatus of perception for the notion that we cannot perceive. It accuses our organs of consciousness of being obstacles to consciousness. How bizarre. And how mean-spirited.

Our perception may be imperfect, but we certainly can perceive. And just because our brain has an identity and must receive ideas in mediated form does not deny that which it perceives. Implied in Kant's argument is the nonsensical idea that only an identity-*less*, formless knower can truly know. This is also absurd and, therefore, dismissible.

Much that proceeds after this point becomes a case of highly advanced but really fairly idiotic semantics. If you don't agree with Kant's initial

---

24   Immanual Kant, *The Metaphysics of Morals* (Cambridge: Cambridge University Press, 1797).
25   Kant, *Critique of Pure Reason* (Cambridge: Cambridge University Press, 1781).

argument, you need not proceed down the darkened labyrinthine path on which philosophers and epistemologists spent the next two centuries torturing themselves. Just say, "No thanks," and walk the other way. You are allowed to do that, and frankly, you'll be better for it. A two hundred year-long game of pinball might actually have been more fruitful.

3. As Professor Jordan Peterson points out, the postmodernist's initial claim is true: "There is an almost infinite number of possible interpretations."[26] But their secondary claim is false: "And that means there is no viable, single truth."

Peterson points out that evolution puts that idea to bed. Evolution mercilessly kills everything that doesn't singularly work. The end.

Peterson extends this argument on a social level. As living beings, he points out, we have to *cooperate* as well as *compete* with others. And not only a single time. Often, we have to work with the same individual many times.[27]

This fact limits the scope of what is viable. We cannot just continually cheat and apply bad or unworkable answers. This limiting of the scope has been the project of Western thought, philosophy, law, and cultural interaction for a few thousand years. It has been extremely well-refined. The systems work. The postmodernist argument that all is merely self-interested warfare is, therefore, false (and cruel in its assignment of bad motives to everyone and everything).

4. In *Stealing from God*, Frank Turek brilliantly dismantles claims that there is "no singular truth" by forcing advocates to face their own terms.[28] It plays out like this:

Assertion: "There is no single truth."

Response: Is that true?

Assertion: "But all truth changes."

---

26 Ideacity, "Jordan Peterson – Political Correctness and Postmodernism, YouTube Post, 27:51, September 12, 2017, https://www.youtube.com/watch?v=f5rUPatnXSE.
27 Ibid.
28 Frank Turke, *Stealing From God* (Colorado Springs: NavPress Publishing Group, 2015).

Response: Does that truth change?

Assertion: "Well, all truth depends on your perspective."

Response: Does that truth depend on your perspective?

Finally, after disarming every one of these arguments on its own terms, Turek recommends returning to the content of their original thesis or proposal and asking them to qualify how their own point can meet the conditions of truth, given that they believe there are none:

> If you feel you have successfully proven that there is no singular truth, can we conclude that your original point is therefore only *a* truth, which might be completely wrong according to changes and perspectives? For instance, your point was true five minutes ago, but not now, though it may be true again four minutes from now? And it might be true for you, as well as for 41 per cent [sic] of the audience here today, but it is not true for me or for the remaining 59 per cent [sic]? Though it might be later?[29]

These are merely four arguments against postmodernism. A fifth might be: "Create, share, and teach *beauty*," which is arguably the single greatest threat to postmodernism.

Sir Roger Scruton argues that the best way to affirmatively teach our culture is to say to children, "Here, this is something that I have loved. See it for yourself." As opposed to postmodernism's approach, a curriculum of scorn, which teaches only how to deconstruct, to "strip naked and thrash." In order for us to keep the light alive, we must teach the love of the thing. To destroy the light, arm them only with picks.[30]

The rest of this book is essentially the argument that Western systems of values are the most viable and, in many cases, the demonstrably *only* *true* conclusions.

---

29 Ibid.
30 Jordan B. Peterson, "Sir Roger Scruton / Dr. Jordan B. Peterson: Apprehending the Transcendent," YouTube Post, 1:32:35, December 14, 2018, https://www.youtube.com/watch?v=XvbtKAYdcZY.

The best book on this topic: *Explaining Postmodernism:*
Skepticism and Socialism from Rousseau to Foucault by Stephen
R.C. Hicks.

IDENTITY POLITICS AND GENDER THEORY

So, the postmodernist project rejects universal meaning and divides us into warring factions. Some factions have power (and are, thus, characterized as bad). Others are portrayed as having less power (and are, therefore, oppressed). The oppressed are as close to "good" as postmodernism can concede. (Here again, we see an exploitable contradiction. So *why* are *they* good? Isn't everything meaningless?)

This sets the stage—and constitutes the necessary conditions—for modern identity politics, as seriously taught by straight-faced academics today—professors who are genuinely not joking about these ideas.

Objection: If postmodernist ideas lead to total relativism, then shouldn't postmodernists be represented across the political spectrum? And shouldn't postmodernists be okay with *any* belief system whatsoever?

Response: Correct. However, as Stephen Hicks observes in *Explaining Postmodernism*, "Postmodernists are 'monolithically far Left-wing,'" and "hostile to dissent and debate," and "the most likely to engage in *ad hominem* arguments and name-calling," and "the most likely to enact 'politically correct' authoritarian measures," and "the most likely to use anger and rage as argumentative tactics."[31]

From this partisanship, we see that the system is fundamentally dishonest. It does not arrive at the "anything is valid" outcome it recommends. Instead, it follows the formula: invalidate everything, then uphold Leftist PC standards by means of violence. If it were truly honest, it would not display

---

31 Stephen Hicks, *Explaining Postmodernism: Skepticism and Socialism from Rousseau to Foucault* (Scholargy Publishing, 2004).

any need to perpetuate itself but would conclude that any outcomes were fine. Yet it aggressively fights for ideology. Why?

In his lectures on the subject, Professor Jordan Peterson generally expresses it this way:

> The fundamental claim of postmodernism is something like an infinite number of interpretations, and no canonical, overarching narrative. The problem with that is, with no narrative, and no value structure that's overarching or canonical, how are you going to orient yourself in the world? Postmodernists have no answer to that. So, what happens is they default to this loose egalitarian Marxism.

> If they were concerned with coherence, that would be a problem, but since they're not concerned with coherence, it doesn't seem to be a problem. But the force that's driving the activism is mostly the Marxism . . . like an intellectual gloss to hide the fact that a discredited economic theory is being used to fuel an educational movement, and to produce activists.[32]

FOUCAULT TRANSLATES THIS MESS INTO THE MODERN ACADEMIC FRAMEWORK.

Okay, so we're lost and meaningless. Let us now base our entire educational system upon that edifice and teach it to our children, shall we? Enter the academics.

Who is the most cited author in the humanities today? The answer is Michel Foucault. Foucault took the end results of this postmodernist mess and translated them into the foundations for the modern humanities. His guiding principle was essentially, "Knowledge is merely an expression of social power. Therefore, we *should* play the politics game. While you're at it, be a good sport and play it on behalf of the traditionally disempowered."

---

32   Ideacity, "Jordan Peterson – Political Correctness and Postmodernism," YouTube Post, 27:51, September 12, 2017, https://www.youtube.com/watch?v=f5rUPatnXSE.

Think about that guiding principle for a second. If there is no objective truth, and we are urged to fight political fights on behalf of the traditionally disempowered, then here is what *must* happen:

Imagine two groups in contest. One group is morally and legally right. Their claim is true; their cause is legitimate. However, they are *traditionally empowered*. The other group is outright criminal. They are morally and legally wrong. They may even be terrorists. By the academic standards set by Foucault, these biased and socially constituted facts don't matter. They don't even feature. There is no objective right and wrong. There is only narrative. If the evildoers are traditionally disempowered, he advises that *they* should prevail.

Does this take your breath away? Welcome to the academic foundations of political correctness being taught to your children today!

It also leads directly into modern identity politics. Theory derived from Foucault asserts that all relationships are based on power and oppression and that they always represent a zero-sum game. So, for instance, a man and woman are not in a partnership. They are at war. And if he gains anything from the relationship, then it must necessarily be at a cost to her. And rich nations are rich *because* poor nations are poor. There is only a hostile relationship here (which, of course, ignores the billions in aid sent to these countries as somehow irrelevant).

Understanding just this much will help you to understand a great deal about Leftist thought-processes. All is war between groups, and someone who is winning must be doing so at the expense of the other, who must be losing.

But there *are* such things as mutually beneficial relationships, in which no one is used. Both good human relationships and growing market economies represent positive-sum games. A rising standard of living, all by itself, disproves Foucault's catch-all theories. To point out these examples is to dismiss Foucault's great error.

English philosopher Sir Roger Scruton mentions that there is something mentally lazy about arriving at the "zero-sum relationships" conclusion and that it is "not a view that successful people have."[33]

ZERO-SUM WRIT LARGE

The rich are rich because the poor are poor. Here is the same argument writ large: The rich nations are rich because the poor nations are poor. Here is how we should respond to that allegation: If that is true, then here is the problem you are required to solve. Why are the nations least touched by the first world empires the poorest on Earth? And why are some previously colonized nations wealthier than them? And why are some previously colonized nations extremely wealthy?

Before we progress on to the warped fruits of these social justice seeds—that all is war between groups—let's ask a question just out of interest: What *else* did Foucault believe and teach?

His monstrosities of twisted reasoning are the stuff of legend. For our purposes, here is just one more of his questionable ideas, worth knowing so that we can cite it back to the Left:

When France explored the notion of lowering the age of consent (from fifteen, which many Leftist intellectuals found to be too high), Foucault was quoted in an interview as saying, "To assume that a child is incapable of explaining what happened and was incapable of giving his consent are two abuses that are intolerable, quite unacceptable."[34]

Foucault was arguing that it was abuse *not* to let children and under-age minors have sex with adults. This is the leading luminary and most cited thinker in progressive sociology textbooks today and the man whose

33 Jordan B. Peterson, "Sir Roger Scruton/Dr. Jordan B. Peterson: Apprehending the Transcendent," YouTube video, 1:32:35, December 14, 2018, https://www.youtube.com/watch?v=XvbtKAYdcZY.

34 Marie Doezema, "France, Where Age of Consent is Up for Debate," The Atlantic.com, March 10, 2018, https://www.theatlantic.com/international/archive/2018/03/frances-existential-crisis-over-sexual-harassment-laws/550700.

reasoning underpins much of modern academia. Of all the minds teaching your children how to live and think, Foucault is at the base. He is thought of as the godfather of gender theory itself. I feel that that Mafioso-sounding term *godfather* is rather apt. Never has the phrase "meet your maker" rung more ominously. The nature and quality of thinking only gets worse, and significantly uglier, when we get to characters like Herbert Marcuse and John Money.

Today we are given a wash of weird ideas from the humanities departments, based on thinkers of this caliber, most of whom are relying on Foucault's thinking. Their ideas are a blend of the bitter and the bizarre: Gender is a social construct; capitalism and science are evil tools of the exploitative white oppressor; free speech is violence; the Bible is hate-speech; heteronormative couples (a mother and father) raising their children according to their biological gender are transphobic. Everything about the West is wrong and evil and must go. Constant rage, constant revolution, zero reverence for what has been achieved in our history.

In response to this, I am often reminded of the ringing words of King Aragon in J.R.R. Tolkien's fictional *The Return of the King*, charging, "*Stand, Men of the West!*"[35] Daily, I feel that this sentiment grows in importance.

In the U.S. today, schools are currently being pressured to accept LGBTQ history into their curricula, even as the Pledge of Allegiance is deemed offensive. Similar patterns of attack are being enacted in Western nations around the world. To admit Foucault is to poison that tree that has so long sustained us. Best the West learn to stand—and to fight—quickly!

WHERE TO NEXT?

That very brief history brings us up to today. Where will it all go tomorrow? While speculation on this topic will inevitably be derided as "wild conspiracy theories" by those on the Left, there are at least three next frontiers

---

35   J.R.R. Tolkien, *The Return of the King* (Sydney: George Allen & Unwin, 1955).

that are already knocking at our doors: social credit scores, pedophilia, and censoring of conservative speech.

Social credit scores are a lived reality in China. Cameras monitor behavior down to a micro-level, and individuals can lose social credits for wrong behaviors. The results of this can be catastrophic. A Chinese person may lose their job, their right to travel, even permission to do something as simple as buying a bus ticket. In this manner, an undesirable can be rendered effectively inactive, a ghost. A citizen practicing wrong-think can be made to disappear.

It's subtler in the West, but it is still being promulgated. Companies already ask employees to sign codes of conduct forbidding them from practicing political speech on social media. This is a direct contravention of citizens' rights in most Western nations, but it still happens. Companies may even fire people for tweets, views, politics, and all manner of things that should be the preserve of free agents in a liberal democracy. Increasingly, the very concept of free speech is under attack, and those who defend it are recast as acting from hate.

Then there are the liberals who are trying to personally enact such tyrannical programs all by themselves. Like Debra Messing. In 2019, the *Will & Grace* star made a public call for Trump supporters to be outed. And then, Debra? What should happen to these people then?

Catchy Slogans That Promote Tyranny

Have you ever heard this little gem? We are also increasingly told by the Left that "the personal is political." I would like you to pay close attention to this malicious trick and to call it out when you hear it. This seemingly innocuous little phrase changes the dynamics, making your most intimate thoughts, speech, and beliefs public property (a return to group-over-individual and also a denial of property rights) and, therefore, fair game for attack.

Your first response to this phrase should be: "I utterly reject that. It's communist. We live in a democracy."

If you must explain further (which you are not obliged to do), it goes something like this: "Just by citing those magic politically correct words, you get unfettered access to my individual rights? My freedoms? My individual liberties? You can tyrannize me and deny me my human rights—to think, to have a conscience, to speak freely—because *my personal world* equals *your political world* and that grants you access? The answer is no."

Free speech and right-to-dissent are the last bastions.

Right-to-dissent matters greatly, which is why free speech and freedom of conscience matter greatly. They are necessarily the first things to go in authoritarian regimes. Why free speech is even under debate in the so-called free West is a question we should all be asking, loudly and continuously, with pressure placed upon those championing its removal. This battlefront matters above all. Without it securely in place, we cannot even discuss the rest.

Try this Experiment: Ask a young person, particularly a university student, whether it is okay to ban, forbid, or censor speech that hurts the feelings of others. A surprising number of them will agree. Given the importance of right-to-dissent as a bulwark against tyranny, this is a worrying trend.

THE NORMALIZATION AND MAINSTREAMING OF PEDOPHILIA

The second immediate frontier is the logical extension of the gay rights' "Love is love" argument. If all love is equal and if men can sleep with men, then what is inherently wrong about a grown man having sex with a prepubescent boy?

This bastion is under aggressive attack, led primarily by groups like the North American Man/Boy Love Association (NAMBLA), a pedophilia and pederasty advocacy group. It is coming into popular culture, and it is coming in a hurry. It partly informs my motives for writing this book. My personal moral system cannot sanction a world in which pedophilia is normalized and openly practiced without consequence to the perpetrators of what I hold to be child abuse.

As for the future beyond that? If the goal is to invert Judeo-Christian moral and societal norms and if no rationality or science may be admitted to stem the tide, then we may safely prognosticate a varied and colorful catalogue of horrors. Pedophilia may well be just the beginning. The question "where does it all end?" is fairly meaningless in the face of man's capacity to perpetually dream up new and ever more creative atrocities in a universe without laws or meaning.

CENSORING OF CONSERVATIVE VOICES BY LEFTIST TECH COMPANIES

Google does it; YouTube does it; Twitter does it. They all do it. As I write this, Left-leaning YouTube is attempting to censor over two hundred videos by educational conservative site PragerU (whom I highly recommend following).

This is merely *today's* example and will likely be resolved one way or the other by the time you read this. If you are following this issue, there appears to be a new story of this nature on a near-daily basis. This particular issue represents a hot and active war. It is also, perhaps, *the* war.

Practical Debate Tip: From this quick overview of the fads and trends in progressive thinking, we see that the value systems of political correctness constantly change. Changing value systems necessarily implies contradictions. A person who must continually alter their beliefs must also necessarily and repeatedly contradict themselves. Loquacious social justice warriors can rarely resist expressing their outrage in public forums like social media; and with even a small degree of research, you can easily point out their contradictory ideas, thus challenging their relativistic underpinnings. Five quick examples include:

- "Gender is a social construct!" and also "Some men are just born with female brains." So, which is it?
- "Your right to own a gun is not more important than the lives of innocent children!" and also "How dare you infringe on a woman's right to have an abortion?"
- "Women are equal to men" and also "Islam is equal to Western society."
- "Pedophile priests! How dare the Catholic church allow these predators to get anywhere near children? They should know that these monsters will abuse their power!" and also "The Boy Scouts is a bigoted, deeply prejudiced organization! How dare they not allow openly homosexual men to take young boys camping alone in the woods?!"
- "You're not allowed to judge others, you misogynist, racist bigot!" (Progressives would use the Marcuse "inclusion through exclusion" argument to justify this one. We will dismantle that fallacy shortly).

What do we learn from all of these fads?

We have covered the idea that these fads all proceed from atheism, into relativism, and then attempt to recover from meaninglessness by prescribing new norms.

In each case, they attempt to provide a "replacement morality." That morality might be as seemingly innocuous as foodism, or Earthism. It rarely matters what the replacement is, so long as it is not the original. Continual revolution against the original order is the point. Outside of that, anything goes.

PC always tries to replace "inside-out meritoriousness" with "outside-in prescription."

The traditional Western view asserts that all good societies begin with the excellence of the individual and the stability of the family and then proceed outward. Political correctness goes in the opposite direction. It assumes that good societies are imposed from the outside by sets of rules and systems of governance. The Western tradition is about individuals with excellent internal morals. This is held to result in good societies, which inherently have minimal need for tyrannical rules.

The Progressive tradition is about social engineering—new rules, new norms, new compulsions, and new fads and flags to hoist and salute. The desired result is reformed and compliant societies, held in check by large systems of rules.

In *Antifragile*, statistician and logician Nassim Taleb argues that societies are, in many ways, like our immune systems. They actually require stressors and challenges in order to develop and to become stronger or, as he phrases it, to become "anti-fragile" from the inside out. Complex systems, he argues, need inside-out development in order to learn, adapt, and grow. Just as spending a month in bed leads to atrophy of muscles and joints and minds, much of our top-down world does precisely this, prescribing and determining ideas that keep everyone emotionally safe yet, consequently, unable to develop into fully functioning adults, an insult to our anti-fragility systems. We humans are "competence-adaptive systems, which require input and bumps of life to learn and grow. Absent that, we atrophy. This is worse, not better.[36]

So, one is a system of internal standards. It is nurtured and grown in the pursuit of goodness and self-development. The other is a system of external standards. It is imposed by a government and by its thought-police. That, in no small part, is why you feel a sense of uneasiness about each new politically correct idea. At the heart of it, that is what is wrong with the whole enterprise, in any of its manifestations. If you have been raised to begin with moral goodness, and then work outwards, political correctness will necessarily sit badly for you.

Objection: But look at the beautiful, peaceful, prosperous countries today that are extremely liberal. Look at Canada. Look at Sweden.

---

36   Nassim Nicholas Taleb, *Antifragile: Things That Gain from Disorder* (New York: Random House, 2012).

Response: Those nations were not built on politically correct principles. They were built on Judeo-Christian and free-market capitalist principles. That is what made them successful in the first place. Today, their laws and social structures are under attack, but they nevertheless still reflect Judeo-Christian underpinnings. Where they are rejecting these standards, they invite violent terrorism, rises in social crimes such as rape (Sweden recently became one of the rape capitals of the world), increased drug abuse, and family breakdown, among other ills. Insofar as these nations worked, they were Western. Today, they continue to run on that momentum. But they are tearing at their own foundations, and the violent results are beginning to show.

Where are the battle lines drawn today?

The goals of political correctness have not changed. They remain an attempt to find meaningfulness and to organize society in a post-God era. Their means of achieving this are largely Marxist, which is to say, they are about leveling and equalizing people. Under political correctness, no one system of values may be seen as superior to any other. Destroying the old value system is key to ushering in the new value system.

Today, grievances have been transferred from "the working class" to groups like immigrants, gays, women, and racial demographics. Postmodernism ensures that all beliefs, all approaches, all trends, and all fads must be positioned as equally valid. But it also does so dishonestly, preferencing the Left and its particular interest groups and attacking the Right. As such, a person who says, "I believe in yoga and unicorns" must be viewed as holding a worldview equal to the person who says, "I believe in science." A moral system based on the wishy-washy idea, "I'm spiritual but not religious" (which is the same as saying, "I speak, but not any particular language") must be viewed as equally valid to the entire Judeo-Christian tradition and its three thousand years of moral innovations, practice, study, and refinement. So, equalizing and leveling are the goals. Discrediting and discarding the old systems and creating revolutions are the means. The mantra is, essentially, "Anything but the old system."

We see the practical mechanics and thought-policing of this double standard in U.S. schools, where it is okay—and sometimes even compulsory—for children to dress up as Muslims and recite parts of the Qur'an, but the ACLU immediately and aggressively attacks even the slightest reference to the Judeo-Christian God.

And here are the battlefronts.

TWENTY-ONE CURRENT IDEOLOGICAL BATTLEFRONTS IN THE WAR FOR OUR CULTURE

1. "Police are bad; criminals are the noble victims. Christians are bad; the world is oppressed by their irrational superstitious practices. Terrorists are good; they are the understandable oppressed. Sexual deviance is liberation. Abortion is the empowerment of women." Pick an old-world value. Everything must be reversed.

2. "That man is a woman because he thinks he is." Postmodernism claims that anything can be anything. There are no valid points of reference, no real boundaries, no true definitions. All is relative. All is opinion, and all opinion is true. Science, by contrast, demands categories. Interestingly, so does God. We will get to that.

3. "That may be *your* truth, but this is *my* truth." In reality, truth must be singular, or it fails to meet its own definition. Anything outside that scope falls under a different category. It is called "opinion." And opinions can be factually wrong, when compared to verifiable truth.

4. "There is no good and bad. There's only power and privilege." It is no longer about who is qualitatively moral or immoral. All humanity must be re-classified according to whether they have power or privilege. The only thing that may be considered morally bad is privilege. The only people who are morally good are those who are oppressed. Hence, it no longer matters whether a superior force is in the right, legally or morally. It only matters that they are a superior force, and by that measure, they become deemed evil. This tactic is most commonly applied to denigrate wealthy white society. It is also often used against the nation of Israel.

5. "Gender is relative. You decide which gender you are." In 2019, bowing to pressure from social activists, the World Health Organization declassified gender dysphoria as a mental disorder. This was not based on any change in the science. It was a concession to the weight of public pressure and political correctness. We will examine how profoundly this move, based on feelings over facts, harms real people and especially confused children.

6. "What matters is that I'm offended." The promotion of subjective feelings to a position of validity, even primacy, is contra-science, contra-logic, and contra-Western standards going all the way back to the ancient Greeks. However, it makes for a strategically useful slipknot for progressives when facts fail. If feelings are sufficient, then any argument can be won by appeals to imaginary kindness or against imaginary oppression.

An excellent example of imaginary oppression is the assertion of "invisible racism" or "systemic racism." "You simple folk can't detect it. But we liberal elites can, and we will tell you how to re-order your life and your nation in order to avoid being guilty of it." In both cases, advocates may plead the reality of oppression based on subjective feelings, absent any evidence, and without having to point to *where* in a system such oppression actually resides. This argument can also be used to defend a bad policy. "Our facts may be wrong, but our 'greater truth' is not."

7. "Words are violence." Related to the elevation of facts-over-feeling (in fact, *dependent* on it), the idea that feelings must be prioritized leads to an inevitable next step: Emotionally hurtful words and ideas (which can be so broadly defined as to be absolutely anything) must be forbidden by proscription.

These are the practical mechanics of modern censorship in progressive societies. This is how thought-policing begins and how the removal of freedom of conscience is justified. It's as though there are new landmines to be avoided in conversation each day. It is introduced under the ruse of kindness. Absent free speech, there can be no scientific principle. There can also be no standards, for nothing may be debated. Absent free speech, we can simply never arrive at truth. However, by progressive standards, that is precisely the goal. The very idea of truth must be negated, made impossible.

8. "Sex is okay with anybody, with anything, at any time, #loveislove." There is no surer way to destroy families, and thus undermine the old moral order, than to promote sex without boundaries and without consequences. It is also the easiest and most successful strategy for destroying societies because humans have powerful sex drives. A healthy and moderate person may never feel the urge to cheat at gambling or to murder another person. But our sexual urges are hallmarks of good health, and they are so strong that they can be overwhelming. Hence, corrupting them to a purpose is relatively easy.

We will examine the profound and far-reaching consequences of societal destruction through free love many times over. In brief, the inevitable results have been fatherless families, which turn out to be the number one determinant of all forms of crime and moral decay, industrial-level upticks in abortion numbers, decreases in the male sense of accountability, and the total fracture of traditional units of moral transmission. Ironically, de-sanctification of sex is also responsible for *lower* levels of sexual satisfaction, not higher levels. Even as it destroys, the trap fails to deliver what it so enticingly promises. Most damningly, we will see that the "normalcy" of boundary-less sex was sold to society on fraudulent science.

I do not place great blame on the shoulders of notorieties like Hugh Hefner. He was just an honest pornographer. By contrast, the scientists who sold us fraudulent claims about human sexuality, with society-altering consequences, to my mind qualify as the greater transgressors. As we progress, we will speak about the fraudulent science and evil deeds of Kinsey and Money.

9. "I am triggered! Take me to my safe space!" From the year 420 B.C., right up to about 2014, universities were supposed to be provocative and challenge students to contest ideas. Then, according to social psychologist and author Jonathan Haidt, something changed.[37] Not only did it change, but it quickly became mainstream.

Students began to perceive the world not in terms of competing ideas, but in terms of danger and safety. They indulged in a strange combination of extreme fragility and extreme sensitivity. Haidt points out that they were now being taught to think in exactly the way that cognitive behavioral therapists, who are interested in increasing mental strength, teach people *not* to think. They were catastrophizing; they indulged in black and white thinking; they used over-generalizations. College, Haidt argues, has somehow switched to actually making students mentally *fragile*, rather than mentally strong. They now promote a fragile-to-the-point-of-damage call-out culture.

Ben Shapiro adds that this is "the furthest extension of political correctness, that when you say something it's not just me disagreeing with you, it is me destroying your identity as a human being in a way that is akin to violence," which, naturally, justifies the Left's violence in response to hearing anything they don't like.[38]

---

37   Gregg Lukianoff and Jonathan Haidt, *The Coddling of the American Mind: How Good Intentions and Bad Ideas Are Setting Up a Generation for Failure* (London: Penguin Books, 2018).

38   Dan Harris, Ignacio Torres, and Lauren Effron, "Outspoken conservative Ben Shapiro on whether free speech still has a place on college campuses," ABCNews.com, October 20, 2017, https://abcnews.go.com/US/outspoken-conservative-ben-shapiro-free-speech-place-college/story?id=50610394.

So, *why*? Why make weak people? Why use the very institution charged with raising excellent minds to raise fragile and hyper-offended ones, who call for trigger warnings and require counseling after hearing a scary new idea? Because that way, everyone can be a victim.

Remember, this entire project is premised on marginalized victims fighting the system. *That's* why. It proceeds like this: Atheism becomes Marxism. Marxism reinterpreted by the Frankfurt school becomes a social theory. The theory is marginalized and disenfranchised groups destroy the system. To be marginalized and disenfranchised, you must perceive yourself to be weak and oppressed. Teach them to be that. *Et voilà.* It creates your foot soldiers, and it justifies their violence.

We see this indulgent celebration of personal weakness spilling out into popular society. I am fascinated by the preponderance of everyday talk about "healing." When a society constantly talks about healing, it is implying that it is, by definition, perpetually broken, perpetually traumatized, perpetually damaged.

I'll never forget one of my friends on social media—a liberal feminist lesbian, who works in academia in the United States—posting her reaction the day after Donald Trump was elected to the presidency. She spoke about how "now is a time for healing. We must tend to our hurt and try to become whole again, beyond this trauma."

Healing? Trauma? From the results of a democratic election? Perhaps I was still naïve back then, but I couldn't quite understand how these terms could be applied in such a context. Now I do. This personal brokenness is learned. It is codified and taught.

I find the prevalence of "healing" discourse at least slightly troubling, insofar as it plays into the victimhood narrative. You see it down to the subtlest of levels. Today, a social media acquaintance posted about how she was "beginning to come to terms with her role as a mother." This was eight years after the birth of her first child and six years after the birth of her second. She *wanted* both children. Yet the narrative stealthily suggests that she is a "victim" of motherhood, who is now nobly rising to the occasion. So brave. Call me callous, but I don't see that as a tear-inducing act of overcoming. Being a mother is, at the very least, a duty that you take seriously, having chosen it. You are not a victim. As a parent raising a child myself, I have always believed that passing on competence and ability is the point. Otherwise stated, the point is not to raise a child, but rather, to raise an adult.

Whenever I ruminate on this topic, I have two thoughts. The first is for people who are trying to "heal": All right, *then* what? Is there a goal on the far side of this healing? Or is healing itself just a lifelong project of encultured self-indulgence?

Secondly, I am reminded of the weakened and defenseless Eloi of *The Time Machine* and can't help but think there's your path to that outcome. It's worth noting that Jonathan Haidt makes compelling arguments that a recent rise in teenage mental health issues, leading to depression and suicidal ideation, correspond strongly with the increased use of smart electronic devices, social media, and television viewing. By contrast, it appears that five activities have inverse relationships with depression:

- Participating in sports and exercise
- Attending religious services
- Reading books
- Interacting socially in person
- Doing homework[39]

The best book on this topic: *The Coddling of the American Mind: How Good Intentions and Bad Ideas Are Setting Up a Generation for*

---

39   Lukianoff and Haidt, Ibid.

Failure by Greg Lukianoff and Jonathan Haidt.

10. "Poverty made me kill them." Terrorists are recast as victims of oppression. Criminals as victims of poverty. Abortionists are somehow victims, too—either of the patriarchy, or of poverty, or of societal norms (specifically, the societal norm of not killing a baby). Across the board, instigators and perpetrators have no part to play in their own acts, their own stories, even their pregnancies, nor any means of preventing these outcomes. They are victims, and abortion is posed as the only solution. No one, it would seem, is responsible for anything.

Straight-faced news reporters have even attempted to make the case that terrorism is a result of the West's failure to solve climate change and healthcare issues. No one is responsible for their misdeeds—other than, perhaps, the West.

Indeed, Left-leaning academics, and scientists are increasingly making the case that there is no such thing as free will. This neatly excuses everything, yet begs so many logical questions that it boggles the, apparently not free, mind. For instance, if you tell me that I have no free will and I slap you, can I then counter that I had no choice?

However, this same standard pointedly does not apply to the old moral order of Western tradition, which, naturally, is single-handedly to blame for every one of the moral misdeeds plaguing humanity. The end goal of such reasoning, again, is to create helpless victims on one side, or at least, people who perceive themselves that way. They make easy political fodder and great foot soldiers for violence. Then to set up a target on the other side: the West.

By contrast, when I personally speak or train on topics pertaining to human development and personal talent in my capacity as a professional speaker and author, I cite "discipline" as the leading indicator of success. I am not alone among human development specialists in arriving at this conclusion. Discipline is the strong arm of personal accountability, which is at the very root of all personal success.

I train the notion of what I call "pre-loaded discipline," arguing that good decisions and excellent performance happen *in advance of the moment*. Don't follow your heart, which is capricious, injudicious, and biased toward easy pleasure. Instead, make the best decision before the time, then determine the outcome in advance by preloading discipline.

This technique is critical in raising children who are able to resist drugs. Drugs are rarely ever presented by a dark and hostile man in a trench-coat, inviting a child to conspire to do evil in an alleyway. Instead, they are presented as easy and fun, usually in settings perceived to be quite safe and usually by their good friends. A decision made by the heart will lead a child straight into participation. A principled decision made in advance can ward off all manner of problems because the discipline to live up to the decision has been preloaded. The child sees it coming and knows what to do.

11. "To be more inclusive, we have to get rid of the wrong kind of people." The originator and champion of this stunningly warped idea was Herbert Marcuse, a German-born U.S. intellectual who had a great and lasting effect on Western educational ideas. Marcuse was heralded as "The Father of the Modern Left," which should tell you everything you need to know. He originally represented his idea as "repressive tolerance."

His argument goes like this: "An all-embracing tolerance ends up legitimizing an unfair status quo." This is code for: "If you let good ideas be debated long enough, the best ones win, and that's unfair for the bad ones."[40]

Marcuse then proposed that the best form of tolerance is intolerant of anything that is intolerant to everything else. That sounds

---

40   Stephen D. Brookfield, John D. Holst, *Radicalizing Learning: Adult Education for a Just World* (San Francisco: Jossey-Bass, 2011).

complex and confusing. Simply stated, Marcuse wants us to accept everything that accepts everything. He also wants us to deny and exclude anything that doesn't accept anything. In practical terms, if science disconfirms Islam or feminist theory, it is science that must go because it is being exclusionary.

Marcuse went on to recommend that educators should actually avoid ever even engaging with mainstream ideas on the grounds that they were now so "ideologically embedded" (which is code for "so thoroughly argued, debated, vetted, and refined over the centuries as to be considered correct"). Instead, he proposed that educators should *only* engage with the troubling and radical ideas.

Translation, please? Why, certainly. Ignore accepted Western tradition. Dismiss it wholesale. Think about radical ideas only. If you wonder why a modern school seems to completely ignore entire categories such as science, democracy, Judeo-Christian moral frameworks, and every other major institution that has formed the bedrock of our society for two millennia and, instead, only seems to discuss themes like radical feminist theory and Marxism, well, *that's* why. Marcuse taught them to do so.

12. "Walls are symbols of hate!" Here is an example of how the politically correct Left has successfully used propaganda to create a public narrative. They are adept at claiming words like *kindness* as uniquely theirs.

In the nationality debate, they have largely succeeded at creating the narrative that walls represent hate. They do not. In the most basic sense, walls represent care. A wall is created, first and foremost, to protect that which we value. That is the entire point of a wall: to keep out a threat. In the broader sense of a national debate, to assert that a nation may not have a wall is also to assert that it may not have national sovereignty. And when did the Left win that debate?

The Left likes to use the example of the Berlin Wall. The flaw in this argument is obvious. This soviet construction was designed to keep its own people *in*. The guns were faced toward their own citizens. This is the diametric opposite of a wall designed to keep people safe from outside intrusion.

Absent borders and walls, where are the boundaries inscribing a community that has agreed to practices like democracy? Or rule of law? Absent such borders, who is in charge? And what belief system, legal system, political system do they employ? Walls and borders not only protect that which we value, they demarcate a community of people practicing high standards (of law, belief, or politics). They are the delineation of "our place."

The Left also argues that walls represent nationalism, which was practiced by Nazis. Yet nationalism was also practiced by the Allied nations, Britain and America, who defeated the Nazis, in defense of their nations. The argument that nationalism equals Nazism is absurd.

Walls are love, not hate. They represent value and protection, not aggression. Nationalism is morally neutral but can be used for moral good or evil. Protecting your borders does not qualify as moral evil, in the same way that trying to expand them might. Nevertheless, here we see how the progressive Left is anti-nationalism and pro-globalization.

13. "Islam is a religion of peace!" The West has a short memory. In its relatively brief thousand-and-a-half-year history, Islam very nearly conquered Europe. It is numerically the bloodiest religion the world has seen (though its body count still lags way behind that of socialism), and its unyielding tenants of intolerance toward all other belief systems, including liberal democracy, is baked into its DNA.

It is also culturally intolerant. If one enjoys the color, music, pageantry, and unique dress that comprise the wonderfully varied cultural expression of human groups around the world, it is positively depressing to see their subjugation into uniform, black-clothed drabness under Islamic repression.

Liberals eagerly and regularly present Judeo-Christian beliefs and Islam as equivalent. There is no equivalence between them, and it is important to be able to qualify the differences.

For now, here is just one example, based on the names. In the Old Testament, Jacob, one of the patriarchs of the Israelites, is renamed "Israel," which means, "struggle with God." And Jacob/Israel did struggle with God, even to the point of negotiating outcomes with the Deity. Jews take this as a precedent. It is an open invitation to debate, struggle, argue, and haggle with God. The result is that theirs has always been a religion (and culture) of lively debate and of ongoing literary thought and meaningful negotiation.

By contrast, Islam means the exact opposite. The word means "submission." This is not a religion that welcomes debating with God or haggling over ideas. It prescribes only compliance at the threat of death. It is the difference between lively thought versus thoughtless obedience. And that is merely the starting point for each respective faith. The differences grow ever starker as the edifices of each construct mature from these foundations.

Of the various belief systems that the West defeated in their own spheres, such as paganism, communism, and Islam, which are now being welcomed back into the public arena by progressive liberals, Islam is perhaps the one most starkly at odds with their own goals and views. Nevertheless, conflation of Western religion with Islam is a common tactic by progressives, as in the viral YouTube video by a feminist railing against "traditional marriage." She mentions the human rights abuses of forced marriage and child brides.[41] In this, I agree with her. And I strongly recommend she begin campaigning against these things in the Middle East.

---

41 The Guardian, "Women, face it: marriage can never be feminist – Julie Bindel," You-Tube Post, 2:48, May 25, 2016, https://www.youtube.com/watch?v=hRYzl60oxks&feature=share.

14. "He is literally Hitler!" Few people on Earth have ever faced the "modern-day Hitler" accusation as often or vehemently as U.S. President Donald Trump when he came to office in 2016. However, it is interesting to note that the facile hurling of this moniker is nothing new.

In his excellent biography of Ronald Reagan and the fall of communism, Paul Kengor notes with wry amusement how liberal Democrats used precisely the same accusations against Reagan.[42] They then repeated the narrative against Bush. Then Trump.

Democrats have spoken about impeaching every single conservative president since Eisenhower. Calling conservatives Nazis and threatening to impeach presidents is standard operating procedure for liberals. It is just what they do.

Should conservatives shoulder the blame for Nazism? Hardly. As we have seen, Nazism and communism are two revolutionary (read: "progressive," not "conservative") ideologies that arose directly from progressive social theories on the Left. Both are responsible for mass murder. Conservative Westerners, predominantly Christian, overthrew them both.

The Conservative approach to progress is slow and peaceful. The Leftist approach to progress is revolutionary and, if necessary, violent.

The man who founded the first modern democracy on Earth was conservative Christian George Washington. The man who led the overthrow of slavery in the U.S. was conservative Christian President Abraham Lincoln. The man who led the fight against Nazism and communism was conservative Christian Prime Minister Winston Churchill, and the man who finally overthrew the communist Soviet Union was conservative Christian Ronald Reagan.

---

42   Paul Kengor, *The Crusader: Ronald Reagan and the Fall of Communism* (New York: Harper Perennial, 2006).

If you truly want liberty, if you genuinely want to face down and defeat tyranny, if your goal is to abolish slavery, it would appear that what you need are conservative Christians in positions of leadership. (Now there's a politically incorrect thing to say. Still. It is demonstrably true, and we should repeat it loudly and often.)

Despite this, as Jonah Goldberg observes in *Liberal Fascism*, the *New York Times* "leads a long roster of mainstream publications eager to promote leading academics who raise the possibility that the GOP is a fascist party and that Christian conservatives are the new Nazis."[43] The word *perverse* does not capture it.

15. "The world was a utopia of peaceful ethnic tribes. Then white people from Europe came along and conquered everyone! They took their cities and their wealth. White people—they're the real problem."

History is infinitely more complex and more nuanced than this simplistic representation would suggest. Every nation has had slavery. There has not been a place or culture in human history that was free of humans selling other humans into bondage.

Historians record that "North Africa's Barbary Coast pirates captured and enslaved" over one million Europeans in the period between 1500 and 1800. This actually represents more Europeans brought in bondage to *Africa* than there were Africans brought to the United States. Who ever tells *that* story? Yet it happened, and it happened to over a million white, Western Europeans. This does not even count Europeans being bought and sold in the Islamic Middle East.

Or we might ask why *North* America becomes the target of focus for revisionist slavery narratives, when Brazil, in *South* America, imported more slaves from Africa than did the whole of the Northern American territories combined.[44] One might argue that

---

43   Jonah Goldberg, *Liberal Fascism: The Secret History of the Left, from Mussolini to the Politics of Meaning* (New York: Doubleday, 2007).

44   Thomas Sowell, *The Thomas Sowell Reader* (New York: Basic Books, 2011).

America is highlighted because it is especially racist against black people in favor of white people. But really? There are Americans still alive today who will remember discrimination against the Irish. Again, history is more complicated than the caricature we receive from sociologists with a vested interest in slanted narratives designed not to recount truthful history but to attack the Old Order.

So, the fact of the matter is that the West has been a committer of slavery, and the West has been a victim of slavery. That is genuine history, replete with good and bad people in every culture. Historical fact remains unmoved by modern liberal interpretations—it just *is*. And that is how we should study it—warts and all—if we hope to learn from it. Tell the truth.

Nevertheless, there is one more pertinent fact about history that "just is." The fact is the West was the *first* to ban slavery. Similarly, the West was the first to extend full legal and contractual rights to women—a phenomenon still unmatched in many Middle Eastern nations today.

The West's own historical slavery numbers, though appalling, do not approach the numbers achieved by Islamic nations; and as the West evolved, it could no longer morally accommodate the institution of slavery and banned it everywhere. Islamic countries were practicing slavery openly into the 1960s and 1970s, and the practice continues to this day, though not legally. In many of these nations, women still do not enjoy the right to enter into contracts as free individuals, nor do they enjoy equal standing before the law.

In the peaceful pre-Western utopia narrative, we are also not told about cultural inconveniences such as the Aztec practice of sacrificing people from other tribes. How many? Scholars estimate these acts of human sacrifice occurred at a rate of some twenty thousand per year. That continued right up to the Spanish arrival in the Americas. Nor is it ever mentioned that colonization is not a uniquely Western idea. Not even close. Clans, tribes, nations, and cultures have been conquering and colonizing one another since the dawn of recorded history. Quite aside from Islamic slavery, there was Islamic colonialism—the Islamic Expansion—which took place over hundreds of years, destroyed untold numbers of local ethnic cultures, and colonized millions of people. Nor is it stated that in many cases, the white Western colonizers were escaping oppression in their own lands and that is *why* many of them departed for distant shores.

Does this excuse crimes against humanity committed by the West? Not at all. The West is acutely aware of its crimes. But what is disingenuous is the assertion that only the West has a violent past. It simply isn't true.

Another simplistic narrative is that science and Christianity have always been mortal enemies. Even the most cursory look at what actually transpired utterly dispels this notion.

The best book on the subject: *What's So Great About Christianity?* by Dinesh D'Souza.

16. "What she does with her body is her business." Strangest among the liberal narratives is the idea that those who object to abortion are somehow oppressing women. There are two things for which this notion fails to account. As a man, I gain nothing by objecting to a woman having an abortion. I do not gain power over her; I do not gain sexual favor from her; and I do not gain submission from her. There is no benefit to me in opposing abortion. If anything, I would gain freer, easier sex by championing it.

And secondly, the interests I am championing are those of a third party and not my own. If I am successful in opposing abortion, a child survives. This is not my child. Statistically most often, this is a black, female child whose rights I am attempting to uphold.

I might also add that it is harder to oppose abortion publicly than simply not to do so. By doing nothing, I would not face opposition. Hence, the "oppressive patriarchy" narrative is absurd. It also tacitly assumes a couple of additional flaws: that other women do not oppose abortion (They do.) and that men may not speak on a moral issue, insofar as it pertains to females (They can.). Once again, this is an attempt at de-platforming by obfuscation. It doesn't work if you say it doesn't work. Morality does not get subsumed under gender issues. If that were the case, then women should be forbidden from speaking against male crime. They are not, and rightly so.

17. "The problem is not the problem. It's the *stigma* that matters."

I grew up in Africa at the time when AIDS rose to prominence in the public consciousness. Even as a teenager who did not yet comprehend the oddities of political correctness, I was baffled by the liberal ANC government's response to AIDS. In public-health pamphlets and television advertisements, they attacked the stigma of AIDS. The real problem, it seemed, was not the virus itself. Nor the behaviors that transferred it. The real problem was the public stigma surrounding it. Having subsequently studied the messaging created by gay-advocacy groups, I now understand why this was done. AIDS was a big threat to the normalization of homosexuality. That was the agenda.

I recall reading with astonishment the advice given to young people in these AIDS-awareness publications, such as: "Some people are lucky enough to be bisexual. This means you can enjoy having meaningful sex with people of both genders." This was the advice that followed on the heels of how important it was to get rid of stigma. This was supposedly life-saving information for the AIDS generation in Africa. Perhaps it was my adolescent-level of reasoning, but it seemed to me that guiding people away from behaviors that caused their death might have been more important than sparing their feelings. Or championing free love.

Here is another example of the stigma problem: On July 2, 2019, Dr. Drew Pinsky stated on *Fox News*, "Because we made drugs legal, essentially, in California . . . the drug users are here now, because they don't get hassled."

California's homeless and drug problems have been skyrocketing of late, because the state successfully overcame the stigma of homelessness and drug use. The obvious outcomes were more homelessness and drug use. Who could possibly have guessed? This seems obvious to the conservative mind. The liberal mind simply can't seem to see it.

Prioritizing stigma over problem is, in fact, a representative microcosm of the liberal mindset. Immorality, harm, deadly viruses—none of these are as important as hurt feelings about the subject. In this modality of thinking, "don't judge" becomes more important than saving lives. I utterly reject it, and you should, too.

Debate Tip: One of the most common liberal techniques for shutting down an argument is the simplistic directive: "You're not allowed to judge!"
Your response: "Yes, I am." (Sometimes the best counter-argument is simple assertion). Nevertheless, when the argument inevitably proceeds, respond with, "Why not? Judgement forms the basis of justice. Are you saying that we should not base our society on concepts of justice?"
The likely response to this is a trick often used against Christians: "The Bible says you're not allowed to judge!"
Your response: "Nope. It says to judge with righteousness. Go check John 7:24. While you're at it, 1 Corinthians 6:2 says that saints will judge all the world." The likely response to that is: "Well, I don't think you should judge!"
To which you can reply, "That's nice."

---

18. "We need to address your 'toxic masculinity.'" Let us begin with an honest admission. Most wars and most violent crimes are committed by men. Of that, there is no dispute. We do not practice reverse political correctness by pretending this away. The politically correct incarnation of this idea, however, has nothing to do with these realities. "Toxic masculinity" is a different charge entirely.

How can we know this? Because in the most violent cities in the United States—for example, Chicago—violent crime is disproportionately committed by black males. Yet under political correctness, these very males are seen as the "victims" of circumstance, specifically "poverty." No, the demonization of men is premised on something more intrinsic. Their very maleness.

Qualities deemed to be quintessentially masculine become objects of scorn. The perfectly natural and even gentlemanly compulsions to be helpful and to get things done are portrayed perversely as acts that show male strength and dominance over females or as "mansplaining."

If a man sits with his legs apart (biologically more comfortable, given important anatomical differences), he is accused of "manspreading." If he does anything whatsoever that attempts to uphold his own dignity or to represent himself in a favorable light (as women also do, and as all humans being do), then we are immediately told about the fragility of the male ego. This is pure sexism. The Left knows this, and attempts to justify it with a trick.

They pull the same trick with racism. They attempt to incorporate the power dynamic into the definition. It's not racism, and it's not sexism if you are attacking those in power. Their theory is often stated like this: "Racism equals prejudice plus power." On that basis, a black person who hates white people is not racist. Clever, right?

This new tactic of theirs proceeds from feminist theory. It can only work if you fail to notice, or to point out, their ideologically embedded definitions of racism or sexism. Thus, it is disingenuous. It is also a blatant example of self-serving propaganda. You do not get to change terms and definitions to suit your worldview. That is the same as rigging a debate so that you will win.

There are many additional "truisms" presented as part and parcel of the demonization-of-males package. The term "rape culture" proceeds from this propaganda, too. This last must not be taken lightly. In nations like Sweden or South Africa, citizens face some of the highest global statistics of male-on-female rape. In South Africa, most sources agree on one in three, and by some accounts, one in two. These numbers are atrocious and out-perform many war zones in their horror. For that reason, we might legitimately claim the existence of a "rape culture" in such a nation.

In the United States, from which the term proceeds, the numbers presented by feminists and those who would demonize men are simply untrue. The term "rape culture" is applied primarily to U.S. universities, where it is alleged that one in four women are raped. FBI statistics reveal that the actual percentage of women raped on campus is 0.6 percent.

There is another pernicious element to the rape culture notion, and that is what the terminology implies. It implies that men have a networked interest in supporting, aiding, and protecting other men who rape. Here, I turn this one to you as a personal question: Has it been your experience that the men you meet want to help rapists? Or has it been your experience that men are generally violently antagonistic toward rapists? Implied in this term "culture" is a reality that I do not see supported by real-world experience. Contrary to feminist assertion, most men do not hate women, but most men do, in fact, abhor rapists.

The war on men ranges from the grave to the petty, from allegations of a culture of rape and a society-dominating patriarchy, to the petty grievances of man-spreading, "fart rape" (I kid you not—this is the feminist idea that a man's assertive breaking of wind is done to prove his dominance and to force a woman into submission), and even "wrong-face" (Remember the Covington kid who made global headlines for "looking smug" in the face of a Native American protestor? And how it all went quiet after it was proved that the young man was actually the victim? The hatred for him was global and palpable.[45] Why?).

We will explore the ways to untangle this mess and answer coherently. Yet, by far, the best response to anti-maleness is the most visceral. It is society's lived experiences of good, strong men. Nothing defeats feminist propaganda like well-treated women who observe, "It just isn't so." To this end, anti-PC women can do much good by speaking out and not allowing the poison to propagate against the men they cherish. We are grateful when you do.

19. "Capitalism is exploitation! The rich take from the poor."

I have written two books on personal wealth: *Is Your Thinking Keeping You Poor?* and *Poverty Proof.* In both cases, I had to explain to the reader upfront that there are two sets of answers to poverty: the politically correct, kind-sounding, but untrue and the difficult to hear, but valid.

No other area of life contains as much misleading Leftist propaganda as does money. From Karl Marx onward, the Left have despised the rich and have employed every form of lie, deceit, and conflict-inducing con to discredit them. For my money, the ugliest and most violence-generating belief from the Left is this: "Wealth exists, and must be distributed." Every evil book on money has followed this formula, from the writings of Marx and Lenin to the twenty-first century update, Thomas Piketty's *Capital in the Twenty-First Century.*

---

45   Robby Soave, "A Year Ago, the Media Mangled the Covington Catholic Story. What Happened Next Was Even Worse." Reason.com, January 21, 2020, https://reason.com/2020/01/21/covington-catholic-media-nick-sandmann-lincoln-memorial.

The reality—and it is a terrifically important distinction—actually goes like this: "Wealth does not exist. It is generated." I call their flawed idea "the Finite Pool" fallacy. It assumes that all wealth pre-existed in one finite pool. Since then, we've merely discovered it, and we've been divvying it up, unfairly as it turns out.

But wealth does not pre-exist. It is not a finite pool. Instead, it is a constantly growing wellspring, generated through work and innovation that create value. And that fact matters greatly. It determines whether systems of wealth must be predicated on stealing what others have generated or on teaching others how to generate for themselves. The latter system is the most successful idea in all of human history with the most dramatic and demonstrable results. The former idea is the most failed idea in history with the biggest body count of any ideology.

Building on this flawed point, the Left will also imply that colonialists arrived on foreign shores and "took" the wealth. When left unchecked, they will even talk about "stealing cities." In almost all cases, these cities didn't exist. And the pioneers subsequently built their wealth.

This difference in understanding between wealth merely existing or being actively generated is the essential point of departure between the Left and Right economically.

Here's another. Complete this sentence for me: 'The rich are getting richer, and . . . ?" You said it, didn't you? You've heard it hundreds of times. Do you believe it? It is not true. Over the past one hundred years, Western capitalist practices have lifted more people out of poverty, both as a number and as a percentage of humanity, than ever before in all of human history. In the past twenty years alone, prior to the systemic shock of the coronavirus crisis, over a billion people had escaped extreme poverty. Extreme poverty had been very nearly eradicated from the face of the Earth. These days, where it is to be found, it is the almost exclusive domain of tyrannical governments, socialist societies (like Venezuela, which used to be the wealthiest country in South America under its previous capitalist system), or gang-and-drug ravaged failed states. In many cases, where capitalism was interrupted by the Covid-19 crisis, it's back.

The poor are *not* getting poorer. Indeed, the poor are getting much, much, much richer. The past one hundred years have constituted nothing short of an economic miracle, and the credit goes squarely to free-trade capitalism. Still, the Leftist narrative prevails. The greedy rich are constantly stealing from the oppressed poor. To change all that, all we have to do is redistribute (read "steal") their wealth.

Interesting to note: Where liberals are faced with insurmountable arguments in favor of capitalism and against socialism, they will often change *motivations* for their argument. They will switch to how capitalism destroys the environment, then begin their anti-capitalist crusade all over again. "Our theory may not make economic sense, and yours might, but yours destroys the Earth."

Objection: "Even the Bible says that money is the root of all evil."

Response: "That's not even close. The verse actually reads: 'The love of money is a root of all kinds of evil' (1 Tim. 6:10)."

Useful term: In response to the Left's attack on "trickle-down theory," you can correctly position them as advocates for "trickle-up poverty."

---

20. "There's no media bias!" Almost all of the leading mainstream media display a Left-leaning bias. This bias isn't merely limited to the editorial pages or talk shows. Even the supposedly hard-nosed, economic and financial journalists in major outlets like the *Wall Street Journal, New York Times,* and the *Associated Press* are overwhelmingly liberal.

Researchers from Arizona State University and Texas A&M surveyed 462 financial journalists and found a ratio of thirteen liberals for every one conservative. The report goes on to ask, "Whatever happened to ideological diversity?" They observe, "You might want to take it (their reporting) with a grain of salt. That's especially true if the piece seems unduly harsh on the free-market system and its many proven benefits. Or if it lauds socialism as an 'answer' to society's ills."[46]

Also, from Investors.com, we read:

The fact is, Google, YouTube and Facebook have all shown repeated bias against conservative voices and web sites. Google, for instance, used to attach fact-checks on conservative stories from leftist sites. It also tilted the results of searches towards left-wing politicians over conservatives. It even fired a computer tech, James Damore, merely for expressing a non-left opinion over the male-female wage gap.

Worse still, YouTube, a lucrative utility for many sites that seek to make money from their web presence, has "demonetized" conservative sites such as Prager University, whose informative and thought-provoking videos have nothing whatsoever to do with "alt-right" anything. Recent videos include such fare as "Why America Must Lead" and "Why Did America Fight the Korean War." For this, Prager U was kept from having ads on its videos.

Facebook, along with the rest of the far-left "mainstream" media, routinely shuns conservative stories on its news sites and aggressively limited "partisan" sites it doesn't like.

All of them work with the Southern Poverty Law Center, a far-left group that aggressively declares right-of-center organizations as "hate groups." None of the major web giants, to our knowledge,

---

46 "Media Bias: Pretty Much All of Journalism Now Leans Left, Study Shows," Investors. com, November 16, 2018, https://www.investors.com/politics/editorials/media-bias-left-study.

works with a comparable conservative group such as, say, David Horowitz's Freedom Center.[47]

Naturally, big advertisers seem to love their social justice causes, too. We think of Nike supporting Colin Kaepernick kneeling before the U.S. flag or Gillette beginning with their infamous advertisements on toxic masculinity, then progressing to the even worse "trans man's first shave" ad.

To point out what is wrong with just one of these ads, take Kaepernick:

- His protest is against disproportionate killing of black people by U.S. police. Studies conclusively prove this fact to be utterly false.

- Kaepernick, a black man, was himself raised by two white parents who adopted him and gave him every privilege, resulting in his selection to play in the National Football League and become rich and famous.

- He is a multimillionaire sports star, posing as an oppressed victim, perpetuating a narrative that has been falsified.

- Nike is playing off this narrative in order to make money. It has no ethical qualms about victimizing police officers through false accusation as part of its commercial policy.

And that, ladies and gentleman, is why I have never bought another pair of Nike sneakers. At the last tally, Nike had lost $3.75 billion in market capital after Kaepernick was named the face of "Just Do It."

21. Advocacy for big government: "One world!" In many ways, this is what it all comes down to. All Leftism, all socialism, all political correctness must ultimately achieve its end-goal. And that

---

47 Social Media: Is Trump Right About Anti-Conservative Bias? You Bet He is, Investors.com, September 21, 2018, https://www.investors.com/politics/editorials/social-media-trump-conservative-bias.

goal is big, centralized government. *Global* government, if possible. The entire project is designed to put power into the hands of a few.

Leftists do not see the danger in this. They do not even see the irony in their "liberal" efforts to create a big, new, centralized ruler with all the power to dictate the norms of society, including how we think, speak, act, earn, and spend. Instead, Hobbes' *Leviathan* seems like a jolly good idea to them. And where we oppose it, they call *us* oppressors. They comfort themselves with the belief that big government will lead us all to Utopia. Peace. The "end of history." While they are at it, these unquestioned rulers will solve climate change and end war. They will make everyone equal. If they have to shut down some liberties along the way, that's a small price to pay. If they must teach our children that there is no God, then so be it. And if they're forced to get rid of a few undesirable dissidents, well, that's a small price to pay for heaven-on-earth.

And that, my friend, is why we fight.

Side Note: Aside from all the well-known failures and discreditations of socialism, here's one failed promise we rarely think about: Socialist utopians also promised society "more free time." Working together would result in increased freedom to pursue art and culture. Oddly, most art and culture were also banned or severely regulated under socialism, but still, the promise was that we would be more free to pursue higher aims.

Side Note: For a completely fictional and darkly dystopian but brilliantly entertaining look at a progressive utopia as run by a group of mind-controlling elites, read Dean Koontz's five-part *Jayne Hawk* series. I repeat that this series is completely fictional. Nevertheless, Mr. Koontz clearly understands the principles.

Those are the battlefronts. Based on these battlefronts, what are the potential outcomes? What might actually transpire in the real world should we lose these ideology wars, surrender to political correctness, and accede our hard-won culture?

Plainly stated, we might lose the next generation. Memory is precious. Where it fails and where we fail to pass it on, light may simply extinguish. And then our children go on, as they must, but in darkness. The world has seen darkness before. Other people's children lived through it. It is possible that ours could, too. Unless we pass on the precious light of memory.

There is something poignant in the words of an article exploring this possibility, published by the Schiller Institute:

> We will have to face the fact that the ugliness we see around us has been consciously fostered and organized in such a way that a majority of the population is losing the cognitive ability to transmit to the next generation the ideas and methods upon which our civilization was built. The loss of that ability is the primary indicator of a Dark Age.[48]

Let us explore this potential Dark Age nightmare-scape through the example of a single human life, post-Westernism, and after the fall of our culture. We will call our character *David*.

While in the womb, David is already a problem. Not only does he represent yet another resource-draining incarnation of Earth's worst plague—humans—but he is also male. His mother considers whether she should just do the right thing and abort him in order to contribute to the dismantling of male patriarchy and privilege. The mother also does not know who the father is, which raises David's chances of becoming a violent criminal sevenfold.

David is not a miracle. He is not fearfully or wonderfully made in the image of any God. David is a meaningless collection of cells. And a problem.

---

48 Michael Minnicino, *The New Dark Age: The Frankfurt School and Political Correctness, Volume 1* (Washington, D.C.: Schiller Institute, 1992).

And ending his life is the solution. If David's mother opts to kill him, she is taught to "shout her abortion" in order to celebrate his death and overcome any maternal reservations she harbors about the act.

Nevertheless, David survives. He is born, begins to grow, and goes on to enter the schooling system. There, he will be taught that although he may have a boy body, there's actually a chance he really has a girl brain. And this is subjective and based upon feelings, which means that any "girly" feeling can stand as proof to him that he is misgendered.

Once this idea is implanted, David will begin a process of active confirmation bias. Every sentimental feeling he experiences will teach him that he might actually be a girl and not simply a male with a full and healthy range of emotions.

Next week, David's school is taken to a mosque. David's mother has no sense of nor value for a First Commandment, which utterly forbids having any other gods before the Judeo-Christian God, and David's teachers are interested in dismantling Western societal norms. So, David is encouraged to turn toward the East and bow, face down, before the god named Allah. As part of his cultural education, he is told to recite the words: "There is no god but Allah."

Then David hits puberty. Sex and morals have been utterly uncoupled and personal accountability replaced with the idea that he's merely a biological victim of his impulses. Any impulses. And if the realization of these impulses results in pregnancy, see step one: abortion of the next generation of meaningless cells.

David is told that he should experiment broadly. It's good for him. Girls, boys, younger, older, *anything*. There are no boundaries. And because sex with another boy is normal and no sex is to be judged, David can't see anything wrong when he is approached by an older man for sex. The older man is being "kind," and that is the moral basis of David's entire society, so how can it be wrong? Everything is on the table, and the real problem is apparently about stigmatizing sex, so a sexual relationship with his uncle must be okay. If not, why not? Wrong relative to what?

Then David enters varsity, and this is where the *real* indoctrination begins. The idea that there might be a God is stamped out without mercy or reprieve. It is the point of his entire education. We are purely material beings in a purely material universe. There is no meaning, no value, nothing sacred. Science proves this. Above all, this is the thing that David must internalize.

Everything else proceeds from this idea. David must learn that he has no intrinsic worth. Worse, he is a white male, and he must learn that his only role in the modern world is as self-flagellator and confessor for his kind. He is what is wrong with everything.

David—his life, his identity, his entire self—is rendered meaningless, even to him, and that is the arch-lesson that he must learn. This leads David naturally to nihilism, despair, and self-loathing, down the path of taught futility.

Even if David could somehow reason his way out of the demographic trap, he will merely find himself within another, like a pet escaping a cage, only to find itself still trapped within the pet store. You see, David's entire species is the worst thing there is. Nothing destroys Earth like humans. They are a plague. They need to be culled and contained. If they disappeared, Earth would be a paradise.

And David is no greater than any other animal. Per the words of Ingrid Newkirk, founder of the world's largest animal rights organization, People for the Ethical Treatment of Animals, "A rat is a pig is a dog is a boy."[49] Why should *his* oppressive species enjoy primacy?

And David has no access to competing conceptions of the universe. There exists a religious book which would offer David an alternative

---

49   Martin Fletcher, "Ingrid Newkirk, the unlikely extremist," NewStatesman.com, June 26, 2019, https://www.newstatesman.com/politics/uk/2019/06/ingrid-newkirk-un-likely-extremist.

worldview, specifically, that he is fearfully and wonderfully made in the image of a loving God and that all history is a moral play about his species and its search for goodness. That he matters deeply and, above all, that he is precious and his choices are important. But David is forbidden from reading this book.

It has been banned in public institutions and in general under hate-speech laws, promulgated some twenty years prior by LGBTQ activists. David is *not allowed* to read the Bible, not permitted to have these thoughts. They are wrong-think.

This is nothing new, the Bible having always been the most banned book throughout human history. David is simply not aware that there was a time, a brief flash, in which his entire civilization was premised on it. Now, like the peasant living under Catholicism before reform, David is not permitted to access the book or read it for himself. He is allowed only to read the literary critiques of the book, which explain how it was an archetype of male dominance.

With all of this informing his worldview and psyche, David then enters the job market. He receives his first paycheck, only to discover that most of it goes to the government, under the guise of socialism. This is supposed to provide David with excellent healthcare and education. Yet if David were permitted access to such information, he would know that everything had become markedly worse under this system. He suspects that things used to be better. Everywhere, he sees signs of broken and neglected infrastructure, amid the discarded needles and trash, that looked infinitely more modern and advanced than the rudimentary system being offered by his government today.

Nevertheless, his leaders loudly and constantly assure him that he is living in a socialist paradise and that everything is much better now. How can David argue? For starters, he is not permitted to argue. One speaks against the government only on pain of arrest. Wrong-speak is one of the worst crimes he can commit. It shows his lack of commitment to inclusivity, socialism, kindness, community, the new order, and even humanity in general. Wrongthink is primitive and destructive, and it has been outlawed for the sake of peace. Saint Marcuse taught us that.

Besides, there are cameras everywhere. Informants everywhere. One misstep, and David might lose his social-credit standing, and that could lead to starvation. The system began in China, then spread to the liberal free world, which then became the "socialized" world. If he fell afoul of it, he would have his rights removed. He would become a non-citizen, incapable of doing literally anything, ghosted out of existence.

So, David keeps his head down. He complies. He is empty, lonely, meaningless, with no hope of appeal to a moral certainty, an external reference point of truth, a reason for it all to matter. He aches down to the level of his soul, but he is told that he has no soul. He yearns for something that is true, beautiful, meaningful, that has purpose and direction, but he fights the urge to tell anybody about this.

The best he can do is not to get into trouble by thinking incorrectly. Thoughts about souls and beauty and meaning must remain his private secret. His aching, his yearning, his need for a truth or a reason or an ultimate God must be dampened to death on the inside.

This scenario is not unrealistic.

These dystopias have existed under progressive tyranny. In parts of the world, they still exist. China continues to practice, and expand the power of its social points system, powered by non-stop surveillance of its citizens. We cannot allow these forms of tyranny in the West. Sane people must speak up because we love our children and because we want a viable future for them. It seems absurd that we would ever surrender our culture to such potentialities.

In addition to the dystopian David scenario, here is a list of outcomes rendered more probable in the wake of PC's success—some innocuous, some very serious:

1. The death of basic good manners

I want to raise my son to open doors for women and act like a gentleman. Feminism says no. My system actively honors, while theirs merely invalidates distinction. Should theirs win out, the world would become a little uglier.

2. The death of humor

In a world in which "you can't say that," hypersensitivity shuts down humor. We become self-censoring drudges. Life loses a little of its sparkle.

Iconic comedian John Cleese and talk show host and author Stephen Fry are just two prominent personalities who lament precisely this problem with political correctness, pointing out that the politically correct do not seem to understand irony. A YouTube search for either name, coupled with "political correctness" will turn up interesting viewing.

3. An undermining of work ethic

When no one is accountable and poverty is always ascribed to oppression, the human compulsion to try is dampened. If the game is rigged against you, why bother? Our great asset of a good work ethic is undermined.

4. An increase in poverty and subsequent social ills

If socialism prevails, everything gets worse. In addition to the social ills, there is also the dampening of innovation and the slowing of new invention, all of which serve humanity on multiple fronts.

5. The rise of anti-autonomy narrative, leading to a prevalent sense of hopelessness

Nihilism and meaninglessness lurk at the heart of a relativist system. It facilitates thinking that says, "Not only can I not achieve anything, but it would be meaningless even if I did."

6. Religious persecution by government intervention

The cornerstone of the old moral system is the Christian Bible. To overthrow a culture and invert its belief systems, its primary agent of moral direction cannot be left intact. Churches, if not banned outright, must be forbidden from speaking on certain moral issues, censored by hate-speech laws. Already places like California are exploring the possibility of banning the Bible in certain contexts, particularly in relation to homosexuality.

7. The undermining of democracy

In his scholarly work *Why Liberalism Failed*, Patrick Deneen shows that liberalism and democracy cannot co-exist—or at least, that one or the other must face serious compromise when we attempt to combine them.[50]

Here is an example. In South Africa, citizens polled overwhelmingly favor the death penalty for extremely violent crime. But they can't have it. Under a democracy, this should be a simple issue. Under liberalism, it is not.

Liberalism only needs democracy until it achieves power. Then it will assert its principles (Leftist politics) at the expense of democracy (what the majority of people actually want).

Islam makes use of democracy in the same manner. Democracy is useful in ensuring its rights, until it can attain majority power, and then democracy must go.

---

50 Patrick Deneen, *Why Liberalism Failed (Politics and Culture)* (New Haven: Yale University Press, 2018).

8. War between demographics

Every group is against every other in perpetual war. There is no possibility of dialogue between them. No "mutual understanding." Only power and oppression (or "pathological dualism"). The result of identity politics of this nature is "only conflict." By contrast, I believe in a culture in which words can lead to resolutions and to peace.

9. Indoctrination of children

Transgender men reading to children in libraries. Children as young as three being taught that gender is a social construct—a girl might actually be a boy. Nursery school children being taught that homosexuality is natural and normal. Young children being taught that their urges shouldn't be fought—restrictions and self-discipline are the same thing as oppression. The bizarre new idea that a child should never hear the word no, insofar as this might stifle their creativity and represent boundaries. This idea fails because, above all, children need boundaries. Also, they need to learn internal discipline, which can never occur in the absence of no.

Even organizations as seemingly innocuous as Disney tell children that only *they* correctly perceive the world—parents are at best befuddled, but well-meaning, harmless buffoons and at worst, backward-looking, authoritarian oppressors who would deny them the freedom to explore anything. (Sing along with Elsa: "No right, no wrong, no rules for me. I'm free!"[51])

10. The death of standards

Of greatest concern to the scientific and philosophical mind, the death of all possible standards renders everything arbitrary. When we may not even *talk* about male and female, how can we know anything? The same dynamic is of concern in the moral realm, too.

---

51   Idina Menzel, *Frozen*, Walt Disney Records, A5, 2014, CD.

11. The death of beauty

This observation is subjective, but I stand by it. Nothing is uglier than postmodernist art. Art achieved its zenith of beauty under the great Christian masters, when aestheticism, form, and splendor were held to matter.

Postmodernism, by contrast, aims to shock, provoke, and accuse. Its core agenda is the meaningless of everything. It also has no lower boundaries on permitted ugliness (here I think of the infamous *Piss Christ*, in which Andres Serrano submerged a crucifix into a glass of his own urine and called it art. If that's art, I don't need it, and I don't want to live in the same world as it).

12. The assertion that there is no such thing as evil—only difference or misunderstanding

We make a grave mistake by pretending away evil. We dismiss it on the grounds of poverty. As a person who grew up in a high-crime country, I have personal and familial experience with this one. I perfectly concur that poverty may lead naturally and understandably to the theft of the proverbial loaf of bread. But that is not what we saw during violent housebreakings.

I will spare you the details, but I have seen photographs and read the reports of what transpires during, for example, farm murders in South Africa. The depravity reaches even to the theatrical. The cruelty defies explanation by reference to poverty or misunderstanding. And where evil may not be named, it cannot be confronted, with the result that it can simply continue to flourish.

13. A return to paganism

The Judeo-Christian-Greko worldview posited man as a meaningful actor at the center of a purposive universe, striving toward moral and intellectual point and purpose.

The pagan worldview was very different, and it has returned. It posits man as a meaningless also-character, at the heart of a turbulent windstorm of forces, blown this way and that by capricious gods and forces of nature who have their own interests at heart. Insofar as man is able to find meaning, he must find it by divining what the stars are telling him or through the magic of reading entrails and omens.

By this view, there is no point or purpose. There is no moral good or bad. There is only the power of acting agents, who are utterly capricious.

Why would this latter view be a problem? Because it precludes science. The Greek and Judaic worldviews pointed man toward the possibility of understanding the universe. It told man that there were constant laws, which, if he tried, he might come to understand. This was the very birth of science for our culture.

The pagan view, by contrast, is magical. Yet the degree to which people live by this worldview today, either as openly professed pagans, or unknowingly as part of a mere "liberated culture," is astonishing.

To live according to paganism is to live in a post-science anarchy of natures and spirits and gods and warring prides. It is also demonstrably untrue, insofar as we *can* and *do* measure natural laws that govern the universe. Our reality is not capricious. It follows known systems. Hence, paganism is, fundamentally, an untrue and invalidated system. To arrive back at paganism as a belief system, one must buy into emotion over science (and, frankly, stupidity over reason).

THE CHAMPIONS OF POLITICAL CORRECTNESS

Now, who is the person championing these causes? What do they want? How do they think, and what do they say and believe?

For starters, it is important to understand that these people are not unin-telligent. They also do not believe themselves to be evil. They may be riddled with contradictions, and they are often self-hating, but they are, nevertheless, smart enough to have evaluated and internalized the politically correct ideol-ogy that they have been taught.

Next, they may or may not be the beneficiaries of the power generated by political correctness. In other words, they may be the politicians who benefit from large numbers of people buying into PC ideology, or they may be among the large numbers of people propping up the narrative—the "foot soldiers," so to speak.

Above all—and this is key to debating these people—they genuinely be-lieve that they are on the side of goodness. They have been sold and have bought wholesale the notion that their belief system is a good one—*the* good one. Theirs is the system of kindness, in opposition to yours, which by contrast is necessarily the bad system, the system of hate. They don't think that they are doing damage. They believe that they are doing good. And they believe that *you* are doing damage by holding humanity back or by actively oppressing them with your beliefs. So, we have a great deal of psychology to contend with here.

They may also arrive at their beliefs from a multitude of approaches. They might *want* to live as pagans, free and wild and human, and thus, the PC narrative suits them. Or they may be conscientious objectors to cruelty, who have then been presented with the false PC-narrative as the only solution. Or, and this is sadly not uncommon, they may have been hurt or damaged by someone in their past and may simply be in a state of rebellion against all authority. This can lead to unthinking rage, propped up by trauma. Such a person will naturally rebel against all ideas of authority, of God, of laws that imply judgment and of systems of morality generally.

Finally, and this is possibly the most dangerous route, the person may arrive at these beliefs through a love of their own intellect. Intellectuals, who see themselves as superior to the rest of us and who would "prescribe" how we should live, can be a poisonous lot. They are smart enough to justify their arguments, but sarcastic and self-assured enough to be completely repellent to truth where it contradicts their ideologies.

Let us form a composite picture of a politically correct individual, by combining their general patterns of argumentation, their worldview, and their ways of thinking and acting. Naturally, not all people who hold politically correct beliefs will fulfill all of these conditions nor meet all of the descriptors. And of course, some proponents may be extreme, Left-wing communists, while others may be more moderate, middle-of-the-road liberals.

Nevertheless, these are the general traits and forms of thinking typical to the progressive, politically correct Left. Let's begin with the broad labels. While noting that not all labels will apply in all instances, the politically correct person will tend to be an:

- Atheist
- Humanist
- Leftist
- Liberal
- Progressive
- Socialist
- Marxist
- Intellectual
- Revolutionary

Breakers, not conservers

Sir Roger Scruton, an English philosopher and conservative knighted for his services to humanity, observes that the key differentiator between the conservative and those on the Left is the difference between a desire to protect and gradually nurture versus the desire to break and replace. Revolution, he argues, is the favorite mechanism of the Left, which fails to comprehend and value what has been achieved and finds it more exciting to overthrow and destroy.

Yes, the correct term is "more exciting." It is difficult, and the act of a mature mind, Scruton asserts, to tend to something slowly over time, evaluating and accepting what does work, rejecting what doesn't, and gradually learning lessons of improvement. This is the conservative way. It is much more exhilarating to overthrow, to spill blood, to destroy structures and groups, who stand in the way of progress."Manning the barricades!" is more exciting than reading about and learning from history.[52]

It makes for more impactful public theater, too. It is easier to write and more compelling to deliver a fiery, radical, "Join us, Comrade! For the greater good!" speech than it is to deliver a "Let's all think this through reasonably and come to mature conclusions" speech. When you hear a politician speaking about fundamentally transforming society, you likely have a radical Leftist on your hands.

Utopians

Fundamental to the conservative belief is the idea that human beings are not perfect but that we learn over time. We become better as individuals and as larger societies through what we learn. This is why history and memory are sacred to the conservative mind. Therein lie all the most valuable lessons. Therein we see the dragons to be avoided at all costs.

By contrast, liberals are millenarian. They believe humans *can* be perfected in one go. All it will take is the right government, the right rules, enforcement of the right ideals—as prescribed by them, the ruling elites—and finally, everything will be right.

In their most extreme incarnation (radical Marxists), they even believe in an end to history. Once all struggle is completed and once all is leveled and

---

52   Roger Scruton, *How to Be a Conservative* (New York: Bloomsbury Continuum, 2014).

equaled, they argue that we will exist in a perfected society. That concludes history. Ta-da. The end.

The conservative mind sees this as juvenile and utopian. But this does not mean that the conservative mind does not aim for improvement. Rather, again with reference to Roger Scruton, it favors peaceful evolution of ideas over radical imposition of new worldviews. Moreover, the conservative mind does not believe in an end to history. That seems small-minded. After all, then what?

A very vocal minority

I observe that the politically correct tend to be a very vocal *minority*. When President Donald Trump, a conservative and outspoken critic of political correctness, announced his run for U.S. president before the 2016 election, I remember turning to my wife and saying, "He's going to win."

My reason for this assertion was that, by this time, political correctness seemed to be an unending wave of madness on the global landscape. I believed—and was eventually proven correct—that the general population was sick of it. I also believed that the aggressive voices shouting politically correct theories were actually in the minority. However, they held the megaphone.

Right up to Donald Trump's victory, the Left-leaning mainstream media were predicting his defeat by a landslide. They were rocked to the core by how wrong they were. And then we observed on social media, and in the media in general, that liberal talking heads globally were equally rocked to the core by this outcome. They had not seen it coming in a million years. To me, it was obvious, even inevitable.

I believe that this teaches us that they are a very vocal minority. They also exist within an echo chamber, in which they hear only their own ideas. For this reason, they tend to believe that their narrative is the only narrative and also the correct one. They are genuinely surprised to discover that they are wrong. When this occurs, their only explanation tends to be racism.

Morally Different in Their Make-up

In the groundbreaking book on moral differences between conservatives and liberals, *The Righteous Mind: Why Good People are Divided by Religion and Politics*, social psychologist Dr. Jonathan Haidt points out a fascinating insight. In brief, it is that liberals use just three moral pillars to make up their belief systems, while conservatives use six.

The six pillars are:

1. Care and harm
2. Fairness and cheating
3. Liberty and oppression
4. Loyalty and betrayal
5. Authority and subversion
6. Sanctity and degradation.[53]

Liberals and conservatives both believe in the first three pillars. However, they interpret them in different ways. Conservatives typically also believe in the next three pillars, while liberals typically do not.

Understanding these differences is extremely useful in two ways: It helps us to understand and articulate what we believe is "missing" in the liberal mindset and, therefore, to better understand why they express the ideas that they express, and it also aids us when pointing out to them which moral underpinnings are absent from their arguments.

Here is how it plays out:

> **1. Care and harm**—Both liberals and conservatives believe in this moral pillar, but in different ways. Liberals tend to emphasize this particular pillar over all others, which conservatives see as an imbalance. How, for instance, should it interact with concepts of justice?

---

53   Jonathan Haidt, *The Righteous Mind: Why Good People are Divided by Politics and Religion* (London: Penguin, 2012).

2. Fairness and cheating—Both believe in this pillar, but our interpretations are vastly different. Liberals approach this one from a group mindset and see unfairness as one group having less than another group.

By contrast, conservatives define fairness as proportionality. This is the objection to equal outcomes for unequal work. Conservatives will argue: Stop punishing success, stop rewarding failure, stop enabling people's bad decisions, stop providing privilege for those who do not earn it.

3. Liberty and oppression—Both groups care about this concept, but in different ways. This pillar refers to our deep-rooted desire to band together to take down the bully.

This pillar can lead to violence. Conservatives tend to perceive this as best applied against tyrannical big government. Liberals tend to see it being applied against capitalists and class oppressors. Also, when it comes to liberty, it is usually about sexual liberty for the Left but economic liberty for the Right.

Those are the three pillars we hold in common, though our interpretations differ. And at this point, we fundamentally part ways.

Conservatives have a "broader palette" of moral pillars. We introduce more concerns into our total moral decision-making matrix. These additional pillars are:

4. Loyalty and betrayal—This concept is almost irrelevant to the liberal. Fidelity to one's own group is extremely valuable to conservatives but little more than a matter for suspicion for the liberal.

5. Authority and subversion—To the left, insubordination is an inherently good thing. To conservatives, a system can't work if it is in a state of constant revolution, and someone must ultimately be accountable. Stability and growth are preferred.

6. Sanctity and degradation—For the conservative, sanctity matters. A sense of the holy and the revered are important. For the liberal, it is a near non-issue. It is perhaps the difference between "Your body is a temple" versus "Your body is an amusement park."

Haidt gives the example of an Occupy Wall Street protest sign that captures the liberal view: "No thing is sacred." The conservative belief system would find this obnoxious and repellent, arguing that some things are sacred and should be cherished and defended.

From these differing viewpoints, you can already imagine just how many of our ideological conflicts arise.

Take the idea of firm borders as one simple example. The liberal sees nothing within a nation as sacred and precious and to be protected. They might even question the fundamental worth of their own culture and see no particular problem with subverting or altering it. The conservative, by contrast, will greatly value their own culture and view a wall as a necessary means of protecting something important, something valuable.

Haidt mentions that in researching and writing his book, he began by identifying himself as a partisan liberal, who hoped to aid the progressive Democrat party but ultimately became a centrist. This was largely the product of discovering what he did about differences in liberal and conservative reasoning.

As a useful side note, Haidt also argues that humans tend to be persuaded first emotionally, and then only logically. (He is responsible for the famous "Elephant and Rider" analogy of human will, which asserts that although the logical rider is technically in charge, the emotional elephant is big, strong, and takes a long time to turn).

This accounts for why liberals tend to argue from feelings first. It is also why I strongly advise that our side should learn to own the kindness narrative and reclaim the good words, which we tend not to do. Arguing from logic alone is insufficient.

Chemically different in their make-up?

We must treat this next idea with a degree of caution. Nevertheless, repeated studies have quite consistently indicated a correlation between males with lower-than-usual testosterone levels and the liberal worldview. Females are also disproportionately represented in liberal voting.

Males with normal or higher-than-usual testosterone levels are proportionately more represented among conservatives and the Right. Sources ranging from science publications to bodybuilding magazines have pointed out that the three leading contributors to reduction of male testosterone include:

- Mac and Cheese meals
- Soy milk products, and
- Eating and drinking out of plastic plates and cups.

(By contrast, a few promoters of healthy testosterone levels include weight-lifting, eating proteins and fats, and getting enough sunshine and Vitamin D).

Does this translate into a useful technique for us? I believe that the answer is no. It is ungentlemanly to press this advantage. Our aim is ultimately to demonstrate truth and moral goodness, not to mock or degrade, lest we come to resemble our opponent. We should, I believe, simply leave it at the level of being useful to know.

This much, at least, seems clear: Women and low-testosterone males are demonstrably more greatly represented among liberal-voting demographics.

Humorous Aside: During the 2016 U.S. presidential elections, one Dr. Dareld Morris, owner of a medical clinic in Florida, aired an anti-Clinton aid that went: "Hi, guys, Doc Morris here. Most are not aware of the negative effects low-T can have on your mental state, for instance, your ability to focus and think clearly. So, as a community service, I have this special offer: for any guys out there that are thinking of voting for Hillary, I want to offer you a free testosterone test. Just come in and register in my office in Fort Myers and let's see if we can help."[54]

Defectors From Their Own

By all accounts, the liberal's first job appears to be to oppose his own. He will accommodate and excuse on behalf of other demographics the same behavior he must vocally deplore among his own.

The single most politically correct man I know on a personal level exemplifies this dynamic. He is a white male, a self-professed Christian, a family man, and a business owner. From his extensive commentaries and writings on social justice issues, you might never guess any these things. Above all else, he aims his greatest ire at Christians, men, white people, and business owners. His comments on these subjects are not merely of concerned disapproval, but of barely concealed hatred. A self-avowed liberal who openly defends political correctness, he primarily targets almost exclusively his own demographic. I find that this observation bears out when applied more broadly.

It appears that liberals draw a sort of perverse moral gratification from this dynamic. They like to publicly show themselves to be against their own. Equally, they like to publicly show themselves to be for the other. This seems to constitute a form of strange righteousness for them.

I am not the only one to have detected this dynamic. It gave rise to the popular phrase "virtue signaling," which is regularly employed against liberals. Academic literature produced by liberals tends to follow this pattern, too. All things Western must be deplored, or at least played down. All other things must be celebrated and played up. Fair comparison is out of the question.

---

54   Sam Wolfson, "Looking for Mr T: the politicization of testosterone," TheGuardian.com, July 28, 2019, https://www.theguardian.com/global/2019/jul/28/looking-for-mr-t-the-politicisation-of-testosterone-and-toxic-masuclinity.

And it's all over the history books.

In *The Myth of the Andalusian Paradise: Muslims, Christians, and Jews Under Islamic Rule in Medieval Spain*, historian Dario Fernandez-Morera provides just one example of this bias, which leads to dishonest historical revisionism in liberal literature. The Muslim conquest of Spain is often called expansion, Morera explains, and every effort is made to highlight the notion that the result was not a conquered and subdued people, but rather, the establishment of a peaceful cooperative.[55] (The author thoroughly disproves the truth-value of this claim. Nevertheless, the claim itself is interesting).

By contrast, European expansion into Africa or the Americas is consistently labeled "conquest and colonialization." So, why the double standard?

Muslims, per liberal writers, brought peace and plurality, science and enlightenment. Europeans did not bring science, medicine, schools, and literature (all of which are to be ignored), but only oppression, based on evil motives.

These games with language, which have important ideological outcomes casting villains and heroes, are almost always the product of white European or American liberal writers. Their desire to hate their own is overwhelming. Their desire to justify and even elevate the other is embarrassing. What would be more honest? Just tell the truth.

Liberal academics appear to see their role in the great historical play as being that of confessors and self-flagellators on behalf of their own. In addition to using words dishonestly themselves, liberals also accuse their opponents of using coded words. This is an act of transference. *They* are guilty of doing it, so they assume that *we* are, too. Just observe the academics and news reporters reminding us that words like "national" and "country" are codes for white.

There is a convention in philosophy that asserts that in order to arrive at good thinking and productive debate, one should interpret the ideas of the

---

55   Darío Fernández-Morera, *The Myth of the Andalusian Paradise: Muslims, Christians, and Jews Under Islamic Rule in Medieval Spain* (Wilmington: Intercollegiate Studies Institute, 2016).

other in their most generous and strongest representation. Only then should one engage with discussion about the merits of the ideas themselves. When the Left asserts that our most innocuous words—"my nation"—are actually code for sinister, racial, terrorist groups, they transgress this convention. The results are inaccurate thinking (on their part) and false accusations (against us).

Noble in Their Public Persona, But at No Personal Cost

There is another element to the grandstanding popularly termed "virtue-signaling." It is generally done at no cost to the person displaying their fine character and transcendent morals to the world. They will, for instance, talk about the evils of people who own land or who possess large amounts of money and how land and money must be given to the poor. However, they do not mean *their* land. They do not mean *their* money. Instead, they are nobly volunteering sacrifice on someone else's behalf. Naturally, this forms one easy way to catch them out in argumentation. Simply charge them with the challenge: "You first."

Emotionally Charged, Arguing a Worldview of Constant Sweeping Accusation

Ask any liberal whether they agree with the moral precedent of the phrase "Live and let live," and they will eagerly concur. However, this is not their real-world practice. Instead, constant outrage and revolution against the Old Order tend to be their lived habit.

There must always be something wrong with the undesirable other side, and no grievance is so petty that it shouldn't be publicly leveled, as though critically important. "Live and let live" refers to absolutely everything, except anything whatsoever pertaining to the Old Order.

Adherents to Arbitrary Rules and Norms, Which Continually Change

If you want to know what your progressive friend will believe, passionately and to the core of his being, next week, just read *this* week's liberal op-eds. In doing so, you will find out what he believes at the same time that he does. This is to say that the liberal belief system does not—indeed, cannot—follow an eternal, universal, unchanging set of well-codified rules. Liberalism is built on constant revolution. That means it must always have something to revolt against, something to overthrow, week after week, or it ceases to have any point at all.

This philosophy is not incidental. It was baked right into the DNA of communism by Marx and Lenin, who prophesied that there should never be a settled outcome to their belief system, other than their assertion of the end of history. Instead, revolution was supposed to continue indefinitely, with good Marxists ever digging up something new to vilify and level in the human community.

Does it seem to you as though there is always some bizarre, new politically correct cause every new week? Well, that's why. The system needs it. It feeds on outrage and revolution; and if it can't find any, it must manufacture it. Without it, liberals have no power because they have no relevance. There has to be something to rage against. The alternative is merely maintaining and improving best practice, and that is conservatism. With that, you now understand a key pillar of the PC world that you experience every day.

Eager to shut down speech based on demographic

"You don't have a womb? Sit down. You don't get to speak on women's issues!" This argument makes no logical sense, yet it is employed all the time. It only works if you fall for it. The argument is so flimsy that it fails in the face of simple rejection. Respond to "sit down" with "No!" and to "You don't have a right" with "Yes, I do," and simply continue.

I recall an instance of a social justice warrior using this technique on a well-meaning person in an incident in South Africa. At a private school, a young, black student had been told that her hair didn't comply with school standards. These standards applied to everybody, but the student identified this policy as a racist rule that targeted her personally and asserted that it was because she was black, and she rose to national prominence for her refusal to comply.

In my personal view, this did not deserve to become headline news. The school could either have decided to permit her hairstyle or insisted she comply with the rules—their choice entirely—and that should have been the end of it. Nevertheless, the student in question went on to be featured in television advertisements, holding her fist up in the defiant, revolutionary pose, the poster-child for resistance against oppression (you know, because she refused to tie up her hair).

In a social media argument on the topic, I witnessed a liberal, white man attempt to shut down the opinion of another man by saying, "You don't have African hair, so you don't get to speak. Sit down, shut up, and try to learn something." Those were his words, verbatim.

I found this moralizing particularly entertaining on the grounds that not two weeks prior, this same man had used his progressive ideas to tear into parents raising white boys. Per his narrative, white boys were the earthly incarnation of all evil in the world. Curiously, though, he did not have any white boys himself, and yet he felt perfectly entitled to address parents who did. Why shouldn't *he* himself "shut up, sit down and try to learn something?"

Not only is this argument easily refuted (simply by saying no), but it is also easily used against its perpetrator. It is not possible for a society to function if demographic groups may not view, address, critique or interact with one another. For that reason, the social justice warrior will slip up and commit this same act himself.

Finally, good governing principles are universal. Anything deemed to be not universal and, therefore, outside the realms of your commentary is operating deviously. In the previous example, it's not about *African hair*. That is secondary and a distraction. It's about school standards. Those apply to everyone. Sorry if you don't like it.

I will also add that it's the height of gall to claim oppression while enjoying all the privileges of a private school education and *simultaneously* refusing to abide by the code of conduct, which you or your legal guardian will have signed. But remember: the outrage machine needs constant feeding. Any excuse to rage against the Old Order.

Fascists Posing as Victims

This characteristic applies both figuratively and literally. Let us begin by looking at the literal sense. If you study actual fascist philosophy (as proposed by Giovanni Gentile and realized under Mussolini), no modern-day organization more faithfully carries out both the precepts and the methodologies of fascism than Antifa, the organization whose name ironically derives from the term "anti-fascist." Still, its proponents fail to see the irony.

In August of 2019, after yet another round of violent Antifa protests in Portland, Oregon, Representative Dan Crenshaw of Texas, a former Navy SEAL, observed, "In Hong Kong, antifascists wave American flags, demand freedom and actually fight fascists. In Portland, "antifascists" burn American flags [and] demand violence in the name of Socialism."[56]

The best book on this topic: *The Big Lie* by Dinesh D'Souza explores the founding philosophy, history, and tactics of actual fascism, starting with its founding philosopher Giovanni Gentile. He so convincingly makes the case that Antifa is, in fact, fascist, that their mission and existence is rendered a bad joke. Antifa is the literal modern-day incarnation of fascist posing as victim.

The figurative version is subtler, yet still pervasive. It is the person who accuses everyone who disagrees with him of being a Nazi and whose response to all enemies is, "You can't speak! We should assault you!" Nowhere is this

---

56 Dan Crenshaw, Twitter Post, August 18, 2019, 7:48 p.m., https://twitter.com/dancrenshawtx/status/1162873906132398081.

more prominent than on modern university campuses, where fascist mobs use blare horns and mass interpersonal violence to shut down guest speakers with whom they disagree.

As an article by The Schiller Institute observes: "With the collapse of the Soviet Union, our campuses now represent the largest concentration of Marxist dogma in the world. The irrational adolescent outbursts of the 1960s have become institutionalized into a 'permanent revolution.'"[57]

I first encountered this particular dirty trick many years ago, before I was even aware of the notion of political correctness. I started witnessing the rise of an argument technique that is not an argument technique at all, but rather, a language trap. It was the act of calling another person a hater.

Do you remember when you first heard this term? *Hater* is an interesting word. It is a fascinating tool of warfare. It presupposes all qualitative objections as invalid and simply accuses the person on whom the label is being pinned as operating from bad faith, assuming the worst possible motivation on their part. It precludes the possibility that they may have a point, any point whatsoever, and moves directly to the invalidation of the entire person as its form of response. "You're just a hater." It dismisses and ends all conversation by throwing paint over the scene.

No properly constituted debate society would sanction such a technique. It would immediately be called out as an *ad hominem* argument (the fallacy of avoiding genuine discussion of a topic by instead attacking the motives or character of the other party), and the person offering the argument would be chastised or disqualified, or they would simply lose the debate. But this argument *is* used in the public forum, where fairness is not moderated by a third party.

I was young when I first heard this word, but it troubled me. I could see that it was a dishonest technique. Today, I would know to call it out as an *ad hominem* argument. The real problem, of course, is that an angry Leftist mob, brandishing placards about haters, blowing airhorns, throwing rocks and Molotov cocktails (no exaggeration—go watch the footage online), and attacking passersby, including the elderly, does not typically permit the airtime for someone to make this argument. That's how terrorism works.

Still, pointing this out to others after the fact strengthens the public perception of the Left as fascists posing as victim, and that in itself is useful. This battle is not won strictly in the setting of academic debates. It is largely a war of culture and perceptions. So, let them be seen for who they are and point out their techniques where you can.

Conservative speaker Ben Shapiro has been the target of many such riots on varsity campuses. He points out: "The headlines were nuts! I mean, headlines like 'Berkeley braces for Shapiro visit.' Really? Was I the one who was going to be smashing ATMs?"[58] He is right to point this out, and we should be proactive in pointing it out, too.

These violent protestors, and the supporting liberal media, hand the violence back to Ben. This is perverse. Ben is simply a speaker who delivers a conservative lecture. *They* are the rioters, looters, and destroyers. *They* should be identified as such and held accountable. It is disingenuous to hand the accountability for the public disorder back to the conservative, who is not guilty of it.

The more we hand accountability for liberal hysteria back to the violent Left, the less they can hide behind their veneer of kindness and professed love of peace. They are warlike and instigators of riots, and they must be called out as such every time they commit these crimes. By contrast, of course, the challenge should also be raised: "Show me the conservative riot."

---

58   ABC News, "Outspoken conservative Ben Shapiro says political correctness breeds insanity," YouTube Post, 9:14, October 20, 2017, https://www.youtube.com/watch?v=vj5JXrpwsZs&list=PLYoabUsEB4c2j0kT_LQta0adH1XjWxVEj.

As social media page Caldron Pool put it: "About 10,000 people gathered in Sydney on Tuesday night to protest abortion. Astonishingly, not a window was broken, not a person beaten, not a car set on fire. No vulgarity and immorality on parade. Just 'dangerous' conservatives and right-wing fanatics, singing 'Amazing Grace.'"[59]

Objection: The alt-right march in Charlottesville turned violent, and then deadly!

Response: True.

Objection: So . . . how do you defend that, then?

Response: I don't. The alt-right is nuts. Why would I defend *them?*

This leads into a discussion about their misunderstanding, by which they see a duality: Liberals versus the alt-right. The group in the middle are called conservatives. They overthrew slavery, defeated Hitler, and faced down communist dictatorship. They are not the alt-right.

Unable or Unwilling to Distinguish Between Skin Color and Ideology

"Skin color is exactly the same as ideology" goes the tacit argument. If you don't accept a new ideology, you are, by default, obviously a racist who hates people based on nothing more substantial than the pigmentation of their skin. This is the ultimate strawman argument: We will simplify your objection to the point of absurdity, then attack that absurd representation. As an added bonus, we get to accuse you of hate, based on our mischaracterization.

Conservatives, scientists, Christians—all those whom political correctness generally opposes—do not have any intrinsic or doctrinal issue with skin color. Science must see it as largely irrelevant, value-neutral, though perhaps interesting from a genetic perspective. Even healthy from a genetic perspective, insofar as mixing of races leads to stronger, improved

---

59   Peaceful Demonstration in Sydney, Twitter Post, August 22, 2019, https://twitter. com/CaldronPool/status/1164368247824633856.

genes. The Jewish faith welcomes people of any ethnic background who wish to become Jews, without reservation. The Christian text openly advises: "There is neither Jew nor Greek, there is neither slave nor free, there is neither male nor female; for you are all one in Christ Jesus" (Gal. 3:28), negating even the perception of difference based on skin color. And most average people around the world today simply don't care, want to live in peace, and have little to no interest in outmoded progressive eugenic theories of race difference.

The problem arises when ideology is smuggled in under the guise of skin color. The two have nothing in common. A white European male can, in principle, be a militant, Islamic terrorist. The damage to society then occurs when the new ideology becomes a protected idea as a result of the slight-of-hand played by those who would deem it a race issue.

Try this scenario:

Liberal: "Including more black people in television shows makes our society more inclusive. And take this young lady. She's albino. Shouldn't she be able to be a model?"

Conservative: "Good. Sure. Absolutely. No argument from me."

Liberal: "Glad you agree, so we'll start teaching your children Islam. You know, in order to promote better race relations."

Conservative: "Um . . . what?"

Liberal: "And if you complain about being raped, you're a racist."

Objection: So what's the way forward, then? Are we just saying no to multicultural societies?

Response: The distinction is this: Multi-ethnic? Yes. Multi-cultural? Well, that one doesn't receive automatic approval. We must know what the alternate culture believes and practices. If child brides are an acceptable practice, then the answer should be no because that is not a moral standard we can tolerate. If you disagree, please explain your acceptance of child brides.

Hypocritical Accusers of Divisiveness

There is incredible hypocrisy in saying, "You're being divisive!" This accusation typically occurs after the damaging liberal idea has been put forward and in response to the conservative objection thereto. Yes. I don't want communism. And I don't believe that fighting against it is a bad thing. If that divides, then that is a good divide. Finally, the conflict began when you *proposed* communism, not when I *opposed* it.

Let's play "Your Contradictions are Showing." It goes like this:

"We must celebrate diversity!"

"Okay, men and women are different, and that's beautiful."

"How dare you say that men and women are different, you oppressive misogynist?! They're exactly the same in every way; and if you mention the idea that genders exist, you're a hateful bigot."

"Um . . . what happened to celebrating difference? Also, that fact—of male and female—is at the center of life itself. Without the existence of two genders that come together to procreate, there is only an absence of all life. Nothing but death."

"You Nazi! How dare you speak such violence! Now, leave me alone; I need to go join my mob and beat up people who refuse to celebrate diversity."

"Okey dokey. Have oodles of fun."

Proponents of Simplistic Narrative Views of History

This generally follows this pattern: Every place on Earth cradled a peace-loving ethnic tribe, living in harmony with nature and in peace with one another, until Europeans arrived with their slavery and their capitalism and stole their cities.

Real history is more complicated, more nuanced, and messier than that. Every nation, every grouping, every culture has its good and bad, and it is important to be able to speak candidly about that, otherwise we preclude ourselves the possibility of learning from history. Even the broad characterizations in the new narrative are at least problematic. For instance, the reference to "white people" creates the impression of a unified, homogenous, and undifferentiated blob, all with the same intentions. And worse: an *invading* unified blob.

Close examination splinters this blob narrative into impracticability. By white people, what exactly is meant? The Picts who were bred out by the Celts? Or the Celts who were conquered by the Romans? And do we mean the pagan Romans, or the later Christianized Romans? Or the Romans who were overrun by the pagan Germanic tribes? Do we mean the Bretons who were conquered by the Angles and Saxons and then again by Scandinavian Vikings? Do we mean the white people who practiced slavery, or do we mean the white people who fought against those white people and abolished it? Do we mean the communists of Eastern Europe and Russia or the fascists and Nazi white people of mainland Europe? Or do we mean the white people who fought the largest war in human history against precisely those people?

The exact same splintering into unending fractionality occurs if you attempt to pull the same simplistic trick with any other race group. That is why color doesn't matter. Ideology does. Belief does. There have been groups of white people who have practiced slavery. And there have been white people who died in their tens of thousands to oppose slavery. There have been white slaves. There have also been black slaves, and there have been (and still are) black slavers.

To rail against racism is legitimate. I will gladly join you on that score. To rail against white people is racist. On that score, I will oppose you, insofar as racism is unacceptable to me.

To say "white people" is to paint a picture of a group—usually for demonizing ideological reasons—that doesn't exist as a cohesive whole. I have never attended a "white people meeting" in my entire life and, happily, wouldn't know where to go to find one. This would surprise the average viewer of CNN who might believe that there are candlelit and coordinated cell meetings all over the world.

Of special note here: This book does not favor so-called "white people" or any other ethnic group. It favors correct thinking, wherever that is to be found. White people have had some astonishingly bad cultural ideas deserving of criticism (bullfighting, just offhand). Thus, "white" is not a protected group in this book. But neither is any other group protected from critique of its bad or harmful ideas by simple virtue of skin color. What we want to emerge from our critique of political correctness are good ideas, not a winning skin tone.

Ever Ready to Assume Bad Faith on the Part of Anyone Who Doesn't Agree with Them

This is the go-to technique for lazy thinkers. The premise is this: Everything I don't agree with must be generated by your fear or your hate. It is not conceivable that you might be operating in good faith, nor that you might actually believe what you are saying, nor that you might actually have a point.

Here is an example from *Time* magazine. The headline of an article on their site, dated June 27, 2019, boldly asserts: "Evangelicals are supporting Trump out of fear, not faith."[60] It couldn't possibly be that they agreed with his policies. It couldn't possibly be that they perceived him to be keeping his election promises. It can't be the record high employment levels or the barrier-breaking prosperity. No, it must be fear. They love him because they are full of fear and hate. *Time* says so. The end.

The reasoning is so blatantly prejudiced, so glaringly partisan, so classically Leftist in its assignment of assumed motives, that it surprises me a

---

60   David French, "Evangelicals Are Supporting Trump Out of Fear Not Faith," Time.com, June 27, 2019, https://time.com/5615617/why-evangelicals-support-trump.

supposedly high-level source of journalism like *Time* could allow this to go out under their name. How embarrassing for them.

If you are looking for it, this technique also presents in subtle variants. I once attended a public debate, at which two self-professed Christians contested the notion,"Does the Bible restrict marriage to a man and a woman?" Anyone who predicted that the progressive liberal would open with a statement indicting conservative Christians for their fear and hate would not have been disappointed. He began by saying, "I understand that this issue causes you uncertainty and fear." Translation? "I'm subtly accusing you of operating from emotion. And in particular, from *bad* emotions. Maybe one day, you can be like me, free of your emotional prejudices, existing on a higher plane. Until you agree with me, you are in the position of fear, ignorance, and hate. Here, have a biscuit."

Fortunately, his opponent caught it and called him on it. The fear and hate narrative, a grotesque descendant of that simplistic word *hater,* assumes its own correctness from the outset and precludes the possibility of the opposition holding valid, qualitative objections.

I similarly recall a friend on Facebook expressing her disgust that the U.S. military did not want to admit transgenders. Her exact words of dismissal were the predictable, "It's just fear and hatred." No, it is actually not. There is a valid reason for the objection. The military demands unique levels of mental strength and endurance. Half of transgender people attempt to commit suicide. Can you logically send them into a combat scenario? And further, entrust the lives of fellow soldiers to them, a demographic with a fifty percent propensity for self-destruction?

There is no fear and hate in arriving at such a conclusion. It would be illogical not to. It would be unjust not to. Furthermore, the underlying liberal assumption that the military is just another social club, to which anyone should have immediate access, is also dubious. The military serves a purpose, and that purpose is to protect an entire nation. It is not there simply to act as a social justice experiment bent on equality. That is not its foundational purpose. If anything, it is a highly refined killing machine, not an "all-welcome," egalitarian social club.

Still, that is the narrative they will present: Everything *you* do is based on fear and hate; everything *we* do is enlightened and inclusive. And the person presenting that narrative will persist in believing that they are obviously enlightened and you are obviously ignorant, even in light of positive refutation. In this, they are immune to logic. They view their "truth" as being greater than your facts.

Lovers of Offense

Welcome to the Woke Wars: I'll win because I'm more offended by absolutely everything than you are!" Offense is viewed on the Left as a sort of right in itself. If you are morally outraged, this must mean that you hold the high ground. It turns out that it is perfectly plausible to be highly indignant and, also, wrong.

Haters of Form

Progressives increasingly champion formlessness. They are against definitions, divisions, borders, and positive constitution. Definitions are considered to be violence, and difference and distinction are re-characterized as oppression. No borders. No labels. No genders. All is blob. We are the Borg, and you will be assimilated. (They would say all is free, but their definition of free is different to ours).

Re-casters of Blame

This technique is highly characteristic of the outraged liberal. Their side creates the problem and then casts blame for it. "Free love! But we're angry because men don't value women. And single moms are martyred heroes. And now we need abortion. How dare you disempower women by denying them the right to kill the baby that they're having out of wedlock because of the morality that we destroyed while trashing the institution of marriage, which would have prevented all of this from happening in the first place? You clearly hate women and children!"

"No. Actually, our system was just better."

As another example, many scholars today blame liberal policies for deepening the U.S. Great Recession of the 1920s and extending it by four more years. At the time, and since, socialists blamed this on capitalism, true to their pattern.

Perverters of Fairness

In a YouTube video by Project Veritas, a Google executive openly explains that they perceive fairness to be the "elevating of marginalized voices." They do not perceive fairness to be the same as hearing the voices of those already in power.[61] What?! Their definition of fairness is not the same as the universal understanding of that term. Theirs is based on demographics and on their characterization of who is powerful and, therefore, oppressive and who is marginal and, therefore, oppressed. It's not about right and wrong. It's about power. This is incredibly significant because they are a major controller of the public narrative.

Holders of Double Standards

Here is perhaps the most egregious example of liberal double standards. They will rail against the one-to-many extrapolation, while also using it when it suits them.

For instance: "Just because 1 . . . 2 . . . 3, 60,000 Muslims have carried out terror attacks, you can't call Islam a religion of terror." However, if a white person says something racist, all white people are racist; and if a white person carries out a terrorist attack, then the biggest threat in the world is white men.

---

61   Old Soul Rebel, "Project Veritas Expose Google," YouTube Post, 25:10, June 25, 2019, https://www.youtube.com/watch?v=TyC5fz2UoAI.

From all of these characteristics, we see that *liberal* no longer means what the word states. It now means orthodoxy. It is not about freedom. It is about prescription. It is not what you choose. It is what we tell you to believe or face our social justice rage.

Those are a sampling of qualities typical of the politically correct person, along with their arguments and methods. So, by contrast to all this, who are *we*?

THE PERSON INVESTED IN ARGUING AGAINST POLITICAL CORRECTNESS

Interestingly, many different demographics have an interest in this project. A person invested in opposing political correctness may fit one, or some, or many of the following types:

- A scientist, who cannot, in good faith, agree that classifications and categories do not matter, that biology is irrelevant, and that emotional claims can supersede factual ones.
- A philosopher, who refuses to concede that magical thinking can be superior to reason and logic.
- A psychologist, who sees that politically correct prescriptions for thinking contravene accepted standards of mental health and degrade the quality and maturity of our thinking.
- An economist, who is troubled by the resurgence of Marxist principles in economies that have proven the value of free-market systems.
- A common-sense citizen, who prefers to speak and hear the truth in discourse and who senses that political correctness is concealing harmful developments, lying about outcomes, and doing so in the service of an ideology with an agenda.
- A practitioner of the Jewish or Christian faith, who sees these ideas as a direct assault on their system of belief, perceiving that political correctness is good being called evil and evil good.

- A person of color, who does not see themselves as a victim, who is sick of being told that they are oppressed, and who believes that all this social division does not reflect reality nor help to pave a healthy way forward.

- A white person who abhors racism and prefers not to see color, preferring the principle of judging a person "according to the content of their character, not the color of their skin," and who assesses the new and heightened emphasis on seeing nothing but skin color as racist and counter-productive.

- An entrepreneur or business owner who is troubled by talk of socialism, massive taxation, redistribution, or general vilification of those who drive economies.

- An individualistic thinker, who refuses to be bullied into believing something that is visibly and demonstrably untrue, simply because the "outrage mob" asserts that they must.

- A person who is troubled by the idea that there is no such thing as evil, but that all bad acts are mere results of poverty or misunderstanding and who believes that denying the existence of evil permits the conditions for it to flourish.

- A citizen who is concerned by the rise of Islam within their previously Westernized nation.

- A high-achieving Asian, who is discriminated against academically under affirmative action.

- Someone who appreciates beauty and finds postmodernist art and expression vulgar and ugly.

- Someone who sees the violent protests, mass marches, and aggressively vitriolic standards of social justice warriors and finds them to be morally unsettling.

- A person of moderate views, who does not see utopianism as viable, but prefers a society that gradually learns and corrects itself.

- A pro-life woman (or man), who believes that casual abortion transgresses an important, transcendent, moral order.
- A proponent of the importance of families, who is concerned about familial breakdown and the resultant social consequences.
- A parent raising a child in what they perceive to be an increasingly crazy, new world.
- A liberal who is beginning to feel that their own side is increasingly crazy and that they did not sign up for this, who feels like the proverbial frog in the heating pot, realizing that they must soon jump or boil.
- Someone who has seen an interesting YouTube video by personalities who fight against political correctness (perhaps Ben Shapiro, Jordan Peterson, or Dennis Prager) and is intrigued to learn more about this subject.

To fight against political correctness, you need not be perfect yourself. Indeed, we shall see that one of the opposition's tactics, first proposed by Saul Alinsky in *Rules for Radicals*, is to force you to uphold impossible standards, even as they do not.

We will deflate this technique right up front, with the admission that we are not perfect but that our system is demonstrably superior. We will also point out to our opponents that it is easy to criticize an existing order when they are comparing it to their imagined perfect utopia. However, where their utopia has been attempted in the real world, it consistently devolves into a nightmare.

Even their desire to unite governments in order to solve climate change lacks credibility at the smallest level. In the U.S., liberal-run cities like San Francisco and Baltimore are currently descending into health hazards, where officials are concerned about the Bubonic Plague. Where liberals are in charge, they are often unable to clean up their own streets, let alone an entire planet.

We will discuss all of that. I will arm you with tools, arguments, and techniques for managing yourself. I will point you in the direction of the resources you might need to win a specific fight. But win we must. And we can. If our arguments are correct (and they are) and if their arguments are flawed (are they ever!), then with courage, patience, and persistence, common sense can prevail. Raise your hand. Raise the objection. Raise your voice. And when you see someone else bravely venturing to do the same, get into their corner and back them. Do not let them stand alone.

With that, let us jump into the "street fight" section of this book.

PART II
HOW TO DISMANTLE AND DEBUNK POLITICALLY CORRECT IDEAS

HERE IS THE FIRST THING to know: The political Left has created an entirely new and different framework of argumentation. It doesn't relate to reality. It doesn't rely on truth. It uses justice words dishonestly, and it creates its own definitions. Then it *wins* by its own definitions. It uses emotional reasoning, *ad hominem* arguments, strawman techniques . . . every trick in the book for winning an ideological argument unethically.

Fortunately, if you understand what they are doing, it is easy to counter their poisoned points, to identify their flawed premises, and to deflate their damaging proposals. And the very fact that their arguments are fundamentally dishonest can, and should, be used to weaken their position. It matters that we do so regularly, passionately, and with persistence. Solomon once observed, "The first one to plead his cause seems right, Until his neighbor comes and examines him" (Prov. 18:17).

Absent our challenges, these people seem right. They seem reasonable. They seem credible, and they seem truthful. Dreadfully, their ideology prevails. Intelligently challenged, however, their agendas quickly unravel, and those looking on see the lie. They also learn how to see the lie again in future.

135

We debate not merely for the progressive in question, but also for the watching audience.

In this section, I will provide you with thirty-six detailed examples of strategies designed to counter politically correct Leftist arguments and ideologies. I will go into some depth on each. Thereafter, I will provide a small handful of additional examples, but in quick overview, because by this stage, you will be familiar with the underlying patterns and will likely only require a quick how-to prompt or two.

Naturally, the specific arguments you face will continually evolve (shall we say, "metastasize"?) over time. But after this, you should be able to see the underlying patterns and fallacies in *any* argument, regardless of how it is specifically presented. You will analyze it and say, "Oh, that's the *Marlboro Man technique.*" Or "Oh, I see they're using Herbert Marcuse." Or "Oh, they have indulged in "concept creep" in order to create a victim class," and so forth. Their patterns of argumentation are all very similar. They are all basically the same thing. Once you get the hang of it, you will be able to adapt the techniques accordingly.

CHAPTER 1
WALK TOWARD THE FIRE.

OUR FIRST TECHNIQUE HAS TO do with how you orient and conduct yourself. Shocked into silence, dumbfounded into unresponsiveness, intimidated by stinging vitriol until we simply do not speak—this is precisely the wrong way to react. It is how you surrender a civilization.

U.S. author and political commentator Ben Shapiro is quite possibly one of the world's finest when it comes to debating against political correctness. Shapiro is entertaining to watch on YouTube, and we can learn a great deal from observing how fearlessly and effectively he confronts bad ideology. (Don't think, however, that the fact Shapiro is Jewish prevents the PC police from calling him a right-wing Nazi or a white supremacist. How's that for irony? Shapiro himself points out that the Left appear to be irony-impaired).

I recommend watching Ben Shapiro in action and studying his technique. He is singularly brilliant in debates. Not just his logic, but his confidence, too. So, what is his guiding mantra?

There are two things that Shapiro has mentioned as internal prompts—guiding heuristics—which I find inspiring. First, he believes that his role is to contribute to society via mental acuity. It is an interesting phrase, and it captures something rather wonderful. He sees his role as providing the service of good thinking.

Second, he tells the story of how his own mentor taught him not to shy away from debates out of fear, but rather to always "walk towards the fire." Ben argues that it is worse to evade and avoid and actually easier to confront the fight head-on. And besides, each time you debate, and each time you fight, you learn, and that makes you more effective the next time. Ultimately, if everyone does it, and does it well, it turns the tide, and that is our goal.[62] This philosophy makes Shapiro seem fearless, and that is a great asset in this arena.

How you manage yourself in these debates certainly does matter. Choosing to walk toward the fire is an excellent start.

Here are a few additional pointers and principles from people with experience in this field. Some of these techniques are highly assertive, while others are empathic and actually quite considerate of your opponent. That may initially sound contradictory, but each has its place. Our purpose, after all, is to win the day for a superior worldview and *not* simply to "crush and destroy" our opponents. Winning matters. But winning hearts and minds for our vision of civilization is the ultimate goal.

Let's begin with a high-assertiveness technique. I would like you to take this one to heart, because in a high-pressure scenario, it can make or break you. The principle is this:

Do not apologize and do not back down.

Let me clarify: This is not the same thing as failing to concede a point if you are factually or logically incorrect. The truth must prevail. Instead, what I am saying is that when you make a stand for a principle, you will inevitably face a politically correct backlash. You will face outrage. It always happens, and you can count on it. The very worst thing you can do is to become intimidated by it, to apologize, and to back down. If you imagine that issuing an apology and backing down will diffuse anger at you, you are wrong. It will make it worse. They will never let you forget it, and you will forever be compromised. Do *not* do it.

An example of this comes to us from the real-world horror story of a varsity student named Olivia, whose family immigrated to the States from

---

62   Ben Shapiro, *Bullies: How the Left's Culture of Fear and Intimidation Silences Americans* (New York: Simon & Schuster, 2013).

Mexico. Olivia wrote an essay in which she pointed out that she felt marginalized because the blue-collar workers at her university were overwhelmingly Latino, while the administrators, professors, and professional staff were overwhelmingly (in her words) "grounded in western, white, cis-hetero-normative upper to upper-middle class values." Olivia herself was not like that. This was the accusation she leveled against this school. This was its crime.[63]

The dean read her article and reached out to her. Here is the dean's email, verbatim:

> Olivia,
>
> Thank you for writing and sharing this article with me. We have a lot to do as a college and community. Would you be willing to talk with me some time about these issues? They are important to me and the DOS staff and we are working on how we can better serve students, especially those who don't fit our CMC mold. I would love to talk with you more.
>
> Best,
>
> Dean Spellman

Olivia spent two weeks stewing over this email. She did not go and speak with the dean, as per the invitation. Instead, she focused on the term "mold," which she interpreted as confirming that Olivia did not fit in. This is despite the fact that Olivia herself intimated that there was a "prototype" with which she did not align. That was her entire premise in the first place, and the dean merely reflected her own idea back to her in the most validating and accommodating manner.

Ultimately, Olivia posted the private email on Facebook, along with her manufactured outrage. She instructed others to share it and to add their outrage. The results were catastrophic for the campus, which erupted in protest.

---

63   Lukianoff and Haidt, Ibid.

There were marches, demonstrations, demands for Spellman's resignation; and two students even went on a hunger strike, vowing they wouldn't eat until Spellman was fired.

In one scene, which can be viewed on YouTube, students formed into a circle around Spellman and other administrators, who had made themselves publicly available to listen, and the students spent an hour shouting at them, using bullhorns. The students did not accept the dean's attempts at an apology. In fact, her concession to the very idea that an apology was due legitimized the students' accusations. It made everything worse.[64]

In *The Coddling of the American Mind*, Jonathan Haidt points out that at one point in this shark frenzy, a student berates Spellman for supposedly "falling asleep" during this public haranguing with bullhorns. The video shows that Spellman was not, in fact, falling asleep. She was trying not to cry.[65]

As disproportionate as the students' actions were in this instance, they were even worse, and even further disconnected from reality, in a similar story that played out at Yale at roughly the same time.

Erika Christakis, lecturer at Yale Child Studies Center, wrote a gentle and carefully considered email, questioning whether it was a good idea for administrators to give students advice regarding appropriate and inappropriate Halloween costumes, as the dean's office had done. She left the email open-ended, suggesting that students should consider debating what they felt was right, rather than just allowing the faculty to provide guidelines.

The email sparked the social equivalent of the bomb at Hiroshima. This happened because a very small group of students opted to manufacture offense at the idea that Christakis was "in favor of racist costumes." A careful reading of her email reveals no such idea. It simply isn't there. Her offense was essentially refusing to back authoritarian rules that catered to arbitrary

---

64   The CMC Forum, "CMCers of Color Lead Protest of Lack of Support from Administration," YouTube Post, 57:06, November 11, 2015, https://www.youtube.com/watch?time_continue=1232&v=OlB7Vy-lZZ8&feature=emb_logo.

65   Haidt, ibid.

social justice whims. For failing to do so, Christakis was deemed "obviously a racist."

This one turned ugly. Over 150 students gathered outside her home to protest, writing in chalk on her walls, "We know where you live!" Christakis and her husband were accused of stripping people of their humanity, of creating an unsafe space, of denying people the "right to exist," of every evil and depravity. The students accused her husband of "wrong-face" when he smiled in their presence, trying to speak with the students.

In another YouTube scene that went viral, one student screamed at him. As part of her profanity-laden diatribe, she included the words: "It is not about creating an intellectual space. It is not! Do you understand that? It is about creating a home here."[66]

Fascinating.

Several thoughts spring to mind for me:

- Never apologize to Leftist bullies. You are not dealing with fair-minded players. You are dealing with a mob. Your apology will be taken as tacit proof that the mob was right, and, as in the global nature and grand tradition of bullies, they will smell your weakness and attack.
- The phrase "fascists posing as victims" has never had clearer representation.
- Social justice warriors in action are indistinguishable from terrorists. They would argue that their ends are noble and that this justifies their means. But so would terrorists.
- Who raised these children? Or, better phrased, who failed to?
- Where were the police? And why was there not a single arrest made, even after students (and even faculty and staff!) later admitted on social media to participating in beating conservatives during their riotous crime spree?

---

66   ReasonTV, "Yale Professor Attacked Over Halloween Costumes Says We've Evolved to Get Along," YouTube Post, 32:48, April 5, 2019, https://www.youtube.com/watch?v=f56xgHHZQ_A.

I believe that the correct response from Spellman in the Olivia issue should have been:

> As previously expressed, I am very keen to talk with Olivia about her concern. The invitation to do so was issued two weeks ago, and, to date, Olivia has not taken me up on my offer to converse and find a productive way forward. Nevertheless, my offer remains open. Olivia, you're welcome any time. I look forward to speaking with you.
>
> Kind Regards

If you find yourself at the center of a storm as a result of your stance or even as a result of the social justice mob's manufactured outrage at no particular crime on your part, I want to encourage you to do one thing and one thing only: Stand your ground. You absolutely must stick to your guns. Keep your composure and breathe. But do not, under any circumstances, apologize to the mob. The mob doesn't want an apology and won't accept it. The mob wants blood. The pressure will pass. The storm *will* abate.

Moreover, as we will shortly see, Leftist social justice tactics actually *depend* on your reaction. They are a form of bating. Saul Alinsky argued that "the action is in the *reaction*" when explaining his principles of agitation for radicals.[67] The teaching is "Keep agitating them until they react. Then use their reaction to destroy them."

So, don't react. Your reaction is the entire point, so far as they are concerned. Do not give it to them. If you simply stand your ground, you will eventually experience something heartening: the inevitable counter-backlash, in which reasonable people who actually agree with you begin to fight back against those who took you on.

This much remains: When you are speaking the truth and when you are standing up for your principles, there is no value in backing down. Ultimately,

---

67 Saul Alinsky, *Rules for Radicals: A Practical Primer for Realistic Radicals* (New York: Vintage Books, 1971).

social justice frenzies don't actually matter, unless you validate them. They are not real. They are shout-storms. They only work if you let them work. If feasible, call in authority, such as the police, and have violent mobs arrested and charged. Then get on with your life.

That is arguably the first principle of interaction with a hostile force, and it is one that I want you to take to heart. Do not let them put you under pressure. The pressure is fake. It is manufactured by design. It is made of wind. Do *not* apologize.

It is not our job to crush people.

Now comes the next principle, and we receive it courtesy of Professor Jordan Peterson. In retaliating, use only the minimal necessary force. It is enough for you to win. You do not need to ruin or destroy. That's what *their* side does. The point *is* to win, and I want you to push very hard toward that end. But the point is not to hurt the other person. Do that, and it leads to counter-reaction and escalation.

Also, when people viciously attack you on a personal level, it can lead to sympathy for you. If you humiliate and destroy the other, it can lead to sympathy for them. Thus, fight to win, but don't fight to destroy a human being. Your conduct is also visible to others.

Peterson points out that we need to remember that our opponent may be taking a chance, going bravely out on a limb, in speaking what they believe is the truth, even if *you* know their argument to be incorrect. They may *not* be acting from bad faith.[68]

So in a debate scenario, don't discount the possibility that your interlocutor might actually have an honest desire to know the truth. Therefore, don't destroy them. Rather, share the truth. And if they try to tell you in return that you are an idiot and a moron and biased and "literally Hitler," smile inwardly

68   ManOfAllCreation, "Don't Build Your Own Enemy / Jordan Peterson," YouTube Post, 11:49, November 3, 2017, https://www.youtube.com/watch?v=ErEbqG2DGxU.

at the fact that they have not learned this skill. *Their* behavior is being viewed, too. Hold your peace, keep calm, continue to make your points.

Christian apologist Ravi Zacharias makes a similar point when he says, "Never forget that behind every question is a *questioner*."[69] If someone is comparing belief systems with you, they may earnestly be seeking truth. There is a real, thinking, feeling, and possibly even *hurting* human being behind the question, with his or her own backstory. Not every question is an attack on you, even the most seemingly vicious ones. Some questions are an honest attempt by a lost soul or a wounded person to find the light. Show them nothing but barbs, and you could actually repel them from the light. Show them truth with sincerity and concern, and you just might win them for the light. That's a best-case scenario.

So, there are times when, like Ben Shapiro, you should go on the relentless offensive and eviscerate. But there are also times when a more useful and productive response plays out like this:

"I can see from your argument that you are a kind and caring person. Your value system appears to be based on empathy and social consciousness, and I applaud you for that. My issue is not with your values. I *agree* with your values because they're excellent. Instead, it is the specific policy that I find problematic. And this may surprise you, but I find it problematic *because I share your concern for people*. Here is how the policy, even though it looks kind, ends up hurting people, not helping them . . . "

So, by all means, be relentless in attacking the corrupt idea. But try to be kind in handling the human being behind it. It's a tall order, but then, standing up for an entire civilization was never going to be child's play. Nevertheless, in this fact, there lies a strangely comforting observation: You have to be the adult. You have to be the leader. You have to be the voice of reason. Their welfare is, in part, in your hands. And that's not a bad mindset

---

69 100huntley, "The Underlying Questions Behind Faith Based Questions / Ravi Zacharias," YouTube Post, 15:09, January 4, 2016, https://www.youtube.com/watch?v=cGtaTDBznUo.

by which to enter a debate. At the very least, you must emerge from this fight looking like the responsible adult, not like the angry radical.

Do not be held to be a moral exemplar.

A crude but oft-used technique of the Left is to point to the corrupt capitalist and, in so doing, dismiss capitalism, or to point to the imperfect Christian and, in so doing, dismiss Christianity.

In response to any attempt to use you, *personally*, as the moral exemplar, I recommend immediately deflating the balloon before they can pop it: "I'm fallen and imperfect. These are the standards I try to live up to. Like you, I'm aspiring to be better. I do not always succeed, and that is why you can't judge the value of the ideas based on my life, just as you are not a perfect example of morality in your world. But I see the value of these ideas, and that's why I champion them. I hope I can help you to see the value of the ideas, too. If you then choose to follow them, you will also not be perfect. But you will be striving to become better, and that is sufficient."

And don't be deterred by accusations of "creating division."

Objection: Listen, I'm tired! Both sides just keep fighting and creating division. Can't you just stop? Can't we all just be tolerant?"

Response: If I stop fighting, then my stance on all moral issues is effectively capitulation to the radical interest groups and Marxist ideologues. That's not a value system. That's surrender. Also, the Left teaches Marcusian techniques designed to exclude us from society. So, no, we can't stop fighting. If we do, they push us out. If *they* stop fighting, however, we can all live in peace. Our goal should be to get them to stop fighting.

Side Note: A value system based on tolerance is necessarily a value system of defeat, which tends toward the lowest common denominator.

To make the statement, "My value system is tolerance" (usually twinned with the noble-sounding: "My religion is love") is to say that on every important moral and ethical issue, I capitulate in advance, and insofar as my voice matters, I submit my society to the decisions of others. If my value system is reactive tolerance, then the active value systems of others will always win out. This includes aggressive systems such as Islam, Marxism, and Radical Feminism. Moreover, to say "my value system is based on tolerance" is to admit to having no boundaries.

What do you *not* tolerate? The answer to that cannot merely be intolerance because then you have on your hands the formula for inviting and accepting every evil, every debauchery, every harm and wrongdoing. So, let me ask again: what *is* your value system? If you can't answer that question, please at least get out of the way while we wage the war for goodness.

CHAPTER 2

KNOW THE HISTORY OF THEIR IDEAS: ROUSSEAU, KINSEY, ADORNO, PIKETTY, AND MARCUSE.

POLITICALLY CORRECT ARGUMENTS ARE ALWAYS built on houses of cards. One bad assumption is piled on top of another. There are many, many weak or unproven premises propping them up. Find them, and the house of cards falls.

By and large, progressives are not aware of their own history of ideas or the assumptions upon which they are founded. Often, they have simply accepted the now-socialized outcomes, without understanding the background or the underlying theory. If *you* know the history of these assumptions, that knowledge alone can be sufficient to illustrate that an entire category of ideas is simply wrong, or at the very least, that the so-called "science" upon which it rests is shaky.

The best books to read on this topic: *Intellectuals* by Paul Johnson and *Fake Science* by Austin Ruse.

Let's take the examples of four men, each of whom did great damage to Western society and each of whom are held in reverence by the Left: Rousseau, Kinsey, Adorno, and Piketty.

The politically correct ideas these men brought down upon society were:

- Collectivism is a good idea.
- Man is an unfaithful, polysexual being, and all sexual expressions are normal. Fidelity to family is an illusion which must be deconstructed.
- The average, patriotic family is deeply fascist.
- The top one percent are stealing resources from the rest of us. Equality, not solving poverty, is the correct goal, and confiscation and redistribution alone will solve the ills of the world.

All four of these now-mainstream ideas were conceived and perpetuated by deeply dishonest players. Showing how these ideas began and what the vested interests were for each founder can discredit all the notions that follow on from them.

I believe that in our bid to topple political correctness, we should know these four characters, and we should be able to cite their stories on demand. Much of the garbage that follows can be swept away when we understand the illegitimacy of these four men and their conclusions:

Genesis of Bad Idea Number One: Collectivism is Best for All.

Our first example is collectivism. Collectivism, as we have seen, is the tendency to think "community first and community as the basic unit," rather than "individual first." This is consistently the genesis of tyranny. To achieve even its most basic ends, it must always infringe on individual rights.

The seeds of modern state socialism, the political incarnation of collectivism, were first sewn by French philosopher Jean-Jacques Rousseau. Rousseau had a self-interested reason for proposing his belief in state collectivism—namely, he didn't want to raise his own children.

His story is explored in sad detail by English historian Paul Johnson CBE in the book *Intellectuals*. In brief, Rousseau wanted to live as a pre-modern "natural" man, having sex whenever he wanted *with* whomever he wanted. He justified this habit via noble-sounding appeals to the supposed purity of pre-modern man and with eloquent arguments about how "oppressive" and "foreign" modern moral norms were to the good of the human spirit. The predictable result was that he had multiple children by more than one mother.[70]

This, Rousseau felt, also oppressed *him*. He didn't *want* to raise his children. However, he had a public image to protect as a champion of humanity, and so he needed a *reason* for rejecting accountability. He fabricated one. Rousseau invented the notion of collectivism, ideally under state jurisdiction, in order to show how his children should be the responsibility of someone else, while he continued to gift humanity with his unique genius. This worked, after its fashion. All four of his children ended up in orphanages. Also, all four died young.

Adding perversity to Rousseau's philosophy was his extensive writing (and this we must call what it was: social grandstanding) on the topic of child rearing and child development). Rousseau rhapsodized about what a great parent he might have been, had he opted to go that route (instead of abandoning his children to death in impersonal institutions). As a father myself, I look at all this and can't help but feel contempt for this man. Rousseau liked to look good. But he didn't like to be accountable.

In his areas of greatest personal failings, of greatest moral depravity—some of which cost the lives of his own children—his philosophical writing soared to its noblest heights. In his lifetime, his tactic effectively worked. He was largely perceived as a hero of the social contract, a shining light of child development, and a force for the freedom of good and natural humans against the tyranny of moral and societal norms. Hurray.

The most cynical view of all his body of work, which I tend to hold, is that it was all done *in order* to look good, particularly in his areas of greatest weakness. Rousseau, the child-abandoner, is also Rousseau the child-development luminary. And we fell for it. He introduced collectivism onto the political scene, and we allow him to guide our social theory to this day.

---

70   Paul Johnson, *Intellectuals* (London: W&N, 1988).

Side Note: This double-standard most bears out with most radical Leftist intellectuals where it matters most: Marx, the great representative of the working man and advocate for socialized taxes, never had a job and never paid taxes. He also paid his family servant an appallingly low wage. In this, he shares commonalities with Bernie Sanders, the modern-day U.S. hero of socialism and the minimum wage, who in 2019, got into hot water for failing to pay his campaign staff a minimum wage.

Here are some additional charming, little observations made by Rousseau:

- Love is messy, exclusive, and preferential. Straight-forward sexual mating is better.

- The general will is more important than the individual will, and the State should impose its will upon the selfish individual for the good of all. Collectivism is the appropriate way forward.

- If it is expedient that an individual die for the will of the collective, then the State must make it so. (A few hundred million dead people later on down the road, could their voices be heard, might turn to Rousseau, the father of collectivist philosophy, and say, "Thank you for that.")

Karl Marx later drew on Rousseau's rudimentary ideas of state collectivism but took them much further. Marxism and communism owe their genesis to the ideas of Rousseau, who in turn wrote his formulations in order to excuse his abysmal performance as a moral human being. If we have communism and its death toll, we have Rousseau to thank for its seeds.

When we are aware of all this, we are better prepared to argue against all collectivist ideas, using the opening salvo: "Do you know why collectivist ideas exist in the first place? They were introduced by a man named Rousseau. And do you know why?"

A prototypical example of the modern progressive liberal, Rousseau shared moral ideas that were intended as prescriptions for others, but not for him. He very nobly offered material sacrifice and selfless service on the part of the masses, who should live according to his precepts, but he didn't do these things himself. Spot this trend in the modern liberal. You will find it every time.

Genesis of Bad Idea Number Two: Man is a Hopelessly Immoral, Sexual Animal.

Our second idea pertains to sex. Many liberal progressives hold the idea that all forms of sex are valid, that nothing is unnatural, that humans are generally polysexual beings, and that our only real hindrances are the oppressive norms unnaturally imposed upon our sexual expression by society and religion. Freud first expressed this idea, and today, it is taken as gospel by the Left.

"Love is love," they say, holding all expressions of sex to be equivalent. "The world will be a better place when sexuality is completely liberated." (To this we must ask, "At what cost?" and then be able to quantify the costs, starting with fatherlessness and child-neglect/abortion).

This worldview leads to assertions that have been accepted without question, such as that one in every seven heterosexual males has engaged in homosexual sex. Today, many people believe that the number of gay people in society is as high as one in three. It isn't. The actual number is about one in one hundred.

There are many "known" beliefs about sex outside of monogamous, heterosexual relations that turn out to be fabrication. And we owe the research—and, indeed, the entire sexual revolution of the 1960s, which led directly to the boom in abortions, the increase in sexually transmitted diseases, and the breakdown of the nuclear family—squarely to one man: a scientific fraud and sexual psychopath by the name of Dr. Kinsey.

In the late 1940s and early 1950s, when U.S. society was arguably at the height of its innocence, Dr. Alfred C. Kinsey published two reports, *Sexual Behavior in the Human Male* and then, later, *Sexual Behavior in the Human Female.*

The findings were astonishing and included ideas of this nature:

- While American men of the World War II "greatest generation" pretended to be faithful and monogamous, ninety-five percent actually qualified as sex offenders, according to 1948 law.
- Eighty-five percent of males had sex prior to marriage.
- Nearly seventy percent had sex with prostitutes.
- Thirty to forty-five percent of husbands had extra-marital affairs.
- From ten to thirty-seven percent had engaged in homosexual sex (the stat used as the cornerstone for the Gay Rights movement. This movement succeeded. After that success, the number was utterly debunked. How many people are actually gay? It is approximately one percent. Nevertheless, the Gay Rights movement no longer cared, having achieved its end).[71]

These are merely the *numbers*. The *narrative* was worse, including graphic descriptions of the specific acts men supposedly engaged in, which were portrayed as lurid, shocking, depraved . . . and commonplace.

Women were equally portrayed as sexually aberrant and "just like men" in their desire for gratuitous and meaningless sex, any time and at any cost and with anything, contrary to most women's felt experience of tying sex to concepts of love, intimacy, partnership, and meaningfulness. Women are squarely the losers in this equation. The result for them has been getting more of what they were told they want, at increased personal risk, while getting less of what they actually want.

Next, and most shockingly, Kinsey "proved" that children were supposedly sexual from birth, enjoying healthy, sexual feelings, acts, and expressions, practically from the crib. The news media hailed him as a scientific pioneer and a liberating hero. The Left still does to this day. For this alone, we should call them evil. You will see why shortly.

These findings rocked the United States, and indeed the West, to its moral core. Its inescapable conclusions were that marriages, across the nation, were

---

71   David Kupelian, *The Marketing of Evil* (Cave Junction: WND Books, 2005).

a sham, that morality itself was an illusion, that people were little more than animals. The honest way forward would be to relinquish our delusions of standards, to see ourselves for what we really were, and to act accordingly. It may be depraved, but at least it is *honest*. The only thing is, these findings were utterly fraudulent. They were a lie.

Kinsey presented his findings as "representative of everyday men and women." He was, he intimated, merely holding up a mirror. He was just showing us who we were.

Here is how Kinsey constructed his "mirror":

His results were biased in advance because he selected for his interviews an eighty percent aberrant male population, including two hundred sexual psychopaths, fourteen hundred sex offenders, and hundreds each of prisoners, male prostitutes, and promiscuous homosexuals, whose sexual promiscuity rates we now know to be incomparably disproportionate to those of average heterosexual men. These men Kinsey used as representative of the average Joe.

So few normal women would even *talk* to Kinsey, that he had to make a plan. So, he opted to label women who had lived for over a year with a man as married. He then also reclassified data on prostitutes and other unconventional women as representative of the average suburban American wife and mom. Based on this, Kinsey then found women, in general, to be cheating, bisexual, sex fiends, who committed every imaginable deviant act as a matter of course. His depiction of "normal sexual behavior" among "average women" was based on this intentionally distorted data set. He preloaded the conditions, then got the outcome he wanted.

The next development is almost unbelievable. It took until 1981 before a sole researcher, Judith Reisman, posed a simple question: How did Kinsey acquire his findings about infant sexuality? Children are "sexual from birth"? How could Kinsey know that? His research indicated that these children had been sexually touched and erotically stimulated by adults. But by who, exactly? And how was that arranged and tested? Was that not the very definition of child sexual abuse? Yes, it was. And Kinsey had hired a pedophile to do it. In fact, he corresponded with a number of pedophiles around the world, actively encouraging them to sexually molest up to two thousand toddlers and infants in order to report their findings to him.

One part of his research shows that when the babies cried, as a result of being stimulated to orgasm multiple times per hour by a pedophile, Kinsey characterized this as a "typical orgasmic response." In other words: perfectly normal.[72]

Does this take your breath away? Can you come to any conclusion other than that this was a profoundly evil man? To this day, the North American Man/Boy Love Association holds Kinsey as their guiding hero and uses his research in their attempts to normalize and mainstream pedophilia.

Reisman asked the obvious questions: Why did no one ever question this information? Why wasn't Kinsey arrested and charged? Who were these children, and where were their parents while all this was going on? How on earth could this "research" have been accepted on face value?

Reisman points out that despite the manner in which both of Kinsey's biographers seem to fawn over this progressive hero, both nevertheless agree: Kinsey was a sadistic bi-homosexual, who seduced his male students and coerced his wife, his staff, and his staff's wives to perform for and with him in sexual acts, which he turned into documented pornography.

His fellow researchers were also bi-homosexual married men with a vested interested in proving the legitimacy of their sexual appetites by disproving the legitimacy of the existing moral norms, which they described as a "narrow, procreational, Judeo-Christian approach to sex." They *wanted* to arrive at their findings; they skewed the data sets in order to do so; and they succeeded in their goal. And we all fell for it.

---

72   Judith A. Reisman, Ph.D., "Kinsey: Crimes and Consequences," Dijg.de, https://www.dijg.de/english/reisman-kinsey-crimes-consequences (accessed January 20, 2020).

Kinsey himself had a vested interested in proving the outcomes at which he fraudulently arrived. He was a sexual psychopath, who set out to show society that everyone was as sexually debauched as he was. This whole experiment was a sort of therapy for him: "Look. Everyone is like me." It went mainstream, and it kickstarted the entire sexual revolution.

From this, we learn that modern humanity was *not* a sexually seething cauldron of bizarre and aberrant practices, hiding snakelike in the dark, waiting only to be welcomed into a state of honesty by brave progressives and their light of truth. Instead, these new ideas were *prescriptive.*

We were not *like that* before Kinsey. We have been taught that all this is normal by a dishonest player with an agenda. And our behavior has followed, with catastrophic consequences. This "science" was not revelatory of some pre-existing truth. It was aggressively prescriptive and actively taught people behaviors previously completely unnatural to society but perfectly common to rapists, pedophiles, prostitutes, and prisoners. *We* now live out *their* standards, as progressives believe we should and the media teaches us to. Kinsey did not *reveal our behaviors.* He *taught us theirs.* And we fell for it.

For my money, the level of outrage aimed at Kinsey today is insufficient and requires amplification. This man's name, findings, and reputation should become mainstream discussion, and not in the fawning manner in which the media treat him to this day.

For our purposes, this knowledge is useful in broad terms. In any debate in which a politically correct proponent points out the broad and boundaryless nature of human sexuality or argues for the normalization of practices we once considered disdainful, there is an objective, scientific response to their argument, and it is to be found in the history—the very genesis—of the sexual revolution: The whole thing was a lie.

We did not "discover" that most people have broad, ranging, aberrant, and boundary-crossing desires. Instead, we were *taught* this myth. If we can

observe the "truth" of it today, it is because we are following the prescription.
Next, of course, we should ask: "At what cost?"

Side Note: Modern politically correct beliefs around sex contain
some strange and contradictory ideas. On the one hand, per Kinsey,
there are perceived to be no acceptable moral norms. Anything
goes. However, on the other, because the world must be viewed
through the lens of "power and oppression," (the Marxist technique, which psychologists would label "pathological dualism")
it is increasingly not permissible to portray women as sexual objects. This applies even down to a petty level, at which an image
of an attractive woman pointing to a car is considered sexual exploitation and deemed unacceptable by political correctness. So,
we see an uneasy mix of total moral permissiveness with oddly
puritanical standards around depicting women in sexual roles.
As ever, political correctness is riddled with contradiction.

Debate Prompt: Being able to rebut Kinsey is a good start. It
shows the flaw in politically correct culture. Then learn how to
go on the offensive by showing why your culture is superior. We
do this in the next chapter when Denis Prager shows us how to
demonstrate the superiority of Judeo-Christian moral norms.

Genesis of Bad Idea Number Three: Conservatives are Fascists.

The mainstream media loves this argument and uses it to this day.
Relentlessly. Do you love your nation? You must be a fascist. Do you believe in
a sense of community? Salute a flag? Take pride in your heritage? Play sports?
All of these and more were reframed as necessary conditions of fascism. This
idea is flawed on the most fundamental level. It essentially follows the formula: "Hitler had a dog, and you have a dog, so you must be Hitler."

Fascism was a highly specific ideology practiced in Italy in the early twentieth century. Elements of fascism were also shared by Nazism. Later, Spain
spent some forty years under a fascist dictatorship led by Francisco Franco.
And that is where fascism begins and ends.

To argue that a love of country is the same thing as fascism—when most people throughout history have, to varying degrees, loved their country—is like asserting, "The Italian fascists ate ice cream, and I see that you are eating ice cream, so you must be a fascist!" It is concept-creep to the point of propaganda.

It is worth noting that Adorno, the author of *The Authoritarian Personality*, was a critical theorist. Remember that idea from the Leftist Frankfurt School? A critical theorist has one job: to tear down by critique. That's it. Adorno saw his job as serving postmodernist Marxism by attacking its enemies. He was, to say the least, biased.

Knowing this is an adequate rebuttal. Citing it in argumentation says, "I know the history of the fascist accusation better than you do, and it is laughable. It comes from critical theory, and its whole job is to tear down Western culture. Don't be its patsy."

> **The first and worst book on this topic:** In 1950, Theodor Adorno unleashed his polemic *The Authoritarian Personality*, in which he argued that the American people possessed many fascist traits and that anyone who supported American culture was psychologically unbalanced.

Genesis of Bad Idea Number Four: The Top One Percent are Stealing From the Rest of Us.

Meet Thomas Piketty, author of what might just be the deadliest, most radical book on economic ideas since *Das Kapital* and *The Communist Manifesto* and, frankly, one that is not all that different. In 2013, Piketty published his voluminous work, *Capital in the Twenty-First Century*. The book is massive and reaches a broad range of conclusions. I have read it and will spare you the boredom. Beneath barren stretches of verbiage and endless charts, tedious to the point of being coma-inducing, its most significant conclusions were:

- Wealth is concentrated among the super-rich, who are hoarding the resources of the world.

- Their assets help them to produce more assets in a never-ending spiral, which will hold them perpetually atop society.
- This represents tyranny and oppression and must be stopped, for the good of society.
- The goal is not to solve poverty. The goal is to solve *inequality*.
- To solve all of this, a global tax and redistribution policy must be put in place. Taxes on businesses and wealthy individuals should be cripplingly punitive. Assets should be seized. Even your children should not be allowed to inherit from you.[73]

The flaws in Piketty's work are numerous. They are moral, philosophical, and procedural. The moral one is obvious. You are not allowed to steal from people. Like all Marxists, Piketty pretends this away with a terminology switch. It's not stealing. It's "redistribution." If you prioritize individuals, this holds no water. If you are a collectivist, well, then everything changes.

Let us dismantle some of his assumptions, which derive directly from Marxist theory.

HIS PRIMARY CLAIM MAY NOT EVEN BE TRUE.

This first observation is perhaps the most interesting. Lord Mervyn King, former governor of the Bank of England, was quoted in a *Financial Times* article saying, "The principal weakness of the book is that the carefully assembled data do not live up to Piketty's rhetoric about the nature of capitalism."

The *Financial Times'* own investigation revealed "many unexplained data entries and errors in the figures underlying some of the book's key charts. These are sufficiently serious to undermine Professor Piketty's claim that the share of wealth owned by the richest in society has been rising and the

---

73   Thomas Piketty, *Capital in the Twenty-First Century* (Cambridge: The Belknap Press of Harvard University Press, 2014).

reason why wealth today is not as unequally distributed as in the past is simply that not enough time has passed since 1945.'"[74]

After referring back to the original data sources, the investigation found numerous mistakes in Piketty's work: simple, fat-finger errors of transcription, suboptimal averaging techniques, multiple unexplained adjustments to the numbers, data entries with no sourcing, unexplained use of different time periods, and inconsistent uses of source data.

Together, the flawed data produce long, historical trends on wealth inequality that appear more comprehensive than the source data allows, providing spurious support to Professor Piketty's conclusion that the "central contradiction of capitalism is the inexorable concentration of wealth among the richest individuals."[75] This sentiment was echoed by an article in *The Guardian*, headlined "Thomas Piketty's economic data 'came out of thin air.'"[76]

EVEN IF HIS CLAIMS WERE PROVED TO BE
CORRECT, PIKETTY THEN ASSUMES THAT WEALTH
IS A COMMON, PUBLIC RESOURCE.

Wealth simply "exists" and should, therefore, self-evidently be equally distributed. Piketty has little to nothing to say about how wealth is originally *generated*. Who made it? Why can you take it away from them?

This is the fatal flaw in all Marxist thinking. It is the fallacy of a man who imagines economics as equivalent to approaching a picnic table situated in isolation and declaring, "Here is some wealth. Now, how shall we share it fairly?" Such a man has missed (or worse, intentionally ignored) a number of important questions, which have legal and moral consequences: Who made

74   Chris Giles, "Piketty Findings Undercut by Errors," FinancialTimes.com, May 23, 2014, https://www.ft.com/content/e1f343ca-e281-11e3-89fd-00144feabdc0.

75   Ibid.

76   Jamie Doward, "Thomas Piketty's economic data 'came out of thin air,'" The Guardian.com, May 24, 2014, https://www.theguardian.com/business/2014/may/24/thomas-piketty-economics-data-errors#:~:text=Thomas%20Piketty's%20economic%20data%20'came%20out%20of%20thin%20air',-This%20article%20is&text=Only%20a%20few%20days%20ago,the%20world%20at%20his%20feet.&text=Based%20on%20a%20simple%20premise,economists%20and%20business%20leaders%20alike.

the picnic table? Why is it ours to take? Doesn't their ownership matter? Why is it okay for us to take from them? Shouldn't we be focusing on learning how to create our own picnic table, rather than fixating on confiscating theirs? And so forth.

Piketty reasons as though the mere tableau of wealthy people, viewed from the outside and perceived as very bad, is sufficient to justify their disintegration. But wealthy people are not a public relations exercise for us to judge as good or bad. They are individuals who have each generated their fortunes in a multiplicity of ways, over which it is not our place to morally preside. Would these rich people, by the same token, be permitted to judge how poor people acquire or spend their money? Imagine the outrage if they tried. So why the double standard? Why are we permitted to judge their personal financial affairs? Because it presents a "bad tableau"?

As economist Thomas Sowell points out, "No third parties can possibly know the values, preferences, priorities, potentialities, circumstances and constraints of millions of individuals better than those individuals know themselves." Sowell proposes that people who attempt such redistributionist arguments tend to confuse *merits* with *productivity*, as though wealth were about values of equality and not about carrying out the business activities that generate wealth: "An economy is not a moral seminar authorized to hand out badges of merit to deserving people. An economy is a mechanism for generating the material wealth on which the standard of living of millions of people depends."[77]

PIKETTY CONFLATES WEALTH WITH POWER, AND IN SO DOING, HE DISMISSES EVEN THE POSSIBILITIES OF DEMOCRACY AND RULE-OF-LAW.

His assumption is that those with money will always and necessarily win at the games of law and democracy. In this assumption, there is a definite

---

77 Thomas Sowell, *Economic Facts and Fallacies* (Hachette: Basic Books, 2008).

grain of truth. This can and does happen. However, Piketty points to it as the always applicable, never-refutable rule of life.

He also errs in using this basis to argue that *capitalism* must therefore be reformed, not *law* or *democracy*. Objectors would use the same basis to argue a very different point: If there are instances when money can buy law or power, then it is the law and the democracy that need reform toward honesty. It is not the case that the monied should be destroyed. Piketty is thus focusing on the wrong side of the argument.

PIKETTY PRETENDS AWAY THE GREATEST ECONOMIC MIRACLE IN HISTORY.

Piketty flat-out ignores and, in some key ways, falsifies and disguises, the fact that capitalism has lifted more people out of poverty in a shorter span of time than any force in history. Perversely, he not only fails to acknowledge and applaud this miracle, but he also actually turns capitalism into the enemy of the poor. This is a gross perversion of truth and a terrific disservice to the poor.

THE POOR ARE GETTING RICHER, TOO.

Piketty ignores and, in some key ways, disguises the fact that although the super-rich are indeed getting richer at an exponentially increasing rate, the poor are getting richer, too, just not as quickly. He fixates on the difference between the two, not the improvement. To do this, he must revisit the old communist technique. It used to be about meeting need. When capitalism does that beautifully, reframe the argument as being about equality, and not against poverty.

This, again, is the classic error (or worse, *deception*) of the Marxist economist. *Difference* is not a bad thing. *Poverty* is a bad thing. And even *increasing difference* is not a bad thing. It would only be a bad thing if the numbers of people in poverty were trending downward. They are not. They are trending upward. Thus, increasing difference points to incredible new breakthroughs in market growth and business innovation. These are good things.

"EAT THE CAPITAL!"

Piketty is essentially proposing that the world eat the excess capital, rather than using it for further growth. He proposes that the wealth be redistributed to meet the needs of the poor. This represents a *consumptive* view.

By contrast, entrepreneurs and economists know that the best thing to do with excess capital is to utilize it for innovation and growth, to make new things possible. This is a *generative* view. This is what the one percent tend to do. Their growth, therefore, actually represents a heightened capacity to contribute to humanity, not a hoarding of resources.

ONE GOING UP MEANS ONE GOING DOWN.

Finally, Piketty commits another common Marxist error in his simplistic assumption that the gain of one implies theft from the other. This is simply not how free markets work. The wealthy do not take wealth from the rest of the world. They generate value anew.

The former idea implies that there once existed a set amount of wealth, and the rich have simply been gathering it to themselves since then. Eventually, they will have all of it, and none will be left. This is nonsense. It doesn't work that way.

Take the simple example of the richest company in the world in 2019-2020—Apple. They became the richest company in the world by providing useful products and services, all of which we freely buy from them of our own will, and all of which contribute to making us more productive and, hence, wealthier. Apple did not "find" a pile of wealth and confiscate it. Instead, they generated value. Then, as a result of using their products, the people who purchased them generated value in different ways, via their own work, as enabled by Apple products. Not only do we gain value when we buy from them, but we also use what we have bought to create more new value still. Piketty refuses to see this.

He also presumes that the rich hoarding all the resources means that there is no potential capital available to anyone else. Writing for *Forbes* magazine in an article titled, "Six Ways Thomas Piketty's 'Capital' Isn't Holding Up to Scrutiny," Kyle Smith argues that this is simply not true: "A huge pool of potential capital is widely available to the non-rich."[78] Moreover, many of the rich also use this capital to fund new start-ups and venture businesses. In this way, the capital available to the rich *becomes* the capital available to the poor. The richer the rich get, the more capital they make available to the poor.

A Curious Side Note: Using flawed arguments from the likes of Piketty, proponents of political correctness will tend to lay the blame for this "corporate greed" that "creates one percenters" at the feet of conservatives and those on the right. "*Your* greedy big businesses," they will say. The weird thing is, *they* are at the top of the hierarchy.

In 2018-2019, the top five wealthiest companies on Earth (Apple, Microsoft, Amazon, Google, Facebook) were all strongly Left-leaning and all headed by progressive liberals. Facebook in particular has faced legal censure and public hearings several times for their questionable bias against conservative customers.

The best book on this topic: *Zucked: Waking Up to the Facebook Catastrophe,* in which Roger McNamee describes "an unmoored business sector inadvertently creating a political and cultural crisis."[79]

It is curious that the Left would blame us when their own organizations are, by far, the richest and, hence, the worst offenders by their own standards. (They also see no irony in expressing moral outrage toward high-earning

---

78 Kyle Smith, "Six Ways Thomas Piketty's 'Capital' Isn't Holding Up to Scrutiny," Forbes.com, May 1, 2014, https://www.forbes.com/sites/kylesmith/2014/05/01/six-ways-thomas-pikettys-capital-isnt-holding-up-to-scrutiny/#3ccb4bcf380d.

79 Roger McNamee, *Zucked: Waking Up to the Facebook Catastrophe* (London: Penguin Press, 2019).

CEO's who are accountable for many thousands of employees, while Beyonce alone out-earns such individuals on a scale of ten to one). There are many additional flaws in Piketty's reasoning.

The best book on this topic: *Equal is Unfair.* Alternatively, pick any other title about refuting Piketty. I find economist Thomas Sowell to be brilliant at this task.

Turn the tables and go on the offensive.

As we have seen, it is not sufficient merely to pick holes in the opposition's position. We must demonstrate why ours is superior. Begin with the assertion that free-market capitalism has lifted more people out of poverty than any other system in history. That is the utilitarian argument, and it is also the kindness argument.

Proceed from that to the moral argument. It goes like this: Socialism is immoral, insofar as it is compulsory confiscation from those who generate wealth. Free-market capitalism, by contrast, is highly moral.

Nothing promotes peace like free-market capitalism. First, it is a strong deterrent to wars between nations. Second, it is a strong incentive for disparate groups to overcome their differences in the interests of mutual cooperation and mutual benefit. Third, its operating conditions are premised on trust and fidelity. It compels us to learn to trust one another and to live up to the trust expected of us in turn. When we break faith or betray trust, we lose our capacity to do future business. This weeds out the bad faith players in a process similar to evolution. It gradually improves societies.

In *The Better Angels of our Nature*, cognitive psychologist Steven Pinker argues that it is the greatest peace-keeping and civilizing force in human history. It is a virtuous cycle. It actively makes us better and actively promotes good behavior.[80]

---

80   Steven Pinker, *The Better Angels of Our Nature: Why Violence Has Declined* (London: Penguin Books, 2012).

Finally, the free-market system spurs innovation and is responsible for every life-saving invention you care to name. Every good product that helps people, keeps children safe, increases our medical care and our standards of living, or saves lives started with a capitalist incentive or was made possible by free-market demand.

Side Note: The moral superiority argument can be used against the entire enterprise of liberalism itself. For example, democratic republics, in contrast to liberal democracies, better promote diversity, and may thus be argued to be morally superior, even by liberals' cherished standards.

Liberal democracies *claim* to promote diversity but are structurally anti-diversity because they are premised on egalitarian principles, which are more restrictive, more leveling, and more homogenizing and, hence, less tolerant of differentiation.

Republics naturally have a higher internal diversity because they can also incorporate undemocratic institutions (such as churches or social groups, which liberal democracies generally attempt to transform into their own image).

Curious Side Note: Piketty's ideas have been debunked so often now that there exists an entire subcategory of books dedicated to pointing out the problems with Piketty. However, try this experiment: Walk into any bookstore and see whether his original is on the shelves. Then see whether the refutations appear on the shelves beside it. I have always found that to be at least curious. It is almost as if the original misinformation is being presented as current and uncontested through simple insistence. Why? By whom? And to what end?

Those are our four dishonest players and the politically correct but logically and morally incorrect ideas they visited upon society.

It is worth noting that a strong contender for father of Bad Idea Number Five is John Money. He does, in fact, fit into this list, as the fraudulent and child-abusing father of the notion, "Gender is a social construct."

Nevertheless, we will save Money for a later chapter and dedicate a little more time to him.

So, although it is possible to win debates about specific aspects of larger-scale constructs, such as socialism, gender-theory, or the one-percent debate, it is also possible to ward off their necessity in advance by proving that the entire thought-structure was a con from the get-go.

To use an analogy from the sci-fi book *Ender's Game*, this would be the act of "aiming for the planet," rather than taking on each hostile alien one at a time.[81] Collapse the entire house of cards right at the outset, and you won't need to argue each bad idea on top of it. Kill the queens, and it's "game over."

The best book on the overall topic of flawed but long-held assumptions: *Fake Science: Exposing the Left's Skewed Statistics, Fuzzy Facts, and Dodgy Data* by Austin Ruse.

---

81 Orson Scott Card, *Ender's Game* (New York: Tor Science Fiction, 1994).

CHAPTER 3
BE ABLE TO DEFEND YOUR CULTURE.

THE GREEK AND JUDEO-CHRISTIAN TRADITIONS give us more of our modern benefits than we are even aware of. In addition to the necessary-for-life, society-creating forces of democracy, rule-of-law, individual rights, science, and medicine, these traditions gave us a few additional surprises.

How about, for example, romantic love?

Dennis Prager wrote an award-winning essay on how Judaic morality (in contradiction to, essentially, every one of the rest of the world's cultures and religions) introduced moral revolutions that enabled the West to rise in the first instance. He wrote:

> When Judaism demanded that all sexual activity be channeled into marriage, it changed the world. The Torah's prohibition of non-marital sex quite simply made the creation of Western civilization possible.
>
> Societies that did not place boundaries around sexuality were stymied in their development. The subsequent dominance of the Western world can largely be attributed to the sexual revolution initiated by Judaism and later carried forward by Christianity. This revolution consisted of forcing the sexual genie into the marital bottle. It ensured that sex no longer dominated society, heightened male-female love and sexuality (and thereby almost alone created the possibility of love and eroticism within marriage), and began the arduous task of elevating the status of women.

Throughout the ancient world, and up to the recent past in many parts of the world, sexuality infused virtually all of society.[82]

Prager proceeds to show how practically all of the gods of the ancient world were shown engaging in sexual relations. The God of the Torah, by contrast, was asexual and, uniquely, insisted on moral sexual norms for humanity. This changed everything.

There are other high-points of the Western tradition that happened nowhere else. Perhaps, most importantly, contrary to pagan belief systems, both the Judaic and Greek traditions posited an *orderly universe.* We cannot overstate the importance of this idea, nor how unusual and revolutionary it was.

An orderly universe, governed by a set of predictable and universal laws, which could be understood by investigation, was something new in the world of thought. This idea was astonishingly important and unique to these two cultures: Greece and Jerusalem. Taken together, they gave us the necessary conditions for the birth of science. This did not happen in any other culture or anywhere else on Earth, where gods were held to be capricious activists and nature to be beyond comprehension.

Finally, we have already seen how the notion of "man created in the image of God" and Jesus declaring, "Whatever you want men to do to you, do also to them" (Matt. 7:12) informed the genesis of human rights and the cornerstone of modern law. Interestingly, you can also see how these ideas contradict the "for the good of society" and "group-over-individual" ideas that have always been the cornerstones of tyranny and mass murder. Judaic ideas directly contradict this dangerous form of thinking. They are, at their very core, anti-socialist—indeed, a safeguard against Marxism. This, naturally, is why socialists so pointedly target Christianity.

---

82   Dennis Prager, "Judaism's Sexual Revolution: Why Judaism (and then Christianity) Rejected Homosexuality," Volume 11 [8], *Crisis Magazine,* September 1993, https://www.crisismagazine.com/2018/judaisms-sexual-revolution-judaism-christianity-rejected-homosexuality.

Some qualities are universal; others are not.

Modern multiculturalists excel at demonizing the West. Their narrative explains the world this way: "The reason the West has been the dominant culture for the past five hundred years is because the West is evil. It practiced slavery and colonialism. Those were the mechanisms of its ascent, and they are the only aspects of Western culture worthy of study, in that they are unique to the West."

Once again, we see the framework of viewing all things through the prism of power and oppression only. It's our old friend, the fallacy of pathological dualism. All qualitative notions of good and bad, all ideas about merit or excellence are vacuumed out of the discussion to leave a simplistic black-and-white caricature, a cartoon parody of real-world complexity.

The problem with their thesis, though, is not just its oversimplification. The problem is that it simply isn't true. Slavery and colonization are in no way uniquely Western concepts. To say otherwise is to lie openly. *Every* culture has practiced these institutions, since the dawn of recorded history.

Economists like Thomas Sowell and authors like Dinesh D'Souza have each dedicated several books to the exploration of this topic. D'Souza advises us to take just the example of India.[83] The Western colonial power of Britain certainly did colonize India. That much is indisputably true. However, this is also true: Prior to the British conquest of India, it was conquered by the Persians. The Mongols did the same. So did the Muslims. Do we study *their* "uniquely Islamic mechanisms of slavery and colonialism"? Why not? They practiced both institutions extensively—arguably much more so than the West. Why, then, does the West receive the ignominious and erroneous label of only transgressor? While we're at it, D'Souza, points out, Alexander the Great also conquered India. Depending on your definitions and geographical delineations, the British are either the sixth or seventh power to occupy India, not the first.

---

83   PragerU, "Are Some Cultures Better Than Others?," YouTube Post, 5:23, September 18, 2017, https://www.youtube.com/watch?v=m9vBJCMD69w.

And then we turn to slavery. It, too, was prevalent in every culture. It was practiced in ancient China. It was practiced in ancient India. It was practiced in every one of the world's early civilizations in Mesopotamia and across to Egypt. It was practiced in Greece and Rome. It was practiced in Africa, and still is in certain places. It was practiced by tribes in South America. It was practiced by tribes in North America, long before Columbus arrived (which is interesting in itself. Europeans did not introduce the concept of slavery to North America. It predated them on that continent. Mention that when historical revisionists talk about white people "introducing" slavery to America). Slavery's global leading practitioner was and, in some cases, still is Middle Eastern Arab Muslim nations.

The multiculturalist silence on this issue is quite baffling (or would be if you assumed multicultural apologists to be honest players acting in good faith).

Colonialism and Slavery are not uniquely Western. So, what is uniquely Western?

The answer is: The *abolition* of slavery. *That* is uniquely Western. It began with evangelical Christians in England and America.

What else distinguishes the West? What else is *uniquely* Western, and might account for Western global primacy? The answers are the institutions of democracy, capitalism, and science. Formalized education derived from these institutions. The rule of law was premised on the sanctity of the individual. These institutions developed because of the interplay of Greek and Judaic ideals and their defining notions of classical reasoning and ethical morality. They arose in the West because of Western culture and ideas. They became a culture, a worldview, a set of legal parameters and a way of raising every generation of our children to out-perform the generation that came before it. Taken together, they made the West incomparably efficacious.

But what about America? It is the leading Western power, and it is multicultural.

Dinesh D'Souza explains this one best. He points out that skin color is not important, a thesis I completely agree with. Instead, *thinking* is important. The United States is founded upon Western *thinking* and not upon Western *skin color* (which would be what, exactly?). It is not, in fact, founded upon ethnic differences, but rather upon shared values. Western values, in particular.

He then proceeds to say (in his capacity as an ethnically Indian American citizen married to a Latina woman from Venezuela) that "we don't want America to be a multicultural society. We want it to be *a multi-ethnic* society."[84] That is, a society comprised of descendants of many nations, races, and colors, who *all agree* on the Western values and principles of freedom and democracy. Such a formula, as it turns out, is a recipe for becoming the leading nation on Earth.

Objection: Yes, but what about the Crusades?

Response: Good question. Did you know that the Crusades were a response to Muslim conquest?

After Muslims besieged, sacked and colonized the city of Jerusalem and further attempted to colonize Christian Europe, the Crusades constituted a response to their aggression.

Also, were you aware that Islam invented the concept of a "Holy War" and that their use of it predated ours? In fact, our use of "Holy War" was a *reaction* to theirs.[85]

Objection: Okay, fine, but children raised without religion show more empathy. I've seen, like, a hundred articles that say that.

Response: Ah, yes! The old 2015 "Current Biology" study. On the Current Biology website, where it was published, you will see that the authors have retracted it because of inaccuracies.[86]

---

84   PragerU, "Are Some Cultures Better Than Others," YouTube Post, September 18, 2017, 5:23, https://www.youtube.com/watch?v=m9vBJCMD69w.

85   Richard C. Csaplar, Jr., "1,400 Years of Christian/Islamic Struggle: An Analysis," CBN. com, https://www1.cbn.com/churchandministry/1400-years-of-christian-islamic-struggle (accessed July 23, 2019).

86   Jean Decety, et al., "Retraction Notice to: The Negative Association between Religiousness and Children's Altruism across the World," *Current Biology*, Volume 29 [15] August 5, 2019, page 2595, https://www.sciencedirect.com/science/article/pii/S0960982219308759.

So, what actually happened? Researcher Azim Shariff spotted some oddities and omissions while pouring through the original study's datasets. The datasets did not control for cultural differences (between, say, Middle Eastern Muslim families and non-religious Chinese families). Once these rather stark cultural differences were controlled for, the discrepancies in generosity between religious and non-religious children disappeared. The thesis was completely disproven. The findings are not true.[87]

It is also worth noting that the data set for religious families was largely comprised of Middle Eastern Muslims. When the article with these findings is shared in Western nations, we are tacitly led to assume that we are talking about differences between *Christian* children and non-religious Western children. This was also not the case in this study. The difference is subtle. Nevertheless, we often see the umbrella term *religion*, including Islam, used as a weapon against Christianity. If you can tar religion by incorporating the non-Western tradition of Islam, then you can duplicitously challenge the notion of the Christian West by transference of crimes.

Debate Technique: Here is another interesting liberal contradiction, which you can use in argumentation. Point to any demonstrable or qualitative difference between cultures, and progressives will immediately label you a bigot. They will point out that your motives must be hate. Yet a study that supposedly finds qualitative differences in good and bad between religious and non-religious children is welcomed as "science"? How does that work? Are they saying that qualitative moral differences between groups are back on the table and admissible for discussion? Oh, good! I have a few I'd like to discuss. Oh, they're *not* back on the table? That's bigotry, you say? Fair enough. Then you

---

87   Guillermo Campitelli Guillermo, "Nonreligious children aren't more generous after all," ResearchGate.net, January 16, 2017, https://www.researchgate.net/blog/post/nonreligious-children-arent-more-generous-after-all.

can't have the results of a study such as this one. By your own standards, that's hate speech.

Side Note: Muslim as "right wing"? Watch out for this fallacy: When studies talk about "right-wing terrorism," you should immediately ask this question: Do you include Islamic terrorism under the term "right-wing"? They often do, arguing that such acts are religious in nature and, therefore, right-wing. Press a researcher, or an analysis, for the answer to this question and do not accept equivocation on the matter. The answer changes everything. The Left has little compunction lumping Islam in with the right, then blurring the terms and saying, "See? Right-wing terrorism is significant. The real problem is white men, and our numbers prove it."

I'm not sure about you, but as a conservative, Western male, I am not okay with being held accountable for Islamic terrorism. It is, in fact, perverse when the prime target of Islamic terrorism tends to be the West. If you unearth the deception, you disprove the argument and reveal the dishonesty of the players. You also show others what to look for in future encounters.

A final note on defending your culture: Flip the "oppressor" argument.

Begin by illustrating that specific Greek and Judeo-Christian principles led to the rise of human rights, science, democracy, and individual liberty. End by flipping their argument about the oppressor. In any cultural debate, the conservative side will inevitably be accused of being the oppressor. This is the core thesis of the multiculturalist.

In response, ask them whether they know who is the most oppressed group on Earth today. The answer is: Christians. State this overtly: Not only are you speaking on behalf of the most liberating, slavery-revoking, democracy and human-Rights establishing belief system in all of history, but you are also speaking in defense of the world's most persecuted people: "Christians are the most persecuted religious group on earth, re-search reveals."[88] [89] [90] [91]

The atheist and progressive response to this, as I've experienced, is to at-tempt to minimize it. Using various dilutions, they will try to say that "it's not as bad as it's made to sound." The correct response to this is sarcasm is "Oh, I'm sorry. Not enough of us have died yet? Please stand by. We're doing the best we can to meet your exacting standards. Maybe if you help Islam along a little by apologizing for it."

You might also follow this with a quantitative argument: "Your side used the figure of six thousand women dying per year of botched abortions to change the law of the United States and legalize baby murder. And it's worth noting that this number was dishonest, anyway. The real number was around three hundred per year. Nevertheless, that was sufficient grounds for great moral outrage and a complete change to the law of the land, resulting in over three million new abortions per year.

"But your argument *now* is that only *x* number of Christians are being slaughtered per year? That's not enough of an outrage for you? May I ask you to please quantify how many would be too many? Give me a number. While you're thinking about it, let's discuss your understanding of basic concepts of morality and why you feel it should relate to numerics."

The best book to read on this topic: *Because They Hate: A Survivor of Islamic Terror Warns America* by Brigitte Gabriel.

---

88 Debbie White, "UNDER ATTACK Christians are the most persecuted religious group on Earth, research reveals," TheSun.co, April 23, 2019, https://www.thesun.co.uk/news/8920568/christians-most-persecuted-religious-group-on-earth-pew-research.

89 "Christian persecution 'at near genocide levels,'" BBC.com, May 3, 2019, https://www.bbc.com/news/uk-48146305.

90 Rita Panahi, "Christianity is the most persecuted religion in the world," HeraldSun.com, June 24, 2019, https://www.heraldsun.com.au/blogs/rita-panahi/christianity-is-the-most-persecuted-religion-in-the-world/news-story/fccadd1f30733117c2d9dd338a27e7cc.

91 Jennifer Wishon, "Global Persecution Report: 'Christians Are the Most Persecuted . . . and It's Accelerating,'" CBN.com, September 22, 2019, https://www1.cbn.com/cbnnews/politics/2019/april/global-persecution-report-christians-are-the-most-persecuted-and-its-accelerating.

CHAPTER 4

DEMONSTRATE HOW INCLUSIVENESS-THEORY HOBBLES KNOWLEDGE AND HARMS HUMANITY.

WE PREVIOUSLY MET HERBERT MARCUSE, the so-called Father of the Modern Left, and his notion of "repressive tolerance." Marcuse proposed that the best form of tolerance is intolerant of anything that is intolerant to everything else. He also recommended that educators avoid "ideologically embedded" mainstream ideas, and teach radical ones instead.

The net result of such an approach is this: You can have science, or you can have Marcuse, but you can't have both.

Marcuse's theory, which presents itself as being all about the welcoming of people into the realm of academia, and nothing more, is doomed to failure on several fronts. First, it simplifies human demographics into mere caricatures. Second, it poses jarring and ultimately insurmountable contradictions in the world of knowledge, ideas, and academic integrity.

First, the human subjects. His theory reduces people into mere blobs and globules, operating on "power and oppression." This is called Pathological Dualism. It is a technique of Marxist theory. It pretends away all qualitative ideas. It pretends away differential morals. It pretends away good and bad and individual story.

Then, perhaps more problematically, it pretends away everything that has been accomplished by a slow tradition of the vetting of the quality of ideas, as though centuries of academic debate and dispute were best regarded as irrelevant.

Its assumed premises are:

- Everyone should just get along.
- Whoever—or whatever—prevents this highest ideal for any reason must be bad by default.

The responses are obvious: Should we get along with rapists? How about murderers? And how about (and here it becomes directly relevant as a societal and educational issue) Islamic terrorists? Must we get along with them and stop being so exclusionary? Moreover, must we all get along at the *cost* of true knowledge? If a cultural superstition conflicts with a scientific paradigm, given that the cultural superstition is held by an ethnic group, is it the science that must go?

Under Marcuse's model, the answer is: yes. This, of course, is absurd, and harmful to humanity's attempts to progress in cumulative knowledge.

Marcuse's moral frame casts heroes and villains. It assumes that anyone who objects to someone else's viewpoint, feelings, superstitions or cultural beliefs is, by default, bad because such exclusionary tendencies are the cause of "not-get-alongness."And per Marcuse, not-get-alongness is the worst thing there is.

The Ultimate in Anti-science

Under Marcuse, the best ideas *can't* win. Also, under Marcuse, the worst, ugliest and most evil ideas *can't* be excluded. The attempts to do so, on the part of the very best, by definition position the very best as the new evil, which must then be pushed out. Welcome to the fairground, mirror-hall world of a liberal academic who put his thinking cap on upside down, then told us to follow him, barking, into the twilight.

For some bizarre reason, academia nevertheless accepted his ideas, rather than doing what they should have done, which was to say, "We've read your proposal, and you appear to be wearing your pants on your head."

The Conditions for Anti-meritocracy

In the weird, wacky, wonderful world of Marcuse, *embedded* means "obviously wrong." In academia, *embedded* actually means "most vetted, debated, and broadly accepted as proven." It means "most meritorious." Nevertheless, this provides an excellent specific example of how progressive thought is demonstrably anti-progress and anti-meritocracy.

A Father of Antifa

The ugliest modern incarnation of Marcuse is Antifa, who, escalating the core premise of including through excluding, use violence to stop violence. The oddity here is that their definition of violence in the second instance is words they don't like and in the first instance is actual physical violence. At the time of writing, the U.S. presidency is discussing labeling Antifa as a terrorist organization. Why they have not yet done this defies comprehension.

In the final tally, Marcuse is simplistic and should be dismissed. He really hasn't thought this through. Or if he has thought this through, then he is operating in the service of evil, helping humanity into a course that, by definition, leads us without escape to the lowest common denominator.

I propose a better system. It's based on science, logic, and open debate. Its formula is "the best idea wins." Its necessary conditions are free speech. And when free speech is permitted and good ideas win, we should hear and adopt those good ideas, not pretend them away as "oppressive."

This approach is very different to globular get-along-ness. It can still perfectly accommodate good manners and civic societies and even differences of opinion. But, critically, what it can't accommodate are terrible ideas being accepted into society and a trend toward the lowest common denominator. It aims us upward, not downward; and for my small part, I insist on that.

Where we see Marcuse's ideas, we should call them out as flawed. We should also help others to understand *why* they are flawed that they may avoid falling for them, too, and they, too, may oppose them.

Side Note: Even if Marcuse's ideas were deemed comprehensible, they are still dishonestly *applied* in modern liberalism. Islam is the ideology which might be demonstrated to be least tolerant of everything, which excludes, forbids, and often even proposes murder against everything that is not Islam, which is somehow, nevertheless, included into the narrative in liberal social discourse. How does that work?

Debate Tip: Add a little flare. "Ah, I see you've introduced the Marcuse argument. In the next minute, I will show you why Marcuse's idea is not only fatally flawed, but also evil. But that's not even the interesting part. The interesting part is that once I point this out to you, you still won't abandon it. Let's begin."

Side Note: The radical says, "You must always question ideas." The scientist responds, "True. And when the ideas are proven to be correct, you must then *actually accept them.*"

The best book debunking Marcuse: There are many. But a good one is *The Coddling of the* American Mind by Gregg Lukianoff and Jonathan Haidt.

I believe we should push hard against Marcusian tactics. For instance:

You: "So, why is gender bad?"

Them: "Because it's not inclusive."

You: "We've been gendered all through our history. Male and female is the fact at the center of our existence. Not just our existence as a species, but also even your personal existence. Why do you believe it's not inclusive now?"

Them: Some rambling answer.

You: "So you're saying that inclusivity is the highest value and should supersede all competing values? What exactly will we be including?"

Side Note: Watch a feminist journalist attempt to use the "So, you're saying . . ." technique on Jordan Peterson and fail terribly

by typing "Jordan Peterson on the gender pay gap, campus protests and postmodernism" into a YouTube search. The technique
only works when the target has relativistic morals or cannot
properly explain their position. Mr. Peterson is significantly too
smart for that. One commentator described the interviewer as
"hallucinating his responses."[92]

Idealizing Alternative Cultures

The Left loves to idealize alternative cultures. Remember: *anything but
the Old Order*. It is useful to be able to refute their most common representations. For instance, Islam is a religion of peace.

For starters, the word *Islam* means "submission" or "surrender" (to the
rule of Islam). It is a religion of peace only insofar as you define peace
as "the absence of resistance." Muhammad's famous phrase *aslim taslam*
means "surrender, and you will be safe." These words were included by
him in letters sent to various rulers offering them peace if they surren-
dered to Islam. Far from carrying a peaceful meaning, this term was a
barely veiled threat.[93]

> **Objection:** But the term *jihad* is supposed to be about an inner
> struggle to live up to God's standards. And I've seen plenty of
> verses about peace in the Qur'an.
> **Response:** Yes, the Qur'an does use the term *jihad* that way. But it
> primarily uses it as a direct incitement to war and murder on the
> part of Muslims against non-Muslims.

When responding to Muslim apologists, look for this trick: They will cite
verses from Mohammed's early career—when he was trying to win over the
Jews and Christians as proof of his desire for peace. When he failed to win

92   Channel 4 News, "Jordan Peterson on the gender pay gap, campus protests and
     postmodernism," YouTube Post, 29:55, January 16, 2018, https://www.youtube.com/
     watch?v=aMcjxSThD54.
93   Time Dieppe, "Is Islam a religion of peace?" ChristianConcern.com, November 7, 2018,
     https://christianconcern.com/resource/is-islam-a-religion-of-peace.

them over and the Jews and Christians saw him as a fraud and a false prophet, Muhammad changed policies. Thereafter, his preachings were overtly violent. In Islamic tradition, the later verses are understood to supersede the earlier verses. But they won't *tell* you that. They will simply show you the verses that speak about peace.

Here are some of the religion's exhortations to violence:[94]

> *Fighting is prescribed for you, and ye dislike it. But it is possible that ye dislike a thing which is good for you, and that ye love a thing which is bad for you . . . Indeed, those who have believed and those who have emigrated and fought (jihad) in the cause of Allah – those expect the mercy of Allah. And Allah is Forgiving and Merciful (Q 2:216-218).*

> *"Not equal are those believers who sit (at home) and receive no hurt, and those who strive and fight in the cause of Allah with their goods and their persons. Allah hath granted a grade higher to those who strive and fight with their goods and persons than to those who sit (at home). Unto all (in Faith) hath Allah promised good: But those who strive and fight hath He distinguished above those who sit (at home) by a special reward" (Q 4:95)*

The best known example of a peaceful verse is Q 2:256: *"There shall be no compulsion in [acceptance of] the religion. The right course has become clear from the wrong. So whoever disbelieves in Taghut and believes in Allah has grasped the most trustworthy handhold with no break in it. And Allah is Hearing and Knowing."*[95]

This was later abrogated by this verse: "But when the forbidden months are past, then fight and slay the Pagans wherever ye find them, and seize them, beleaguer them, and lie in wait for them in every stratagem (of war); but if they repent, and establish regular prayers and practise regular charity, then open the way for them: for Allah is Oft-forgiving, Most Merciful" (Q 9:5).[96]

---

94   Tim Dieppe, "Is Islam a Religion of Peace?" Christianconcern.com, November 7, 2018, https://christianconcern.com/resource/is-islam-a-religion-of-peace.

95   Qur'an, Sahih International, Verse 2: 256, English Translation, http://corpus.quran.com/translation.jsp?chapter=2&verse=256.

96   Ibid.

Surah 9 is the last chapter to be revealed in the Qur'an and is held as abrogating earlier instructions. Surah 9 is also the most violent chapter. Consider these verses:

> *Fight those who believe not in Allah nor the Last Day, nor hold that forbidden which hath been forbidden by Allah and His Messenger, nor acknowledge the religion of Truth, (even if they are) of the People of the Book, until they pay the Jizya with willing submission, and feel themselves subdued (Q 9:29).*

> *O Prophet! strive hard against the unbelievers and the Hypocrites, and be firm against them. Their abode is Hell, - an evil refuge indeed (Q 9:73).*

> *Allah hath purchased of the believers their persons and their goods; for theirs (in return) is the garden (of Paradise): they fight in His cause, and slay and are slain: a promise binding on Him in truth, through the Law, the Gospel, and the Qur'an: and who is more faithful to his covenant than Allah? then rejoice in the bargain which ye have concluded: that is the achievement supreme (Q 9:111).*

> *O ye who believe! fight the unbelievers who gird you about, and let them find firmness in you: and know that Allah is with those who fear Him (Q 9:123).*[97]

Note that these are open-ended commands without qualification. This is very different to the Hebrew Old Testament, in which exhortations to any kind of violence were highly specific, limited in time and place, and almost always included eradicating a town that practiced human sacrifice.

Tim Dieppe, head of public policy at Christian Concern, notes, "In total, there are well over a hundred verses advocating violence in the Qur'an."[98]

Be wary of attempts by apologists to counter that there is more violence in the Bible than the Qur'an. This fails to ask: are these references *descriptive* or *prescriptive*? There are numerous descriptive verses about violence in the Bible, which are matters of historical record, not injunctions. In many

---

97   Dieppe, Ibid.
98   Ibid.

cases, these references were deplored by that Deity and overtly used as instruction against violence. To equate them with injunction to violence is dishonest, like accusing a guide to excellent table manners of describing bad table manners.

Objection: "You're a racist."

Response: Islam is not a race. It's a religion. If you're saying that you are pro-Middle Eastern people, then I'm with you. Now, let's get back to discussing the religion.

Objection: Why can't you just let them have their religion?

Response: Good question. Here is why. Within the belief system, Muhammad is held to be the perfect man, and Muslims are repeatedly urged to be like him. He had a child bride, whom he married at the age of six and had intercourse with at the age of nine. He also plundered caravans, murdered the tradesmen carrying the goods, and took booty.

Next, a woman's legal standing in the Qur'an is held to be half that of a man. And that is under good conditions.

Finally, the Qur'anic verses Mohammed uttered are open-ended instructions to wage violent war against us, indefinitely, until there is no religion but Allah.

Can *you* accept those conditions? If you can, why? Why do you not see the value in protecting children from sex trafficking? Why do you not see the value in protecting lives from terrorism? Why do you not see the value in protecting women from discrimination?

(Now go on the offensive): Your question, "Why can't you just let them have their religion?" is akin to asking, "Why can't people just abuse children? Or oppress women?" But perhaps you are insinuating that it is okay for people with a different skin color to do these things? Maybe you don't think they can or ought to live up to Western standards? Or maybe you don't think that those values—protecting children, uplifting women—are as *important* as skin color? Please clarify which it is.

The Socialist Paradises

"But Cubans are among the happiest people I've ever met." "But Sweden works perfectly," and so forth.

Let's start with the happiness argument.

I personally grew up in apartheid South Africa. The system fell apart when I was about twelve. Under apartheid, black people were among the happiest people I ever met. And so, one of two things must be the case here. Either socialism is a wonderful idea in the same way that apartheid was a wonderful idea, or observed, individual happiness is no indicator of the oppression of a governing system.

Leftists will often tell romantic stories about how Cubans play dominoes in the streets. How very neighborly. Forget that they couldn't express politically banned views. Forget that their books were prescribed for them. Forget that all of their media and entertainment were vetted by the communists and that they weren't free to leave. Forget that they had to queue for basic amenities. Playing dominoes in the streets trumps all of that!

Quick question: Are we not allowed to play dominoes in the street in our culture? Or is it just that we have better things to do?

Sweden

With regards to Sweden and the Scandinavian states being socialist paradises, there are many important points to understand. As I explained in my book *Is Your Thinking Keeping You Poor?*:

> People in Sweden typically pay 60 to 70 percent of their income in tax, and enjoy among the highest standards of living on earth.

> Here's what the advocates don't tell you: although these nations are undeniably socialist, the wealth didn't come from socialism.

> In a period that Swedes term their golden age, between about 1870 and 1970, Sweden enjoyed a particularly low level of

government regulation and a free-market system. As a result, Swedes employed their excellence, innovation and hard work and became one of the top three wealthiest nations on earth per capita.

Then they implemented a socialist system. Almost immediately, Sweden dropped out of the top 10 wealthiest nations on earth per capita. They are still doing well, and their socialist country enjoys a high standard of living, but not because of socialism. If anything, they are only able to sustain socialism *because* of the prosperity-creating free-market system that preceded it.

It's also worth noting that since about 2007, Sweden has been relaxing its socialist systems. They, too, have recognised that collectivism is not necessarily the Utopia that left-wing thinking purports it to be.

So, in a best-case scenario in which a free-market system has already created immense prosperity, socialism depletes the wealth of the whole. In countries that did not enjoy high levels of prosperity prior to the implementation of a collectivist, socialist system (such as China, Russia and Cuba), socialist systems have been nothing short of ruinous. Tens of millions have starved to death under their jurisdiction.[99]

It is also worth noting that the definition "socialist state" is in many ways a bit of a stretch in their example. Sweden, for instance, has *less* regulation over its businesses than the United States. Its free market system is actually freer than America's.

There is much more to understand about the Sweden myth. For a video that begins to unpack this issue, type "Yaron Answers: How Can Scandinavian Countries Perform So Well Economically?" into a YouTube search.[100]

---

99 Douglas Kruger, *Is Your Thinking Keeping You Poor?* (Cape Town, SA: Penguin Random House, 2016).

100 Ayn Rand Institute, "Yaron Answers: How Can Scandinavian Countries Perform So Well Economically?," YouTube Post, 7:00, July 1, 2013, https://www.youtube.com/watch?v=JTOpBPIoL-g.

The Utopia of the 1960s

Many of today's establishment liberals—and professors, in particular—were social revolutionaries in the 1960s and hold this time period in reverence. It was—they emotionally state—the era of free love, the dismantling of the patriarchy, peace, and brotherhood. Yet the 1960s are the very genesis of nearly all things corrosive in today's social climate, including the very things that these later-day hippies lament as evil.

Let us take just one example. Economist Thomas Sowell points out that crime among black Americans, like crime among white Americans, was declining for years before the 1960s. During the 1960s, something significant changed, and crime rates began to skyrocket among both blacks and whites.

How badly did this affect black society? In Detroit, for example, the poverty rate among black people was only half that of blacks nationwide. It had the highest home-ownership of blacks in the entire nation. Its unemployment rate for blacks was 3.4 percent, lower than that among whites nationwide. Then it *became* an economic disaster area after the 1960s riots. It became significantly poorer. Also, it became significantly more violent.[101]

This is curious, given the liberal narrative that such cities are disastrous because of a legacy of slavery. They were, in fact, way more successful *prior* to the liberalizing 1960s. They became economic and social disasters areas *after* the liberalizing 1960s.

The 1960s were also the beginning of massive family break-ups, which, through fatherlessness, lead to most forms of violent crime ravaging black communities today. Prior to the 1960s, the primary value system of black families in the U.S. was Christianity. Under this value system, their conditions were on an upward trajectory. After the 1960s, the competing value systems of radical race theory, liberal anti-Christianism, free love, family disintegration, and social welfare entered the value system for black Americans. Their trajectory immediately headed downward into crime and poverty.

---

101 Thomas Sowell, *Discrimination and Disparities* (New York: Basic Books, 2018).

If we were to perform a simple SWOT analysis on black communities and the two competing systems—Christianity and progressive liberalism—we would quickly conclude that Christianity places black communities on an upward trend, while liberalism places it on a downward trend. Yet curiously, despite its decimating effect on black lives, liberalism claims the high ground here, arguing that it has done nothing but liberate and uplift black people. History shows this assertion to be false. If anything, so far as black communities in the U.S. suffer with poverty and crime today, they can thank the progressive movement for defeating their upward trajectory.

The 1960s were not a utopia. They were an absolute disaster, morally and socially. Their legacy is of destruction and the reversal of an upward trend toward economic success.

The "Singing" African Utopias

Ever come across this one? I've seen at least ten variations on this story on social media, fawningly shared with comments like "Sooo beautiful!" The legend begins: "There is a village in Africa . . ." (Just Africa, mind you. Africa is a rather large continent, with over fifty sovereign nations, so a little specificity might help. Nevertheless . . .)

"In this village, a woman will sit beneath a tree and 'sing the song of her child' before she falls pregnant. Then she will go to lie with a man and conceive the baby. The song she sang will be his song for life. All through his days, the young man will know his song. And when he does anything selfish, or anything that brings harm to the people of his village, or anything that takes him out of harmony with nature, then every member of the village will all gather together in a circle of trust around him [crying, if we are to believe the pictures on the poster]. They will sing his song to him to remind him of who he is and to remind him of his place among the people. And that is why these people need no laws, no courts, and no police. Their very identity is their greatest strength."

Liberals eat this sort of flaming horse manure for breakfast. They also tend to cling fast to an outmoded picture of Africa, dreaming up unspoiled villages populated by the child-like, eco-loving, and suspiciously socialist "noble savages" of Rousseau's fondest fantasies.

Your average citizen of Gabon would be perplexed by this image. And jumping into her car with her take-away coffee in one hand, laptop in the other, the working woman in Gaborone would be perfectly bemused. This fabrication is actually quite racist in its own way.

CHAPTER 5

MAKE SURE YOU FRAME THE ISSUE, NOT THEM.

WINNING A DEBATE IS OFTEN about framing the issue. Without a clear set of agreed parameters, a debate can wash around aimlessly. Or worse, if *they* set the parameters, they can force a win. When we know and agree on what the parameters are, there is a point of reference, a "measure" by which one party or the other can actually prevail in any debate. Therefore, do not simply charge into the elements of their argument. Insist on starting by framing the issue.

Take the topic of monetary systems. The Left is endlessly enamored with Marxist and socialist principles and will fight for them with unflagging passion, even in the face of their perpetual and predictable failure. Their desire to fight for these principles is premised on at least three of their characteristics, including "communal thinking," in which society is put before the individual, "notions of kindness," and "animosity toward the old value system," which in this case amounts to learned animosity toward capitalism.

To win this debate, start by framing the issue. It would play out like this: A PC apologist makes a specific argument, either about a bad element of capitalism or about a good element of socialism. You then begin by zooming back in order to properly frame the issue: "Before we even get into that specific idea, let's establish what we want here. So, what *do* we want? I propose that we should choose the system that works best, and we should choose the system that is most moral. What we should *not* do is choose the system that works least effectively. And we should *never* choose the system that is funda-mentally immoral. Does that sound acceptable to you?"

You are unlikely to elicit clear agreement on this statement. But it ac-tually doesn't matter. You have already articulated clear terms, off which you can now bounce your *own* arguments. And you can invalidate theirs according to this framing, whether or not they have clearly submitted to the criterion.

Your work is now done in this respect. It will now become possible for you to illustrate *why* your system of belief is superior and *why* theirs is infe-rior, according to a set of parameters that the opposition would have to dis-mantle in order to prevail. And to dismantle those criteria would render them somewhat ludicrous, which would be easy to point out: "So, you're saying we should choose the *least* effective system?" or "So, you're saying we should choose the immoral system over the moral one?"

Framing the issue upfront is important and can determine who wins or loses a debate. Failing to frame the issue is deadly because it leaves the op-portunity open for them to do so. They unerringly will, and they will frame the issue according to kindness and cruelty or power and oppression. You cannot allow them to do this because by these vague and subjective terms, they will win.

Debate Tip: If you spot their framing of the issue by these terms, you must begin by actively *dismantling* their framing *before* you engage in the argument.
It would play out like this:

"I see that you have framed this as a 'kindness' issue. That's very noble of you, but I believe it's shortsighted. First, I will show you how your system is not inherently kind, but actually does more damage than good. But before we get to that, I propose a differ-ent approach. Rather than choosing the 'kindest' system—which socialism is not, anyway—I propose that we look for the system that does two things: It should be the most effective at lifting poor people out of poverty, and it should be the most moral. I will show you how it is entirely possible to be kind and, simultaneously, completely *immoral*. Even *evil*."

Now you have dismantled their framing and established your own. Once again, they are unlikely to fawningly accede to your terms. At best, they will allow cautious and tentative willingness to hear you out. At worst, they will be hostile to your terms.

Once again, though, it doesn't matter. You have now stated your terms, and at the very least, *you* get to argue according to those terms. You have reframed the issue. And even if they decline the debate, you have effectively won because your framework still stands, in that case, unchallenged.

Debate Tip: The best words to use in order to regain the reframing of the issue are "That's the wrong question." Use this phrase even if they didn't ask a question. You reframe their statement into a question, then provide a different question. For instance, they say, "We should care about the poor people in those countries!" You respond, "That's the wrong question. The question isn't 'Should we care?' Of course, we should. The question is 'Does sending aid improve their situation or make it worse?'"

Debate Tip: Care to indulge in a little theatrics? Seal a page into an envelope and keep the envelope with you. When they respond with a predictable line, such as, "Yes, but real socialism has never actually been tried," open the envelope and show them the large headline, "Yes, but real socialism has never actually been tried!" Below it, list the countries in which it was tried and where it made people poorer. The same effect can be achieved with a PowerPoint slide. Here's the list of failed socialist (communist) states and economies:

Algeria

Angola

Argentina (in the process)

Bolivia

Burundi

Cambodia

China—The worst death-toll by starvation in history (currently a dual economy)

Cuba

Ecuador

Equatorial Guinea

Eritrea

France (in the process)

Iran

Iraq

Libya

Nicaragua

North Korea

Republic of Congo

South Africa

Sudan

Turkey

USSR

Venezuela

Zimbabwe

Here is another option. You can actually view their own argument as perfectly valid, and then use that against them, once more employing a little theatrics:

Objection: Real socialism has never been tried.

Response: You mean to say that the socialist experiments we've tried so far were the *diluted* versions? And even *they* managed to murder over one hundred million people. Just imagine how much damage the *undiluted* version could do! Thanks for the heads up. We'll definitely be sure not to try it now that we know that.

Now, let us explore the moral component of capitalism. Here are some talking points that you can unpack, one by one, to illustrate that free-market capitalism is the most moral, pro-people economic system in the world, in contrast to their failure and moral tyranny of the alternative:[102]

1. Free-market capitalism has increased the standard of living like no other global force. Countries that have freer economies have higher GDPs (gross domestic product), life expectancy rates, and per capita incomes. Here you can see opportunities to respond to their kindness narrative: "Why would you be so *unkind* as to deny this to poor people?"

2. Countries with free markets tend to offer more human rights to citizens, as well as lower levels of child labor, gender inequality, and illiteracy. (Once again, tell me about your kindness?)

3. Free markets give people the opportunity to pursue their dreams. You can be whatever you want to be in a capitalist society. The government doesn't tell you what to do. There are no "labor quotas." The opposite is true in centralized systems, which is tyranny.

4. Free markets allow people to rise out of poverty. If you want a better life for yourself, you can work for it and earn it. No one will stop you (but government regulation might).

5. When you are industrious, you get to benefit from the fruits of your labor. You do not have it confiscated at gunpoint for redistribution (which is immoral and certainly unkind).

6. When I personally speak on business innovation (as the author of two business books on the topic of business innovation published by Penguin), I point out that that the most successful organizations use customer-centricity to generate new innovation. By definition, capitalism creates a success-criterion based around helping people and on constantly improving.

---

102 Turning Point USA, "Free Market Capitalism Improves People's Lives," YouTube Post, 3:02, July 6, 2020, https://www.youtube.com/watch?v=plm6XqTjbKw.

7. Finally, every nation started out as poor, and in that sense, every nation started out as third world. Therefore, poverty is not the interesting thing and not the point worth studying. Rather, the point worth studying is how wealth was *created*. Studying that topic leads us to useful answers for humanity. If we understand how it is done, we can replicate it—to the good of all. That is the correct debate to have, and that is a good way to frame the issue.

Debate Tip: Respond to the accusation of imperfection. After displaying why our system is superior and theirs inferior or non-existent (imaginary utopias), you ultimately end by saying, "You don't get to make that argument."

So why do the youth keep falling for socialism and economic redistribution? The youth are sold the idealistic kindness aspect. This works for a few reasons: Adolescents are looking for meaning at this stage in their lives. They are in the most ideological phase of their development. Righteous anger comes easily.

Thomas Sowell urges us to look deeper into things that look good on the surface: "Undefined words have a special power in politics, particularly when they invoke some principle that engages people's emotions. 'Fair' is one of those undefined words . . . Who, after all, is in favor of 'unfairness'?"[103]

Also, the youth typically have not yet begun earning their own money, so the fundamental unfairness of a socialist system, to them, is not immediately obvious. Socialists play on these emotions: It's only about "greedy, rich people" (whose crime is wanting to keep the money they have earned).

Nor do the youth yet have much education or experience, and so they are not aware of the history of tyranny behind this idea. They genuinely do not see a problem. Hence, socialism allows them to feel righteous rage on one side and altruistic compassion on the other. This idea is, therefore, easy

---

103 Sowell, *Economic Facts and Fallacies.*

to sell to them. It is all based on emotional thinking. And advocates will use dishonest techniques to make their arguments: "Look at this particular evil corporation (and ignore the thousands of others providing employment and creating useful things)."

Yet socialism has been defeated—both in theory and in practice. Today, the correct war to wage on this terrible idea is the *moral* war. Our job is to show that our system is the moral one; theirs is the immoral one. That is the correct battlefront, particularly in the minds of the youth. For their part, all of the good that capitalism achieves is summed up and dismissed using the disingenuous phrase, "competitive exploitation."

BACK TO FRAMEWORKS

Following this diversion into a specific topic, let us return to the idea of framing the issue. Specifically, there is a common Leftist framing tactic that I would like you to be aware of and be able to debunk.

Do not allow them to frame the fight as a duality.

"You're either an evil fascist or a good socialist! Those are the options." In creating polarities only, they push everyone to one side or the other. And in doing so, they redefine conservatives as right-wing. This, in turn, places you in an unnecessary defensive position. In arguing against political correctness, our most likely descriptor is either conservative or classical liberal. Or simply: "Stop trying to label me."

If you are forced onto the Right by their framing, you will face the Nazi charge. But if you detect and dismantle the narrative, you will point to the middle, where, once again, we find the conservatives who founded America on freedom, overthrew slavery, fought and defeated the Nazis, and faced down and overthrew the communist Russians.

The Left uses the tactic of presenting an "only option" in a great many spheres. It is always a mistake to permit them to frame the issue as though theirs is the only option.

A silly example: Barbie recently introduced a range of new special edition disabled and black Barbies. I have little issue with this. In its own way, it does something rather sweet for children. The issue is subtly different. What stopped someone from making their *own* black dolls? Or their own dolls in wheelchairs? Why did they *have* to have Barbie?

On a larger scale, the same applies to affirmative action programs. The liberal government essentially argues, "There is no possibility of creating a new business. Instead, the only option is for you to give away half of yours." We see this dishonest "only option" tactic used over and over again.

"If you build a wall, how will these poor people immigrate?"

Answer: Legally.

"If you deny abortion, how will women prevent birth control?"

Answer: By using any one of a variety of means of contraception that *do not* kill a baby, such as condoms, the pill, or a diaphragm.

The Left further evolves this technique into arguments for permissiveness. For instance, "The government is trying to stop illegal immigrants. But look! A homegrown, white man just committed a terrorist act!"

Response: It's not either/or. Governments should stop illegal immigrants *and* homegrown terrorists. You are presenting a false dichotomy, as though we should choose one or the other.

In these instances, it is useful to overtly call out the technique they are using: "Ah, yes! I see you're using the old 'only option' argument. I'm surprised you would argue from such a point of weakness because it's so easy for me to invalidate, but you have. The 'only option' argument goes like this . . ."

Turn their use of "only option" arguments against them.

Ask them why they *want* this evil. They appear to be championing the immoral option *only*, as though that were the most desirable outcome. Provide a range of alternatives and then question their motives for choosing only the evil one.

Finally, reject their attempts to blame our side for problems they created.

"Look at this poor, single mother with six children! Who's going to take care of her? You heartless beasts!"

Now, ask this person whether they supported the sexual revolution. In one of their more egregious twists, the Left has little compunction blaming others for problems that they created. Here are some examples from not too long ago:

"America is a warmongering bully! Just look at how our missiles are pointed at Cuba and the Soviet Union! And at China. And at North Korea!" This is said with no heed for the fact that these are, or were, extreme-leftist governments, against which the US then had to defend itself. If the Left would stop raising up these dangerous tyrannies, no such response would be necessary.

"A woman's body is not 'holy,' you puritanical fundamentalist. Stop sexually oppressing her. It's like you're literally trying to make her live in *The Handmaid's Tale*." This is closely followed by: "Why do men treat women's bodies as though they were nothing more than sexual objects? There's no value, no respect!"

"Cops are pigs! Don't cooperate with them!" Followed by "How come you don't do any policing in our community? Is it because you're racist?"

"We need social welfare! People are suffering." Social welfare programs are then implemented, predictably incentivizing and increasing the numbers of the poor. Their response? "See? The numbers of poor people are increasing. We need more social welfare."

"We need to relax the petty laws. Who cares if homeless people defecate in the streets, or throw rocks, or do drugs? We need to stop criminalizing them. It's the stigma that's the problem." Followed by: "Look at the increase in violent vagrants on our streets. We clearly need less prosecutorial police and more socialism."

The Obama administration imposes a record number of new regulations on businesses. President Donald Trump comes into power and takes a hatchet to them. He removes the red tape, repeals the rules and restrictions, and frees up the market. Within two years, businesses are booming, and unemployment virtually disappears within the United States. The previous president, Barack Obama, stands up before the cameras and says, "Actually, I did that." No, Barry. No, you didn't. That's not how free-market capitalism works.

These are just a few examples of past problems created by the Left. Here is one they are busy creating right now: The Left insists that any man who decides on subjective emotional grounds that he is now a woman must be permitted to compete against biological women in sporting and athletic events.

"But I am a woman."

"Sure. Other than your penis and your *xy* chromosomes. That, I guess, leaves your *feelings*, which apparently must be taken as the true indicator. Hashtag science."

These men, of course, grew up with the benefit of testosterone. After transitioning into women, they then go on to obliterate women's records. Leftists tell us that we must all cheer wildly, and isn't it amazing how well these women are performing? Wow, a new record!

As we all stand by pretending that the king is wearing clothes, women become oppressed by progressives and are mocked as transphobic if they lodge legitimate complaints. And the damage to women does not end with denying them the right to win at their own sports; in many cases, the physical violence enacted against biological females by these physically stronger biological males is nothing short of a liberally sanctioned forum for men to batter women. We should accuse liberals of their crimes of enabling assault against women.

For their part, the liberal progressives stand by this new norm, which directly oppresses women. When they speak of uplifting women, or of anything whatsoever to do with "oppression" of women, this double standard should rightly be used against them.

Objection: But it's more inclusive.

Response: No, it *excludes* women from their own events and marginalizes them in their own spheres. It's oppressive. You've got this one wrong.

"Well, then, where *should* these transgenders compete? Tell me that!"

And yet again we see the phenomenon of Leftists creating a new problem, then trying to hand it to us.

Framing is powerful. Framing the issue allows the framer to win because they create the terms. The Left will even go so far as to frame issues of their creation as our problem.

Let us now proceed to consider one of the most commonly employed framing techniques used by the Left. It is a trick of language, and it is used often. It is called "Concept Creep."Understanding this one can be half the battle won.

CHAPTER 6

CALL OUT CONCEPT CREEP

CONCEPT CREEP ALLOWS THE LEFT to reframe even the most innocent and innocuous as malevolent or actively violent. It is the act of expanding definitions so far as to encompass *anything* the proponent wishes. Without concept creep, their enemies disappear back into rationality, and so they must engage in this technique feverishly.

Just being able to label this technique—to say, "that is concept creep"—is enough to defeat it. After that, *you* get to reframe the issue. First, though, you have to spot it.

An example: A sign indicates that one bathroom is for males and one is for females. A liberal points to the signs and yells, "Oppression!" That word, "oppression," is concept creep. The signs do not actually constitute oppression in any real sense, except under the most imaginative and credulity-stretching circumstances, and wouldn't qualify under any reasonable definition. (Also, that is how you know that the kindergartners are truly in charge.)

Critical theorist Stanley Fish calling opponents of affirmative action "bigots" and lumping them in with the KKK is another example.[104] So is radical feminist Andrea Dworkin insinuating that all heterosexual males are "rapists."[105] "Rapist" is a serious accusation, and it has corresponding conditions that must be met. Dworkin's broad description of sex as fundamentally

---

104 Stanley Fish, "When Principles Get in the Way," NYTimes.com, December 26, 1996, https://www.nytimes.com/1996/12/26/opinion/when-principles-get-in-the-way.html.

105 Michelle Goldberg, "Not the Fun Kind of Feminist," NYTimes.com, February 22, 2019, https://www.nytimes.com/2019/02/22/opinion/sunday/trump-feminism-andrea-dworkin.html.

exploitative on the part of the male does not meet these terms. As such, it is simply a false accusation. My value system has a commandment against that: "You shall not bear false witness" (Exod. 20:16).

Another shop-worn phrase that the Left employs is "denying their right to exist." Its cousin is "denying their humanity."

Try this. Post a thoughtful comment critiquing one of the Left's protected groups (that is, anybody whosoever outside of the Old Order). You will inevitably elicit at least one comment from a liberal that you are "denying them their right to exist." This has to be some ultimate extreme in the linguistic game of concept creep, in which your words are equated with genocide. It's ludicrous. But they do it.

Jonathan Haidt describes a letter from the students at Pomona University in which they explained why a certain female speaker shouldn't be allowed on campus. (To this, lecturer Lucia Martinez Valdivia says, "No one should have to pass someone else's ideological purity test to be allowed to speak.") Nevertheless, this paragraph appeared in their letter: "Engaging with her, a white supremacist, fascist supporter of the police state is a form of violence. . . If engaged Heather MacDonald would not be debating on mere difference of opinion, but the right of Black people to exist."

Haidt points out that this single, little paragraph contains the following errors and fallacies:

- Dichotomous thinking (Us versus Them)
- Fortune-telling, as the students predict what a person will say
- Catastrophizing: There again we see that phrase: "denying them the right to exist." How exactly will she do that? Their language inflates the horrors of her words far beyond what the speaker might actually say
- Labeling run wild. Serious accusations made without supporting evidence
- *Ad hominem* argumentation.[106]

---

106 Lukianoff and Haidt, *The Coddling of the American Mind.*

The letter also ended with a demand that the president must send an email—not just to them, but to the entire faculty, student body, and staff—apologizing for her patronizing statement (read: defense of academic freedom). So, in addition to the fallacies of reasoning above, we can also add bullying and amplification.

Response: I'm denying them their right to exist? Let's test your theory. If you're right, now that I've done it, they don't exist. Yet it turns out, they do still exist. So, you must be wrong, and as such, I will accept your apology for your false accusation. You see, speech and ideas do not work that way. You are committing the logical error of *catastrophizing*. You are taking simple debate of ideas, and forcing it to perform the gigantic leap to being an act of genocide. You have made the conscious choice to view me in the worst possible light, and that's very ugly of you. Debate about ideas is not genocide. It is actually the core of science and sound reasoning, by which we arrive at the best ideas. To call debate genocide is emotional thinking in its most ridiculous incarnation.

Forcing speech is basic bullying.

The "denying their humanity" and "denying their right to exist" arguments are also a subtle form of bullying and should be called out as such. They follow the formula: If you don't do what they want you to do, you are the abuser. The precise opposite applies when an ideology forces one to do something against their will. I don't want to call a man "she," but you force me to do so; *you* are the bully, not me.

Concept Creep

In 2016, Australian psychologist Nick Haslam wrote an article titled "Concept Creep: Psychology's expanding concepts of harm and pathology."[107]

---

107 Nick Haslam, "Psychology's Expanding Concepts of Harm and Pathology," in *Psychological Inquiry*, Volume 27 [1], January 2016, https://www.tandfonline.com/doi/full/10.1080/1047840X.2016.1082418.

He found that concepts had expanded in two directions: downward, to apply to less severe situations, and outward, to encompass new but conceptually related phenomena.

Haslam provides an example, using the word "trauma": Psychiatrists previously used this term very strictly to describe a physical agent that caused physical damage. In 1980, DSM 3 recognized Post Traumatic Stress Disorder, a non-physical trauma, for the first time. This represented a change. Nevertheless, the qualifications were extremely specific.

DSM emphasized that to qualify, the event could not be based on subjective feelings. It had to include such recognized trigger events as war, rape, or torture. Even divorce and bereavement did not qualify. These experiences were considered to be sad and painful, but they were not the same thing as trauma. It was believed that people could, in the course of time, recover quite adequately without therapeutic interventions.

By the early 2000s, however, the concept of trauma had crept down so far in parts of the therapeutic community that it included anything "experienced by an individual as physically or emotionally harmful or threatening and that has lasting adverse effects on the individual's functioning and physical, social, emotional, or spiritual wellbeing."[108]

The *subjective* experience of harm became ingrained in the definition of trauma. As a result, *anything* could be "trauma." This was a shift to a completely subjective standard. As such, it was an error on the part of many unprofessional medical practitioners. Nobody else could decide what trauma was (and was not), including the medical practitioners themselves. If it felt that way to *you*, then it was. Your own subjective assessment became sufficient evidence.[109]

Do you see the problems?

Here's the first one: This vastly expanded definition entails a massively expanding group of "mentally unwell" students. This, in turn, implies an

---

108 Ibid.
109 Ibid.

enormous need to grow the campus counseling framework. *Everyone* is mentally ill! Mental illness is on the rise! *Oh, no!*

Except that, really, they aren't, and it isn't. Not even close. They're just sad. Or angry. Or any one of a range of other normal emotions that adolescents must experience in order to grow and mature. Still, this way they get to be victims, entitled to counseling.

But that is not the worst consequence. These traumatized patients also qualify as victims, who are now entitled to recourse. They have been "wronged." The bad feelings represent an injustice, a violation, an act of violence, a crime. Someone made them feel something, and now that person must be punished for the damage they have caused, for their "violence."

The phrase "rape culture," is another example. Proponents argue that misogyny is endemic to American culture. Hence, *everything* is rape. Opponents of this view (that's us) argue that this expanded definition trivializes true sexual abuse cases by "crying wolf," thus cheapening the validity of legitimate rape claims.

Rape claims are extremely serious and should be taken seriously. Genuine rape is a horrific crime—one of the very worst. As violations of a person's sovereignty go, this is one of the most egregious, the most disgusting. Cheapening rape claims by arguing that everything is rape damages the legitimacy of the law in this regard, and thus hurts its victims.

Moreover, it turns normal, non-transgressing males into perpetual criminals, even if they merely flirt with women. If it is subjective, it begs the question: What qualifies? If a man tells a woman that he thinks she is beautiful, does that qualify?

Finally, and this is no trivial matter, it also precludes, unexamined, the possibility that some women might actually *like* being found attractive.

Proponents of this idea, like radical feminist Andrea Dworkin, believe that their personal subjective emotions are representative of women universally. Yet even a single woman who enjoys being found attractive belies this bias. And finally, let's take Dworkin's theory to its logical ends, and ask: "Therefore, *what?*" No flirting? No approaching women? No finding women attractive in the first place?

One is led to assume that radical feminists truly believe that all heterosexual sex is bad. Problematically for Dworkin and her ilk, this fact of male-female attraction and the need to approach in order to initiate it is at the center of our species' existence. It is our most important biological convention. It is at the center and genesis of her personal existence, too. If it goes away, there is only death.

Can this debate—as to whether rape is indeed endemic on varsity campuses, literally a "culture"—be answered? Yes, it can. Both in concept and numerically.

Conceptually, one must begin by contrasting the United States, where this accusation is so freely thrown about, with countries in which rape really is endemic and openly tolerated (such as parts of Afghanistan, where women may be raped, then arrested for it, and then shunned by their family afterwards). The United States, in principle, does not tolerate rape. It punishes it legally. When rape occurs, this is in contravention to the law of the land. By definition, we can already state that the U.S. does not represent a rape culture. Rape is illegal in the U.S.

Progressive college students, however, don't want to hear this argument. The argument itself, they say, is violent to them, insofar as it contradicts their lived experience. It would thus "damage" them to hear that America is not a rape culture. A threat to beliefs is a threat to mental wellbeing, and that qualifies as trauma. Emotions win. Emotions are "truer than facts." This is postmodernism at its most ridiculous.

Haidt argues that the culture of safetyism is based on a fundamental misunderstanding of human nature and of the dynamics of trauma and recovery. He says, "It is vital that people who have survived violence become habituated to ordinary cues and reminders woven into the fabric of daily life. Avoiding triggers is a *symptom* of PTSD, not a treatment for it."[110]

Conclusion? Political correctness does more harm than good. Even to those it purports to protect. Even at a medical and psychological level. That is the core premise of this book.

Research on post-traumatic growth shows that most people report becoming stronger or better in some way after undergoing a traumatic experience. The Leftist approach, if allowed to flourish like a poisonous rash, will not permit this to happen. It will hold people in their trauma and reinforce their victimhood.

Now, let us look at the issue of rape culture statistically, and the evidence is damning for the radical feminist case:

> Gender activists, academics, and politicians insist that one in five women at U.S. varsities will be sexually assaulted. It turns out, rates of rape in the U.S. are very low and have been declining for decades. In 2012, it was at under twenty individuals per one hundred thousand. This is by no means an "acceptable" number. However, accurately stated, this is 0.02% of the population. Some recent estimates put the number at 3 per 100,000, which would be 0.03%.

The U.S. Bureau of Justice Statistics estimated that at college campuses, the percentage of female college students reporting rape or sexual assault was 0.6%.[111] Again, this is not an acceptable number. There is no acceptable number. But it is an order of magnitude less than what the progressives are claiming.

Side Note: In nations like South Africa, which had the highest rape rate in the world in 2020, one might readily argue that there is, in fact, a rape culture. Rape statistics are off the charts there

---

110   Lukianoff and Haidt, *The Coddling of the American Mind.*
111   Tierney Sneed, "1 in 5? Data and the Debate about Campus Rape," USNews.com, December 16, 2014, https://www.usnews.com/news/articles/2014/12/16/1-in-5-data-and-the-debate-about-campus-rape.

compared to fully developed Western nations (other than Sweden, where immigration has caused a formerly low-crime Western nation to register in the top six for the globally highest rape stats).[112]

For our purposes here, we are defending Western culture. Western culture has lower rape stats than Arabic or African culture. This, of course, begs the question: Why the feminist rage against Western rape culture, but total silence regarding African or Muslim rape culture? The answer is: political correctness. And where we may not speak the truth, the problem cannot be addressed. That is how political correctness protects rape. Yet even though the U.S. stats are now widely known, when they are presented in social justice articles, they are nevertheless dishonestly portrayed.

I saw a fabulously dishonest example of this in an article shared on social media. The piece boldly stated that the U.S. was among the top five rape capitals of the world. This seemed extraordinary to me, and so I read the article carefully, playing my favorite game: *Find the Fallacy.* I found it very quickly.

What they had done was to collate the statistics for violent rape in every country on Earth. Then, when it came to America, they combined *two* sets of stats. The first was America's actual violent rape statistics. And the second was a broad survey of women who reported feeling "uncomfortable" in the workplace. They added the two together and used the number as a total for America. And so, discomfort at off-color comments in an American workplace was conflated with gang rape in a back alley somewhere in a third-world nation.

Talk about concept creep. A man saying something sexually suggestive and thereby making a woman feel uncomfortable is akin to rape? How extraordinary.

Perhaps the most egregious aspect of the rape culture narrative is how it disempowers women through sweeping stereotypes. All women, the narrative suggests, are cowering victims of brutal, scary men. All sex, the narrative

---

112 "World Population Review: Rape Statistics by Country 2020," WorldPopulationReview.com, https://worldpopulationreview.com/country-rankings/rape-statistics-by-country (accessed July 22, 2020).

continues, is oppressive rape, in which the male dominates the female. The mental image is one of women scattering into the bushes, as T-Rex-like salivating males go marauding by. "Here, cower beside me, Martha, as we hope and pray that they don't spot us!"

The narrative does not even permit the *possibilities* that women might enjoy sex themselves, or initiate it themselves, or find men and male attention enjoyable, or, in the simplest terms, be capable of standing up for themselves and saying "no, thank you" to unwanted advances. By the Leftist narrative, every woman is a helpless victim. Remember, to understand the collectivist Left, think "group," not "individual." They think "category of women," not "individual woman."

"White supremacists are everywhere!"

Possibly the worst example of concept creep today is the term *white supremacist*. *Everyone* is a white supremacist. Did you know? And *everything* is white supremacy. Astonishingly, even black, female, conservative presenter Candace Owens, who has made a cause and career out of calling out Democrats for their condescending "Black people are victims" narrative is, herself, a white supremacist.

Debate Tip: Here is the best way to explain what is wrong with the concept of "Micro-aggressions." This relatively new term was popularized by an article written by professor Derald Wing Sue of the University of Columbia in a 2007 article. Drawing on popular understandings, micro-aggressions were defined as "Brief and commonplace daily verbal, behavioral, or environmental indignities, whether intentional or unintentional, that communicate hostile, derogatory or negative slights or insults."[113] (It originally ended with "toward people of color," but concept creep means it also now applies to everyone). Can you spot the fallacy? It is in the words "intentional or unintentional."

---

113   Derald Wing Sue, et al, "Racial Microaggressions in Everyday Life," *American Psychologist*, May-June 2007.

The fatal flaw in this idea is its introduction of "non-intentional" as a form of recognized violence. If I bump you on purpose, that is assault (though a very mild form). If I bump you by accident, that is not assault, although the other person may *mis*-perceive it as one. The term *misperceive* is key here. "Perceive" is not accurate. Their perception was wrong, and therefore, the term *misperceive* better applies. The term *micro-aggression* attempts to elevate the unintentional bump into malicious assault. Therefore, *everything* is assault, and *everyone* is a victim, all the time.

No society can function this way. Legally, the concept fails, too. You cannot hold a person maliciously accountable for accidental acts. If I bump you, and you fall off a cliff and die, that is a tragic accident, but my life goes on. If, however, I push you off a cliff, I will be jailed for life, and rightly so. Intent matters. Haidt describes this absurdity as the triumph of impact over intent.[114]

Just one of the awful outcomes of normalizing this idea is that it prescribes that you should *always* choose to see the worst in people, by assuming bad motives on their part. What could possibly go wrong? This idea is anti-peace, anti-community, and, frankly, full of hate. When we hear the term, this should be our response to it, as we claim the moral high ground and accuse them of lowering societal norms in the interests of ugliness.

Reject their corrupted version of "human rights."

Human Rights. One of our most laudable ideas. Human rights are at the heart of our value system, which posits the individual as inviolable. Once an individual is held to be sovereign and inviolable, the legal rights of that human then follow.

Here is where the concept goes wrong in the hands of progressives. A right can only be predicated on the inviolability of the individual. In other words, legitimate rights only prevent others from doing negative things to

---

114   Lukianoff and Haidt, *The Coddling of the American Mind.*

you. What can *not* properly qualify as a right is anything that imposes an *obligation* on anyone else. Why? Because that violates *their* rights.

The U.S. Constitution correctly identifies inalienable rights as "things the government may not do to the individual" and "things individuals may not do to one another." Obama criticized this approach as being reactive only, a "charter of negative liberties," and failing to proactively make promises to people.[115]

By contrast, the U.N.'s progressive "Universal Declaration of Human Rights" charter does just that. In fact, it does something quite sneaky. It includes entitlements. It argues that individuals are *entitled* to certain things. This entitlement implies that someone else must provide these things, which creates an obligation on another. The entire trick being played here is basically a justification for socialism.

If entitlements are human rights, then somebody has to provide those entitlements. So, logically, who? Well, a big socialist government, of course. And with that, we are back to collectivism. The perversity here is that they use the concept of individual rights and the inviolability of the individual to introduce and justify collectivism, which, in turn, creates tyrannical obligation.

The Left uses the term human rights to denote something that doesn't qualify. When, for instance, transgender people try to compel speech using their preferred pronouns, they are not asking for a right. They are asking for a special privilege for their group. They are, in fact, asking for legal sanction to shut down your freedom of speech and conscience and legal sanction to compel you to obey their wishes. None of these things constitute rights. They constitute ideological bullying. This is a subtle and cunning use of scope creep, in which bad ideas are smuggled through inside of good ones.

---

115   Heather Higgins, "Barack Obama's Poor Understanding of the Constitution," USNews. com, November 3, 2008, https://www.usnews.com/opinion/articles/2008/11/03/barack-obamas-poor-understanding-of-the-constitution.

Punch a Nazi.

Perhaps the most egregious, violence-justifying, and patently absurd example of concept creep on the Left is their now-popular pithy little phrase: "Punch a Nazi."

Let's explore both the concept creep and the built-in errors of reasoning in this glib little phrase in the form of a conversation. It plays out like this (Feel free to copy and paste on social media. You will find an easy to copy-and-paste version available at www.BreakingWoke.com.

Punch a Nazi—Exploring Social Justice

By: Douglas Kruger

"Dude! Punch a Nazi!"

"Um . . . Just a second. It sounds like you're advocating public violence in the form of an assault of strangers. Isn't that illegal? And immoral?"

"Well . . . maybe it's not legal, but it's definitely moral."

"Okay, so we've established that it *is* illegal. You *are* propagating an illegal, violent act."

"Well, the thing is, it's *moral*."

"Why is it moral?"

"Because they're Nazis!"

"So, as long as they're part of the correct demographic, it's okay to assault them?"

"Yes."

"Got it. While that might not pass any legal test, let's assume that your argument is basically correct and move forward. Now, have you ever met a Nazi? They have party membership cards and wear specific uniforms, and they're alive and active in the 1930s and 1940s in Germany."

"Well, I mean, not a REAL Nazi, like that. But people who are LIKE Nazis."

"Okay, so we've established that you are advocating illegal public violence against a specific group of people, based on their demographic, but it also seems that you're a little shaky on who exactly those people are. So, what is the exact qualification for someone to be 'like' a Nazi?"

"Well, they're racists."

"Okay, so we've changed track now. You're actually advocating that people should punch racists?"

"Yes. Totally."

"So, you were just using the term *Nazi* to be inflammatory?"

"They deserve it because they're racists."

"Right, so we've established that it's the *racism* that is the real issue here. So, you're saying that we should find racist people who are like the Nazis—say, for example, those who oppose the Jewish state of Israel—and punch them?"

"Um . . . No, I think Israel is a Nazi Apartheid state. Most of today's real racists support Israel."

"So, we're not talking about Nazi-style racism against Jews? And your belief is that the *real* Nazis of today are those who support Jewish Israel, which was founded as a result of the actual Nazis chasing the Jews out of Germany? That, in fact, the Jews *themselves* are Nazis? That seems contradictory."

"Well, I mean, I'm talking about racism in general. Not just with Jews."

"Fair enough. So if, for example, someone uses a derogatory term about white people, someone else should punch them?"

"No, definitely not. It's the other way around."

"Ah. So, you should actually ignore racism as a broad category and only use it selectively. You should only punch people of the *correct color* who make derogatory comments?"

"Yes."

"Isn't that racist?"

"No."

"I see. So, we've established that you're advocating illegal public assault, based on a double standard, against a poorly defined group of people, who generally support the people that Nazis most opposed. So far, so good. So, what exactly qualifies these people as racist Nazis, in the context of it being the right *kind* of racism to meet your qualifying criteria?"

"Their hate. They're not inclusive."

"That sounds like a very broad, vague, and flexible definition, given that the outcome is so certain and so violent. It's also completely subjective. It almost sounds like *you* get to decide who meets those criteria, and then *you* get to enact violence upon them as a result. You're both judge and executioner to perfect strangers, whose backgrounds, lives, values and stories you don't know."

"Well, you know racism when you see it!"

"*How* do you know it when you see it?"

"They talk about things like border control; and they're nationalistic; and they deny that minority groups are victims."

"Those sound like political beliefs."

"Exactly!"

"So, you should punch people for their political beliefs?"

"Yes, their political beliefs make them Nazis."

"But those political beliefs are not inherently racist or hateful. They're also not inherently Nazist. Controlling a nation's borders is normal. All nations do it. It provides security. Being nationalistic just means you love your country, which includes all its minority groups. And telling people that they are not victims empowers them. Conversely, continually telling them that they are victims disempowers them."

"Well, my sociology teacher told me that those things are racist. They're exactly how Nazism began."

"Your sociology teacher is a radical Marxist, who doesn't know his history. He appears to have re-defined normal, moderate families and concerned citizens—and even normally functioning nations—as 'Nazi.' That's called 'concept creep.' And based on that fantastical imaginary stretch, you and he are fermenting violence together. He is the political ideologue, and you are his foot-soldiering thug. You even have a violence-promoting slogan for your misguided civic views: 'Punch a Nazi.' Have you ever considered that *you* might be the oppressor?"

"No way. Everyone thinks the way I do!"

"And if they don't, you punch them, to *make* them think like you?"

"Um. Well, if they're Nazis, then yes."

"That's exactly what a Nazi would do. Your message is 'conform to my political worldview, or I will carry out violence upon you.'"

"Well, I think all those things they believe are racist."

"But I don't."

"That's because you're a Nazi."

"Then go ahead and try it, junior. Don't be surprised if you wake up in a hospital ward."

CHAPTER 7
REJECT THEIR IDEOLOGICALLY-EMBEDDED DEFINITIONS.

AS WE HAVE SEEN WITH concept creep, words matter. Their accuracy is important, and so we should be aware of terminology and how it is used. Another linguistic trick the Left likes to pull is to embed ideas with foregone conclusions built into the words themselves. If the word is accepted, then the embedded ideology is smuggled into the debate, along with its foregone conclusion, like an ideological Trojan horse.

Take the example of the relatively new addition to our language: "hetero-normative." This term has a built-in ideology. It reaches ideological conclusions before even charging out of the gate. The term *hetero-normative* subtly accuses people of the "crime" of trying to "normalize" heterosexual relationships, as though they were the standard. They *are* the standard. And they have been the standard for a very, very long time—since the dawn of our species, as it turns out. This norm is, in fact, the very reason for the continued perpetuation of our species and always has been. The word implies that this isn't so and creates a false picture in which everybody used to be pansexual, until conservatives came along in the recent past and began the sinister project of "normalizing" man/women relationships. To allow the word is to accept the conclusion.

The term *cisgender normative* performs the same trick. It relates to whether or not a person "identifies with" their biological sex. Over 99.7 percent of people do. Most stats indicate that 0.3 percent of people don't. This makes cisgender a global normative paradigm. Heterosexual relationships and cisgender individuals are overwhelmingly the norm, overwhelmingly the standard, overwhelmingly the template for humanity, and have been so throughout history, even accounting for notable anomalies like the Greek predilection for soldiers having sex with their young male apprentices.

They are the norm both biologically and numerically. Biologically, they account for perpetuation of the species, and boy, that's normative. But they are also the norm numerically. The number of non-heterosexual people is only around two percent of the population. And as we shall see, a disproportionate number of those individuals report being sexually assaulted by a member of the same sex as children, disparaging the notion that they were "born that way." This demographic cannot make such an assertion in the face of disproportionately high abuse stats.

A Plethora of New Phobias

The Left's new phobia words pull the same trick. Take the well-known term *Islamophobia*. It contains several foregone conclusions, which are:

- Islam is obviously perfectly acceptable. There are no problematic issues there worthy of discussion. This issue is settled and beyond dispute.
- Negative reaction to Islam is necessarily predicated on fear or racism.
- This fear is phobic, insofar as it is not a valid fear, notwithstanding Islam's documented history of violence nor its internal prescriptions for radical proselytizing.
- *Et voila*, within one word, we have a complete ideological defense of a system that might not actually withstand intellectual scrutiny, but which defense goes even further and becomes attack, defacing and vilifying those who would dare to raise the concern.

Islamophobia is a hard-working word indeed. It is also a dishonest word. Do not let them introduce their own revised definitions, which contain embedded ideology.

Another popular example is their new definitions for old words. For instance, we have long held a universally understood definition for racism, which is hatred based on skin color. But now, from the halls of academia and radical social theory, there is a new definition for this old word, revised to the following formula: *Racism is prejudice plus power.* No, it isn't. That's a brand-new definition. It comes from radical social theory, and it has new premises, which are designed to achieve a new agenda. We reject such terminology, just as we reject the agenda. A racist is a person who hates people of another skin color. This applies regardless of the skin colors in question. It cannot be selective without having a biased agenda.

Debate Tip: Look out for words like *condemn* and *categorically reject*. They represent a weakness on the part of your opponent and an opportunity for you. Clear thinking and academically sound debaters should generally not use these words. The words themselves are replacements for the argument or differently phrased refusals to even engage with the ideas. Pointing this out highlights dishonesty on your opponent's part or signals their inability to present a cogent argument. Look out for such words and use them on the offensive.

In addition to words that come with assumed conclusions, there are also some *causes* which liberals assume are uniquely theirs, but which are not. Here are a few examples:

RAPE

To listen to the mainstream media, one would assume that liberals are the only people who care about rape, while conservatives are supposedly blasé about it. In my entire life, I have never met a fellow conservative who is not passionately anti-rape. If anything, conservatives tend to propose the death penalty for this crime, while liberal sensibilities do not extend this far. And conservatives remain eternally baffled by the Left's unwillingness to condemn rape in Islamic and African societies. Thus, I contend that this one of our great causes, more than it is one of theirs.

CHEATING CORPORATE COMPANIES

Since medieval times, small Christian towns have held the idea of mercantile laws and business contracts to be inviolable. Without the upholding of contracts and without the conditions of trust which they enforce, everything falls apart.

Capitalists know this. Good law, sound contracts, protection of property, prosecution of corruption, and so forth are of paramount importance to the entire system of capitalism. Deal-breaking, law-breaking, cronyism and underhandedness utterly ruin the system. When the system works, it uplifts societies like nothing else we know of. Everyone prospers. Its integrity *must* be maintained, and that is not a Leftist principle. It is a conservative one.

BUYING LEGAL OUTCOMES

It is the same story with the capacity for interest groups to "buy" legal outcomes. That undermines the sanctity and efficacy of the law, which is what upholds society (and capitalism). There are few greater threats to a successful conservative society than the capacity for some to buy preferential treatment.

RACISM

This one is actually insulting. The Left obsesses about race and continually attempts to paint its opponents as pathologically hung up on the topic. Conservative Christians were the first people on Earth to fight against slavery—both in England and then in the U.S. A conservative president enacted the Emancipation Proclamation, then fought a Civil War in order to uphold it.

Contrary to a never-ending tirade of propaganda from the Left, conservatives don't care about race. And for my part and for that of the conservatives I associate with, I have never heard anything but outright condemnation of racism. It is evil. But remember, if the Left doesn't own it, then they cannot create victimhood groups. It is, in fact, not in their interests to solve the actual problem of racism. It is in their interests to maintain it as a perpetual issue.

> **The best video on this topic**: Anything by Candace Owens. But start with this one: "Candace Owens: Race has become a business."[116]

116   Fox News, "Candace Owens: Race has become a business," YouTube Post, 4:21, May 4, 2018, https://www.youtube.com/watch?v=8Am-1IHSGWo&list=LLqP3ZTiYUWbZL3p 23LCQg_A&index=849.

CHAPTER 8
CHECK THE TRUTH-VALUE OF THEIR CLAIMS.

THERE IS SOMETHING A LITTLE sad about the fact that this technique must be stated. It implies we must expect dishonesty. The unfortunate reality is that the opposition has little compunction about twisting data or presenting ideas in revised formats. When you are presented with stats, quotes, findings, or outcomes, do not begin by arguing them on their own merits. They may not be true. In fact, if they sound politically correct, they are probably not true. Instead, begin by investigating the claims. When you start looking for them, the falsehoods range from the small (social media studies misrepresenting social norms) to the enormous.

Here's one famous one from liberal mythology still in use today. Perhaps you have heard of how the American founding fathers "separated" church and state? How they created a "wall of separation" between the two? It is a wonderful mythology. It is also a complete lie and a pernicious one, which was used to force prayer out of schools, in a perversion of the original intent of the First Amendment.

The First Amendment does not contain the words "wall of separation between church and state." In fact, it does not even contain the words "separation of church and state." When it was adopted in 1791, the point of the clause was twofold. First, it was meant to prohibit the federal government from setting up its own national church and then imposing that church upon the people. Then came the second part of the clause, which was a flip side to the first. Liberals utterly ignore this part and, in fact, openly contravene it. The flip side was that government was also prohibited from preventing people from openly practicing religion (for example, in schools).

As The Freedom Forum Institutes explains: The establishment clause separates church from state, but not religion from politics or public life. Individual citizens are free to bring their religious convictions into the public arena. But the government is prohibited from favoring one religious view over another or even favoring religion over non-religion.[117]

Perversely, liberals used a misrepresentation of this clause to arrive at a brand-new conclusion: The government should ban the open practice of religion in schools. They even gave it a catchy label: "separation of church and state." How's that for using your own rules against you? And how's that for clever labeling?

Or how about this one? The Black Lives Matter movement was launched to combat the epidemic of white police officers executing black people, for no crime other than the color of their skin. Do you recall the frenzied CNN reports? They seemed to go on for weeks. This sort of alleged violence leads to serious inquiries, as it must. The trouble is, the inquiries came back with disappointing results for social justice activists and for CNN.

As Heather Mac Donald reported in *The National Review*, "There is no epidemic of racist police shootings."[118] Her article referenced a study published in the *Proceedings of the National Academy of Sciences*, which found:

> White officers are no more likely than black or Hispanic officers to shoot black civilians. It is a racial group's rate of violent crime that determines police shootings, not the race of the officer. The more frequently officers encounter violent suspects from any

---

117   "The First Amendment Says That the Government May Not 'Establish' Religion. What Does That Mean in a Public School?," FreedomForumInstitute.org, https://www.freedomforuminstitute.org/about/faq/the-first-amendment-says-that-the-government-may-not-establish-religion-what-does-that-mean-in-a-public-school (accessed February 29, 2020).

118   Heather Mac Donald, "There Is No Epidemic of Racist Police Shootings," NationalReview.com, July 13, 2019, https://www.nationalreview.com/2019/07/white-cops-dont-commit-more-shootings.

given racial group, the greater the chance that members of that racial group will be shot by a police officer. In fact, if there is a bias in police shootings after crime rates are taken into account, it is against white civilians.[119]

The study found that of police-officer-involved fatal shootings, "fifty-five percent of the victims were white, twenty-seven percent were black, and nineteen percent were Hispanic. Between ninety and ninety-five percent of the civilians shot by officers in 2015 were attacking police or other citizens; ninety percent were armed with a weapon."

The article points out that earlier studies have also disproven the idea that white officers are biased in shooting black citizens, yet the "the Black Lives Matter narrative has been impervious to the truth," but "the persistent belief that we are living through an epidemic of racially biased police shootings is a creation of selective reporting."[120]

These results are now widely known and established. However, it is curious to note that CNN did not subsequently spend weeks frantically correcting these perceptions and pointing out the truth. They simply moved on with the result that the "racist police shootings" narrative still stood in the public consciousness. Damage done.

Could that have been why, when George Floyd was killed by police in 2020, the popular narrative still stood, and the resultant outrage and protests then exploded around the world? Incendiary narratives can have global consequences.

Finally, how about this one from New York Times columnist Tom Wicker? Wicker used per capita income statistics when depicting the success of the Lyndon Johnson administration. He then used family income statistics in order to depict failure for the policies of Ronald Reagan and George H.W. Bush. The variation over time in sizes and composition of what constitutes a family can and does completely change the picture, which Wicker used to selective effect.[121]

---

119   Ibid.
120   Ibid.
121   Sowell, *Economic Facts and Fallacies.*

Economist Thomas Sowell points out that similar tactics have been used to depict progressive administrations as economically successful and conservative administrations as stagnant or trending downwards for decades. It requires a canny mind to a) suspect this deceit, and b) go looking for the differences in applied categorization.[122]

One trick of this nature that is a favorite of the Thomas Pikettys of the world is to point to a stagnant-growth demographic and to use this as evidence against capitalism. They will point out how, for instance, wage earners haven't had an increase in a ten-year period. What they will not tell you is that these have not been the same individuals over the duration of that period. Instead, the ones measured at the beginning of the ten years have typically been promoted out of that category. The ones represented at the end of the ten years are newcomers, who may just have started their working careers or who have progressed from poverty to earning this wage. There is a continual upward flow of people through this supposedly stagnant category. For the most part, the lives of the individuals depicted here are steadily improving, not remaining economically stagnant, as the category itself would suggest.

So, check everything. Check the claims. Check the numbers. Check the nature of the study. Check the conditions by which these conclusions have been reached and whether these terms are applied consistently or selectively.

Check on whether militant Muslims have been included under the category "right-wing terrorists." Check whether "uncomfortable banter" has been placed in the same column as "rape." If the commentary includes outrage or attack, the diligent reviewer is more likely than not to find these transgressions. You are arguing with an ideologically motivated opponent and one not known for its scruples.

---

122 Ibid.

CHAPTER 9

LEARN ALINSKY'S "RULES FOR RADICALS," SO THEY CAN'T BE USED AGAINST YOU.

SAUL ALINSKY'S *RULES FOR RADICALS* has been used against conservatives for nearly half a century, to devastating effect. Yet the principles are easy to counter, if we are only aware of them. Once you are aware of them, you will see the liberal Left using these tactics all the time, from mass movements that sweep liberal presidents to power, to simple arguments on Facebook.

I strongly encourage you to learn these techniques, to understand them, and to teach others how to spot and refute them. They are vicious; they are unethical; but they are common, and they are effective. I would even go so far as to say: If you see these techniques being used on someone else, insofar as you will shortly know how to step in and defuse them, please do. Don't allow another person to be bullied into submission simply because they don't understand the methods being employed against them.

Meet the author of The Art of War, *repackaged for Modern Progressives.*

Saul Alinsky was essentially an American activist for communism who never openly identified himself that way. His goal was the same old progressive fair: break society. If you break it, you can then rebuild it the way you want. Tear everything down through constant use of critical theory, of relentless social attack, and of never-ending pressure on your opponent. Agitate until they crack, then pounce.

The key to understanding Alinsky's method is this one guiding principle Alinsky repeatedly tells his students: "The action is in the *reaction*." What he means by this is that the real good stuff is to be found in how *you* react to the attacks carried out against you. An Alinskyan is encouraged to attack their opponent using any means. Slander. Name-calling. False accusations. Mobs mobilized to stand outside your business. Weeks of frenzied news media reporting. Anything. Just agitate. Start by poking. Then when the target begins to react, that's where the gold lies. A target that is constantly reacting is, by definition, on the defensive. They are scared. They are pressured. They are rendered insecure. Eventually, they will either apologize, which is like an admission of guilt, or make a mistake. And that is when you take them down.

Alinsky is a proponent of the "ends-justify-the-means" ethics. So, for instance, it doesn't matter if your opponent hasn't said anything racist or bigoted. Your ends are important and, therefore, morally justified. Accuse them of saying such things anyway. You can even accuse them of saying things *in advance* of their having the opportunity to do so, as Obama did on this occasion, highlighted in Jeff Hedgpeth's book on how to defeat Alinsky tactics:

> Democratic presidential contender Barack Obama said on Friday he expects Republicans to highlight the fact that he is black as part of an effort to make voters afraid of him.

> "It is going to be very difficult for Republicans to run on their stewardship of the economy or their outstanding foreign policy," Obama told a fundraiser in Jacksonville, Florida. "We know what kind of campaign they're going to run. They're going to try to make you afraid. They're going to try to make you afraid of me. He's young and inexperienced and he's got a funny name. And did I mention he's black?"[123]

---

123 Jeff Hedgpeth, *Rules for Radicals Defeated: A Practical Guide for Defeating Obama / Alinsky Tactics* (Scotts Valley: Create Space Independent Publishing Platform, 2012).

In *Rules for Radicals,* Alinsky outlines thirteen techniques, thirteen "rules," by which to destroy your opponent. They can be used in combinations or in isolation. They can also be adapted and changed according to the scenario. Simply being aware of these techniques will go a very long way to prevailing against them. Most people who become targets of Alinsky tactics have never heard of him and are thus blindsided and baffled when they get taken down. This need not happen to you.

Here are his thirteen rules:[124]

RULE 1: POWER IS NOT ONLY WHAT YOU HAVE, BUT WHAT THE ENEMY THINKS YOU HAVE.

Liberals and social justice warriors are generally in the minority. And so, they must be loud. They must find ways to puff up, like an animal in nature. This could mean organizing shout mobs. The goal is to look like they have big numbers, and therefore, public support, even if they do not. The rule suggests that even when they are a small group, they can still bring great pressure to bear on opponents, even if the pressure is actually fake. Indeed, especially if it is fake.

"We, the people!" is actually "We, the hired protestors, here to express manufactured outrage for the cameras in order to sway public opinion by looking as though we *are* public opinion." Socialist billionaire George Soros has been known to sponsor such groups.

Entrepreneurs are familiar with this basic principle: If your coffee shop is struggling, hire three fake couples to sit in it. More will then follow because of the perception that this place is "obviously popular." The technique definitely works.

Conservatives tend to miss this trick in their bid to play honestly. But we actually go too far the other way. We won't even "like" someone else's status, for fear that the mob might attack us, too.

---

124 Ibid.

Not only do we fail to prop up our numbers for the sake of perceptions, we don't even show our numbers. This is wrong. Representation *is* important. At the very, very least, don't let bad ideas stand uncontested. At best, use this technique against them (but honestly, and not with hired actors).

RULE 2: NEVER GO OUTSIDE THE EXPERIENCE OF YOUR PEOPLE.

Keep bringing debates, fights, or social issues back to what your side is sure of or confident with, even if it means arbitrarily changing the subject. Ever been in a debate with a social justice warrior, who simply switches to another topic entirely, mid-debate? You were discussing marriage when your opponent suddenly throws out, "Yes, but your side is destroying the rainforest!"

That's Alinsky.

RULE 3: WHENEVER POSSIBLE, GO OUTSIDE THE EXPERIENCE OF THE ENEMY.

Building on Rule 2, this rule suggests that you should keep the enemy constantly off-balance. Force them to fight on topics and issues that they are not familiar with, so that they will slip. If they slip, you pounce. The action is in the *reaction*.

As before, this means introducing new topics arbitrarily. Basically, go straight for the jugular of what you find to be "weak" about your enemy's entire situation, culture, position, or worldview. Then destroy them on those grounds and not on the grounds of the original argument.

RULE 4: MAKE THE ENEMY LIVE UP TO THEIR OWN BOOK OF RULES.

"Yes, but I know a Christian who sleeps around!" Alinsky says, "You can kill them with this, for they can no more obey their own rules than the Christian church can live up to Christianity." This tactic is disgusting, in that it is an *ad hominem* argument. But if you don't know that, it can work.

Hedgpeth describes this one as "the tactic that the right has allowed the Left to own without a fight." He is correct.

Remember the number of times I have spoken about flipping the power dynamic and getting them to openly defend a position that they have been dishonestly and tacitly defending? I will explore it a few more times as we progress. If you *don't* do this, they will use relentless pressure on you, forcing you to defend your position as they swarm and bite like piranha. The response to this rule is to flip it, then flagellate *them* with their own inconsistencies.

Debate Tip: Once you force the Leftist to defend their position, you are then positioned to use Alinsky's technique against them.

Imagine a scenario in which you are debating sexual norms. You have forced them to defend their own stance that "love is love."

"So, you're saying that all love is equal. There is no morality governing sex. It's okay for you to have sex with an underaged child."

"No, I'm not saying that. Obviously, you can't have sex with a minor."

"So, you're saying that there *are* moral laws governing sex?"

"No, I'm saying . . . I mean . . . In *that* case, between two men, it doesn't apply."

"So, you're saying that love is love but only defined according to what you, arbitrarily, believe qualifies as love, here and now? Maybe it will change tomorrow?"

And so forth. The action is in the *reaction*. Force them to defend the indefensible, and they must ultimately undo their own shaky logic.

Send out the hit squad.

The Left also use this tactic by proxy, and via other actors, even as they morally distance themselves from it. This way, their hatchet job goes ahead, yet they continue to look impeccable.

Obama used this technique against Alaskan Republican candidate Sarah Palin. Palin spoke in favor of family values. Her daughter, Bristol, was pregnant out of wedlock. Obama's campaign beat Palin over the head with her own book of rules. Yet simultaneously, Obama himself feigned sympathy for Palin and her family. The formula is to send out the hit-squad to do the dirty work, then stand before the cameras clucking sympathetically about the shame of it all, and for extra virtue-points, publicly promise not to use it against her.

Finally, they will even attack you for the inconsistencies of others in your camp. You are a member of *this* group. And another member of this group has said *this*. Therefore, your side is immoral.

Hedgpeth observes:

> Have you ever seen politicians or even business leaders peppered with questions that seem irrelevant? Have you ever been blind-sided in social media by questions and issues with which you know little or nothing? Have you ever seen the mainstream media dwell on seemingly inconsequential issues when covering Conservatives? All of these are textbook examples of the second and third rule. Ignore any strong points made by your opponent, and simply overwhelm him with tangential questions that might exploit some weakness. Even if you never exploit an issue in your favor, you have changed the subject from your weakness, and pushed the momentum of reaction in the direction of your opponent.

I believe that this tool, reversed, is a gift to conservatives who are not afraid to use it, given that the Left is shot through with contradictions. We should use it! It is also worth noting that the Left thinks that by holding no morality, they are exempt from moral standards. So accuse them of having no morality. If that is their position, force them to own it. And push them on it, hard, until they unravel.

RULE 5: RIDICULE IS MAN'S MOST POTENT WEAPON.

Alinsky states, "It is almost impossible to counterattack ridicule. Also it infuriates the opposition, who then react to your advantage." And as we know, "the action is in the *reaction*." And so, the entire point of using ridicule is just to get you to react.

If you don't, or even better, if you maintain your calm and dismiss them with humor and wit of your own, you win. At the very least, don't fall for the bait. Just ignore it.

RULE 6: A GOOD TACTIC IS ONE THAT YOUR PEOPLE ENJOY.

"If your people are not having a ball doing it, there is something very wrong with the tactic." Under Alinsky tactics, this rule essentially translates to "Go ahead. Call people racist. Call them stupid. Mock them. If it feels good, do it." It is an "incite the mob" principle.

RULE 7: A TACTIC THAT DRAGS ON TOO LONG BECOMES A DRAG.

People get bored easily. Alinsky advises continually providing them with new targets. A new revolution. A new enemy. A new group to swarm and destroy. Keep your people invigorated. This is in contrast to the conservative project of slowly growing and nurturing a good and healthy society and "if it isn't broken, not fixing it." Our side is deeply anti-revolution and wants conditions of peace to get on with our private lives.

RULE 8: KEEP THE PRESSURE ON WITH DIFFERENT TACTICS AND ACTIONS AND UTILIZE ALL EVENTS OF THE PERIOD FOR YOUR PURPOSE.

Once again, we see that the Alinsky mode is all about pressure. Unrelenting, never-ending pressure. And you can use any excuse to keep up that pressure. Remember, "the action is in the reaction."

Switch tacks by switching tactics. Just keep the pressure on. If three years of screaming, "Russian Collusion!" doesn't work, just switch to "Racism!" and scream all the louder. Achieve your goal any which way. Just achieve it. Keep pushing.

Alinsky added to this, "Utilize all events of the period for your purpose." This is commonly phrased, "Never let a good crisis go to waste."

Anything that happens can be turned into "proof" of your narrative, so long as you are not bounded by honesty. Penguins in Madagascar died in a jet ski accident? "See? We need socialism!" People are crossing the Mexican border into America? "See! It's because we haven't solved climate change!" It doesn't matter if it doesn't make sense. The point is pressure, pressure, pressure.

RULE 9: THE THREAT IS USUALLY MORE TERRIFYING THAN THE THING ITSELF.

Rule 9 is typically carried out with threats of boycotts. It is generally premised on shock value. So, stay calm. Don't be pressured. This rule relates to the very first rule about making it look as though they have more power than they actually do. Don't be pressured. Your insecure reaction is the entire goal.

RULE 10: THE MAJOR PREMISE FOR TACTICS IS THE DEVELOPMENT OF OPERATIONS THAT WILL MAINTAIN A CONSTANT PRESSURE UPON THE OPPOSITION.

We agitate. You react. We react based on your reaction. You react to that. And so, we keep the pressure on, systematically and unrelentingly. It must be turned into a cycle.

RULE 11: IF YOU PUSH A NEGATIVE HARD AND DEEP ENOUGH IT WILL BREAK THROUGH INTO ITS COUNTER-SIDE.

This is based on the principle that every positive has its negative. Alinsky states, "We have already seen the conversion of the negative into the positive, in Mahatma Gandhi's development of the tactic of passive resistance."

He follows that by explaining that Gandhi, and later Dr. Martin Luther King Jr., discovered the power of the negative to accomplish positive results.

Hedgpeth explains:

> When faced with clear inequities it is common to choose some display of force as the remedy. It is human nature to push back when pushed. The revolutionary methodology of Gandhi was to resist force not with force, but with passivity. In addition, as with Martin Luther King Jr., a new method of revolution was discovered and implemented. By using a negative, they were able to bring about profoundly positive change. While the concept was not new, dating back to the teaching of Jesus and others, it was a fresh execution of these tactics in a vastly different world.

Alinsky himself explains:

> One corporation we organized against responded to the continuous application of pressure by burglarizing my home, and then using the keys taken in the burglary to burglarize the offices of the Industrial Areas Foundation where I work. The panic in this corporation was clear from the nature of the burglaries, for nothing was taken in either burglary to make it seem that the thieves were interested in ordinary loot – they took only the records that applied to the corporation.

> Even the most amateurish burglar would have had more sense than to do what the private detective agency hired by that corporation did. The police departments in California and Chicago agreed that "the corporation might just as well have left its fingerprints all over the place."

> When a corporation bungles like the one that burglarized my home and office, my visible public reaction is shock, horror, and moral outrage. In this case, we let it be known that sooner or later it would be confronted with this crime as well as with a whole series of other derelictions, before a United States Senate Subcommittee Investigation. Once sworn in, with congressional immunity, we would make these actions public. This threat, plus the fact that an attempt on my life had been made in Southern California, had the corporation on a spot where it would be publicly suspect in the event of assassination.

RULE 12: THE PRICE OF A SUCCESSFUL ATTACK
IS A CONSTRUCTIVE ALTERNATIVE.

Here is an example of an Alinsky rule that contains within it the seeds of its own destruction. Alinsky rightly points out that if you are going to attack a system, you had better be able to propose a better system. Mostly, the Left cannot. Thus, if this rule is flipped, they are in trouble.

Hedgpeth explains: "One of the ways in which a 'target' can wriggle off the hook is essentially to throw his hands up in the air and say, 'You're right. Now, what should we do about it?'"

He gives an example of how this one nearly backfired on Alinsky himself, discussing a situation in which Alinsky was trying to bring integration into public schools (a goal that both Hedgpeth and I actually agree with).

> They chose to target the school superintendent to be the face of the segregation problem in that area of Chicago. Alinsky says, "They took the position that they did not even have any racial-identification data in their files, so they did not know which of their students were black and which were white. As for the fact that we had all-white schools and all-black schools, well, that's just the way it was. If we had been confronted with a politically sophisticated school superintendent he could have very well replied, "Look, when I came to Chicago the city school system was following, as it is now, a neighborhood school policy. Chicago's neighborhoods are segregated. There are white neighborhoods and black neighborhoods and therefore you have white schools and black schools. Why attack me? Why not attack the segregated neighborhoods and change them?" He would have had a valid point, of sorts; I still shiver when I think of this possibility.

The superintendent could have simply removed the target from his own chest.

> The superintendent would have been essentially saying, "It's not my fault. Yes, you have the wrong guy, but you've also got the wrong goal, and what's worse, you don't have a solution." It is no

wonder that a response like that would have Alinsky shaking all those years later. He knew that by not fully understanding what to do with a reaction from his opponent, he was setting himself up to have the tables turned on him.

RULE 13: PICK THE TARGET, FREEZE IT, PERSONALIZE IT, AND POLARIZE IT.

Let's start with the terms.

Targeting means selecting a person who can be used to represent a larger group, like the school superintendent in the example above.

Freezing means keeping a person frozen in place as the representative of the group to be attacked. Don't let them have a legitimate reason for transferring the blame on others. They must be frozen in place as the icon of the group.

Polarizing means turning as many people against the target as possible.

So, pick a target, freeze them in place so they can't escape, put pressure on by throwing as much ridicule as possible at the target. Then wait for them to react. "The action is in the reaction."

Here is an example. In 2019, as Britain fought over the Brexit issue, one member of Parliament was caught in a photograph "lounging" on a front bench during a debate. A friend of mine shared the photo with an indignant comment. She said, "If this country goes into a recession or you or someone you love is impacted by Brexit just think of this rich entitled snob who doesn't [care] about the people." She is probably not even aware of it, but this is Alinsky's Rule 13. Do not engage with the merits of the debate. Instead, pick a representative, freeze them in time, use them as the icon around which to rally hate, and attack.

Those are Saul Alinsky's thirteen *Rules for Radicals*.

Preparing for Battle

If you find yourself in the heat of battle, or if you are about to enter it, gather your trusted people and go through these ideas. Use them as a sort of

SWOT analysis (Strengths, Weaknesses, Opportunities, Threats). Debate how your opponent might use them against you. Decide how you will react if they do. Determine where you might flip this dynamic and force it upon them (ethically). Be prepared for it. And above all, do not submit to pressure. The pressure, for them, is the entire point.

Expert Tip: If you can inject a little charming wit or sparkling humor, you will defuse the "pressure" of an Alinsky tactic. Few things say, "I am not under pressure" quite like playful banter. Think of Ronald Reagan. When asked if he was too old to be president, he quipped, "I will not make age an issue of this campaign. I am not going to exploit, for political purposes, my opponent's youth, and inexperience."[125]

---

125 "Reagan Quotes and Speeches," Reaganfoundation.org, October 21, 1984, https://www.reaganfoundation.org/ronald-reagan/reagan-quotes-speeches.

CHAPTER 10

IF THEY WANT THE MORAL RIGHT, INVITE THEM TO TAKE THE CORRESPOND-ING ACCOUNTABILITY.

IN 2019, ARKANSAS WAS ONE of the U.S. States attempting to oppose abortion with the introduction of a "heartbeat" bill. As a result, we suddenly began to see social media posts, unrelated to the topic of abortion, depicting how cruel these states were and what monstrous and mean-spirited human beings lived there. This represented pure, manufactured outrage, yet unfortunately, many people did not perceive the link and took the bait.

I recall one particular outrage meme that did the rounds on Facebook. It spoke about how authorities in Arkansas had used bleach on food destined for the poor in order to prevent them from eating it. It was accompanied by a moral rant, accusing such people of stealing from the most vulnerable, of being soulless monsters, and instructing them that they should go back through their own lives and try to work out when they went wrong. The rant was laced with expletives and shared liberally by social justice warriors around the globe.

When I first saw it, I instantly assumed it to be a lie, being somewhat jaded on the topic of social justice rants, and went looking for the truth of the matter. It took me all of fifteen seconds to research what had actually transpired. It turned out that authorities in Arkansas *had*, in fact, added bleach to food in order to prevent its consumption. But that was half the story. As a health authority explained: Some large batches of chili had been deemed a health threat. The director of health explained that it was determined to be at risk for E. coli, salmonella, and listeria.

Authorities knew that homeless people tended to rummage through refuse and eat such food, so it could not simply be discarded. They further argued that homeless people whose systems had been compromised by bad food tended to die of exposure outside in the elements as a result. To ward off that outcome, they intentionally made the food inedible.[126]

This is not even close to being the same thing as "ruining good food to spite the poor." It was actually an act of humanitarian concern. But the outrage mob chose to represent it that way.

When they do this, we can easily unravel the "mean-spirited" narrative by researching *why* those who were accountable made the call. Contrary to the social justice narrative, most people on Earth do not act from evil motives. They do not twirl their mustaches and cackle in sinister delight, while ruining food for poor people. To assume that they do is rather childish.

So, what *were* their motives? Find out. Then remind the SJW that, if they felt they could have made a better moral decision, they should go and work for that council. That way, they can also bear accountability for the outcomes of their "remote-controlled morality" (which here would have been poisoned poor people). When they refute the suggestion, return with: "So to be clear, you would like total freedom to make righteous judgements that damn perfect strangers, but you would like to do so with no corresponding personal accountability? You don't have to face the problem. You just want to judge those who must?"

---

126 Alexandra Klausner, "Health department poured bleach on food meant for the homeless," NYPost.com, November 12, 2018, https://nypost.com/2018/11/12/health-department-poured-bleach-on-food-meant-for-the-homeless.

CHAPTER 11

DO NOT ALLOW THEM TO REDEFINE "SOCIETY'S MOST VULNERABLE" BASED ON PERSONAL INDULGENCE RATHER THAN INNOCENCE (ADDRESSING ABORTION).

PERHAPS ONE OF THE MOST fruitful definitions of civilization proposes that healthy civilizations are defined by their protection of their most vulnerable. Political correctness interprets this primarily to mean protecting those who indulge in unconventional sex. In doing so, it imagines that these groups are victims.

Traditionally, though, the notion of protecting society's most vulnerable was meant to connote something very different. It designated as its target of concern a genuinely innocent and vulnerable group, such as the elderly, the frail, or the very young. It also set out to protect these vulnerable groups from a great deal worse than hurtful negative words.

This leads us to what is probably the most sensitive topic in this book: defending the unborn. There are two ways to approach this argument. The first is via logic, and the second is via the heartfelt appeal. I believe that the latter technique is actually much more effective. For this reason, I applaud the people who attempted to have ultrasound videos of unborn babies shown in Times Square, New York. Nevertheless, for two reasons, I am going to stick to the former here.

The first reason is that this book is intended to be primarily a series of intellectual counter-arguments, rather than emotional appeals. The second, if I may expose a moment of honesty, is that delving into the emotional side of this topic is a little too much for me. I am a parent to a three-year-old, and explicit discussions about the real-world stories, and suffering, of babies during abortions is taxing.

I believe it is effective for you to offer emotional arguments and to display the videos and photographs that reveal to the world what they are actually excusing whenever they use abstract and emotionally distancing words like "fetus" and "termination," rather than "baby" and "murder."

The painful reality does not correspond to these abstract words. There is struggle and fighting and even crying from these children when abortions are carried out. One abortionist who defected from Planned Parenthood pointed out that she learned to cut the vocal chords of the baby first to avoid hearing the crying noises.[127] [128] And there I will stop because that's already enough for me.

Removing the layer of abstraction opens people's eyes. You should do it. Allowing abortionists the leeway to use their abstract words distances humanity from the reality of what it is doing. Use emotive techniques extensively; they work.

The best book on this topic: *The Marketing of Evil* by David Kupelian. I listened to the audio version of this book, and I played the chapter on abortion while I was driving (through Sir Lowry's Pass, Cape Town, as it happened). I will admit that

---

127 "Babies May Start Crying While in the Womb: Crying Behavior Recorded in 3rd Trimester Fetuses," WebMed.com, September 13, 2005, https://www.webmd.com/baby/news/20050913/babies-may-start-crying-while-in-womb#:~:text=13%2C%202005%20%2D%2D%20A%20baby's,the%2028th%20week%20of%20pregnancy.
128 Kupelian, *The Marketing of Evil*.

I cried a little when I listened to this chapter. It is hard going. Still, the chapter provides some critical insights. In America, for instance, the history of abortion is little known. A small team of people intentionally set out to overturn the abortion laws and employed blatant lies in order to do so. Learning the history is always useful for undoing the narrative, so I would exhort you to do so.

So, how do you debunk the logical fallacies, poor reasoning, and factual errors inherent to this topic? We proceed as follows, in each case:

"It's not a person. It's a meaningless collection of cells."

The first response to this assertion should be: *"You're a meaningless collection of cells. Prove me wrong."*

Your opponent will find this idea shocking. However, it's a valid challenge. *Why* are they *not* a meaningless collection of cells?

"Well, because I'm alive and walking around."

"The baby is alive. It *will* walk around."

"Yes, but it's not walking around yet."

"Okay, so *not walking* is the criterion for murder. If I sit down, can you kill me?"

"No, because you've walked before."

"So if a one-year-old hasn't walked yet, we can kill it?"

Invite them to enumerate the differences between themselves (as evidently meaning*ful*) and a baby (as meaning*less*). There are no differences. They must descend into absurdity as they scramble to respond. Or they must use Nazist arguments to back up their claims:

"It's not yet fully mentally developed."

"Ah, so it's okay to kill people with low levels of mental development?"

Ultimately, this line of argumentation must arrive at the following determinant: What, exactly, confers meaning? Is it God? Is it the law? Or is it the purely absurd? As Ben Shapiro asks, "Does the vagina magically confer personhood?"[129] And prior to passage through a vagina, is one not a person? What if one is born via Caesarean section? Do they become perpetually a non-person? This line of argumentation puts your opponent on the defensive and forces them to confront their own arbitrarily delineated standards.

Here is the second potential response to "It's a meaningless collection of cells":

"It may have been possible to hold this view in a pre-scientific age, when humans were ignorant. We could not peer into the womb. Today, we have ultrasound technology that allows us to see pre-born babies. This meaningless collection of cells yawns, stretches, dreams, sucks its own thumb, plays with its own toes, and even sometimes cries itself to sleep within the womb. It experiences non-stop human emotion."

The argument that this is a meaningless collection of cells is outdated, anti-scientific, and prejudiced toward violent ends. We reject it outright as absurd. It also begs the same question: What changes a "meaningless collection of cells" into an actual human being?

Here is a simpler response to your assertion. "You do not get to deny humanity to a human being based on the stage of their development. If you did, who decides which stage of development? An infant can't walk, so is that a meaningless collection of cells? A teenager hasn't gone through complete brain development, so is that a meaningless collection of cells? When are you prevented from killing people on those grounds, and why? Because the *law* says so? The law has been steadily creeping backwards and allowing later and later abortions. So, we see that the law is arbitrary. No, this must be determined by a moral standard, and since you appear to have none, we will step up on this issue. Those 'cells' are human and have their own heartbeat and unique brainwaves. Those cells are already thinking."

129 Hank Berrien, "WATCH: Ben Shapiro Debunks Transgenderism and Pro-Abortion Arguments," DailyWire.com, February 10, 2017, https://www.dailywire.com/news/ben-shapiro-debunks-transgenderism-and-pro-hank-berrien.

Response: "Yes, but they're not thinking very much."

Counter: "Ah, yes, the old 'kill all stupid people' argument. Very popular in 1940s Berlin."

"It's not a person. It's a fetus."

Sure. And by the same token: it's not a person; it's a Jew. It's not a human being; it's a gay, a black, a gypsy. The argument that proposes denying personhood to another on the grounds of terminology substitution (which is nothing more than wordplay) is Nazist. History has always judged people who committed this fallacy extremely harshly, and rightly so. What will future generations say about our glib use of the term "fetus" to dismiss an entire human life? They will call us monsters. They will be right.

"Okay, so it is a human being. But it's not yet viable."

A two-year-old is not yet viable. He cannot live without the love, care, and nurturing of his parents. Absent their care, he will die. Any argument from "viability" is also an argument for infanticide.

Here we also see why you do not even need Judeo-Christian morals as a reference point to judge abortion immoral. We are *mammals*. First and foremost, mammals are defined by care of their young. To deny care to our own young, indeed, to actively murder our own young, on the simple grounds that they are "not yet self-sufficient" is contrary to nature. It is fundamentally wrong, even by animal standards. Caring for our young is what we do, as mammals, and it is taken to a higher calling among more developed *human* mammals, who go to such lengths as sacrificing our own convenience so that we may educate, nurture, and raise our young.

"It's not yet fully conscious."

We are not permitted to murder an unconscious human being. We are not even permitted to murder a person in a full-blown coma. Now imagine this scenario: A person is not "fully conscious," but we know from science that they *will* be fully conscious in nine months' time. Does their present, not-fully conscious state endow us with the right to kill them?

Also, prove that they are not fully conscious. They wake; they sleep; and they wake again. What, exactly, makes you believe they are "not fully conscious"? It appears, from the evidence, that you are flat-out wrong.

"It's about giving a woman a choice."

No. Abortion presented as an issue of "choice" is nothing more than the dishonest suggestion that abortion is the *only* choice. There are many forms of contraception available today, many for free and available to the poorest of the poor. In South Africa, which is an emerging nation, even the poverty-stricken can acquire free contraception from clinics. It is doubly not an issue of choice because an entire human being is denied the choice to live, and every other subsequent choice they might have made had they not been murdered. In this case, the choice to have an abortion removes another human being's choices in totality. To say that this is an issue of choice is akin to saying, "It's my choice to kill you." That is not a choice. It is a *crime*.

Additionally, are there some "choices" that society forbids? You typically do not extend this same "choice" regarding the death penalty. Why? Because you regard the outcome to be too horrible to qualify as worthy of being a choice. Well, same here.

"It's her body, her choice."

This one differs slightly from the version above. While that incarnation focuses on the fallacy of "choice," this one focuses on the fallacy of the issue being exclusively about "her body." It posits the body as sacrosanct and inviolable. These are also the exact conditions by which it fails:

"I completely agree. That is an excellent principle. Now, tell me, what is your other brain thinking right now?"

"Other brain?"

"You say it's your body. And you're right. Bodies are inviolable. No one may cause them harm or violate them. Your body currently contains two brains, each with a measurable set of brain waves, each with distinct brain activity. It's your body. You are asserting that it is not somebody else's body. So, tell me, what is your other brain thinking about right now? If you cannot, perhaps that is because it is *not* your brain, and perhaps that is because it is *not* your body. It is someone else's body."

"It's a health issue for the woman."

No. Abortion increases the risks of breast cancer in women. It makes health worse. It also results in significant psychological harm to a great many women later in life. It is only a health issue insofar as it makes women's health worse.

The number of abortions performed to "save a woman's life" are vanishingly small. Also, when we discuss elective abortion, we are not even discussing abortion as a life-saving measure, and so, suggesting that it is is dishonest.

"Abortion is a matter between a woman and her doctor."

No. The suggestion of such a procedure is deceptive. A woman does not "meet with an objective doctor" who guides her toward the correct decision for her. Instead, staff at family planning clinics are trained to sell abortions, actively and aggressively. That is how they make their money. They will make every caring and understanding utterance necessary in order to guide a woman down their sales funnel and toward this goal of achieving a sale.

Read the story in *The Marketing of Evil* of the highest-earning consultant in a Planned Parenthood clinic, who was able to "cry on cue" when consulting with her young, female inpatients. This sales rep used this ruse exclusively in the service of ensuring she closed the deal and sold an abortion every time.[130]

---

130 Kupelian, *The Marketing of Evil.*

"Well, I'm not necessarily pro-abortion, as such. I'm just pro-choice."

Analogous arguments include:

- "I'm not *pro*-slavery. I'm just saying let every potential slave owner make up their own mind."
- "I'm not pro-murder myself. I'm just saying we should let every potential murderer make up their own mind. It's a very personal choice, you see, between a murderer and their potential target. It's not really for me to judge."

The correct response to this moral cop-out should be, "Given that you have no morals, step out of the way and let us lead."

"Abortion helps the poor and, in particular, black people."

Ah, yes. This the old, liberal, "better dead than poor" argument. In this decade, more black babies are aborted in New York City than are born alive. Abortion helps the poor only if you define "help" as "prevent from living."

This argument is also elitist, insofar as it assumes that it is better to be dead than to be born a poor, black person. By contrast, we believe that *all* lives are intrinsically valuable and not measured in racist, privileged, socio-economic terms. We reject as disgusting the thinking that says, "A poor, black person has no value and is actually better off dead." You do not get to make that call on a baby's behalf.

Moreover, as we have seen, extreme poverty has almost disappeared from humanity. This narrative appears to assume that the "poor are getting poorer" and that to be born into poverty will only cause a downward spiral. The global trend is toward an *upward* spiral. This child is more likely to *escape* poverty than to spend a lifetime in it.

"You're discriminating against women."

Around the world, there are overwhelmingly more girls aborted than boys. I'm trying to save their lives. And I have no vested interest, other than concern for humanity. I gain nothing from taking up this cause. In fact, I face scorn and ridicule from you, which is surprising, since you purport to be pro-woman. In fact, it sounds like I am pro-woman, and you are not.

Men gain nothing from taking up this cause. If anything, being pro-abortion helps men to get more sex and not face the consequences thereof. If anything, we have a vested interest in being pro-abortion.

Yet I am anti, at my own public cost and for no personal gain. So why? Because I care about women, enough to fight against the possibility that the smallest and most defenseless girls continue to be murdered in large numbers before they can even live. I am a champion for women's rights.

"But it's inconvenient for her to have a baby right now."

This is the "my convenience is worth more than your life" argument. In what humane society has "convenience" ever qualified as acceptable grounds for murder?

"Well, it's not murder. The law doesn't define it that way."

"The law is a manmade set of definitions. In this instance, the law was championed by liberal progressives like yourself. You *made up those terms* and definitions. It is not murder according to the law because you created the law so that it would not be murder. Your terms and definitions are circular and self-serving. And your corresponding act also meets every condition of murder. Here you are simply wrong."

"But science says abortion is okay."

"Really? Science now gets to have a say in moral decision-making? That's new." First, you are committing a logical error by anthropomorphizing science. It is not a living thing. It can't make decisions because it isn't an intelligent entity. It is actually nothing more than a system for disproving untrue ideas. Worse, you are making science a god, with the power over human life. Communists did that, and Nazis did that. It ended badly for human life.

Next, science does not qualify as science if it is morally prescriptive. Real science is merely a process of falsification. It can tell you how to cure a disease or launch a rocket into space. It cannot tell you if you *should* cure a disease or launch a rocket into space. It cannot speak on issues of human morality.

But let us assume it could. Let's assume that your argument is, contrary to all logic, somehow correct. Based on that flawed assumption, let me ask you a few questions: What is the moral matrix upon which it operates? How does it weigh values? If it deems anything whatsoever to be morally wrong, how does it apply that standard? Relative to what? Couldn't science argue that survival of the fittest is the only reasonable standard, derived from evolutionary biology? If so, wouldn't it be morally okay, according to science, for *my* family to kill and eat *your* family?

Actually, this fallacy isn't new. The "science" of racial supremacy propped up the Nazi Holocaust. And the "science" of communism propped up the genocide, and then death by starvation, of tens of millions of people in Russia and China.

Science has no place in moral decision-making. Where it has been smuggled into the decision-making matrix, it has consistently done more damage than good. Science, as a moral tool, kills people. It did for the Nazis; it did for the communists; and it does in the case of abortion. Viewed objectively, science as a tool for morality appears *always* to lead to human death. On those grounds alone, we should reject its authority in the sphere of morality. It has a single-outcome track record.

Finally, explain to me precisely which scientific law makes abortion acceptable. Now point it out to me. Is it one of Newton's principles? Einstein's formula for relativity? Show me the law derived from science that negates the moral problem of killing a baby. Science does not do that. This issue is outside of its scope. This is a moral issue, and that means one of two things:

1. We decide it according to whether or not there is a God and if so, He says two things on the topic: "Before I formed you in the womb I knew

you," (Jer. 1:5) and "It would be better for him if a millstone were hung around his neck, and he were thrown into the sea, than that he should offend one of these little ones " (Luke 17:2).

2. In the absence of God, we decide it according to naturalistic principles. At this point we return to the idea that we are mammals, whose primary characteristic is to care for their young. Either way, abortion is morally unacceptable.

We might argue that there is a third option, which is: "I don't know." That is an honest position to take. In such an instance, when we are not sure whether or not abortion is murder, should we not err on the side of life, rather than death? To come down on the side of death when uncertain seems remarkably irresponsible, possibly even criminally negligent.

"Once you take emotion out of the issue, there's no real problem."

Absolutely true. Psychopaths are able to murder people without any concern whatsoever for how such people hurt, cry, and beg for their lives. Babies being torn apart cry, too. The ones born still alive—and it happens—kick and fight to breathe, until they suffocate and die. But if you switch off your emotions, their slow death doesn't matter. There's no real problem.

"Yes, but what about rape?"

Good question. Before we proceed to entertaining that extreme scenario, can we agree that all abortion outside of rape is morally wrong? If we can't, then there is no point in entertaining a sub-set. It would seem that you are attempting to use extreme, outlying cases to justify the broad main category. Specifically, you are trying to use rape cases as an excuse to justify casual abortions. This is dishonest. If, by contrast, you are saying that abortion should be banned, except in the case of rape, then we have an honest and potentially fruitful discussion on our hands.

Additionally, rape is very obviously morally wrong. It is a crime of violation. Our goal, therefore, should be to solve *that* problem, and to that end, the conservative is on your side. Many conservatives, myself included, would propose the death penalty for rapists. This goes further than what most liberals would be willing to do to solve the problem. However, the problem of the crime of rape does not justify another crime: the murder of a baby.

"But what about absent fathers who don't provide child support?"

Here, again, I am on your side. That is why I fight for traditional values and nuclear families, largely the point of this book. There are few things more disgusting than a father failing to provide for his child. Fathers *are* accountable for their children. Abandoned mothers *are* victims, with a legitimate and very substantial grievance about a criminal and immoral act. Once again, the correct way forward is to focus on the right side of the problem: irresponsible fathers and holding them accountable.

It does not follow from this legitimate complaint that the right thing to do is to kill the baby. If it did, the same argument could be made in favor of infanticide: "Well, the dad just left, so I guess I'll kill the child."

"But it doesn't actually hurt the baby."

Have you seen the videos? Have you read the books? Do you know what actually happens? Go find out, and not from the people with a financial incentive to keep the reality of it from you. Have you personally ever experienced suffocation? Have you ever had a limb pulled off? Have you ever been crushed and forced through a tube?

The truth is heartbreaking. If people actually knew what we were dealing with here, they would never allow it. That is why the reality is kept from the public and couched in euphemisms.

"But if you ban abortion, women will just do it illegally."

"If you ban guns, people will just kill one another with knives." We are not interested in the legal versus illegal question. That is a red herring. We are interested in the moral versus immoral question. It is immoral to kill a baby, whether it is carried out legally or illegally, "safely" or "unsafely."

In this latter instance, the "safety" argument also fails because a baby is murdered, and that is not safe. Essentially, people making this argument are saying, "While killing someone, the perpetrator should be kept safe." No, they should not.

"But feminism is important. We are trying to uplift women."

What is increasingly being packaged and presented as feminism in the West has little to do with the original proposed values of feminism. In many ways, the latest incarnation of this ideology runs counter to the original ideals.

I grew up in Africa. The continent has high rape stats, and in many nations, women still have low legal rights. Such places desperately need feminism—in its original, intended incarnation. But the feminist movement in first-world countries such as America, where there is no legal distinction between men and women and no difference in rights between the two genders, feminism is almost exclusively about abortion.

Why? Why is *that* its only goal? This movement disingenuously makes the argument that men want to control women's bodies and to control their reproduction. In saying this, they create a narrative of the "evil patriarchy."

The reverse of this narrative is true. People who object to abortion, including myself, have no desire to control women's bodies or reproductive habits. Of the plethora of forms of contraception available at very low cost, or even for free, there is only *one* to which we object: abortion. We are okay with the use of condoms. We are okay with the use of the Pill. We are okay with diaphragms and any other non-murderous intervention.

"You're trying to control women's bodies and women's reproductive rights."

The exact opposite is true. Far from asserting a desire on our part to control women's reproductive habits, if anything, we are saying, 'Please take control of your own reproductive habits!" That way, you won't have to abort a baby.

If the societal goal is for women to be in control of their bodies and in control of their reproductive habits, then we are all on the same page. I want that, too. Now, please stop killing babies. That is the only thing to which we object.

A variation on this theme is the assertion by abortionists that society is trying to "manage women's wombs." Feel free to manage your womb any way you wish. This does not include killing another living person. That person is not your womb.

"But only three percent of what family planning clinics like Planned Parenthood do are abortions."

First, that is factually untrue. Defectors from the organization point out that this is simply PR fiction, and that *most* of what they do are abortions. It is a similar cosseting fiction to labeling a baby-slaughtering warehouse a "family planning clinic." The perversity of this ironic label beggars belief. And the cynical technique carries over further into the soft décor, welcoming pastel colors and pictures of happy families in the corridors, all outside the doors of operating theaters in which babies are pulled limb from limb or suffocated in saline solutions.

These people work extremely hard at making the century's greatest evil look like a whimsical episode of *Winnie the Pooh*. But babies still die, and horribly, regardless of the reassuring Enya music, soft lighting and chamomile tea.

Second, even if the numbers *were* accurate, which they are not, this argument would be akin to a profligate serial killer saying, "Don't worry, folks. Only three percent of what I do is murder. The rest of the time I deliver muffins to the elderly." Well, *that's all right, then!*

"But the Earth is already overcrowded."

This is an entirely different argument, a different topic. It does not follow that abortion is okay. The point may or may not be valid, but it can and should be effected by personal choice not to have children, or not to have very many children, or to use contraception rather than procreating. It is untrue to posit that abortion is the only solution because the planet requires it. It is also utopian and elitist: "Once we kill off all the poor babies, the educated elites can rule a much-reduced earthly paradise."

"But the people who oppose abortion aren't adopting unwanted babies!"

This is truly one of the ugliest arguments around. The fallacy lies in the assertion that *objecting to murder* transfers responsibility *to the person objecting.* To refute this suggestion, represent it back to the person making it using a different character:

"You decide to murder your grandmother. I object on moral grounds. You then become self-righteous and morally puffed up, telling me that the only way I may validly object is if I am personally willing to take your grandmother into my house and care for her in perpetuity."

Moral right and wrong exist independently of our personal relationships to a victim. And it is untrue to frame the issue as though the only alternative to your committing murder is for me to take accountability for the person who is a problem to you. This technique is doubly disgusting in that it attempts to subtly accuse those speaking up for the innocent of some kind of culpability in the crime of the murderer, or at least, of neglect for the other person's victim.

The argument is also functionally impaired. By this I mean, it is also not true on its own terms. Many anti-abortion advocates *do* adopt. According to American Adoptions, "Some sources estimate that there are about 2 million couples currently waiting to adopt in the United States—which means there are as many as 36 waiting families for every one child who is placed for adoption."[131] But you don't have to provide these numbers. Challenge *them* to provide the numbers. "How many people do, and how many people do not?" *They* raised this assertion—it is their job to prove it.

---

131 "How Many Couples Are Waiting to Adopt?," AmericanAdoptions.com, https://www. americanadoptions.com/pregnant/waiting_adoptive_families (accessed August 2, 2020).

"If abortion is murder, then so is a wet dream."

Colorful.

Nevertheless, let us entertain this proposition as though it were a serious argument because I have seen it, and cruder versions of the same idea, presented as one.

Here is the fallacy: This argument equates male ejaculation with a living baby. It is an inaccurate comparison because male sperm is only half of the recipe. By itself, it cannot create a living baby. The correct comparison here would be to the female reproductive byproduct—the egg, which is shed during menstruation.

Just as a woman's period does not constitute the "murder" of a baby, because no baby existed, so, too, with sperm.

"What do you mean I'm arguing from privilege?"

Finally, this argument goes on the offensive, instead of simply reacting to theirs.

"I'm amazed that someone with your level of privilege would make an argument for abortion."

"What do you mean, *my level of privilege?*"

"You're alive. That is the ultimate privilege. You were given this gift, and you were not aborted. Yet you, in your privilege, would deny this same outcome to other humans. It's disgusting."

I advise that when a person repeatedly switches arguments and you have dismantled a sufficient number of them, you turn the tables and put the pressure on them.

"You have presented all of these easily dismissed arguments in favor of abortion. In each case, I've pointed out the humane alternatives. Yet after I dismiss each one of your arguments, you switch to a new argument in favor of abortion. It seems apparent to me that you *want* the evil option. You are not happy with *alternatives* to baby-killing; and after each one of your justifications for killing is revealed to be flawed, you switch to another one. Why? Why do you so desperately *want* this evil? Why do alternatives not satisfy you? What's driving you?"

Going on the Offensive on Behalf of Society's Most Vulnerable

In a clever forcing of liberal value dissonance, PragerU sent a reporter to ask people to sign two petitions. The first was to save eagle eggs from harm. People eagerly signed it. The second was to keep human babies from being aborted. In the face of the ensuing uncertainty, the presenter posed the question: "Is an egg more valuable than a baby?"[132]

132 PragerU, "Is An Eagle Egg More Valuable Than a Baby?," YouTube, 3:21, September 4, 2019, https://www.youtube.com/watch?v=ZR9Ye_Uk-x8.

CHAPTER 12

RESPOND TO THE "CATCH-ALL" ARGUMENTS.

"YOU'RE A RACIST, SEXIST, MISOGYNIST, ablest, homophobic, Islamophobic, bigoted, Nazi, white supremacist, colonialist transphobe! You're denying our right to exist, and you're literally Hitler!"

"Goodness! You left out the part where I kicked puppies, stole candy from a baby, and single-handedly melted the polar ice caps. You should have me arrested and imprisoned for life immediately! It's all *me. I'm* the problem!"

All of these labels are designed to do one thing: dismiss. If a person really is, for example, a fascist, then one need not engage with them. They can be written off wholesale. That is the point of these labels. They help the Left to avoid engaging with actual ideas.

Remember that it often doesn't matter to your opponents on the Left whether or not the accusations are *true.* Combine the fallacy of concept creep with the poison of Alinsky tactics, and hurling invectives becomes little more than a knee-jerk reaction. Fortunately, it is an obvious strategy and also a fairly weak one.

Your first option is what I call the "Tim Technique." In response to a long and vitriolic social justice rant, my friend Tim Ohai once memorably provided as his complete response the three-letter answer: "LOL!" In its failure to create a useful *reaction,* this brusque dismissal is a form of genius. It hints at the fact that you don't have to rise to every challenge, nor even respond to every criticism.

If you do, though, another option is to point out their strategy:

"Ah, I see you're using postmodernist tactics. Okay, let me do the same as you: *You atheist, communist, mass murderer! You are literally Stalin.* I mean, it's not true, but that doesn't matter according to your standards, does it? Alternatively, may I propose a more productive way forward? How about we actually stick to facts, rather than engaging in crazy *ad hominem* personal attacks and slinging wild accusations? Would you agree to that?"

Then force the issue: "No, before we proceed, *do you agree to that?* If you don't agree to that, then you're giving yourself permission to keep on calling me "literally Hitler" like a screeching parrot, and that's a dishonest tactic. I would like you to prove that you are willing to be a responsible adult here."

They can't agree. But they also can't not agree. If they do agree, they can be held to a higher standard of honesty. If they refuse, you can point out their refusal to use logical arguments and to proceed as an honest player, dismiss them as morally unworthy, and walk away.

Use Humor and Theater.

Because these liberal reactions are shopworn and predictable to the point of being trite, you can use humor and theater to respond to them.

Jeff Hedgpeth responds to such arguments with the line: "How can you tell when a liberal is dead? They stop calling you a racist." And also: "Calling people racist—it's the liberal 'get-out-of-logic-free card.'"[133]

The above quotes are actually useful counter-arguments. By using them, you exit the Alinsky trap, which was: "The action is in the *reaction.*" It represents a refusal to engage with them on their grounds, and once again, it constitutes pointing out what they are doing, thus calling their bluff.

You can extend the humor technique further by apportioning your opponent three race cards (or bigot cards, or Nazi cards, or whatever the case may be). In response to their first instance of name-calling, you hand over

---

133 Hedgpeth, *Rules for Radicals Defeated.*

their first race card (literally using props, or as a meme online, or figuratively through language) and point out that they only get two more; after that, they will have to start using facts like a big person.

A sense of theatrics can be your friend here. If you have a blackboard behind you, draw three large cards, with the letters "RC" on each. Do not provide an explanation. After their first outburst, cross one out, and say, "That's your first race card. You get two more. Then you have to start using facts."

"You're so prejudiced!"

"Thank you. The world absolutely needs prejudice. Now, ask me why."

A world without prejudice is a world without standards. Prejudice is a desire for better standards for humanity. Lack of prejudice means no standards whatsoever. You'd be amazed what can go wrong in a world without prejudice. It does not lead to peace and harmony and happiness, as you seem to think it does. Now, let us talk about the specific qualitative nature of the prejudice because some prejudices are bad, and some are good.

The same response applies to the terms *discriminatory* and *biased*: "Correct. I believe in merit, and I believe in acceptable standards of behavior. Your stance reflects that you do not believe in merit and that you reject acceptable standards of behavior. Why do you believe in fundamental unfairness? Why do you have no standards? Please explain it to me."

"This is about tolerance!"

"Interesting. Could you please specify for me what it is that we will be tolerating? Tolerance implies difference. What are those differences, specifically? If they amount to different recipes for the preparation of food, from different places on earth, count me in! I love me some foreign falafel! But if you're saying, 'Well, they're a bit rapacious And they kind of believe that we should be slaughtered just a touch in order to make us submit to their religion,' then my answer, and every sensible person's answer, is going to be 'No, I won't be tolerating that. I'm surprised you would ask me to. It makes your motives appear questionable.' So, let me ask you: What *are* your motives? Why would you encourage us to tolerate something that causes us harm?"

With this, you have flipped the questioning. They must answer. Then you can play, "So you're saying . . ." as you pick apart their unexamined and poorly formulated ideas.

"People like you just lack empathy!"

"Actually, the conservative value system rests on six moral pillars. One of them is, in fact, empathy. The liberal moral system only has three. You are accusing me of lacking a component necessary for justice. The reverse is true. Allow me to explain, by informing you of the work of psychologist Jonathan Haidt."

"Check your privilege!"

"Ah, I wondered when Herbert Marcuse would appear. My response to you, and to Marcuse, is no."

"Who?"

"Glad you asked. Allow me to explain. (See page 78).

Alternatively, you can begin by having them *qualify* your privilege. The answer will be a spew of trite postmodernist insults. Following that, you regain the high ground by using this barrage to prove *their* bigotry. It plays out something like this:

"Ah, so the problem is that I am a white male. Your arguments amount to bigotry against my culture and sexism against my gender."

"I see that you are attempting to *accuse* me of my own culture, in order to deny me my right to speak. That's a disgusting tactic. Instead of responding to my point, which you are proving you can't do, you are committing the fallacy of an *ad hominem* argument, in which you attack the person making the point instead."

"You've gotten personal, haven't you? You've become vicious. You have chosen to attack the culture and tradition that I was born into, and you are reframing it as though it would be valid to accuse me of my own heritage. Would you do the same with a Jewish person? A Muslim? A Chinese person?"

"In using this ugly tactic, you are not only failing to acknowledge the good points in my culture, but you are actively vilifying everything that's best about it. *Privilege,* you say? You are vilifying all the education and all the learning that my ancestry has worked for and bequeathed to my generation over the course of centuries."

"Calling me privileged is Leftist bigotry. It is the mean-spirited act of in-validating everything my culture ever did to get this generation to where it is now, as though all past progress were to be considered a point of shame, not a point of pride. And yet uplifting our children, and making things better for the next generation, is really the very *best* thing that we do as a species. In this, liberal progressives like yourself invert reality and re-label our highest good as a form of evil to be maligned. 'Privilege.' Well, I say, nice try. Pity about your bigotry. Now, see if you can address my original point, preferably without being so racist."

(Here, you can introduce a second technique, such as forcing them to openly defend what they were tacitly and dishonestly defending previously):

> "Now, you tried very hard to avoid my point about Islamic violence by calling me Islamophobic, and then you committed the fallacy of an *ad hominem* argument when you tried to call me 'privileged,' based on my race and ethnicity. Both techniques were dishonest on your part, and both techniques failed. Let's return to your de-fense of Islam. You have positioned yourself as its champion. You are pro-Islam. I want you to answer some questions about the spe-cific beliefs that you are defending."

"You're a white supremacist!"

"Goodness me! That sounds serious. Let's engage with your accusation. As I haven't done a single thing to make white people 'supreme,' we can safely say that that part doesn't qualify, and we can dismiss it. So, what's left? I guess you must be accusing me of being white, which is an immutable characteristic of my birth. Explain that to me."

This proceeds into their faltered explanation, in which you get to play, "So you're saying . . . " and pick apart their logic.

They might come back with this one:

"Straight, white men are at the top of the dominance hierarchy!"

"Ah, I see. You practice tribal thinking rather than logic. You're interested in spreading conflict through an 'us versus them' mentality, in which you, subjectively, get to choose the good guys and the villains. And here I thought you wanted a useful discourse about the excellence of ideas. Turns out you just want to stand with your tribe and throw stones. That's Saul Alinsky again. If you'd prefer a useful discourse about excellent ideas, I propose the following . . . " And then you set the parameters. If the parameters are reasonable, they can't obey them. Yet they must or be called on it.

Alternatively: "Explain to me what you mean by white. You seem to be implying a monolith, where one doesn't exist, and it shows simplistic thinking. So, let's be specific. Do you mean Celtic? Or Anglo, or Saxon, or Breton? Do you mean Frankish, or do you mean Germanic? Perhaps, you mean Slavic? Or Latino? Or maybe Nordic? Which particular group are you referring to? Oh, all of them, you say? So, if I can point out one of those groups that is not at the top of the dominance hierarchy, then your theory falls apart, agreed? Or would you prefer to better defend your theory by specifying which particular ones are at the top?"

It is Heisenberg's uncertainty principle. The closer you look at it, the more it falls apart. Remember that their thinking tends toward dualism and division into good versus bad. If you are not fawningly pro, then *de facto*, you must be an evil oppressor. Pointing this logical fallacy out defeats it. "Now let me ask you this: Is there anyone in the middle? Or are all people divided into evil oppressors and the saintly oppressed? And have you ever in your life held a single 'oppressed' person accountable for their own deeds, or is everything they do our fault as well?"

Alternatively, go on the offensive when they say that you should check your "male" privilege. Use these talking points from conservative commentator Paul Joseph Watson. He is English, and the exact numbers he cites may vary from nation to nation; but the principle of his argument is useful:

- "I love how my male privilege entitles me to be 11 times more likely to die in the workplace than a woman.
- I love how my male privilege entitles me to contribute to the 99.9 percent of combat deaths and casualties.
- I love how my male privilege entitles me to be 5 times more likely to commit suicide than a woman.
- I love how my male privilege gives me just a 15% chance of winning custody of my children.
- I love how my male privilege means I'm three times more likely to be homeless than a woman.
- I love how my male privilege means I get more than double the prison sentence than a woman for the same crime."[134]

"You're a racist!"

"Here's your first race card. You only get three. While I'm handing it to you, let me ask you a question: Are we talking about race or are we talking about ideology? These are two different things, and you don't get to use them interchangeably. If you don't currently understand the differences, I will be glad to explain them to you . . . Now would you like to have a useful discussion about the *ideological* problems I've just pointed out—for example, how they oppress women—or would you like to blindly stick to your deceitful tactic by which you insist that I'm talking about skin color? I don't care about skin color. I care about ideology. If you're not interested in engaging on the

---

134 "I Love How My Male Privilege," Digital image, iFunny, April 13, 2016, https://ifunny. co/picture/r-paul-joseph-watson-if-m-w-i-love-how-dH4M5O2n3.

ideology, I have some questions for you about why you think oppressing women is acceptable. Does skin color dismiss that standard in your view? If so, doesn't that make *you* a racist?

"You're literally Hitler."

Ben Shapiro responds to this one by pointing out that the issues with Nazism are evils that both the Left and conservatives agree are wrong. This is a good framework for responding. List the evils that both sides oppose, such as tyranny against a populace and demonization of a racial grouping and frame the issue as a matter of morality. In doing so, you claim moral high-ground, while also setting standards for debate that cannot be dismissed without contradiction.

Provided the video has not been removed, watch Shapiro take the topic apart by searching "Everyone Reading This is a Bigot," on YouTube.[135]

Finally, just call their bluff.

"If I'm a bigot for standing up for oppressed women in Islamic societies, then so be it. I'm a bigot. You should become a bigot, too."

---

135 The Daily Wire, "Everyone Reading This is a Bigot," YouTube Post, 6:03, August 30, 2019, https://www.youtube.com/watch?v=Bmd8F_xSWQs&feature=youtu.be.

CHAPTER 13

HAND FASCISM AND NAZISM BACK TO THEIR RIGHTFUL OWNERS.

Objection: Okay, before you even begin, the very first people that the Nazis arrested were the socialist communists.

Response: That is perfectly correct. They arrested these people because they were fishing from the same pond. Marxist socialism was too close to national socialism to be comfortably accommodated. It was a directly competing system, and it had to go. It had to go, so that the "right kind" of socialism could win in Germany.

Pick an Antifa mob, any Antifa mob. Somewhere amid their masked faces and SS-style clothing, you will inevitably see this legend: "No Trump, No KKK, No Fascist USA." The Left is utterly convinced that these are right wing ideas. Be sure to be able to explain why they are, in fact, Left Wing.

Stephen Crowder expresses it this way in his videos: Point to a single Nazi policy that wasn't Leftist. They wanted gun control, centralization, socialism. They were anti-religion; they shut down freedom of speech; and they controlled the media. They were trying to create a more progressive, utopian society. And you don't get to point to racism because that is not a conservative value; it is a progressive value, beginning with the eugenicists of the democratic, progressive, American South, who inspired the Nazis and whom the Nazis openly wrote about as their ideological forebears.[136]

Debate Tip: Force them to clearly define *fascist*. Begin with "How dare you?" Then proceed to, 'That is a serious charge" and then require of them, "Define fascism, since you are accusing me of it." And then watch them flounder. The term fascist is so vague and so poorly delineated that even scholars of fascism can't agree on what it actually is. George Orwell wrote: "The word Fascism has now no meaning except in so far as it signifies 'something not desirable.'"[137]

Go one step further: Take a workable definition of fascism along with you. Any accurate definition will prove it to be a Leftist phenomenon.

In his historical account of fascism, Jonah Goldberg observes that "fascism, properly understood, is not a phenomenon of the right at all. Instead, it is, and always has been, a phenomenon of the left."[138]

So, why do we think of fascism as right-wing today?

Here's why: Mussolini began (and continued) as a roaring socialist. But in Italy, he realized that dividing people according to workers didn't fit. So, he came up with a variation on the socialist theme. It was still socialism, but as with Nazism, it prioritized its own nation—national socialism—rather than aiming for a global worker's utopia. It was socialism for Italy.

This angered the Left, who wanted to distance themselves from him. Anything they disapproved of had to be pushed to the Right, so they started calling him right-wing. And it's been that way ever since. It isn't true by any measure. But it's useful, insofar as you can disavow yourself of a brand of socialism that you disapprove of.

The best books on the topic: *The Big Lie* and *Death of a Nation*, both

136 Ashtyn&Jon2.0, "Yes, Hitler was a Liberal Socialist Loud With Crowder - REACTION," YouTube Post, 7:43, February 3, 2016, https://www.youtube.com/watch?v=EN1V8onC-Oo.
137 George Orwell, *Politics and the English Language* (London: Penguin, 1946).
138 Jonah Goldberg, *Liberal Fascism: The Secret History of the American Left, From Mussolini to the Politics of Change* (New York: Doubleday, 2008).

by Dinesh D'Souza. These books go into painstaking detail about the definitions and history of both forces. It concludes with little wiggle room that these are progressive, Leftist ideals. Remember: thousands and thousands and thousands of angry repetitions of a line do not make it true: "Trump is Hitler; Trump is a fascist."

Another good book on this topic: *Liberal Fascism: The Secret History of the American Left, from Mussolini to the Politics of Change* by Jonah Goldberg.

Objection: A lot of self-identified alt-right activists do identify themselves as neo-Nazis today.

Response: True. And we oppose them, too. We offer no defense for them because they're nuts. Anyone who follows those ideologies is crazy, Left or Right. But the ideas come from the Left. "What do you mean they come from the Left?"

Here Again is the Progression: Crisis of faith in God leads to atheism. Atheism leads to progressivism. Progressivism gives rise to collectivist ideas. Collectivist ideas took three forms: socialist communism, Nazi national socialism, and Italian fascism. All three were evil. All three came from the Progressive Left. Today, the Left is still enamored by its own collectivist ideas. It *still* loves socialism. That's why we oppose you. Your ideas are evil, and they have a body count of over one hundred million so far. We fight you because you are immoral, and your ideas consistently lead to tyranny, not freedom.

Of course, not every predictable catch-all phrase from the Left is an accusation. Some are presented in the form of defenses. For example:"The science is settled." The very phrase "the science is settled" is profoundly unscientific. Point out to them that their use of this phrase betrays their misunderstanding of the most basic underpinnings of science. Science is about constant reevaluation, not conformity to consensus. It is about the constant falsification of theses, until we arrive at the best idea. To say, "the science is settled" is not dissimilar to saying, "I don't understand the concept of science."

CHAPTER 14

FORCE THEM TO ANSWER THE QUESTIONS: "AT WHAT COST?" AND "WHO DECIDES?"

ACCLAIMED ECONOMIST AND POLITICAL COMMENTATOR Thomas Sowell points out that the liberal consistently fails to answer the question: "At what cost?"[139] Responding to their ideas, presumptions, and proposals with this question forces the weakness of the thinking out into the open.

When you do force them to confront this question, it is useful to have concrete examples of the costs. If you argue a particular issue often, by all means, start a file on that topic. Media clips and specific story-examples will go a long way. Even bullet-point factoids will do.

Here are a few. We begin with a broad description of "costs" in a chapter from *The Marketing of Evil*:

> Today, in the rarified but toxic air of multiculturalism and political correctness, all cultures and all values are of equal value. The most ignorant, oppressive, suffocating, women-hating kind of culture—where people's hands and feet are amputated as punishment for petty offenses—is now worthy of equal respect to Western culture, which has provided most of the world's knowledge, progress, food, medicine, technology, quality of life, representative government, and liberty.[140]

---

139 WideWorldOfWisdom, "The Difference Between Liberal and Conservative," You-Tube Post, 4:31, March 17, 2010, https://www.youtube.com/watch?v=5KHdhrNhh88.
140 Kupelian, *The Marketing of Evil*.

The chapter goes on to provide the example of all religions being considered equal and how that played out in a liberal society: Britain's Royal Navy permitted an officer to perform satanic rituals on board one of its ships, the frigate *Cumberland*. A twenty-four-year-old naval technician and non-commissioned officer was given his own satanic altar where he could worship Lucifer.[141]

So, what? Well, consider the very reasonable notion that the majority of the rest of the sailors derive from a Christian background. Would they not be able to legitimately consider such a ship to be "cursed"? Even if, as an atheist, you do not see their complaint as legitimate, at the very least, consider its impact on morale.

Or how about this one, from *The New York Post*? In response to malformed notions of tolerance, we should ask, "At what cost?" and then give an example like this:

> American soldiers are being punished for blowing the whistle on the systematic rape and enslavement of young boys at the hands of brutal Afghan Muslim military officials. Honorable men in uniform risked their careers and lives to stop the abuse. Yet the White House—which was busy tweeting about its new feminism-pandering "It's On Us" campaign against an alleged college-rape crisis based on debunked statistics—is AWOL on the actual pedophilia epidemic known as bacha bazi.
>
> On Thursday, Obama administration flacks went out of their way to downplay Afghan child rape as "abhorrent," but "fundamentally" a local "law-enforcement matter."
>
> This is the price the innocents pay for blind multiculturalism.[142]

Here's another example: "So why can't you just use someone's preferred pronoun? What does it really cost you?"

---

141 Ibid.
142 Michelle Malkin, "Yes, our troops were ordered to ignore Afghan pedophiles," NYPost.com, September 25, 2015, https://nypost.com/2015/09/25/yes-our-troops-were-ordered-to-ignore-afghan-pedophiles.

This was the issue that launched psychologist, author, and speaker Jordan Peterson to prominence, and he rightly pointed out that it's not the pronoun—calling someone *he* or *she* or *zhe* or *a bowl of yogurt*, according to their made-up ideas of gender. The real issue is that this has become *legally compelled* speech.[143]

It would not be new to ban a certain form of speech. That has its own problems, but it's not new. For instance, we ban talk about explosive devices in airports. Fair enough. But this is different. This legally prescribes what you *must* say. It compels you to endorse an ideology. That is contrary to basic freedom—of speech and of conscience and of religion. Once you transgress those rights, the slippery slope begins. As Peterson points out, this is no small issue. This is at the very heart of freedom versus tyranny. We cannot permit any government the ability to legally compel our speech and to do so at the expense of prison time. It is thought-policing, and it is the definition of tyranny.

Or even a simple example, that begs a number of questions. In June of 2019, Britain legally banned "harmful gender stereotypes in adverts."[144] What's the downside? Well, for starters, who gets to decide what qualifies as "harmful"? Will it be the radical feminists and politically correct progressives who originally proposed the policy? Undoubtedly.

So, what might *they* consider a "harmful gender stereotype?" How about a loving scene in which a mother and her daughter play with dolls? A radical feminist could easily make the case that this promotes outdated ideas that denigrate women, invalidates interracial families, and propagates harmful notions of women as nurturing, and on and on.

How about a man and woman falling in love? Could we show that in an advertisement? "Do you mean, perpetuating heteronormative, patriarchal, anti-LGBTQ, male-dominating rape culture?"

---

143   LBC, "Jordan Peterson on Why He Refuses to Use Special Pronouns For Transgender People—LBC," YouTube Post, 3:53, May 22, 2018, https://www.youtube.com/watch?v=s_UbmaZQx74.
144   "'Harmful' gender stereotypes in adverts banned," BBC.com, June 14, 2019, BBC.com, https://www.bbc.com/news/business-48628678,

Do you see the problem with this? At what cost? And who decides? This is the precise mechanism by which liberal democracies become increasingly *intolerant*.

Moreover, the next problem in line is that the new normal will be prescriptive. You can't show a loving father disciplining his child (heaven forbid). But you *can* show a lesbian instructing her infant to rebel against the system and break out of rigid social norms by defying society.

In imitation of the Kinsey dynamic, by which *Sexual Behavior in the Human Male* taught society how to behave like pedophiles, prisoners, prostitutes, and rapists, the newly sanctioned "social justice-approved" ads will not merely reflect, but also actively *teach* society its new norms, the actual norms having now been forbidden.[145]

The justification for this Marxist social engineering? Why, it can only be . . . you guessed it! "Inequality!" And what must Marxists do to get an equal society? They must level those who are unequal.

As Advertising Standards Authority chief executive Guy Parker so innocuously explains: "Our evidence shows how harmful gender stereotypes in ads can contribute to inequality in society, with costs for all of us. Put simply, we found that some portrayals in ads can, over time, play a part in limiting people's potential."[146]

I could pick that statement apart six ways from Sunday. It "costs for all of us"? That sounds like an emotional assertion. Precisely how does it cost for all of us? Quantify the cost. It "limits people's potential"? An advertisement can do that? I didn't realize they held us in such bondage. If that is true, we should ban all advertising immediately. And your "evidence shows that?" I'd like to see this evidence because I do not believe you. Was it written by Engels?

---

145 Kinsey, Ibid.
146 "'Harmful' gender stereotypes in adverts banned," BBC.com, June 14, 2019, https://
www.bbc.com/news/business-48628678 .

Sweden revisited

Liberal progressives are unanimous in their views about immigration. Failure to open borders and allow other cultures to pour in is equated with racism. Here Thomas Sowell would remind us to ask: "At what cost?"

Take the nation of Sweden. A few decades ago, it had one of the lowest crime rates on Earth. Today, it is one of the rape capitals of the world. How progressives, who claim to oppose oppression of women, can elevate the supposed and completely manufactured *need* for multiculturalism over the significance of rape is quite probably one of their crimes of the century. Yet they do. I will never forget the social media post in which a young progressive held up a sign reading: "Will take rapists over racists."

One is forced to reach two conclusions:

1. This young woman has never personally been raped.
2. It is curious that she believes she gets to make this assertion on behalf of other women who will be raped.

When liberals say, "multiculturalism," we should respond: "You mean *permitting rape culture*." Then add: "Our side is opposed to that kind of violence against women. We think it's criminal that you would encourage and enable it. It's quite possibly your crime of the century."

And who decides?

Similarly, Thomas Sowell and Ben Shapiro point out that we should also force liberals to answer the question: "Who decides?" Their principles are generally derived from emotion, and that renders them vague and subjective. So, who ultimately makes that call?

We have repeatedly seen that the conservative value system begins with the inviolable individual. The Marxist and liberal value systems begin with "the group." Here is just one more reason why the concept of the inviolable individual matters so greatly. It forms the basis of ownership laws, and ownership laws form the basis of everything. If an individual is inviolable, then such an individual's property belongs to them, and them only, and cannot be taken away. So, too, with their thoughts and ideas, which are held to be a form of property. It sounds abstract, but to deny someone their thinking is to deny them something that is supposed to belong to them.

By contrast, if you think *communally*, then property can easily be seized. Thoughts, even private ones, can easily be forbidden. The concept of "individual ownership," which is as at the cornerstone of the law, must be violated. And once we acquiesce to this violation, the question then arises again: "Who decides?"

How much land can be taken? From whom? At what cost? How often? On what grounds? The liberal response would be: "The government decides." Yet such a government, by definition, is already immoral. If it fails to uphold the sanctity of the individual and the property rights that follow from that cornerstone, then that government is already a tyranny. Anything they decide or enact after that point is merely paperwork in the service of evil.

The answer to the question "Who decides?" is necessarily relativistic. Having posed this question and having forced them to justify their assertions, we should now go on the offensive.

"Actually, that is the wrong question. The question should not be 'Who decides?' The question should be: 'Do we uphold human rights or not?' Human rights equals individual inviolability. Individual inviolability equals property laws. Remove one chink from the armor, and your justice structure falls apart. So does your proposal uphold human rights, or are you happy to flagrantly flout them?"

Who really does decide? Increasingly, the worst of the worst

Under liberalism, the answer to the question "Who decides?" must always tend toward the lowest common denominator and maximum tyranny, *just in case*. As Paul Joseph Watson often argues, "The culture of inclusivity is a race to the bottom for humanity."

In the ultimate irony, Paul Joseph Watson's videos, making such points, are regularly taken down by YouTube. His viewpoint is being excluded.

Yet it is a valid observation. To be tolerant, we must always be asking: What more can we tolerate? What worse? What standards no longer matter? What additional ugliness must we now celebrate in order to call ourselves tolerant? Where is the bottom? Or do we just keep "tolerating downward" indefinitely? What is tolerance's limiting principle?

After explaining this, we should add, "And that is how you are in the service of making society much worse, and that is why we oppose you."

CHAPTER 15

BE ABLE TO CITE THEIR SLIPPERY SLOPES IN DETAILED FORM.

AN EXTRAORDINARY AMOUNT OF LIBERAL policy is based on *permissiveness*. This permissiveness tends to head downward, toward the lowest common denominator, which is one of our chief complaints about liberalism. Once again, it is *anything but the old system*. Proof of this tendency is the rise in numbers of openly practicing witches and Satanists in the West today.

We have already seen that a good response to their proposals is: "At what cost?" The typical liberal response to concerns about permissiveness, you will repeatedly find, is cavalier mockery. They will dismiss objections as "little more than fear-mongering by backward-looking fundamentalists." There is, they will assert, "no slippery slope." They have been saying this for decades, even as we accelerate down into the funnel.

Side Note: It is worth pointing out that they are first to use the slippery slope argument. In their case, it generally takes the form of reacting to even humorous commentary with the hammer of disapproval, and if they can muster it, state-sanctioned censorship. They will argue that even permitting off-color jokes is the beginning of a slippery slope that will lead to oppression of a victimized group. Forcing them to face this contradiction is useful.

And so, in order to dismantle this narrative, it is expedient to have a few specific examples of completed slippery slopes, ready on hand, in order to prove your point.

Here are three common ones. They are easy to learn in story form and useful if you can cite them on demand:

- Gay rights don't impose on your rights. If you don't like gay marriage, don't get gay married.

  Here is the slippery slope: The gay rights movement began by presenting itself as a meek call for tolerance. Today, having achieved tolerance, it has turned aggressive and is attempting to destroy millennia-old values and institutions. Gay rights activists in places like California are trying to have the Bible legally banned as hate speech. We see headlines like, "Lawmakers want to force churches to embrace LGBTQ ideology instead of the Bible."[147]

  There's your slippery slope. From requests for nothing more than tolerance, to legal action against your right to read and believe in the Bible.

- #LoveIsLove—All expressions of love are valid.

  Here is the slippery slope: A man loving a man is just as valid as a man loving a woman. All love is equal.

  This is precisely the line of reasoning that the North American Man/Boy Love Association is using to legalize pedophilia. And quite frankly, how can we stop them? If we accept the liberal premise that "love is love," then there is no logical reason that a consenting eight-year-old boy should not be permitted to sexually submit himself to the advances of a fifty-year-old man.

  The law says it's not okay? Well, gay people had the laws changed, too. Laws are quite easy to change, once we buy into a guiding principle, such as, "Love is love." What could possibly go wrong?

---

147 Ben Davis, "Lawmakers want to force churches to embrace LGBTQ ideology instead of the Bible," CaldronPool.com, June 20, 2019, https://caldronpool.com/lawmakers-want-to-force-churches-to-embrace-lgbtq-ideology-instead-of-the-bible.

- Abortion is not a slippery slope.

  Here's your problem. When you begin to introduce gradations into the value of life and to argue that life is valuable or invaluable based on, say, a certain level of development, or lack thereof, you immediately face this problem: There is no argument for abortion that is not also an argument for child infanticide. "Not yet viable? My two-year-old is not yet viable. He also can't fend for himself."

  But it gets worse. Life judged in gradations leads straight to Nazist principles: "Well, that man is old and infirm. He must go." Or "That woman has a low IQ." Or "This conservative doesn't believe correctly," or "'that one doesn't work hard enough."

  It couldn't happen here, you say? History is littered with the astonished dead, all of whom made that mistake. These slippery slopes show us the problem with allowing things that supposedly "don't affect us." They create precedent. The same precedent can then be used against us.

  We have already seen that the "science" around modern gender theory, positing that gender is a loose construct, is fraudulent. However, in Canada and the U.S., certain places have made it illegal to try to help people who are struggling with their gender identity to come to terms with their biological gender.

  Clinics that treat gender dysphoria (by trying to help the *mind,* rather than surgically alter the sex) have been shut down and caring clinicians put of practice by government force. The result of that, in addition to the harm to the doctors, is further perpetuation of the problem of gender dysphoria. If it is not classified as a problem, and it is illegal to help you, then there can be no hope. Ideology wins one hundred percent, and mental illness proliferates by design. This leads us directly into the fifty percent suicide rate of transgender people, coupled with a government-enforced prohibition on treating it. Thank you, political correctness. And there is your slippery slope.

So, we've seen how gay rights seemed innocuous. Then they were legalized. Then speaking against them became a hate crime. Now there are genuine attempts being made to have the Bible banned on the grounds that it constitutes hate speech. How much further could the slippery slope go?

Can you see the direct link to a scenario in which you may no longer teach your children Christian principles, at home, *by law*? I can. Easily. That is how slippery slopes work. That is how entire cultures are lost.

CHAPTER 16
RESPOND TO DENIAL TACTICS WITH DETAILED EXAMPLES.

JUST AS THE ARGUMENT THAT "there is no slippery slope" can be debunked with detailed examples, the tactic of abject denial can be undone with the weight of evidence. Here again, it is useful to pick your cause and then to begin collecting examples. The more examples you have, the stronger your argument becomes.

Here are some sample causes, along with a few example articles:

"There's no war against men!"

An article in *The Guardian* details why more men should wear skirts. The rationale provided, in the headline, is that "masculinity is a trap." This constitutes a direct attack on men. It presumes that "maleness" is inherently bad. That's called sexism. It is a direct attack against men. Collect more examples, present them on demand, and your case is made.[148]

"But feminism is just about equal rights for women."

Really? Is that how out of touch you are? You mean it's not about lesbians drawing a figure of Christ with their own menstrual blood in order to mock the Judeo-Christian patriarchy? Maybe you're thinking about feminism from

---

148 Arwa Mahdawi, "Masculinity is a trap – which is why more men should wear skirts," The Guardian.com, June 19, 2019, https://www.theguardian.com/commentis-free/2019/jun/19/masculinity-trap-why-more-men-should-wear-skirts.

the 1940s? Or maybe you are, in fact, aware of the direction in which feminism has gone, but you're being dishonest by pretending that you are not.

It is easy to find YouTube videos and articles about what is wrong with third wave feminism. A good example to start with is "Is modern feminism starting to undermine itself?" by Jess Butcher.[149]

"There's no war on white people!"

Start with this article example from *Clash Daily*: "Open Season on White People: The New Politics of Racism."[150] Add more to your file.

Side Note: Just as it is useful when good women stand up against the male-bashing narrative, it is highly effective when black people stand up against the white-bashing narrative. By the same token, white people should do precisely the same against black-bashing narratives, and men should do the same when women are scorned. I express my personal gratitude to conservative black voices like Candace Owens for doing just that. You are a hero, Candace.

"There's no war on Christians!"

Collect articles like this one: "Religious freedom expert: global war on Christians intensifying."[151]

In real-world debates, what tends to go wrong when liberals make these assertions is that, although we know them to be untrue, we falter for examples. So have the examples at hand. If you know you will be debating a particular issue, collect a set of headlines and quotes, collect numbers and stats, and have them at hand in bullet point form. It is extremely effective to

---

149 TEDx Talks, "Is Modern Feminism starting to undermine itself? / Jess Butcher / Tedx-AstonUniversity," YouTube Post, 16:39, September 5, 2018, https://www.youtube.com/watch?v=lgIgytWyo_A.

150 Ed Brodow, "Open Season on White People—The New Politics of Racism," Clash-Daily.com, August 8, 2018, https://clashdaily.com/2018/08/open-season-on-white-people-the-new-politics-of-racism.

151 Caleb Parke, "Religious freedom expert: Global war on Christians intensifying," FoxNews.com, April 23, 2019, https://www.foxnews.com/faith-values/religious-freedom-christians-sri-lanka.

provide a staccato rapid-fire delivery of counter-examples, one after the other. Just doing that constitutes a complete argument.

In the "war on Christians" debate, one can easily point out that every single thing the Left has ever done has constituted a war on Christians:

- Rousseau creates ideas about a collective that can and should "put to death" any dissenters. This informs the progressive, liberal French Revolution, which instantly turns into a bloodbath. The Revolution openly declares war on Christianity and tries to purge it from the nation, replacing it with the secular faith of "liberty, equality, fraternity." That's the first thing progressive politics ever did. Day one, step one.
- Rousseau's collectivism leads to Karl Marx and communism. Communism declares war on Christianity, bans it by state decree, and tries to exterminate Christians in its territories.
- On a different prong of the same progressive fork, eugenic theory asserts that some races are superior. This leads to the sterilization or murder of black people and Indian people in the U.S. and to the rise of Nazism in Germany, which targeted Jews and Christians
- Today, Leftist political policies push Christianity out of schools, and liberal, homosexual activism targets Christianity above all for special persecution.
- The Left supports, excuses, and sanctions Islam. It welcomes Muslims into its own culture *en mass*, against protestations from its own constituents, leading directly to a rise in anti-Semitism in places like France and Germany, and enabling via silence the killing of Christians in Muslim countries.

"There is no war on Christians?" Actually, it's all the Left ever does. There are more examples, but this represents a starting point overview.

CHAPTER 17

POINT OUT THAT THE NEW LIE IS THE SAME AS THE OLD LIE.

WE HAVE NOW SEEN A couple of examples of the wrong, but difficult to quantify arguments from the Left, such as the Slippery Slope and Denial Tactics.

Here is another. Progressives will take an old lie, repackage it, and then present it as new. This, too, can be difficult to respond to—but not impossible. With the weight of a few specific stories, or quotes, or examples, we get the job done. It is only in the absence of any examples whatsoever that the lie gets to live on.

Here is one of the most popular re-packagings of an old lie today: "It's not socialism. It's *democratic* socialism."

Golly, then it must be the better version, right? Placing it beside a good word must make it good. And also, fundamentally different.

The trouble for that line of argumentation is that from its very founding over a century ago, socialist Marxism has *always* called itself democratic socialism. It's just that most teenagers today don't know that.

In *Dictator Literature*, Daniel Kalder points out that as far back as 1898, when the first major socialist movement was founded in Russia in Minsk, it called itself the Russian Social-Democratic Workers Party. Out of interest, Lenin himself was saddened to have missed the founding convention, exiled, as he had been, to Siberia.[152]

---

152 Daniel Kalder, *Dictator Literature: A History of Bad Books by Terrible People* (New York:

If you know this, you can simply deflate the argument: "It's been called democratic socialism for over one hundred years. The communists who took over Russia called it that. And they even called it that more than fifteen years *before* the revolution. It's the same rubbish today. Our issue is not with whether or not people willingly participate in it. Our issue is with Marxist collectivism itself, which is evil and deadly, whether or not it is democratic."

Your average social justice warrior, not knowing terribly much about history, will be unlikely to have a response for that. You should then progress on to the moral argument, framing this as a question of good versus evil.

Side Note: There is another approach you can use to respond to this specific argument. Instead of pointing out the error, you can actually go on the offensive. The argument proceeds like this:
"You are saying that democratic socialism is not the same thing as communist tyranny. But I have a different belief. I believe that even what we have now, *politically correct liberal democracy*, is nearly indistinguishable from communism. What we *already have* is bad enough. You want to go even further and make it even worse." Can we justify this assertion?
Here is an extract from *The Demon in Democracy: Totalitarian Temptations in Free Societies* by Ryszard Legutko, who not only lived under communist tyranny in Poland but also then worked in the liberal democratic European parliament. He should know. He explains:
Communism and liberal democracy proved to be all-unifying entities, compelling their followers how to think, what to do, how to evaluate events, what to dream, and what language to use. They both had their orthodoxies and their models of an ideal citizen. . . . As for liberal democracy, the belief still lingers that it is a system of breathtaking diversity. But this belief has deviated from reality so much that the opposite view seems now closer to the truth. Liberal democracy is a powerful, unifying mechanism, blurring differences between people and imposing uniformity

---

Simon & Schuster, 2018).

of views, behavior and language. . . . The nascent liberal democracy significantly narrowed the area of what was permissible. Incredible as it may seem, the final year of the decline of communism had more of the spirit of freedom than the period after the establishment of the new order, which immediately put a stop to something that many felt strongly at that time, and that, despite its elusiveness, is known to everybody that has an experience of freedom—a sense of having many doors open and many possibilities to pursue. Soon this sense evaporated, subdued by the new rhetoric of necessity that the liberal-democratic system brought with itself. . . . My subsequent experience of working in the European Parliament only endorsed my diagnosis.[153]

Quote this passage, or a story that exemplifies the same idea, and then return to your proposal: "What we already have is bad enough. In many appreciable ways, it already resembles a communist tyranny, and the similarities are growing. Yet you want to openly move further in that direction. I think your proposal is evil."

A Few Additional Similarities Between Liberalism and Communism

- The European Union overrides local interests (making it anti-democracy) by saying that it knows best what is good for a Europe as a whole (such as importing millions of Muslims). Communism did the same: "We're suspending your rights, denying you representation, and overriding your will. But don't worry—it's because we know what's best for you."

- Both promised to reduce government interference into life. But both increased it on a scale unseen before in history.

The best book on the counter-arguments to socialism:
Arguing with Socialists by Glenn Beck.

---

153 Ryszard Legutko, *The Demon in Democracy* (New York: Encounter Books, 2016).

CHAPTER 18

DO NOT FALL FOR EMOTIONAL FRENZY.

AS WE DEBUNK AND DISMANTLE Leftist ideas, it is worth noting that we are not only dealing with factual arguments here. We must also face up to frenzied tornadoes of emotion. The danger is in falling for emotion, as though it mattered. That is the pressure of Alinsky again.

In 2019, the social media world was awash with posts about how "The Lungs of the World are Burning!" The stories reflected large-scale fires in the Amazon jungle, which were said to be destroying the entire rainforest. We had weeks of frenzied fear-mongering about this topic, including guilt-ridden rants about how capitalists (naturally) would destroy the entire world that very week, and we would all suffocate to death.

Then NASA published some figures that threw water onto the frenzies. They pointed out that these fires, while large, were no different to the patterns of burning experienced in the Amazon each year for the past fifteen years.[154]

My friend Ziggy Whitehouse put it this way:

> From NASA: As of August 16, 2019, an analysis of NASA satellite data indicated that total fire activity across the Amazon basin this year has been close to the average in comparison to the past 15 years.

---

154 "Fires in Brazil," Nasa.gov, August 13, 2019, https://earthobservatory.nasa.gov/images/145464/fires-in-brazil.

Based on what people have been sharing on FB, I thought the entire Amazon had been burned to the ground. Should I believe NASA or random people on Facebook?

It wasn't just the facts that were wrong. The emotive language, referencing the "lungs of the earth" was flawed as well. Forbes debunked that one in an article titled, "Why everything they say about the Amazon, including that it's 'The Lungs of the World,' is wrong."[155]

We fall for these emotional frenzies all the time because they seem so urgent, so irresistible.

I can recall five years ago, how all the bees in the world had apparently disappeared that year, and we were all going to be dead by the next year. We might also cite Dr. Paul Ehlrich's famously wrong book, *The Population Bomb*, which predicted that we would have used up the Earth's resources and begun starving to death in our hundreds of millions by the 1980s.[156] The opposite happened, and we are now feeding more people, more effectively, than ever before, despite our growing numbers.

Emotional frenzy is a common part of the Leftist narrative. So far, we are supposed to have died of nuclear winter, acid rain, eating all the resources of the Earth and then each other, melted ice caps, white people, and Donald Trump, who, presumably, will blow us all up, or steal our bees, or some such.

In highlighting this particular issue, my suggestion to you is this: Don't take the frenzies at face-value. They serve a larger agenda. There may well be a kernel of truth in each of them (the fires in the Amazon were massive by any standard), but the conclusions ("We're all going to die!") are consistently way off.

155 Michael Shellenberger, "Why Everything They Say About The Amazon, Including That It's 'The Lungs of The World,' Is Wrong," Forbes.com, August 26, 2019, https://www.forbes.com/sites/michaelshellenberger/2019/08/26/why-every-thing-they-say-about-the-amazon-including-that-its-the-lungs-of-the-world-is-wrong/#3882e1a05bde.
156 Paul Ehlrich, *The Population Bomb* (San Francisco: Sierra Club/Ballantine Books, 1968).

"But they're shouty and self-righteous and, therefore, scary!"

Our human tendency is to respond to the indignant with wariness and even respect. Don't. Their manufactured outrage is not the same thing as maturity, and it is not analogous with justice. It should not be accorded or rewarded as such. Do not react to them as to the stern and scolding schoolteacher. We do not grant dignity on the strength of righteous indignation manufactured against us.

Instead, react as to a petulant child in need of correction. Mentally reposition yourself as the adult. Instead of: the opponent is very angry and, therefore, to be respected, it becomes: they are very angry and, therefore, need to learn to control their emotions better, like grown-ups. You can help them with that. React accordingly.

There will always be a new frenzy because there always has to be a new rallying cry (against capitalism, against humanity, against the Old Order—remember, the point is constant revolution). The nature of the attack will continually change. But it's always just the same old rubbish at core. When you see it, take a deep breath, look for the fallacy, wait for the real reports, ignore the emotion. Their entire point is to create fearful frenzy and to unite all groups against the Old Order. Don't let it work on you. And certainly, don't contribute to sharing the froth.

Positive frenzy

Not every use of the frenzied, emotional tsunami comes in the form of a fear-mongering negative. It is also presented in the form of an emotive positive. A sort of "glee wave."

In late 2019, over 130 of the world's most prominent musicians—Lady Gaga, Miley Cyrus, Katy Perry—signed a petition aimed at combating attempts at legislating against abortion. The message was essentially, "We're famous, so *yay, abortion!*"

What are their arguments for why abortion is morally okay? Or their counters to the arguments for why it is evil? What new information do they have proving it is okay for a baby to suffocate to death? There were none. That is not how this tactic works. Instead, it was simply the weight of many glossy, famous people all saying "Hurray!" together. That's it. An argument comprised of wind and glitter. Jazz hands. Approval as argument.

We must teach our children in particular to see through this, and not to fall for arguments from feelings from famous people. Children, who are looking for role models, are the most vulnerable to this dishonest tactic, and they also struggle to see through the importance of loud music and impressive lights. (But Miley says it's fine, and the stage looked amazing!).

This is how progressives use fear, and also popularity, to sell ideas, absent valid arguments. The point is to override logic by tapping into feelings. In the next chapter, we will see how this technique is used in debate scenarios, particularly via the identity of the speaker.

CHAPTER 19
ANTICIPATE THE "MARLBORO MAN ARGUMENT" AND CALL THEIR BLUFF.

IN *THE MARKETING OF EVIL—HOW Radicals, Elitists, and Pseudo-Experts Sell Us Corruption Disguised as Freedom,* David Kupelian explains how progressives sell toxic ideas, simply by presenting them in the hands of attractive proponents. It is perhaps the ultimate argument from emotion: the bikini model offering the poisoned apple. We will call it the "Marlboro Man technique."

Here's how it looks in action, as explained by Kupelian:

> You are invited on to a debate. Your job is to defend traditional marriage. Your opponent is a highly attractive, highly educated, well-spoken lesbian.
>
> She begins by stating that she loves her country. She points out that she has served in the military. She pays her taxes and obeys the laws, and she has been in a monogamous relationship with her partner for 18 years.
>
> She comes across as warm, personable, reasonable and clear-spoken. She's even very attractive. *And so,* she asks, *what's so wrong about just allowing her to marry her partner and live in peace?*[157]
>
> How would you currently respond to that argument? Does it leave you somewhat deflated? At a loss for an answer? That is because it is *designed* to do so.

---

157 Kupelian, *The Marketing of Evil.*

The correct response is to point out she is using the Marlboro Man technique and then to steer the discussion back to a qualitative investigation of the salient point.

Here is how the Marlboro Man technique works:

Selling tobacco is difficult. The stuff is poisonous and obviously bad for you. And yet it is still sold in vast quantities and has been for a long time. The bestselling brand in the U.S. for many decades was Marlboro, as a result of its clever advertising campaign. The campaign would show highly desirable imagery of a wonderful lifestyle: America! Wide, open spaces! Beautiful mountains, and a crystalline stream. An American eagle in full flight, and a manly cowboy admiring it all! Tobacco!

Do you see the bait-and-switch? Marlboro sold wonderful, positive imagery, *not the tobacco itself*. It presented *attractiveness* as the core argument, and then, when we bought into *attractiveness*, gave us tobacco instead.

In a practical debate, this would be the proper response: "I see that you are using the Marlboro Man technique. That's very clever. In order to sell poisonous tobacco, Marlboro presented us with attractive images of a cowboy, of America, of freedom, and then concluded: 'Tobacco!' But the *goodness* of tobacco does not logically follow from the images of America, freedom, and a cowboy. They are unrelated.

"In your instance, you have presented us with the image of an attractive, kind, good, and law-abiding citizen. And it worked! The audience clearly likes you. Hey, *I* like you, and I'm here to debate against you. You are a very likable person. But at the end of your Marlboro advertisement, you handed us lesbianism. It doesn't logically follow.

"So in the same way that a responsible and clear-thinking person must examine tobacco on its own merits, and not in a halo of fish-eagles and freedom, so, too, we must examine lesbianism in and of itself and not as exemplified by *you*, a very likable, very reasonable person. And when we take the Marlboro Man technique out of the equation, we discover a number of things about the lesbian community as a demographic, which may or may not pertain to you as a highly likable individual."

1. Lesbians commit abortion significantly more often than heterosexual women. I am not okay with the murder of babies, and as a demographic, lesbians commit this act disproportionately. Naturally, this is also a curious fact, as it entails sex with a man, which calls into question the narrative of being "born this way." Apparently, there is some deception at play there.

2. Fatherlessness is the number one determinant of crime and of violent behavior globally. A child raised in a very caring, very nurturing household by two women, who are to be lauded for their efforts, nevertheless has a grossly inflated chance of becoming a violent criminal and of spending time in jail. Children *need* fathers; and where fathers are absent, the results are significantly worse, not only for the children themselves, but for society as a whole.

3. *You* may not personally be a radical individual. In fact, you come across as extremely sensible, which is why you were selected to be here today. However, lesbianism, in general, tends to follow the radical agenda of third wave feminism. And here are the problems associated with that . . . "

The Marlboro Man returns to TV.

You will also see the Marlboro Man argument presented in progressive commercials. It usually takes the form of a series of scenes edited together in rapid succession, intended to depict a "progressive and wonderfully energetic," diverse society. The edits may play out like this:

- A school of dolphins
- A mountain climber
- A female pilot takes to the skies
- A gay pride march
- A baby gets a hearing device and smiles at mom for the first time.

Wow—*Life, progress, technology, and improvement! Helping a baby to hear!* And *homosexuality*. Yet to quote the children's show *Sesame Street*: "One of these things just doesn't belong here."

Meek and humble works, too.

The use of emotion-as-argument works just as effectively when the speaker is meek. A small, trembling persona can be presented in the service of tyranny every bit as effectively as an attractive sex symbol. In this case, the formula essentially goes like this:

"Look at us. We're so small. So fragile. So oppressed by everybody. You should really hand all power over to us. Stop talking about lofty ideas like freedom of speech. Suspend your rights and give us the power. It's best for everyone."

Emotion is *the* argument of the Left. When your ideas are bad, or contradictory, it must be. The question is really just *how* it will be employed and how you can diffuse it. Generally, calling it out—simply labeling it—is the best response.

Branded Babies

A variation on the Marlboro Man argument is the "branded child technique." In this technique, the small, sad faces of children are displayed on memes or on the news, with the parents' ideology shamelessly emblazoned across their foreheads.

Of course, this is not the child's thought, though it is duplicitously represented as such in order to heighten our emotional responses. Perhaps most egregious incarnation is the use of an autistic child as an activist. It reminds me of the Palestinian technique of using school children as human shields: *If you fight back, you will be hurting an innocent child.*

The Flip Side

Liberals also employ the reverse of the Marlboro Man technique against their opponents. They will identify their target with an evil person, institution, or idea, then use shouted repetition to entrench their point. Just as tobacco can be made to look wholesome, the wholesome can be made to look poisonous.

Here is one example from the presidency of Donald Trump: In 2018, more than three hundred newspapers joined together to publish editorials explaining the roles of journalists and amplifying their benefit to society. They directly and collectively attacked Donald Trump, pointing out that the first order of business for a tyrannical government is to try to enact state control of the media. That much is true; it *is* the first order of business for tyrannies.

This, they said, explained Donald Trump's repeated attacks on them. He was a Nazi, a tyrant, the next Hitler, and all the usual shopworn invectives. We know what evil looks like, the messaging went, and this is it.

They were half-right. Donald Trump *was* repeatedly attacking them. But he was not repeatedly attacking them in order to establish his own media or in order to have them banned. He has never made any such move. Instead, he was attacking them for *lying*. Maliciously and repeatedly and demonstrably, on record.

Liberal journalists would lie about Donald Trump, and then, when Donald Trump reacted, would misrepresent his outrage at their duplicity as "attempts to shut down the press." Donald Trump had never banned any media source, nor even endorsed state-run media, let alone trying to launch his own. Here we saw the Marlboro Man technique reversed by masters of narrative manipulation.[158]

Here is another example: In *After the Ball*, the handbook for gay advocacy in America, gay rights advocates encourage their proponents to smear the opposition by equating them to:

- Klansmen demanding that gays be slaughtered or castrated
- Hysterical backwoods preachers, drooling with hate

---

158   Mark R. Levin, *Unfreedom of the Press*, (New York: Simon & Schuster, 2019).

- Menacing punks, thugs, and convicts who speak coolly about the [homosexuals] they have bashed

- A tour of Nazi concentration camps, where homosexuals were tortured and gassed (Interesting point: William L. Shirer's definitive book, *The Rise and Fall of the Third Reich*, points out that many of the Nazi perpetrators were gay themselves. Their numbers were particularly high in the S.S.).

As we saw previously with the Alinsky technique, the solution is to frame yourself in the public consciousness *before* they get the chance, or at the very least, to point out their use of this technique, rather than to argue it on its own merits, which would place you on the defensive.

CHAPTER 20

DO NOT ACCEPT THE OUTLIER AS THE STANDARD-SETTER.

CONTINUING FROM THE PREVIOUS CHAPTER, we will remain with the theme of homosexual relationships. Media, TV, and popular gay narrative would have us see homosexuality as in every way qualitatively identical to heterosexuality. They will point to, elevate, and iconize the two gentle, loving men, living in a beautiful cottage, in a twenty-year faithful relationship. The Marlboro Men. See? Exactly the same!

Except that, when we reintroduce facts into the equation, we see that such idealized, monogamous, and perfectly stable gay couples are *not* the norm. In fact, such examples are way, way outside of the median average for the demographic. If we are going to speak the truth, we cannot accept the outlier as the normative standard setter. Author Douglas Murray, himself a gay man, makes this argument for intellectual honesty in *The Madness of Crowds*.[159]

Emotional story-examples allow this technique to sneak through. Facts and figures completely demolish it. If there exists such a thing as an "average" gay man, based on statistical norms from the demographic, this is what he would look like:

- He was sexually abused as a child. (This one is heartbreaking but lies with undeniable prevalence at the unexamined core of this topic.)

---

159   Douglas Murray, *The Madness of Crowds*, (New York: Bloomsbury Publishing, 2019).

- He abuses alcohol and drugs.[160]
- He has had scores of, and sometimes even several hundred, sexual partners.

A 2012 Seattle survey found that by age thirty-nine, heterosexual men surveyed, on average, had been with ten sex partners. By the same age, homosexual men reported an average of sixty-seven sex partners.[161] One study in San Francisco, cited in *Psychology Today*, found that nearly fifty percent of gay men had more than five hundred partners.[162]

And so, a different picture emerges. Now, let us see what the research actually says about the entire demographic. How many people are gay? With how many partners has each gay person, on average, had sexual relations? If we do not look only at the outlier (the Marlboro Man), what does the real picture look like?

We are concerned with Western culture here, and so our numbers pertain to Western nations. (It is worth noting that in Islamic nations and a great many socialist or tyrannical nations, homosexuality is either illegal or simply "does not exist" per the authorities, and so it is more difficult to examine their stats).[163]

In the U.K., the Office for National Statistics found that fewer than two people in every one hundred are *not* heterosexual.[164] That two percent, plus a small fraction of a percentage, accounts for *everything else* in the ever-expanding LGBTQ-moniker.

---

160 "Gay and Bisexual Men's Health: Substance Use," CDC.gov, https://www.cdc.gov/msmhealth/substance-abuse.htm (accessed April 18, 2020).

161 Sarah Nelson Glick, et al., "A comparison of sexual behavior patterns among men who have sex with men and heterosexual men and women," National Library of Medicine, May 2012, https://pubmed.ncbi.nlm.nih.gov/22522237.

162 Christopher Badcock, Ph.D., "It's the Mode for Men to Have More Sex Partners," PsychologyToday.com, March 2, 2017, https://www.psychologytoday.com/us/blog/the-imprinted-brain/201703/it-s-the-mode-men-have-more-sex-partners.

163 Rachel Banning-Lover, "Where are the most difficult places in the world to be gay or transgender?," TheGuardian.com, March 1, 2017, https://www.theguardian.com/global-development-professionals-network/2017/mar/01/where-are-the-most-difficult-places-in-the-world-to-be-gay-or-transgender-lgbt.

164 Gregory Robinson, "Number of people who identify as lesbian, gay or bisexual at UK high," TheGuardian.com, March 6, 2020, https://www.theguardian.com/society/2020/mar/06/number-people-identify-lesbian-gay-bisexual-uk-high.

When people use the phrase "hetero-normative" in an attempt to imply that backward religious fundamentalists are trying to make heterosexuality the norm, this statistic is a complete rebuttal. Most people—indeed, almost all people—simply *are* heterosexual.

Have you heard people say that it is about one in ten? Or even one in three? It is actually about one to two in every one hundred, depending on which study you choose. The popularly quoted numbers are off by a factor of around ten.

As *The Guardian* newspaper observed in a "Reality Check" segment on this finding, after the first such survey conducted in 2013:

> Do those figures seem low? One reason they might is that the number one in ten has long-persisted in popular culture as a reliable guesstimate of homosexuality rates. That number made its way into public assumptions and poor press reporting through the Kinsey Reports, two books written by a zoologist at Indiana University—*Sexual Behavior in the Human Male* (written in 1948) and *Sexual Behavior in the Human Female* (1953).[165]

Now let us ask a difficult question. Here I believe we are straying into some sad and even incredibly tragic territory. Nevertheless, let us pursue the truth wherever it leads us. How many of those individuals were sexually abused as children?

Does that question strike you as unkind? It is pivotal. The gay narrative asserts that they—as one percent of the population—were "born that way." Yet instances of molestation, abuse, and neglect are far more highly represented in the youthful backstories of homosexual individuals than in those of heterosexual individuals. This at least challenges their claim that gay people are "born that way," but likely completely debunks it.

Here is another problem for the "born this way" narrative. *The Guardian* articles continues: "Those aged between sixteen and twenty-four were by far

165   Mona Chalabi, "Gay Britain: what do the statistics say?," TheGuardian.com, October 3, 2013,   https://www.theguardian.com/politics/reality-check/2013/oct/03/gay-britain-what-do-statistics-say#:~:text=While%201.5%25%20of%20men%20in,compared%20to%203.5%25%20of%20men.

the most likely to say they were gay, lesbian or bisexual—2.7% of them did—a proportion that steadily declines as you inch up the age scale."[166]

Declines. People *decreasingly* identify themselves as gay as they get older. As many as half of young people who think they are gay in university say that they are not by their twenties or early thirties. That, also, seems at least curious. It is also a damaging idea for the "immutability" narrative.

And in the United States? The Center for Disease Control did the research. They came to almost exactly the same conclusion. No more than 1.6 percent of adults in America are gay or lesbian, and that is a generous estimate.[167]

Numbers for transgender people are vanishingly small. Even the LGBTQ-friendly Williams Institute at UCLA, if they may be taken at their word, puts the total population of transgendered individuals at only seven hundred thousand (out of some 320 million). This is two-tenths of one percent. In *Fake Science*, Austin Ruse posits that the real number is probably significantly smaller.[168]

Inborn and innate?

We are told that homosexuality is inborn and innate. Why is that important? Because if so, it cannot change, and only bigots would deny its normalcy. You cannot discriminate against someone who is genuinely born that way. This would qualify homosexuals as a special class of people persecuted for an innate and immutable characteristic. Yet repeated studies have confirmed that there is extremely high prevalence of early childhood trauma among gay people, usually including sexual abuse by older, same-sex individuals. Even to mention this is considered deeply politically incorrect. I believe that is wrong. In fact, I even think it is morally wrong. I go the other way: "How dare we fail to acknowledge this victimization?! It is disgusting that we should pretend it away."

166 Ibid.
167 Casey E. Copen, et al., "Sexual Behavior, Sexual Attraction, and Sexual Orientation Among Adults Aged 18-44 in the United States: Data From the 2011-2013 National Survey of Family Growth," *National Health Statistics Reports*, Number 88, January 7, 2016, https://www.cdc.gov/nchs/data/nhsr/nhsr088.pdf.
168 Austin Ruse, *Fake Science: Exposing the Left's Skewed Statistics, Fuzzy Facts, and Dodgy Data*, (New York: Simon & Schuster, 2017).

In 2011, Boston university professor Emily Faith Rothman carried out a meta-analysis of studies concerning gay or bisexual men or women. She found that 59.2 percent of the men had suffered childhood sexual abuse. It was even more for women, at seventy-six percent.[169] These numbers are significantly higher than for the general population. And these are merely the sexual abuse stats which gay people were willing to admit to. There may be more among those who might not be willing to admit to them. And we do know that other forms are much more greatly represented for them as well, including physical and emotional abuse. And that is even before we get to the topic of neglect by the father figure.

So those are the numbers upon which we are told that homosexuality is "normal," the philosophy upon which rests the idea that it is innate, and perfectly natural. The numbers disprove the narrative, and a qualitative exploration of the abuse dispels the idea that this is all perfectly healthy.

Now, let us progress to the next idea. To be gay is *equivalent.* Gay and lesbian men and women live comparable lives to heterosexual men and women. Is this actually true?

Again, here is what the research says: "One widely cited study found that forty-three percent of homosexuals had more than five hundred sex partners during their lifetime. A similar study conducted in the 1980s put the number at over one thousand in some cases.[170]

Another study reported the following findings:

- Men who have sex with men are more likely to abuse drugs and alcohol.
- Having sex with multiple anonymous partners while on methamphetamine is rising in popularity among the gay population.
- Men who have sex with men are at increased risk for depression and suicide compared to the general population.
- They are more likely to experience and perpetrate partner violence.

169 Ibid.
170 William W. Darrow, et al, "The Gay Report on Sexually Transmitted Diseases," AJPH, Volume 71, [9], September, 1981.

- They are significantly more at risk for sexually transmitted diseases and significantly more highly represented among those infected by STDs. In the U.S., they account for eighty-three percent of primary and secondary syphilis cases.

- This tiny percentage of the population (at most 1.6 percent) contributes over sixty percent of new cases of HIV in the United States. And that is in this decade, not in the "ignorant" eighties or nineties.

- They are seventeen times more likely to get anal cancer than heterosexual men, and significantly more represented among demographics with bowel-based viruses, infection with parasites, gonorrhea, and anal tearing. On this stat alone, we might pose some serious questions about the "it's all perfectly natural" narrative.

- They are more highly represented among cases of suicidal ideation, mental disorders, and substance abuse problems.

- Sexually abused young males are up to seven times more likely to self-identify as gay as are their peers who have not been abused.[171]

One can certainly find long-standing gay couples living together in peaceful union behind the proverbial white, picket fence, with no drug problems and no mental health problems and no sexually transmitted diseases from outside partners. But they are the outliers and not typical of the demographic.

It is at least interesting to note that studies of this nature are now considered hate-speech, and that following the science on this path is no longer deemed acceptable. One must ask the simplest of questions: Why?

Despite all of this extensive (but increasingly disallowed) research every new week, you will read a new post about how "science has confirmed a gay gene." In *Fake Science*, we see that the largest ever meta-analysis of all such studies proves these articles to be invalid—wishful thinking, at best. The

---

171   W.C. Holmes and G.B. Slap, "Sexual Abuse of Boys: definition, prevalence, correlates, sequelae, and management," Pubmed.gov, 1998, https://pubmed.ncbi.nlm.nih.gov/9846781.

desperation to confirm such a gene and the will to ignore the evidence of abuse is telling.

> **The best book on this topic:** *Fake Science* by Austin Ruse. Offering a description of the ugly and dishonest inside politics that went into normalizing homosexuality, this book also debunks every one of the "in the genes" findings one by one.

So, where to?

Does all this translate into the illegitimacy of homosexual people? Does that mean they can rightly face oppression or demonization? No. If anything, it leads us to the exact opposite conclusion. Much evidence would indicate that these individuals are *already the victims* of abuse, neglect, and trauma—indeed, its logical outcome. We should have no interest whatsoever in persecuting them.

We do, however, have a direct interest in *their* not persecuting *us*. We have seen some radical activism from gay-rights groups over the past decade, including the targeting of Christian businesses, persecution of anyone who questions their narrative, and, most troublingly, movements toward classifying Christian doctrine and the Bible as hate speech and, thereby, to have them banned. We are way past the dynamic that is popularly presented to us, of a large and oppressive Christian nation chasing down poor, fleeing homosexuals. It is now active oppression in the other direction.

Here is an example that made the media: "IKEA sacks employee for quoting the Bible after he was told to participate in pro-LGBTQ event: 'I've been hired to sell furniture . . . these aren't my values.'"[172] And another example is "The Ongoing Persecution of a Christian Baker."[173]

---

172   "IKEA sacks employee for quoting the Bible after he was told to participate in pro-LGBTQ event: 'I've been hired to sell furniture . . . these aren't my values," CaldronPool.com, July 1, 2019, https://caldronpool.com/ikea-sacks-employee-for-quoting-the-bible-after-he-was-told-to-participate-in-pro-lgbtq-event-ive-been-hired-to-sell-furniture-these-arent-my-values.

173   "The Ongoing Persecution of a Christian Baker," NationalReview.com, June 12, 2019, https://www.nationalreview.com/2019/06/masterpiece-cakeshops-jack-phillips-persecution.

For a list of articles pertaining to the persecution of people who do not agree with homosexuality, visit Carm.org and search "homosexual persecution of Christians."

To concede the world's largest religion, with over two billion followers worldwide, to the uncompromising demands of a group of people who make up approximately one percent of the population—and very likely make up that percentage due to trauma in their own childhood pasts—is the definition of a tyranny of the minority.

If we take those who are known to have suffered abuse in childhood out of the equation, we are conceding our rights and norms to a group that represents approximately 0.5 percent of our societies. And even this minority is simply "not known" to have been abused. We are taking even this claim at face value.

CHAPTER 21

HAVE THEM EXPLAIN THEIR POSITION FIRST, THEN FORCE THEM TO FACE THEIR OWN CONTRADICTIONS.

REMEMBER ALINSKY'S PRINCIPLE? THE ACTION is in the *reaction?* When you begin an interaction by defending your ideas, it is like appointing them as the police and yourself as the fleeing criminal. You're out front, but only until you make a mistake. And all they have to do is pursue and keep the pressure on, until you trip up.

Don't permit this. Instead, flip the dynamic so that they are the ones on the run, and you are the one keeping up the pressure. Keep up the pressure by pointing out flaws. To do this, get them to explain their position first. It is often their *conclusions* that are more useful than their arguments. For instance: "America is evil and racist!" This conclusion often appears within an argument about illegal immigration.

Use their conclusions against them: "If America is evil and racist, shouldn't you be warning immigrants *not* to come here? For their own good? Or is there a chance that America is not, in fact, evil and racist, but that it is actually good and prosperous? If it is good and prosperous, then your argument in favor of admitting more immigrants makes sense. If not, it doesn't. So, which is it?'

The *opposite* conclusion works just as well: "They deserve to live in freedom and hope, too."

"Just to be clear: America *is* a land of hope and freedom? And not an evil, racist empire?"

The liberal-progressive position is riddled with contradiction and forcing them to defend their own views causes their arguments to unravel.

Here's another example: "There's no such thing as evil. People are just undereducated, oppressed, or misunderstood."

"So, the Nazis were not evil. They were misunderstood. And how about white colonialists? And slave owners?"

"Well, I mean . . . *they* may have been evil . . . "

"Okay, so we have established in principle that there is such a thing as evil, contrary to your initial claim, about which you were simply wrong. We merely differ on what we *identify* as evil. For you, it's Nazis. I share that definition. I, too, believe they were evil. Moreover, I believe that any system that denies individual human rights in favor of group rights and tries to impose ideology by government decree qualifies as evil. Hence, I believe Leftism is one of the world's leading evils today."

Here are a few further examples of contradictions on which they can be pressed:

- "All truth is relative." But: "Postmodernism gives us a more accurate view of reality."
- "The president is guilty of using incendiary language!" But: "I just wish I could blow up the White House. I enjoyed that show about the mock assassination of the president. Here's a picture of a comedian holding up his severed head. We should shoot all his supporters."
- "You're born gay. You don't have a choice." But: "Issues of gender are not set. They are a choice."
- "There's no slippery slope. Stop fear-mongering." But: "We can't allow any inappropriate comments whatsoever. It's a slippery slope that can lead to denying that group their right to exist."
- "All cultures deserve respect. You just don't understand their norms." But: "Western culture is evil and oppressive."

- "There is nothing sacred about sex. People should experiment and have as many partners as possible." But: "Men just see women as sexual objects. They don't place any intrinsic value on the woman herself."
- "Industry and technology are bad and destructive." But: "It's unfair that some have access to technology, while others do not."
- "America is evil!" But: "Let them in to America. They deserve to benefit from the good things, too."
- "Men are evil. They are oppressive rapists." But: "There is no difference between men and women."
- "You're not allowed to judge people." But: "You're not allowed to say that."

Perhaps one of the richest veins of contradiction we may mine on the Left is their assertion that material things are not important (an anti-capitalist stance), paired with the fact that their entire moral system is premised on materialism (redistribution, who owns what, preoccupation with material inequality). Material things matter greatly to the Left, who assert that they do not.

Transposable Arguments

Usefully, Leftist arguments in favor of one cause can be shown up in another. For instance, the argument for being pro-choice turns out to be an excellent argument in favor of slavery. This presents the Left with a serious problem. Either slavery is bad, and abortion is also bad (as we believe, without dissonance); or slavery is bad, but abortion is somehow good (as they believe, with a great deal of dissonance).

Abraham Lincoln came up against this idea long before us. In 1858 in Ottawa, in a debate against Stephen Douglas, of the progressive Democratic party, Lincoln picked apart the argument for slavery. His opponent, Douglas, took what may be called the "pro-choice" position: He said he wasn't "pro-slavery." But neither was he "anti-slavery." His was a stance of public indifference, he explained. "It is none of my business. This is something for each particular state or community to decide for themselves."

Thus framed, the issue was not one of principle. It was one of free choice. This is exactly the trick that abortionists pull: "Hey, people will have differing views on an issue as contentious as slavery. Diversity is the great safeguard of our liberties." Douglas called his stance *popular sovereignty*.

Happily, Lincoln saw through the ruse. He began by showing the radicalism behind the supposedly modest stance by drawing out the consequences one by one. He also exposed the inner contradiction of this stance: "Choice? But you are removing someone else's choice." Choice here is being invoked to cancel out the choice of others. Hence, this act is profoundly anti-choice. Or differently stated, it is "privileged" choice. Pro-choice really means pro-slavery, just as pro-choice really means pro-baby-killing.

Finally, Lincoln pointed out in the debate, the *content* of the choice is a crime. When the content of a choice is a crime, you do not get to make such a choice validly.

Lincoln was particularly adept at untangling and debunking progressive ideas. In 1858, he used this ironic argument, which survives in his handwriting on a scrap of paper: "But slavery is good for some people!!! As a good thing, slavery is strikingly peculiar in this, that it is the only 'good' thing which no man ever seeks the good of for himself." Then he turned the tables: "Nonsense! *Wolves* devouring *lambs*, not because it is good for their own greedy maws, but because it [is] good for the lambs!!!"[174]

The Words Themselves

Before even descending into a specific argument, you can use their own terminology to point out their contradictions. Here's one example:

"We want social justice! And we shall achieve it by gaining control—heart and mind and speech and act—over an *enemy* of social justice."

So, social justice is about bullies controlling victims?

---

174 D'Souza Dinesh, *Death of a Nation*.

UNTANGLE EMOTIONAL LANGUAGE AND POINT OUT THE LIE.

PC ARGUMENTS ARE RARELY UNEMOTIONAL statements of fact. Instead, they are almost always emotionally overblown accusations, based on hyperbolic and faulty language, with very little in the way of supporting facts. They are lies constructed around hyped-up emotion.

As such, it is a mistake to take even the language at face value. In doing so, we are forced to accept the embedded ideas within the language. Instead, we should begin by unraveling the language itself. Often, unraveling the language will unravel the bad idea.

Take this example: "The United States is a heartless bully. It targets and dehumanizes vulnerable people at its Southern border."

If we accept this language at face value, we end up having to defend the idea that the United States is *not* a bully. Yet the language itself, when shown to be inaccurate, will already disprove the core idea.

Take just a single word: "targets." To target someone is to actively seek them out. In this context, it means to intentionally look for someone for the purpose of persecuting them, to "go out of your way." This is a serious accusation. People who target others are malicious, even evil. Using this accusation, liberals will enthusiastically draw comparisons to Nazi Germany: "Germany targeted the Jews, and America targets poor Mexicans. See? It's the same." But as we've seen, *to target* is an active verb. One must plan and scheme, in order to "target" a group of people. One must "go to" these people.

By contrast, the actions of the United States in this context are *reactive.* Indeed, they are reactive to a crime. The United States does not "go to" these people. These people come to the United States, and specifically, they do so illegally. As such, the targeting accusation is akin to accusing a person defending their own home of targeting housebreakers, which would be nonsensical.

It is not a good-faith argument. Instead, it is an intentional twisting of words to portray reality differently and to vilify an innocent party. The United States does not target these people. Instead, it reacts in defense of its borders, just as any nation would. And should.

Words matter. Correct definitions and accurate descriptions are important. When used deceptively, as in this example, they create a villain out of a non-villain. This is injustice. It is unfairness and victimization, premised on inaccurate wordplay.

Before you defend any idea against a PC opponent, start by examining the language itself. Do the words accurately describe reality, or are they being contorted in the service of an ideology? Simple descriptions of who acts, and in what ways, can be twisted to misrepresent reality; and if you don't spot the deception, you will end up arguing *as though what it describes is true.*

If a scenario is being represented emotionally, which will almost always be the case with PC proponents, then you can be reasonably sure that the words employed are being contorted. They are not honest descriptors. Pick them apart. Untangle the words, point out the intentional dishonesty in the terms, and you need not proceed to defend the idea. The idea will already have been disintegrated.

Incredible Claims

One of the U.S.'s most famous transgender teens is Jazz Jennings, born a boy, now a girl. The parents, Greg and Janet, insist that their boy asserted his female identity as soon as he was able to talk, saying that their fifteen-month-old baby would unsnap his onesie "to make it look like a dress."[175]

As a father myself, I can tell you that children unsnap anything that snaps. Their inferring of a child's intentions into this action is extremely telling. But it gets worse. They report that when he was two, he asked them, "Mommy, when's the good fairy going to come with her magic wand and change . . . you know . . . my genitalia?"

I have a three-year-old. His teachers describe him as surprisingly vocal for someone so young. And I will tell you right now that if any parent tried to convince me that their two-year-old had uttered a sentence like this, I would smile politely and say, "Sure thing, sport!" I would react with the exact same disbelief were such a claim to be made regarding a four-year-old.

Here we see how harmful ideology is foisted on children by virtue-signaling, liberal parents. Is there anything sadder than mutilating your child just so that you can go on *ABC News*, become famous, and say to the world, "Look at me"? I believe people who do such things are child abusers and should be called out as such.

Debate Tip: Once you have spotted and unraveled a dishonest word or dishonest language, do not be shy to accuse your opponent of dishonesty. If terminology is intentionally deceptive, say so openly for all to hear. State that your opponent is employing dishonest tactics and lying in the service of their ideology and point out the lie. This will make them more cautious about employing the tactic a second time, and it will point out to observers that your interlocutor must be monitored for dishonesty. It also positions you as the honest player.

Debate Tip: Your opponent retorts, "Are you calling me a liar?" Respond with: "I have just pointed out how you lied. The onus is now on *you* to prove that you are not a liar. To that end, it's not looking good for you."

---

175   Eric Braun, *Taking Action for Civil and Political Rights (Who's Changing the World?)* (Minneapolis: Lerner Publishing Group, 2017).

Your opponent cannot prove a negative, and so, this puts them in an untenable position. The best they can hope to do is to attempt to be more honest going forward, or at least, not be caught lying again.

The Soviet Euphemism

Probably the best-known form of politically correct language is the "newspeak" or "doublespeak" invented and made famous by Soviet propagandists. It is evasive or ambiguous use of terminology, designed to deceive, confuse, or obfuscate.

The word *fetus*, employed in the abortion argument, is perhaps the ultimate example of an ideological euphemism. It commits what philosophy calls "the error of reification," in which human beings attempt to alter the nature of reality via nothing more than words.

Reality does not comply with our wishes when we commit this error. Changing the label on a living being does not actually change the living being—only our social narrative about it. This is self-deception at its finest, with terrific consequence.

The list of euphemistic, deceptive terms is impressive and ever-expanding. Here are just a few that you should never allow through unchallenged:

- To appropriate: to steal
- To expropriate: to steal
- To redistribute: to steal and give away
- Re-allocation: to steal from here and place over there
- Economic Empowerment: Marxist redistribution and job reservation
- To neutralize: to murder
- Enemy of the people: anyone that the government needs "neutralized"
- Subversive: anything that goes against government ideological prescription. Of note, free nations rarely employ terms like subversive or dissident. These terms appear almost exclusively in socialist states.
- Affirmative action: racially motivated and anti-meritocratic job reservation

- Investment: the government apportioning your money to things you did not approve of
- Undocumented: illegal alien
- Pacification: murder of civilians
- Liberation of the people: imposition of communism
- Economic liberation: imposition of communism
- Climate change: A replacement for the discredited global warming
- Progressive: implies forward movement and progress (The acts do not correspond with the definition.)
- Sanctuary city: city presided over by a mayor who refuses to uphold the law
- Giving it back to the people: using dishonest politics to put our party back in power
- Capacitating: firing people
- Developing: third world
- Lobbying: bribing
- Alternative medicine: anything that science can't prove actually works
- Load-shedding: familiar to South Africans in place of "black-outs" or "power failures"

As a popular meme observes: "Calling an illegal alien an undocumented immigrant is like calling a meth lab dealer an undocumented pharmacist."[176]

In *Politics and the English Language*, George Orwell wrote that obfuscatory, political language is designed "to make lies sound truthful and murder respectable."[177] We need not fall for this tactic if we are simply paying attention to the use of words.

The best article on this topic: "From Russia with Euphemisms" in *The National Review.*

---

176 Calling an Illegal Alien An Undocumented Immigrant, Digital Image, iGeek, http://igeek.com/File:IllegalImmigrantTerms.png.

177 Orwell, *Politics and the English Language*.

One Step Further

Now let us take another example. In this instance, it is not individual words or terms that are dishonest, nor a phrase, as is the case with euphemisms. Instead, a deceptive analogy is employed. A picture of comparison is created, which dishonestly portrays a scenario.

I saw this argument employed to explain appropriation of land from white farmers in South Africa under a proposal called "Appropriation without Compensation." (And how's that for a Soviet terminology? Sounds a lot better than "stealing without paying you.")

The analogy put forward was that of a picnic. The argument went like this: Imagine a picnic. All the participants have lots of food, and all are content. Along comes a stranger, who is starving. Wouldn't it be right not only to share some of the food, but also for a few of the picnic-goers to gift their entire meal to the starving person on the grounds that the starving person has nothing and desperately needs the food?

Does this analogy sound deeply flawed to you? I am not kidding when I say that it was related by a man with a doctorate. Liberals seem to love their picnic analogies.

There are several things about the parameters of this analogy that do not correspond with the reality of land confiscation. First, implied in the act of giving away all your food at an event as trivial as a picnic is the idea that the giver should not worry; it's *just one meal*. No big consequences. This has nothing in common with giving away the land upon which you live, which is irreplaceable.

Second, in this analogy, the happy picnic-goers are portrayed as "giving" away their land. In reality, the land would have to be *confiscated*. Confiscation of someone's land by act of law, and at the gunpoint of military officials upholding that law, has nothing in common with an act of charitable giving. The picnic analogy transposes the ideas of giving and stealing.

Third, the sentimentality of the picture—an outdoor picnic—does not accurately portray what it's actually like to really evict an entire family off the farm that they have been tending for generations and to leave them destitute. Picnics sound lovely. Police and military raids less so.

Moreover, the picnic analogy assumes that what is given immediately feeds the needy: "Here, have a cupcake. Voilà! Now you're not hungry." A farm does not work that way. Confiscating and occupying someone else's farm does not immediately feed you nor make you rich. You actually have to *work* the farm before that happens. And so, the underlying analogy of "sharing the wealth" is also flawed. "Sharing the work that creates the wealth" might be a more accurate statement.

Finally, and as with all liberal thought-experiments of this nature, this picnic analogy allows the speaker to look righteous (in this case, in a social media post) without personally sacrificing anything. The weaver of the analogy is not present at the picnic. He is very nobly volunteering "cupcakes" (farms) on behalf of other people. He gets to look generous without personal cost. He recommends eviction for others, but not for himself.

In both of these tactics—dishonest word usage and dishonest analogies—the same basic thing occurs. The principles of what is actually going on in the real world are hidden, concealed, altered, or distorted behind obfuscating words. You do not need to go as far as defending the bad ideas as they are represented. Unravel the language, and you have unraveled the bad ideas.

It is interesting to think of this picnic analogy in the light of what we learned from Jonathan Haidt concerning the six pillars of morality. The liberal, you will recall, operates on the basis of only *three* moral pillars:

1. Care and harm
2. Fairness and cheating
3. Liberty and oppression.[178]

---

178 Haidt, *The Righteous Mind.*

Their understanding of pillar number two—fairness and cheating—is fundamentally different to ours. They see "unfairness" represented in the person of the stranger who does not have food. They do not perceive fairness in the way that conservatives do, which is to say, as a system of proportionality. Therefore, the immorality of taking from someone else in order to give to the stranger does not seem immoral to them. Indeed, the underpinning moral problem is not even a part of their spectrum.

You will recall that the next three moral pillars, which inform conservative values but not liberal values, are:

4. Loyalty and betrayal

5. Authority and subversion

6. Sanctity and degradation.

These values simply do not feature for most liberals. Hence, "So what if I betray my people in taking away their land?" and "So what if taking their land undermines legal principles?" And "What makes land so very sacred to them? It's just land—a resource to be distributed."

CHAPTER 23

DO NOT LET THEM OWN THE "GOOD WORDS."

FOR MY MONEY, THE SINGLE greatest mistake we make in our centuries-long cultural war with the Left is to allow the them to own the "good words." They speak about kindness. They speak about compassion. They speak about being tolerant and understanding—all the love words in a single basket.

The language is pure trickery. The reality of their ideas has nothing in common with what they represent. Over and over, we have seen how their policies devastate kindness (by creating toxic culture), reverse compassion (by denying people the truth, or by impoverishing them through socialism), and actively oppress people (by creating target groups who may be openly attacked).

Yet they claim that they represent the good qualities, and somehow, that becomes enough. It frames them as the good guys. And by contrast, it frames their opponents as de facto bad guys. We absolutely must reclaim the good words.

In fact, doing so makes an excellent starting point for every debate and every public speech and every social media comment. Openly state your premises: "We care about people. And therefore, our goal is kindness toward the poor. And therefore . . ."

After these "claim the good words" statements, you then explain your policy or stance, which actually *does* result in improvement for these groups.

Economist Thomas Sowell argues that if progressive policies were judged by their outcomes, and not their intentions, there would never be another progressive policy.[179]

It is also useful to have at hand specific examples of how the progressive incarnation of "kindness" hurts people.

Here's one from a 2019 Fox news broadcast: San Francisco has new homeless camps strewn across the city. People defecate in the streets near families and businesses and openly shoot crystal meth on the pavements. These acts should be illegal. Yet now, they are not. This was the result of a progressive "kindness" act. The city passed a policy called Proposition 47, which decriminalized petty crimes. Now, when people publicly defecate on the streets, there is no consequence (because it is no longer a legal infraction).

The result of this has been that homelessness, drug abuse, related violence such as crazed men barking at passing civilians or throwing rocks at cars, and anti-social and unhygienic behaviors such as public defecation outside of restaurants have skyrocketed. Typhoid fever has even made a comeback.[180] Liberal kindness could kill us all. It must be stopped.

Side Note: Watch Paul Joseph Watson take on this topic on YouTube by searching "Paul Joseph Watson, Los Angeles."[181]

How Progressive Kindness Isn't

So, the result of a progressive policy of kindness toward the homeless and drug addicts has been more homeless and more drug addicts. Remember the Leftist idea that the "stigma" is the real problem? No, it isn't. Shooting mind-altering crystal meth is the real problem. Stigma is just our feelings about

---

179   Sowell, *Economic Facts and Fallacies.*
180   Betz Bradford, Fox News, Dr Drew Says LA Public Health in 'complete breakdown': 'No city on Earth tolerates this,' Foxnews.com, May 31, 2019, https://www.foxnews.com/health/dr-drew-says-third-world-countries-would-be-insulted-to-be-compared-with-los-angeles.
181   Paul Joseph Watson, "Los Angeles is a . . . ," YouTube Post, 13:15, August 18, 2019, https://www.youtube.com/watch?v=HKCfu4UJQiQ."

the topic. And if our feelings about the topic are negative, that is the correct response to such a scenario. The stigma narrative is one of the most harmful abuses the Left has visited upon people who actually need help.

Objection: But if we don't remove the stigma, they'll get arrested!

Response: Exactly. And then they can be referred for help. Why would you deny them that? (Note how this response reverses the kindness standard.)

I recommend having a real-world example or two of this dynamic up your sleeve, so that you demonstrate precisely how progressive kindness makes things worse, even for those it purports to help.

In his response to the Alinsky tactics, Hedgpeth advises: "Define yourself positively before your opposition has the chance to define you."[182] Based on this observation, I also recommend going beyond just an opening salvo in which you own the kind words. That is good positioning, and it is a good start. But you can go further. Actively accuse *them* of cruelty. Get passionate about it. Display your outrage at their policies, which are so criminally unkind to people in their outcomes. By the same token, you need to be ready to and able to undo their framing efforts, both in terms of how they will position themselves and in terms of how they will frame a victim group.

Remember the term *micro-aggressions*? This is a device used to create victims. Yet you can easily explain how the use of the term *micro-aggressions* constitutes an act of hate on the part of the user: "Micro-aggression call-out culture prescribes that you should always choose to see the worst in people, by assuming bad motives on their part and viewing even the accidental as malicious. This stance is anti-peace, anti-community, and driven by antisocial, blind hate. It chooses always to see the worst in people. Why would you use such a hateful paradigm? By contrast, our side believes in good relationships, based on honesty and equality. That's why we propose . . . "

---

182 Hedgpeth, *Rules for Radicals*.

Side Note: The Hebrew Bible contains active admonitions to judges to practice justice and not social justice. Judges, in their privileged position, are remonstrated from trying to right society. Instead, they must judge each case on its own merits. This is the biblical injunction against social justice, and it informs a superior legal system.

The best book on this: *The Rational Bible: Exodus* by Dennis Prager.

Effective positioning is largely about labels.

We have already seen that positioning, whereby one side or the other frames the issue, creates the conditions for a win or a loss. Labeling is one aspect of positioning, and the Left uses it to brilliant effect. I have demonstrated that they attempt to position even the most detrimental policies as kindness. That is the strategy behind this technique. The specific label applied is the "foot soldier." It then gets the job done.

For example, in late 2019, singer Taylor Swift used her fame to try to get signatures on a petition for something called the Equality Act. Her smiling face and words of compassion, coupled with her music, must represent the ultimate Marlboro Man argument. And what could possibly be wrong with something called the Equality Act? It *sounds* so good. It sounds like *pro-choice*. The words are all positive.

Here is one problematic key idea: It would criminalize discrimination based on gender identity. That, of course, is subjectively and emotionally defined and based on the fraudulent science of John Money. Yet to argue against any of this would then be to take on the Equality Act. And surely, you're not opposed to *equality*, right? That is how the labeling trick works.

Yet consider just some of the damage it would do:

- If parents refuse to permit hormone therapy treatment and genital mutilation for their children who are suffering with gender dysphoria, the state would then be entitled to take their children away from them, citing child abuse (for *not* flooding your child with hormones of the opposite gender), despite the fact that seventy-five to ninety-six percent of children with gender dysphoria simply grow out of it, if left to do so.[183]

- If a man wanted to compete in women's sports, you would not be able to prevent him doing so. At the time of writing, a biological male is the number one ranked NCAA track star.

- If a person with gender dysphoria decided to cycle through an infinite range of genders during the day, then that would become their legally protected right. And if we didn't keep up and treat them accordingly, that would be considered a crime.

- It would create the impossibility of female-only spaces, including locker rooms and changing rooms, resulting in the forced admission of biological males.

- If churches or social groups wanted to hold a single moms' night, they would not legally be permitted to prevent males from attending.

The consequences go on and on, and all of them are damaging. But the labeling—ah, the labeling! It all sounds so good.

One of the greatest mistakes we make in this debate is to allow the Left to label every bad idea they have using good words.

Still, we have got it right a few times:

We labeled our abortion stance "pro-life." That was a good move. Yet we still continue to use their moniker "pro-choice" alongside our own. We should not. We should speak about being "pro-life" or "pro-death" for babies. "Trickle-up poverty" is another good one. This is the label we should apply to leftist economic policies, in parody of the phrase "trickle-down economics."

Still, one of the most overlooked opportunities for our camp is in the labeling arena. We should be actively seeking out new labels for their dishonest techniques, and we should be actively creating new labels that frame their policies.

---

183 Ruse, *Fake Science*.

As an example, take the very issue under discussion here—that the Left likes to claim all the good words and use them to position awful polices as positives. What might we label *that* technique, so that it can be called out in public debate? Our label for that should be colorful, memorable, derogatory, and self-explanatory. It should be easy for listeners to get what the term means very quickly. "Virtue-signaling" comes close. Can you think of something better?

I believe we need terminology for every one of their dishonest tactics, and I believe we need to popularize the negative identifying labels for every one of their bad policies.

Danger Zone: Steer well clear of racial slurs or bigoted descriptors. That is not the point here. There is a chasm of difference between pointing out that someone is virtue-signaling, which identifies their dishonest tactic, versus using something like racist terminology, which would be unethical on our part and instantly give them the high ground.

CHAPTER 24

REJECT GROSSLY DISTORTED COMPARISONS AND REVERSE THE OUTRAGE.

LET'S PROGRESS ONE STEP FURTHER from owning the good words. Liberals will use techniques designed to position *them* as good in contradistinction to everyone else. The "you are literally Hitler" argument is their favorite (closely followed by the "you are exactly the same as a Southern slave owner" gambit).

In this gross distortion lies an opportunity to reverse the framing, pointing out how egregiously they are abusing a human tragedy in order to score points. Return the pressure to them. Accuse them of the immorality of their own ideas. Flip the dynamic.

Here is how I put it once in a small essay:

> There are not many politically-correct progressive arguments that make me genuinely angry. At most, they tend to provide an ironic laugh or a weary eye-roll. Many are useful for the sharpening of one's capacity to spot and dismantle logical fallacies.
>
> But one in particular makes me livid, and that is the Holocaust analogy.
>
> In my books, writing and speeches, you will quickly detect my respect and admiration for the Jewish people, not only as survivors of genocide, but for their values generally. They are a people that I venerate.

Today I've read a number of the usual stock "Trump is Hitler!" posts. These are yawn-worthy in their banality, as tired and threadbare as the knee-jerk: "You're a bigot!" line.

But today, a number of them went beyond mindless repetition of a CNN thought-meme ("Orange Man Bad! TV teach me!"). The meme I saw a number of times today quoted Anne Frank and her firsthand account of terror at SS-led home invasions in which families were separated at night and deported to extermination camps. All this shared with comments like: "See? History is repeating itself!"

History is repeating itself . . .

Here is how we must torture logic and belittle Jewish genocide in order to arrive at the conclusion that history is repeating itself. It is a four-step process:

1. Persons attempting to enter a nation in contravention of that nation's laws must be viewed as holding equivalent legal standing to a Jewish-German citizen whose family had lived in Germany, with full citizenship, for generations.

2. The act of detaining and preventing people from breaking into a nation illegally must be deemed morally equivalent to (read: exactly the same as) the German S.S. breaking into citizens' homes at night and dragging family members away for execution in death camps. Forget that anyone within the U.S. who breaks the law is also separated from their family as a result of their crime, we must now view this separation of individuals as being "like Nazis carrying people away in the night."

3. The rare (but nevertheless tragic) cases of people dying in detention, generally as a result of malnutrition from their perilous desert journeys en route to breaking into a nation illegally, must be viewed as morally equivalent, and even precisely identical, to a planned campaign of intentional mass extermination of an entire demographic via organized execution.

They're the same. *Et voila*. With only that tiny amount of logical convolution, Trump is Hitler.

4.   (. . . And this is the part that truly gets my ire), while making this incredible leap of logic, you must then grandstand about "compassion,"in order to look righteous on social media, even as you denigrate and belittle one of the greatest human tragedies in history for the sake of scoring cheap political points.

I generally believe in responding to poorly structured thinking with well-structured argumentation. Yet in this case, I don't believe it's the appropriate response. I believe the appropriate response to this cheap and nasty bait-and-switch is simply: "How *dare* you!?"

Nevertheless, if we deign to respond to such vile rhetoric with logic, it essentially goes like this:

Consider the President's position. By your logic, the only way to avoid being compared to one of history's worst genocidal maniacs would be to open the borders completely and allow everyone who wants access to pour through. This would have to be done in direct contravention of the oath he took to protect the nation he serves.

Don't screw around with Holocaust analogies. You do not get to dance on those graves.

So . . . who *does* "screw around" with Holocaust analogies? Here is just one example: Radical race-baiter the Reverend Jesse Jackson informed us that survivors of the Holocaust had been targeted "again" in 2000. Why? Because that year's Florida ballot was too complicated for a few thousand elderly voters. So . . . you know . . . Holocaust.

Additional Resource: *The Jewish News Syndicate* published a great article on what real incitement to murder actually looks like.[184]

---

184 Jonathan Tobin Jonathan, "What Real Incitement to Murder Looks Like, The Jewish News.com, July 12, 2020, https://thejewishnews.com/2019/08/16/what-real-incitement-to-murder-looks-like.

CHAPTER 25

CALL OUT THE UNSTATED PREMISES.

THE LIBERAL PROGRESSIVE LOVES NOTHING more than to point out prejudice. Yet their own use of prejudice as an unstated premise for their arguments can be extraordinary.

During Brexit, Britain's exit of the European Union, I recall several liberal commentators sadly shaking their heads at what was "obviously a step backwards." This is, at least, curious, when you consider that the point of the exercise was to regain sovereignty and be more free—to move *away* from tyranny and *toward* democracy.

Nevertheless, about the least vitriolic of the liberal commentary said, "The older voters got their way, and now the younger generation will have to live in this world they have created." The diatribes were often much more aggressively stated than that.

There are a number of assumed premises in these ideas, which were not openly stated, precisely because they are prejudiced notions. For instance:

- Young people are obviously clear-sighted, wise, and highly educated. Old people are obviously fearful, stupid, and backward-looking.
- Young people would have done the right thing for the country. Old people have obviously chosen the wrong thing for the country.
- Young people would have acted selflessly in the general interest of the greater good. Old people have been selfish and don't care about the greater good.

Every single thing about that is wrong. In any society, older people are generally more experienced, wiser, and better educated than the younger generation. They are also less radical and better able to perceive what actually works and what does harm in a society.

It is doubly wrong in this particular society, in which the older generation still remembers fighting the world's greatest war against tyranny for the very purposes of preserving civilization for the next generation. If they personally did not fight, they were raised by parents who passed these lessons on to them firsthand. They understand what is valuable and what should not be relinquished much better than the next generation. To accuse these people of acting selfishly is, frankly, disgusting.

Here is another example. In a now-famous video in which journalist Cathy Newman attempts to bait Professor Jordan Peterson, her fifth question to Peterson is: "Does it bother you that your audience is predominantly male? Isn't that a bit divisive?"[185]

There are several interesting problems with this question. First and most obviously, Peterson can't control who his audiences are. He doesn't choose them. *They* choose *him*. Possibly, the most useful response would be to turn the tables: "Why would that be divisive?"

But of interest to us here is the underlying assumption that a mostly male audience is inherently a bad thing. Why? Is this premised on the notion that men are bad? That having a largely male audience is suspect? There is an assumed prejudice here, and it informs her attack.

She is also assuming that there is active agency here. That this audience has somehow been designed. It hasn't. It is a purely reactive outcome. Nevertheless, it is hard to respond to an attack premised on an assumed prejudice when the Left keeps it under the covers. Our task, then, is to draw it out into the open, by saying it on their behalf. Here you can use the "So you're

---

185   Channel 4 News, "Jordan Peterson debate on the gender pay gap, campus protests and postmodernism," YouTube Post, 29:55, January 16, 2018, https://www.youtube.com/watch?v=aMcjxSThD54.

saying . . . " technique and complete the assumption out loud for them. This provides them with the opportunity to either correct or backtrack. If they simply deny it, they are already on the defensive and must find a creative new way to justify what they just said.

Either way, do not allow assumed premises to go unchallenged, particularly when they rest on the premise of bigotry against a demographic. And once again, you can use the act of pointing out their prejudice to change the framing, showing them to be the bigots.

CHAPTER 26

WHEN THE TRUTH IS PREVAILING, DON'T LET THEM SWITCH TRACKS.

"YES, BUT" IS THE FAVORITE technique of the debating progressive. There is something dishonest in the very phrase, which represents an opportunity for you. "Yes, but" is always employed after you have scored a direct hit. Your argument is cogent, logical, clear, and correct. Your opponent now has no choice but to respond with "Yes, but," and it will generally be followed by something that attempts to deconstruct the entire argument, such as, "Everything is really just a matter of opinion," or "How can we trust what we see?"

Let's take an example. Your opponent has attempted to make an equivalency argument, arguing that "all religions are the same." His specific point is that Christianity is responsible for just as much terror as Islam. You have read, or listened to, any one the following books about Islam:

- *The Politically Incorrect Guide to Islam (and the Crusades)* by Robert Spencer
- *It IS About Islam: Exposing the Truth About Isis, Al Qaeda, Iran and the Caliphate* by Glenn Beck
- *The Truth About Muhammad* by Robert Spencer
- *Preachers of Hate: Islam and the War on America* by Kenneth Timmerman
- *Religion of Peace? Why Christianity is and Islam Isn't* by Robert Spencer.

As such, you know several things. You know that there is no equivalent to Christianity's Golden Rule in Islamic teachings. The closest it comes is the assertion to treat your Muslim brother with fairness.

You also know that the violence in the Old Testament was limited by time and place, with such directives as, "Joshua, go into this place, and kill these people" (almost always as a result of their practice of child-sacrifice). The Qur'an, by contrast, teaches Muslims open-ended violence, exhorting them to use all means to spread terror until there is no religion but that of Allah.

Finally, you know that of all religious wars in history, Islam by itself is accountable for half of the death toll. You point out that the Crusades and the Inquisition were carried out under the authority of the Catholic Church, which forbade people from even reading the Bible. Christians in Europe fought a series of bloody wars to win back this right.

You point out these important key differences.

Your opponent says, "Yes, but Christians have owned slaves."

Your response should be: "Stop right there. Two things have just happened. The first is that you said yes. From this, I take it that we are now in agreement. We have established and agreed upon the idea that your original premise has been addressed and refuted. Contrary to what you said, Christianity is not responsible for as much terror as Islam. Then we can entertain your 'but.'"

If they refute this, you return to your original claims, asking, "Where did I lose you?"

Thereafter, you point out: "The second thing that happened is that you made a new proposal. Having failed at your first thesis, you introduced a brand new one, which was that Christians have owned slaves. This was dishonest on your part. What you've done is to throw mud, and then, when it didn't stick, to find different mud to throw.

"So let me ask you this in advance: After I dismantle your slavery premise, will you change the goalposts again? Will you throw more new mud? If so, can we save some time and permit you the opportunity to be more honest? What will be your next accusation after I've pointed out that your slavery thesis is wrong, too? And finally, the big question: If I can satisfactorily answer all of your charges and prove your theses to be factually wrong, will you change your mind on Christianity? If not, may I then point out that you are simply being a bigot? That you just hate Christianity?"

This technique rises out of the trenches of argument and becomes meta-argument: Arguing *about* the argument. You are pointing out that they are not acting in good faith. You are framing the issue, and you are setting the standards for the way forward. You are creating the conditions by which you will win.

Your interlocutor must attempt to do the opposite. He must attempt to de-frame the issue, usually by deconstructing all terms and conditions and causing the entire discussion to implode into relativism: "Well, it's all just a matter of opinion."

Your response is not to entertain this attempt. "No, it is not a matter of opinion. Real human beings live and die by these beliefs, and I have just demonstrated that there are qualitative differences between them."

A Note on Psychology: In *Explaining Postmodernism*, Stephen Hicks points out that the person arguing from politically correct principles is perfectly capable of cognitive dissonance. They do not mind that the facts do not support their claims. Instead, as taught by Foucault, they believe they are on the side of "greater truth," and not "facts."[186] They are, in other words, quite contentedly self-deceived, premised on their own notions of virtue.

Herbert Marcuse instructed them to use philosophy to achieve "the absolute annihilation of the common-sense world."[187] It is useful to know this. Calling it out may never persuade your interlocutor of their error—they are, again, contentedly aware of it—but it may indicate the absurdity of the position to an onlooking audience in the war for hearts and minds.

Side Note: Another liberal claim is that Muslim terrorists are a small minority. Liberals do not extend this courtesy to white males,

---

186 Hicks, *Explaining Postmodernism*, 2004.
187 Ibid.

who must all be tarred equally even in the face of a vanishingly small number of offenders. The best video debunking the notion of the radical Muslim minority is by Ben Shapiro on YouTube, with the title "The Myth of the Tiny Radical Muslim Minority."[188]

In *Rules for Radicals Defeated*, Jeff Hedgpeth also speaks about the liberal tendency to switch tracks when they are losing. He states:

> You will see this rule played out repeatedly on Twitter and virtually everywhere else a Liberal gets a chance to speak. One of the main ways this rule is used is subject-change. . . . When they're losing the argument in an area where you clearly have the upper hand, they simply pull out something that they are likely to know much more about. Whether it's relevant or not is beside the point. Their aim is not really to win a legitimate debate; it is to keep you on the defensive so they can preach their Liberal talking points as long as possible.[189]

(Remember this idea from earlier? Facts aren't important. It's deeper emotional "truth" that must be put into the foreground.)

Finally, here is *how* they pull out of debates, either when they are losing, or in advance of a debate that they feel they are likely to lose against a more skilled, more honest opponent. They will claim that even having a debate legitimizes the opposing point of view (that would be ours), and so they will not be participating. Respond to this by pointing out which of your premises stand and may now be considered unchallenged.

188 Ben Shapiro, "The Myth of the Tiny Radical Muslim Minority (Ben Shapiro)," 6:17, January 30, 2020, YouTube Post, https://www.youtube.com/watch?v=6L2Jilo3qmI.
189 Hedgpeth, *Rules for Radicals*.

CHAPTER 27

CALL OUT THEIR REASSIGNMENT OF BLAME VIA MISLEADING VISUALS.

IN 2016, GLOBAL FEAR OF Islamic terrorism was running hot. Against that backdrop, *Scientific American Mind* magazine ran a special on terror in their May/June issue. The headline read, "The Mind of a Terrorist," with the word *terrorist* written in enormous text over a man's face. The face was split down the center; one half was left open, and the other half was covered in a black balaclava, showing only the eyes. Yet there was something curious about that face. It was the face of a blond-haired, blue-eyed, Caucasian male. The cover did not specifically reference "white" or "right-wing" terrorism. Instead, this man was merely their selected representative for the concept of terror.

In 2016, the U.S. Department of State statistics show that the number of Islamic terror attacks carried out in just one nation, Somalia, was 359 in that year alone. The Global Terrorism Database concluded that "almost all of the human impact of extremist attacks is Muslims killing or injuring fellow Muslims."[190] Yet this was the editorial choice made by that publication.

This technique is insidious because it is not openly stated. It merely uses visuals to tell a deceptive story in the service of political correctness. Because there is no verbally stated lie to which we might respond, it is more difficult to engage with the implied lie.

---

190 Jack Herrera, "Most Terrorist Victims are Muslim," Pacific Standard Magazine.com, March 18, 2019, https://psmag.com/news/most-terrorist-victims-are-muslim.

Possibly the ugliest example of this was the infamous, and soul-tugging photo of the young, immigrant child washed up on a beach and the Syrian father weeping over his body. The reports implied that cruel Europeans had failed to help and that this was why the child had drowned. Played down, and sometimes not mentioned at all, was the fact that the beach was in Turkey.

At the very least, we can make it uncomfortable for people to continually make these implicitly dishonest choices by calling them out. At the time of the *Scientific American Mind* publication, I took a photo of this cover and posted it on social media with a comment something along the lines of: "You have to be at least this politically correct to work for *Scientific American Mind*."

This particular issue is not a debate, per se. Rather, it is a common dirty tactic, which duplicitously informs cultural norms, tacitly propping up political correctness. It only works if no one calls it out. For that reason, we should. Where it becomes extremely objectionable, we should do what we can do to defund such dishonest players and "vote with our money."

Here are some further ways in which liberals either reassign blame or simply pretend it away.

Take this headline: **"San Francisco board rebrands 'convicted felon' as 'justice-involved person,' sanitizes other crime lingo."**[191] That is merely a comical example of how liberals intentionally frame criminals as victims. Or at the very least, as non-criminals. But the dynamic runs deeper than that, and it is used in subtler ways.

In one of my previous books, *Poverty Proof—50 Ways to Train Your Brain for Wealth*, I begin by speaking about how there are two sets of narratives about poverty: the politically correct but untrue narrative and the "hard-to-hear" but economically true narrative.[192]

---

191   Lukas Mikelionis, "San Francisco board rebrands 'convicted felon' as 'justice-involved person,' sanitizes other crime lingo," FoxNews.com, August 22, 2019, https://www. foxnews.com/politics/san-francisco-board-adopts-new-language-for-criminals-turning-convicted-felon-into-justice-involved-person.

192   Douglas Kruger, *Poverty Proof* (Cape Town: Penguin Random House SA, 2019).

The politically correct one begins by assuming that no one on Earth is responsible for their own poverty. People are poor because of:

- Global warming
- Slavery
- Vaguely defined "oppression"
- Systemic discrimination
- Insufficient government intervention
- Plagues of locusts

Yet extensive research carried out by the Brookings Institution, a Washington policy think-tank, has revealed and repeatedly confirmed that the number one and number two determinants of poverty versus upward mobility have nothing to do with external factors. They are squarely personal choices.[193]

The top two determinants of upward mobility are:

1. Work ethic
2. Faithful maintenance of a family (as opposed to, say, having children out of wedlock).

These are choices. They have an internal locus. They are not externally inflicted. And yet, to even point out that these two issues affect wealth is often labeled as unkind to the poor.

I believe that approach to be deeply flawed and counter-productive. By not telling people which behaviors keep them poor, you may well spare their feelings, but you will deny them the most relevant information that bears upon solving their problem. If they are unaware of these facts, they may keep repeating the corresponding behaviors, thus only worsening their poverty.

That is not kindness. That is cruelty. It is also appallingly elitist, insofar as liberals assume that it is their place to manage the feelings of the poor and to decide what information they may and may not hear.

---

193 Ibid.

I am not the only one who finds this "kindness over truth" narrative flawed. As I mention in *Poverty Proof*, Isabel Sawhill, a senior fellow at the Brookings Institution and author of several books on wealth and poverty, has spent a lifetime studying social mobility. She has won numerous awards for her contributions. Isabel is convinced that personal choices surrounding marriage and work are *the* greatest determinants of upward mobility. Nevertheless, when she points this out, citing studies and statistics that prove it to be true, she is often surprised to find that she is attacked for being unkind to poor people.

Sawhill says that this liberal viewpoint is profoundly misguided. It ultimately does damage to poor people by denying them the truth. Once you know the truth, of course, you can act on it. Until then, you're simply floundering around in the dark, repeating mistakes that impoverish you, or worse, remaining dependent because you have been told that you are a perpetual victim. Sawhill refers to this problem of truth-versus-feelings as "ideology versus reality" and argues that the ideology isn't helping.[194]

There are also cases in which the liberal media play games with words in order to remove blame. On September 11, 2019, the *New York Times* commemorated 9/11 and spoke about "airplanes taking aim at the Twin Towers."[195] Sentience among airplanes must be a relatively new phenomenon. It used to be that terrorists would carry out such attacks, and the planes were merely their means.

And so, we see once again the liberal tendency to remove blame. In the case of offending criminals, it is absurd. In the case of people suffering social ills, such as poverty, it is elitist and cruel. In the cases of major terrorist attacks, it dishonors the innocent victims when you will not even identify the known perpetrators of their deaths.

---

194 Ibid.
195 Keith J. Kelly, "New York Times deletes tweet saying 'airplanes took aim' at towers on 9/11," NYPost.com, September 11, 2019, https://nypost.com/2019/09/11/new-york-times-deletes-tweet-saying-airplanes-took-aim-at-towers-on-9-11.

Debate Tip: Start by establishing shared goals: "Do we agree that lifting people out of poverty is a good idea? Are we both on board with that objective? Then let's ask what are the number one and number two determinants of poverty versus wealth. We have answers to this question, and it is the right thing to do morally to share these answers."

Tell black people they are perpetual victims.

Way back in the 1500s, Machiavelli had already asserted that the best way to control a group of people was to keep them dependent on you. Candace Owens sees this ruse in the liberal parties of today, particularly in America. She excels at pointing out its nuances and falsities on YouTube.

"His motives were unclear."

Similarly, when it comes to Islamic terrorism, we should utterly reject the limpid ploy by liberals and apologist newscasters, who offer us the flimsy: "His motives were unclear."

When a man shouts, "Allahu Akbar"—which means, "Allah is the greatest"—the chances are reasonably good that he is doing this for Allah. That is, by his own admission, his motive. Failing to hold him to his stated motive in the most dramatic act of his life, which may take his own life as well as that of others, is a gross travesty. It is also worth noting that such a man has specified which god he is referring to.

We have already seen how newscasters attempt to lump Islamic terrorism in with "right-wing" activities. They are equally fond of explaining that a man shouted "for God," while carrying out an atrocity. The correct translation is "for Allah." The terrorist himself would agree with this assessment and be offended by any other.

CHAPTER 28

DO NOT FALL FOR THE "SCIENCE" ARGUMENT WHERE NO SCIENCE IS PRESENT.

APPEALS TO SCIENCE APPEAL TO liberals. In their world, science is the ultimate arbiter; and to claim "It's science" is to settle an argument.

There are many problems with their use of the term, though, and it is easy to debunk this tactic.

Three of its most common applications are:

1. Abortion: "It's perfectly okay—it's just science."

2. Climate change: "The science is settled."

3. Gender: "It's a social construct."

Your broad response should be two-fold: "First, I will show you that what you are citing is not science. It is ideology. You are misusing the science label. Second, I will show you that when it comes to questions of human morality and ideology, all the most dangerous liars in history have used the phrase: "It's science."

"There's nothing wrong with abortion. It's science."

"Oh, look, gang! Science gets to decide upon human morality now! Here let me try: Humans are comprised of atoms made chiefly from carbon. Insofar as we cannot observe or measure a soul, there is no scientific reason that it would be 'wrong' to return this person to a state of disassociated matter, comprising the same atoms made up of carbon, especially if it's necessary for the greater good. See that? Everything about that statement is scientifically accurate. And I just used it to justify murder."

The trouble with science is that it has nothing to say about matters such as the intrinsic value of life, or the inviolable rights of an individual, or whether or not we actually have a soul (the impossibility of measurement renders no useful conclusion, which is not a conclusive outcome), or any other Judeo-Christian principle, refined in philosophy, war and experience over more than two millennia. No, science doesn't get to answer moral questions. And where it does, we run into problems in a hurry.

Objection: If it's science, how much damage could it really do?

Response: You sound an awful lot like those hundred million people who thought communism was science. It is *easy* to destroy human life by saying, "It's science."

Let us consider the specific issue of gender-theory. An article appeared on the website of mainstream family magazine *Living and Loving* on August 14, 2019. It asked, "Is this the lifestyle for you?"[196]

The parents who practice this trend are described as "forward-thinking." It cites a "growing pool of research," quotes a psychologist and then a study from the *Journal of Applied Developmental Psychology,* tells you all about the benefits of being a gender creative parent, and then concludes with five "quick and easy tips to raise a gender neutral child."

Doesn't it all sound so lovely? So kind? So inclusive? It is written in the form of a gentle invitation, which "might be right for you." It is all so very enlightened. So scientific. Except that it isn't. Instead, it is fraudulent and evil.

There are many, many things wrong with this article and with this topic. Let's consider six of them:

---

196 Kim Bell, "Gender neutral parenting, is this lifestyle for you?," Livingandloving.co, August 14, 2019, https://www.livingandloving.co.za/family/gender-neutral-parenting-is-this-lifestyle-for-you.

1. THE "SCIENCE" IS NOT SETTLED. NOT EVEN CLOSE. EXCEPT IF YOU LISTEN TO A HUMANITIES PROFESSOR.

Clinical psychologist Jordan Peterson observes that the social constructionist view of gender isn't just another opinion; it's wrong. He points out that to say that there's no causal relationship is palpably absurd, and that 99.7 percent of people who inhabit a body with a biological sex identify with that biological sex, so that the two are incredibly tightly linked.[197] [198] If you can't attribute causality to a link that tight, he reasons, then you would have to dispense with the notion of causality altogether, a problem for science at large.

Of the people who identify as male or female who are also biologically male or female, Peterson says that the vast majority have the sexual preference that would go along with that, and the gender identity and the gender expression. These levels of analysis are tightly linked, and the evidence that biological factors play a role in determining biological identity is overwhelming.

He asserts:

> There isn't a serious scientist alive who would dispute that. You get disputes about it, but they always stem, essentially, from the *humanities*. As far as I'm concerned—I looked at it very carefully— those arguments are entirely ideologically driven. It's a tenant of the ideology that identity is socially constructed, and that's partly why it's been instantiated into law, because there's no way they can win the argument but they can certainly win, let's say, the propaganda war, especially by foisting this sort of reprehensible advertising information on children. That's part of the express intent.[199]

So, here's our first distinction: What do you mean by "science"? If you mean real science, then no, the science does not prove a single claim in this

197 Thinkers, "Jordan Peterson - Gender taught as a social construct in schools: What to do?," YouTube Post, 7:38, October 26, 2018, https://www.youtube.com/watch?v=KGCN7OHeoqk.
198 The Unplugged Observer, "Jordan Peterson on Differences between Genders as Social Constructs," YouTube Post, 4:19, November 5, 2018, https://www.youtube.com/watch?v=IEq3HorOhfc.
199 Kimberly Morin, "Professor Obliterates the idea that Gender is a 'Social Construct,'" YouTube Post, 2:19, May 25, 2017, https://www.youtube.com/watch?v=yASbo5JRmnE.

regard. It overwhelmingly disproves it. But if you mean that a person with a Ph.D. in social sciences says it's okay, well, then, we have a different debate on our hands. And as Peterson rightly points out, it is not a scientific debate. It is an ideological debate, with a person who merely claims to be speaking on behalf of science. "Science," here, is wordplay.

Do you recall the opening lines of this book? "In the beginning, there was a bad idea. Sadly, no one squashed it. It invariably begins with a liberal professor in the university's department of sociology." People like Professor Peterson are trying to squash it. Sadly, the genie appears to be out of the bottle.

2. THE HISTORY OF THIS SCIENCE IS SO EVIL AND SO FRAUDULENT, THAT IF MOST PEOPLE WERE SIMPLY AWARE OF HOW IT DEVELOPED, THEY WOULD ABANDON THIS IDEA.

Meet John Money, one of the most evil and fraudulent scientists ever to cause societal-level damage to humanity. His starting hypothesis was what we hear today as settled fact—namely sex is biological, but gender can be socially conditioned. It is a "social construct."

Money attempted to test this theory, which he pulled from thin air, using an actual baby boy. The baby, one David Reimer, was the victim of a botched circumcision. Baby David's penis was burned off in the procedure.

John Money and the parents conspired to use this child as a test subject for his theory that a boy—any boy—could be raised as a girl. David's testicles were removed. He was put into a dress, which he ripped off the first few times, until he realized that his parents insisted, and so he continued wearing it under duress. They then raised him as a girl, renaming him Brenda.

David (or Brenda) had a twin brother, which maximized the experimental efficacy of the trial. As part of the "treatment," John Money had the two children interact in sexual ways with one another (yes, you read that correctly) and pose in provocative sexual positions in order to "teach them" the "appropriate" sexual modeling.

Money injected the boy with female hormones in order to make him more feminine. He also tried to force the little boy to urinate sitting down, something the boy refused to do.

The experiment was a disaster. It simply didn't work. Yet it was reported by Money as a great success and lauded as a breakthrough by the radical, Leftist, academic community. Yet at no point did David feel like he was a girl. He described himself as being unhappy with his Barbie dolls and wanting to play with his brother's masculine toys. Why? Because he was a boy.

David was in every way deeply unhappy with his female persona. At around the age of fifteen, after finally learning his own past, he told his parents that he wanted to go back to living as a boy. Watch documentaries of these parents talking about this, and you will see the father sincerely recalling how he asked "Brenda" if he was absolutely sure he wanted to make this change. (Change? The boy was a boy all along! He had to endure forced sexual encounters with his own brother, in a feminine role, in order to make him "Brenda" in the first place).

This bizarre case is still why gender theory exists in academia today. It remains the cornerstone of the entire argument and the founding of the statement: "Gender is a social construct."

How did this all turn out? David's brother, Brian, became schizophrenic, overdosed on pills, and died. David later killed himself by blowing off the top of his head with a sawed-off shotgun.

This is the controlled test case upon which the theory of gender as a social construct is based. This is its genesis and remains its founding and primary argument.[200]

Postmodernist author Judith Butler cites John Money in her book, *Gender Trouble*. The now accepted "gender as a social construct" or "gender as a free-floating artifice" finding gets baked into each new progressive academic book,

---

200 Ruse, *Fake Science*.

and so the ideas have continued to be piled on top of this evil and fraudulent edifice, as though its founding instance were actually true.[201]

As we have already seen, quite arguably the most horrifying aspect of this new trend is that when children do display signs of gender dysphoria early on, it usually disappears as they get older. That is, except if virtue-signaling liberals insist on forcing the issue by injecting their children with hormones that prevent the onset of puberty (how is that not child abuse?), and then surgically and irreversibly mutilate their genitalia. After all that, it is permanent and can't go away. Yet in many cases, it *would* have gone away, resolving itself, if merely left alone.

The science is now showing that the vast majority of children simply grow out of gender dysphoria tendencies, if left to do so, with some studies showing a 94% desistance rate.[202] By definition, this means that most gender-reassigned children were wrongly mutilated and wrongly committed to this course.

Again, I pose the question: Knowing this, how are these acts not classified as child abuse? There are plenty of doctors, physicians, and pediatricians who would respond, "They should be."

So, why don't doctors oppose it? Or why don't they do so more aggressively?

What happens when genuine scientists and ethical doctors who are not duped by progressive ideology point out the problems? Dr. Jordan Peterson became world-famous for refusing to tow the line on politically correct usage of pronouns. That already speaks volumes.

Dr. Kenneth Zucker, long-time editor-in-chief of the *Archives of Sexual Behavior* and psychologist-in-chief at Toronto's Center for Addiction and Mental Health, studied and worked with gender-confused children for years. Zucker and a team of researchers found that of the twenty-five girls they

---

201 Judith Butler, *Gender Trouble* (Milton Park: Routledge, 2006).
202 "Research on Children 'Growing Out' of Gender Dysphoria Adds Layer Of Complexity To Transgender Care," Kaiser Health News.org, May 24, 2018, https://khn.org/morning-breakout/research-on-children-growing-out-of-gender-dysphoria-adds-layer-of-complexity-to-transgender-care.

treated for gender confusion, only three still had gender identity disorder later in life. For this, he came under fire from the LGBTQ community. He was fired from his job. His clinic was shut down.

Political correctness won out by sheer bullying. The truth must not be allowed. Not even in "science."

"But don't actual brain scans show differences?"

No. The biggest meta-study of all the data on this topic, conducted by Lawrence Mayer and Paul McHugh and published in 2016, which combined the results of all studies and insights into mental difference or distinction, found "inconclusive evidence and mixed findings" concerning the brains of transgender adults. They describe the results as "conflicting and confusing," and not confirming.[203] So no, the science is not "settled." Right now, the science is not saying anything.

One of John Money's acolytes once claimed to have found a gene variant that supposedly determined transgenderism. Since then, there have been dozens of studies purporting to find that transgenderism is in the brain or that it is to be found in the genes. This is precisely the same as the ongoing attempts to find an elusive (read: "non-existent") gay gene.[204]

If you care for a little more detail, Mayer and McHugh also point out that none of these studies are methodologically sound. None of the studies are serial, longitudinal, or perspective. They are all simply "snapshots in time" taken of small groups, that may or may not have any relationship to the larger population.

These studies are on tiny numbers of people, they don't look at their subjects at regular intervals using the same criteria over the lifetime of the subject. The fact that there may be a difference in brain functioning or morphology at one moment in time does not prove innateness or causality.

All observed differences beg the question: Are these distinctions the *cause* of transgenderism or the *results* of it? These people are generally taking

---

203 Ruse, *Fake Science.*
204 Ibid.

hormones, behaving in scripted gendered ways, and so forth. The brain is plastic and will respond to these conditioning stimuli. Just as London cab drivers' brains are physically altered by their profession, are transgendered people "changing their own brains"? Probably. And even if not, the results are *still* "conflicting and confusing."

Mayer and McHugh conclude that the claims of certitude made by trans-gender advocates "cannot be supported with any scientific rigour." The consensus of scientific evidence "overwhelmingly supports the proposition that a physically and developmentally normal boy or girl is indeed what he or she appears to be at birth."[205]

In *Fake Science,* Austin Ruse points out that so-called "conclusive findings" presented at grade schools and on TV are "ideological journalism masquerading as science," and that these misrepresentations are damaging. Here, the title of this book applies: Political correctness certainly does do more harm than good.[206]

To this day, the trans-suicide rate is off the charts. Just shy of fifty percent of trans people try to, or successfully do, take their own lives. This is *why* gender dysphoria was classified as a mental disorder in the first place. These stats have not changed. So, why is gender dysphoria no longer a mental disorder? Because it is not politically correct to say so. Leftists put pressure on the World Health Organization, who, in turn, declassified it.

When people say, "It's science," *there* is the science on which gender fluidity is built. Child-abuse that led to suicide. I think the best debate technique is to have them look at their own evil. Recount the story of John Money.

It is worth noting, even the debauched and child-abusing Money nevertheless still believed that there were only *two* genders, which he took to be interchangeable. On top of his flawed science, gender theorists have now posited *infinite* numbers of "genders." These are the imaginary constructs of

---

205 Ibid.
206 Ibid.

ideologues in social studies departments. They bare no semblance to science; and when people call it science, they should immediately be called out for their false claim.

The Left, in this instance, is the party of pseudo-science. The "human" argument that they will present here is that the ends justify the means. Breaking down gender barriers makes it all worth it, even if this isn't science. Curiously, this "kindness" does not cause the trans suicide rate to go away.

Key learning? The hypothesis fails. Forcing people to go against their biological gender in a case study resulted in suicide. People who go down this route today overwhelmingly commit suicide.

Could there be something intrinsically important to a young girl about being taught to be a girl? Could there be something intrinsically valuable, even *critical*, to a young boy about being taught to be a boy? For millennia, we've known the answer to be yes. Now, faced with the opportunity to invite a fifty percent suicide rate into our children's lives, we glibly say no and run the counter-natural experiment on a societal level with our children as the guinea pigs.

Parents gladly volunteer their children for these experiments because it earns them social righteousness points among their liberal fellows. They are not even stopping to entertain the question, At what cost?—largely because "the science is settled."

If you will forgive a digression into personally felt emotion, "May God have mercy on our souls."

Debate Tip: When doe-eyed parents mention that they plan to raise a child genderless, your immediate response should be, "Aren't you worried about the suicide rate?"

Response: "What do you mean?"

"Well, do you know the history behind the idea that gender is just a social construct?"

This takes you straight to telling the John Money story, which leads into the suicide of his subjects, which was the study upon which this science was "settled." This then leads into the suicide stats in general.

End with the challenge: "What if there is something intrinsically important about teaching boys to be boys and girls to be girls? And what if failure to teach it leads to increased suicide rates, which all evidence shows *is* the case. What if denying maleness cues to boys and female cues to girls is deeply damaging to them, a denial of a fundamental psychological and physiological need, like denying them milk in their formative years? What if the human mammal requires this input? Why would you want to mess around with that?"

---

3. THE LOGIC IS EMOTIONAL.

"But my son *feels* like he is a woman."

"How does he know—having never actually been a woman? Also, what does it "feel" like to be a woman? Is there a measure? Show it to me."

It is circular reasoning to say that he knows what it feels like to feel like a woman because he feels like one. When the Left props up this idea, are they assuming that certain feelings are feminine? Perhaps softer feelings, such as those of kindness or nurturing? Does that reasoning not fall afoul of their own desire not to perpetuate gender stereotypes? And how do we arrive at the conclusion that a male cannot feel kindness or nurturing or any other feeling stereotypically deemed "female"? Has science proven that men's emotional range cannot accommodate such feelings? If gender is an artificial construct, then there can be no such thing as "what it feels like to be a woman" because they have dismissed that possibility as made up.

Here is an impossible contradiction for the Leftist: If maleness or femaleness is not biologically determined, not genetically determined, not chromosomally determined, and not determined by sex, then what on earth is a man or a woman anyway? A set of made up feelings? But that can't be the answer because those are subjective, and they themselves argue that they are artificial constructs of society. So, now we are left with *no such thing as a woman*. Yet clearly, there *is* such a thing as a woman.

The answer to the riddle is easy once you dismiss the stupidity and return to the truth. A woman is a biological female with two *x* chromosomes and female genitalia. A man is a biological male with *xy* chromosomes and male genitalia. And as for the subjective feelings? Those are called *feelings*. My two-year-old thought he was a dinosaur. He told me he *was* a dinosaur. He roared loudly and acted the role of a dinosaur. He was also wrong. The claim is imaginary.

4. THE "SCIENCE" IS NOT "SHOWING THAT THIS IS A GOOD IDEA."

Rather, your generation of children are the guinea pigs. We will find out in a decade or two whether this unnatural gamble with your child's development returns dreadful and lasting results.

5. THE CHILD IS BEING DENIED A CHOICE.

Goodness, how terrible! Yet when we know what is right for a child, we *never* give the child a choice. My infant son would like to drive my car. The answer is no. That's called being a parent.

Children don't get to choose what they eat or when. They don't get to choose the language they must speak. They poop themselves uncontrollably, and we clean them up. Helping a baby to develop (and to become what correctly becomes of ninety-nine point seven percent of people) is not abusive. It is correct.

Instead, to train a child away from what constitutes normalcy for ninety-nine point seven percent of people, in favor of a point three-percent margin, is *abnormal*. And that point three-percent margin? Up until 2019, the scientific community regarded them as having a mental condition called gender dysphoria.

What changed? Public pressure from politically correct activists. Did reality change? No. Did biology change? No. Did politics change? Ah, now we're on to something.

6. CATEGORIES ARE OF PARAMOUNT IMPORTANCE TO THE BIBLICAL DEITY.

Dennis Prager repeatedly illustrates in his *The Rational Bible* set of books that God is extremely interested in categorization and distinction: Night from day, male from female, life from death, good from bad, clean from unclean, and many more.[207]

For the Christian parent considering these issues, it is important to take the time to familiarize yourself with the nature and prescriptions of your own God. To Him, categories matter and for important reasons.

207 Dennis Prager, *The Rational Bible* (Washington, D.C.: Regnery Publishing, 2018).

CHAPTER 29

COUNTER THEIR ATTEMPTS AT EXTRAPOLATION.

REMEMBER THE FINAL ALINSKY TACTIC? Freeze a target in place while you take them apart.

Gay rights advocacy groups took this tactic one step further in February 1988, when 175 gay rights activists in America met in Virginia. Marshall Kirk and Hunter Madsen turned their public relations plan into a book, *After the Ball: How America will Conquer its Fear and Hatred of Gays in the 90's*. Note, already, the accusation of fear and hate built right into the title. It is not a moral issue, you see. It's an issue of fear and hate. They are already framing the debate.

Their marketing campaign proposed three primary ways to "sell" gay rights, three key techniques for manipulating attitudes:

1. Desensitization
2. Jamming
3. Conversion

Here is what each technique aims to do:

1. **Desensitization**—Relentlessly inundate the public with all things gay through advertising and media on the grounds that "if straights can't shut off the shower, they may at least eventually get used to being wet."[208] Seek desensitization, until they think that homosexuality is "just another thing."

---

208 Kupelian, *The Marketing of Evil.*

2. **Jamming**—Carry out a sort of psychological terrorism meant to silence dissenting opinion. Use outrage mobs, threats of boycott, and intimidation campaigns.

3. **Conversion**—Mainstream the behavior and insist it be treated as an equivalency.

For the purpose of this chapter, we are interested in number two: "Jamming."

Here is how this technique was used by gay rights activists in the real world: In 1998, a University of Wyoming freshman named Matthew Shepard was lured from a bar and severely beaten by two men. He died from his injuries days later. This hate crime was pure gold to the activists. Using the media extensively (and it is to be noted that the mainstream media played accomplice with predictable enthusiasm), they singled out conservative Christians and groups like Focus on the Family as being responsible for the young, gay man's death. Why? Because, as the activists explained, these groups had created an "atmosphere of anti-gay hate," and were, thus, personally culpable for the crime.[209]

This astonishing idea begins with blaming a non-active non-agent, who had no involvement in a situation, for the crime itself. It bypasses the critical legal notion of "innocent until proven guilty" and proceeds directly to "guilty," and it is perhaps the most incredible incarnation of concept creep you will ever witness.

These targeted groups:
- Did not encourage violence against gay men
- Did not participate in violence against gay men
- Were not present at the time of this crime
- Did not condone this crime after the fact
- Did not celebrate this crime after the fact
- Actively condemned the crime after the fact
- Disavowed violence of this nature

---

209 Kupelian, *The Marketing of Evil.*

- Do not prescribe acts of this nature as part of their policy
- Do not go onto media shows and encourage acts of this nature.

And yet gay advocacy groups tried them for this crime in a public forum, accompanied by great emotional outrage, and proceeded to find them guilty.

Once again, I submit my opinion that the modern notion of "Christians oppressing homosexuals" has it precisely backward. By a planned campaign, this was how homosexuals targeted and tarnished Christians.

This claim of guilt by virtue of existence is astonishing. And yet by contrast, when Israel or America are attacked by Islamic terrorists, these same liberal commentators will dismiss, as irrelevant, the Muslims dancing in the streets in celebration in places like Palestine. That, somehow, is not linked, and does not create an atmosphere of hate.

We saw the same dishonest trick played against U.S. President Donald Trump. Every crime committed by every lunatic was directly attributed to President Trump's "creating a climate of hate." Curiously, despite the record number of Islamic terror attacks on U.S. soil during President Obama's campaign and despite his open support of Muslims—"I will stand with my Muslim brothers and sisters"—the liberal media could not find it in their hearts to blame him for every crime, as they did for Trump.

Harkening back to the labeling chapter, we need an appropriate name for this ugly technique.

Debate Tip: Use this knowledge in reverse. When you see it being employed (for example, against Donald Trump), point out that this technique comes from the gay activism book *After the Ball.* Explain that it functions by honing in on a single event, extrapolating backwards, then blaming someone for "creating the climate." Then run through the list of "things the person being blamed did not do." Thereafter, if necessary, point out an equivalency by making up a crime for your opponent and accusing them of it. "You didn't actually do it; I know that. But I'm going to accuse you of it anyway, based on your own standards of legal jurisprudence."

CHAPTER 30

BEWARE THE PRECEDENT OF CODES OF CONDUCT.

RECALL HOW LIBERALS USED THE first amendment of the United States Constitution, which was intended to protect open practice of religion, to *ban* religion. They are very good at using codes of conduct. Indeed, they love and need rules and bureaucracy. An ever-growing government, with ever more rules to follow, props up their power.

Ryszard Legutko observes:

> The EU has become a major regulating power in Europe, and its politicians proudly state that they are responsible for 70% of the national legislation. This legislation is mostly unnecessary in view of the majority of the citizens, but necessary from the perspective of the European institutions. It confirms their power, regardless of whether it is beneficial for the people or not.[210]

In *Why Liberalism Failed*, Patrick Deneen notes that as liberalism expands, so, too, must government and its rules and restrictions.[211] For our part, this is useful to note in two ways:

1. I propose that we should be advocates of the original American conception of the ideal of small, limited government, which upholds law and infrastructure, but otherwise, pretty much gets out of the way. It is not there to do social engineering, or to rule our lives, or to tell us how to

---

210 Legutko, *The Demon in Democracy.*
211 Deneen, *Why Liberalism Failed.*

think. Indeed, it is supposed to have very little to say about our lives whatsoever. That is the tyranny of liberalism.

2. We need to appreciate that in spreading liberal tyranny, rules and institutions are the primary vehicle. Liberals tend to think "institutionally," whereas we tend to think "individually." Our great mistake is in permitting them to own the institutions and then grow their power through the expansion of rules.

We should be aware of this from the highest levels to the lowest: such as school board committees and attempts to bring in new codes of conduct.

It starts off innocuously: "My thanks to the school board for hearing me. I'd like to propose a code of conduct, by which we agree on acceptable norms for social conduct in order to foster mutual respect and a climate of inclusion."

When they say, "by which we agree on acceptable norms," what they really means is, "by which we agree on which norms are *unacceptable*," and thereby use the mechanisms against their opponents.

This use of reverse strategy can take another form: "I would like to propose a free-speech area." Translation: "I would like to propose that every place else be deemed a non-free-speech area."

It can escalate to mass denunciations. We have seen university professors organizing open letters and collecting signatures in order to condemn an individual, or demand the retraction of an idea (unchallenged, which is intellectually dishonest), or forbid a particular group from speaking: "Everybody, point at the witch!"

They create sets of rules, codes, and guidelines, as always, employing the "kindness" narrative, and then use those very rules to persecute the opposition. In a corporate company, this is enough to get conservatives fired. In a school, it is enough to introduce terrible ideologies and push out Judeo-Christian, Western values.

I believe it is important for our side to go to these committee meetings, point out the fallacies, block and reject the attempts at questionable new codes of conduct based on concept creep, and be an active part of how our schools, community organizations, corporate companies, and countries are run.

One simple response to these attempts is to tell the group: "This is a Herbert Marcuse technique. It creates the conditions for a downward slope. Let me explain."

For our purposes here, it is sufficient to note that this is a technique used by the Left and to make a choice to look out for and oppose it and to become actively involved in the institutions of community and democracy.

CHAPTER 31

CALL THE BLUFF OF UNPROVABLE CLAIMS.

HOW ABOUT THIS FOR AN audacious technique? When there is no oppressor present to create victims, just say that there is anyway. Tell people, "It's invisible."

As a labeling act, we might call this one the Left's "Tooth-Fairy Technique": "She exists! We promise she does!" The method itself is simple: Aim bad words at large systems. No proof is required. Just keep the terms so vague that they simply cannot be disproven.

It is most commonly witnessed in the following formulation: "America is inherently racist. It's not out in the open. Instead, it's covert. In fact, it is systemic. The entire legal system works (for example) against black people" (in an unspecified but "obviously racist" way).

The ideas of intrinsic, endemic, and systemic oppression, presented by straight-faced intellectuals and very sincere talking heads on TV, sound perfectly reasonable—until they are asked to point to the problem. Then it all falls apart.

Ben Shapiro excels at dismantling this narrative. He argues that he is *also* opposed to racism, and so he is volunteering to help. Just *point* to the racism. Don't merely say it's "systemic." Show us *where in the system* it actually is, so that we can get on with fixing it.[212]

---

212 Ben Shapiro, Ben Shapiro DEBUNKS Viral 'Systemic Racism Explained' Video, YouTube Post, 17:49, June 10, 2020, https://www.youtube.com/watch?v=TBDfMQ27Asw.

Let me give you an example of this dynamic drawing on an unusual source for our example. We will be considering the lyrics from Queen's "Innuendo." This song is a perfect example of aiming bad words at big systems.

Consider this stanza:

> While we live according to race, color or creed
> While we rule by blind madness and pure greed
> Our lives dictated by tradition, superstition, false religion
> Through the eons and on and on . . . [213]

It is a great song. But boy, does it fail the basic truth-test!

"While we live according to race, color or creed." Sounds dreadful! So, point to how we live according to race or color or creed. Name the law. Identify the institution. Point to the clause. Can you find a single one?

"While we rule by pure madness and blind greed." Goodness! What a curious way to describe, say, parliamentary procedure or how constituents of a democracy vote.

"Our lives dictated by superstition . . . " *Which* superstition dictates our lives? What is it forcing us to do? How is it currently evading our legal systems? What incentivizes us to keep following it, and who are its proponents?

The words are all high-sounding; the pronouncements are all grand. By the weight of sheer declarative conviction alone, the concepts therefore seem inherently true—until you begin to pick at them, at which point they descend into little more than Leftist poetry.

---

213 Queen, *Innuendo*, 1991, Innuendo, Parlophone, 1, 1991, CD.

CHAPTER 32

VOTE WITH YOUR MONEY.

MOST OF THE RESPONSES WE have considered to this point have been intellectual in nature. However, there are further strategies that we can apply against the ills of political correctness.

For instance, when advertisers attempt to ram Leftist ideology down our throats via advertising messages, we can boycott them. We can vote with our money.

In 2018 and 2019, Gillette tried to go this route. Their opening salvo was to pick on "toxic masculinity," with an advertisement that encouraged men to "shave away" the bad behaviors. Men in the ad were portrayed in such a gross light and fundamental maleness so maligned, that I tossed my own Gillette products into the bin that day. I haven't bought and will not buy one of their products again.

Shortly thereafter, they went a step further. Their next advertisement featured a young, transgender man's first shave. The result? Gillette then hemorrhaged a whopping twelve billion dollars in revenue, after which they quietly said that they will likely avoid social justice issues in the future.

So, this technique works. The message, which we can actively send to ideologues in advertising, is: "Go woke; go broke."

I note in passing that this outcome reinforces my stated belief that the PC police are not (to their own surprise) in the majority, but rather, they are a very vocal minority.

For my own part, I will no longer permit my own money to support Nike. UNESCO is another entity that my wife and I used to support, but no longer do, on the grounds of their vilification of Israel. Netflix has come under fire by Christian conservatives as well, for using their brand and financial power to bully Georgia, in the face of that state's attempts to limit abortions.[214] Shortly thereafter, their subscription numbers trended downward for the first time in their history, as a result of canceled contracts.

Voting with your money hurts Leftist causes. It is extremely effective, particularly if you state your reasons in public and encourage others to do the same.

---

214 Sonia Rao, "Netflix becomes the first major Hollywood studio to speak out against Georgia's abortion law," The Washington Post.com, May 28, 2019, https://www.washingtonpost.com/arts-entertainment/2019/05/28/netflix-becomes-first-major-hollywood-studio-speak-out-against-georgias-abortion-law.

CHAPTER 33

LOVE THE PLANET; DON'T FALL FOR THE IDEOLOGY.

POSSIBLY CONSPICUOUS FROM THIS BOOK so far is the issue of environmentalism and its poster child, global warming. The arguments back and forth on this issue are, frankly, tiresome. There is science proving the phenomenon of global warming. There is science disproving it. There are arguments that it is occurring, but that it is part of a natural meta-cycle and that mankind's negative contribution is dismissible as minimal. There is also conflation between damage to the environment—such as littering, which the majority of conservatives would actively oppose—and global warming, which is not the same thing as environmental damage.

This is my take, and I suggest it as a very simple, but—I believe—very reasonable stance:

1. We are supposed to be good stewards and faithful custodians of the planet. That makes scientific sense. It is also a Judeo-Christian value. Finally, it is simply common sense. You can't destroy the place where you live and continue to live there. And excellent stewardship is a virtuous worldview by any standard.

2. It does not logically follow that we should surrender our rights and powers to big government. The socialist element of this argument proposes that we submit to an over-arching governance structure, conceding what were previously self-governing democracies to larger, non-democratic superstructures, in which unelected bureaucrats have

access to all the money and all the power. That is a path to tyranny, and it is also not a solution to environmental damage.

Being a good custodian of the planet is an excellent idea and a value worth teaching to our children. But when presented as a false dichotomy— "The planet is dying! We need socialism!"—the formula is dishonest, at least.

Bowing to fear-mongering of the order spread by politicians like Alexandra Ocasio-Cortez—"We only have twelve years left to save the planet!"—must be held to be a sign of intellectual weakness.[215] As such, her ilk do genuine environmentalism no favors.

Perhaps what troubles me most about the environmental message is when it becomes radical, anti-human, immune to facts, or religious. These we should not permit either.

I recall watching a cartoon with my son. The main characters were anthropomorphized animals. In one emotionally charged scene, one of the characters, observing environmental damage, turned to another and said, "I *hate* these humans!" "Yeah," the other replied. "Me, too."

That was when the channel was changed. I will not have my child indoctrinated into hating his own. That's a liberal quality, and not one for us.

"People are a plague."

"Just to be clear, you are now proposing genocide? If you could kill us all and remove that plague, would *you* press that button? Or are you the sort of elitist who thinks that only *some* people should be disposed of? If so, who? And who decides? It's fun to play God with people's lives, isn't it? To be sure, every genocidal maniac in history has rather enjoyed it. Why shouldn't you?"

---

215   Andrew Freedman, "Climate scientists refute 12-year deadline to curb global warmng," Axios.com, January 22, 2019, https://www.axios.com/climate-change-scientists-comment-ocasio-cortez-12-year-deadline-c4ba1f99-bc76-42ac-8b93-e4eaa926938d.html.

CHAPTER 34

TEACH YOUR CHILDREN THAT THE LEFT'S ENTIRE TACTIC IS RIDICULE.

PSYCHOLOGIST NICHOLAS HUMPHREY ARGUED IN a lecture that just as Amnesty International works to liberate political prisoners around the world, secular teachers and professors should work to free children from the damaging influence of their parents' religious instruction.

Philosopher Richard Rorty argued that secular professors in the universities ought to do all they can to discredit religion and added that parents who send their children to college should recognize that "as professors, we are going to go right on trying to discredit you in the eyes of your children, trying to strip your religious fundamentalist community of dignity, trying to make your views seem silly rather than discussable."[216] Good to know. Thank you for your honesty.

Liberal nations are hardcore about this goal. A friend who relocated his family to hyper-liberal Canada related to us: *"Goal number one* for their educational system is to teach children atheism. They're aggressive about it. It's like that's the entire point, and that's the thing they have to achieve. They drum it into them. Everything else is incidental."

---

216 Vox Day, *The Irrational Atheist: Dissecting the Unholy Trinity of Dawkins, Harris, And Hitchens* (Dallas: BenBella Books, 2008).

Okay, but do they have a point?

Let us play devil's advocate. If science genuinely disproved the existence of God, then would it not make sense to teach atheism to children from Day One? It may hurt feelings, but aren't we interested in pursuing the truth? That is a valid observation, which hinges on one contingency: *Does* science actually disprove God?

In our final chapters, we will explore the Anthropic Principle, derived from the field of physics and taught to us by astronomers. The Anthropic Principle is such a compelling scientific proof of intelligent design that radical atheists of a scientific bent have a problem on their hands. They are now faced with a need to explain away God. The science points squarely in His direction and has, to date, been impossible to disprove. Should we therefore indoctrinate our children into a belief-system based on the science? I am tempted to say yes. And the science is overwhelmingly pointing toward God. So, by all means, let's teach that.

Atheists are, in fact, so desperate to explain away this problem that leading thinkers like Stephen Hawking have even fallen into some fantastical traps of thinking. Hawking has proposed something he calls "imaginary time," in order to make God go away. We will see why later on. With imaginary time, new universes can pop in and out of black holes with no beginning and no end—a necessary condition if your goal is to make a Deity disappear.

There are two problems with imaginary time:

1. It has never been observed and cannot be tested.
2. Hawking did not derive it from observable phenomena or even infer it from plausible principles. He made it up. And he made it up based on his political agenda, in order to achieve an emotionally desired outcome. The only place where imaginary time actually exists is within the imagination of Stephen Hawking.

Based on this kind of "science," luminaries like Hawking assure us that there is no God and bring their influence heavily to bear on the educational system, forcefully urging us to teach atheism to our children as official school policy. When people use science of this poor ilk to declare that such important issues are now settled, we really should be encapsulating that word in inverted commas. And frankly, those little air-bunnies should extend to the horizon in either direction.

Just consider the gall of inventing imaginary time in order to disprove the science that proves God. And then on the strength of that, telling the world that the issue is resolved. Hawking's theory here is quite indistinguishable from magical thinking. And his conclusion is a fallacy of malicious proportions.

Still, our children tend to naturally fear and reverence authority figures. Schools that favor atheism will play on that, and particular Left-leaning teachers will play heavily on it.

They are informed by credentialed intellectuals like Hawking, and they will not hesitate to bring the intimidating force of the entire educational superstructure to bear upon your children's "unacceptable" beliefs. This is intimidating for a child. It is difficult for them to hold onto the idea that they might be right (as science actually indicates) in the face of such unyielding, authoritarian scorn.

Therefore, it is imperative to teach them that bad authority figures exist, that big people can be wrong—very wrong—yet simultaneously very sure of themselves, and that they *will* face such scorn; it is the nature of this cultural war. Their teachers and professors *will* mock, and they will probably refuse to actually engage with the counter-arguments, which is intellectually dishonest and, frankly, points to a teacher who does not understand the role of teaching.

Instruct your children ahead of time that this is dishonest on the teacher's part and that mockery and moral posturing are not the same thing as being right, no matter how confidently the mocker carries himself and no matter how much he calls you a sheep.

Your children need to be mentally tough enough to understand that being derided is not the same thing as being wrong. In fact, derision is just intellectual bullying. That's what the *bad* guys do, and it is one of the ways you can identify them.

In stark contrast to the atheist paradigm about the discussion of beliefs ("mock them; shut them down"), here is what the biblical apostle Peter said on the same topic: "But sanctify the Lord God in your hearts, and always be ready to give a defense to everyone who asks you a reason for the hope that is in you, with meekness and fear" (1 Peter 3:15). That actually sounds a lot more scientific to me. And a lot more respectful.

And the big tech giants are leading the charge.

In 2018-2019, a commission for journalistic integrity called Project Veritas busted Google for a systematized, institutionalized bias in favor of so-called "progressive" liberals and specifically against conservatives, whom the Google executives expressly say must be stopped. Google executives apparently feel that it is their duty to do this.[217]

This is in direct contravention of their legal status as a mere platform, a status which provides them with certain exemptions. The moral of the story: they are not legally entitled to guide or frame the narrative according to any political bias. Yet they do.

After the Google executive was recorded making these comments and after an inside whistle-blower leaked documents confirming this policy, Google got hauled before the U.S. Congress. Responding to these allegations, the representative casually admitted that she hadn't read the report before appearing to testify. Why? Because, in her words, "she has a day job." Here is the mockery and dismissive tone, applied at the highest levels.[218]

So, no big deal, then. Just the culture-framing policies and norm-perpetuating viewpoints of most of the world at stake. *Meh.* Of particular interest

---

217 Maddie Crichton, "Project Veritas and Politicians Accuse Google of Anti-Trump Bias," Roguerocket.com, June 27, 2019, https://roguerocket.com/2019/06/27/project-veritas-and-politicians-accuse-google-of-anti-trump-bias.
218 BlazeTV, Sen. Ted Cruz GRILLS Google Exec on Political Censorship," YouTube Post, 5:18, June 25, 2019, https://www.youtube.com/watch?v=Dx2wjCz4SyY.

to me was how they perceive and construct their notion of "fairness." It is not the same as what we might understand by the idea. In a video published on this same scandal by commentator Glenn Beck, we learn that *their* understanding of fairness is not centered around truth or accuracy. It is centered around IDENTITY. Specifically, fairness to them means elevating the voices of those who are marginal, while suppressing the voices of those in power. That is a radically different interpretation of the concept. It is tribal, rather than truthful. It is also Marcusian.[219]

The conclusion is this: You can have political correctness, or you can have truth. But by the Left's own standards of fair-play, you cannot have both.

---

219   Ibid.

CHAPTER 35

LEARN HOW TO DISTINGUISH THE FOOT SOLDIERS FROM THE HIGH PRIESTS.

LIBERALISM IS DEPENDENT ON A certain relationship. Understanding that relationship helps us to perceive the whole ideology more effectively. The relationship is that between policy-prescribing high priests and their ideological foot soldiers. There are the puppet-masters and the torch-bearers, the gurus and the acolytes—pick your metaphor. This structure is necessarily the case because the enterprise springs from a crisis of faith. In the absence of guiding lights, progressives must create their own or feel lost in the universe.

At the genesis of all totalitarian systems is this desire for "someone bigger to take care of me." It is the seed of the welfare state, the wellspring of communism, the birthing condition of national socialism.

Most Left-leaning individuals you will meet are not priests. They are puppets. Their task is to validate the expert elites and to provide followers. As for the elites, they cannot exist other than upon the power granted by followers.

Why does it matter to know this? It alters psychology. When you are debating with the foot soldiers, you should know a few things about them. They are insecure about their place in the universe. They desperately want to be right. They want reliable guides who can show them the way, and they are scared when their foundational beliefs are rattled. They are, in every sense, the frightened child who needs a parent.

The priests are different. Here we are not dealing with earnest and searching insecurity, but arrogance. These people take delight in showing others the way. The "way" changes all the time, but their sophistry helps them to show why they are ever right and how important it is that you follow them.

The first group can be won over. They are earnestly seeking human beings. They have an undefined need, which they are trying to fill by following the priests. They may still be open to hearing the truth.

The second group are dangerous. They are reinforced by their own narcissistic sense of certainty, and they exist in mutually-congratulatory echo chambers, where they may rub rarified elbows and congratulate themselves on intellectual superiority and indisputable correct-think.

The great danger in the face of this latter group is that we treat them as they wish and, indeed, *expect* to be treated—with reverence. Their opening play will be to claim the "authority ground," to position themselves in the role of the parent. That is what they do. If we fall for it, we respectfully diminish ourselves into the position of politely inquiring child: "But don't you think that maybe . . . ?"

This is the wrong approach. When authority is constituted on factual error or manifest deceit, we do not grant that authority the respect it craves. We may speak civilly to such a character, but we also speak as if in the presence of an intellectual bad smell, not a beacon of reason.

When approaching these situations, I want you to learn to think, speak, and act as though you are the adult and the high priest is the misguided child. It changes everything.

Liberal: "Aren't you open to learning?"

Implications: I'm obviously right, you're obviously wrong, and I am trying to help you.

Response: "How astonishingly condescending. You are factually incorrect but attempting to speak as though you had moral authority. Or credibility. Yes, I am open to learning, but not from someone as misguided as you. Here is what is wrong with your proposal . . . "

The phrases they will use will range from the patronizing to the outright hostile. The body language and smirk are part of it, too. From the time of Moses, the high priests have had their snakes and their mirrors, and they have known how to position themselves as legitimate and to whisper and hiss with just the right drama. Their entire aura is based on theater. It is all a positioning technique. See through it. Calmly speak the truth, as an authority correcting a child. You are the adult. You are the one speaking the truth. All they have are academic words, scary voices, intellectual airs, and dramatic lighting. For someone armed with the truth, it's not that much, after all.

Remember, Saruman, the corrupt wizard, spoke with the incontestable tones of ancient wisdom and the certainty of dark force. But he was wrong. And the little Hobbits won in the end anyway.

CHAPTER 36

DON'T LET THEM USE SIMPLE INSISTENCE AND ACT AS THOUGH THEY HAVE ALREADY PREVAILED.

IN SOUTHERN AFRICA, THE NATION of Rhodesia underwent a liberation struggle, then renamed itself Zimbabwe. A Marxist-Leninist and African nationalist by the name of Robert Mugabe came to power. The nation began its slow descent into the bowels of hell.

Few countries have ever experienced such a dramatic devaluation of currency, other than where similarly Marxist national experiments were conducted, such as in Venezuela. And in Zimbabwe, as in Venezuela, the police and military were regularly deployed to quell and subdue the population. Leftist policies, in the hands of an African dictator, made for a potently anti-human mix.

I will never forget a simple thing that I personally saw in the early 2000s, when living conditions in Zimbabwe were comparable to those of any war zone. It was a state-sponsored t-shirt, proudly worn by a surprising number of Zimbabweans, emblazoned with the legend: "Mugabe was right!" And that was the complete argument. He was right. That's all.

The Left is immune to truth. Their own failure does not matter to them. It does not even reduce the energy behind the arrogant smirk. Disproving every one of their arguments, one by one, rarely converts them, and their abysmal track record is no catalyst for an altered course in their politics.

This resistance to useful feedback is not merely a deficit; it rises to the level of technique. They don't argue over wins and losses. They simply act as though everyone has already agreed that they have won the culture wars, and they display surprise when you don't comply.

We see this from the big things—"Mugabe was right!"—down to the small things:

- "What do you mean you don't want our kindergarten to do a day trip to a mosque? Why ever not? Don't you know that multiculturalism has won?"

- "Well, obviously we need to include everyone's culture." In other words, everyone's but our own, and so we will act as though we have tacitly agreed that our values don't matter, and we will vacuum our identity out of this institution in order to invite their norms to prevail.

It is only obvious that their conclusions follow if we permit it to be obvious that their conclusions follow.

Like many people born on that continent, I was saddened to see South African President Cyril Ramaphosa publicly hail Mugabe as a "gallant leader" upon the latter's demise in 2019. As my friend Shelley Walters put it: "Sometimes political correctness is a moral mistake."

PART III
HOW TO UNRAVEL THE FOUNDATIONS OF THE PROGRESSIVE LEFT

IN THE PREVIOUS SECTION, WE elaborated on the most common tactics, techniques, and attacks by the Left; and we explored ways of disproving, debunking, and defending against them.

In section three, we will now take a very quick look at a few more common Leftist tactics; and while I will not go into great detail on each of them, I will at least point you in the direction of strong responses. By now, it is my hope that you perceive the recurrent underlying patterns and themes and that you will already be able to unravel just about any of their arguments.

After that, we will attempt to do something dramatic. We will consider whether it is possible to prove the existence of God. Why? Because if it is, then every progressive argument that proceeds after the "crisis of faith" can be dismissed wholesale, as fatally flawed from its genesis.

Finally, I will provide you with some personalities to follow and a few suggestions for the way forward.

Let us begin by considering some additional Leftist arguments and brief responses to them:

Quick solutions to other PC problems:

1. Don't accept points on the calendar as arbiters of morality.

This technique is most commonly employed in the abortion argument.

Objection: "I can't believe we're even discussing this in 1990 . . . or 2015 . . . or 2025!"

Response: Why? Do dates determine the morality of murder? Is the calendar the appropriate arbiter of morality?

Analogous argument: "In the 1920s, communists spoke with great and arrogant scorn and sweeping pride about how 'only a fool, or the unscientific, could believe in the outdated and disproven notions of capitalism today. All history is inevitably moving toward communism. It's obvious. It's science."

Response: You are merely the next generation of liberals to pull the arrogant "calendar proves our morals" fallacy.

2. "That's cultural appropriation!"

Professor Jordan Peterson observes that there is no difference between cultural appropriation and learning from one another. They are the same thing. He makes the argument in detail here in a YouTube video titled "Jordan Peterson – The idea of cultural appropriation is nonsense."[220]

Furthermore, imagine this scenario: An Arab in the Middle East sets up a lab in order to practice "Western" science. We immediately shut him down. "Ah, that's cultural appropriation. You're being a racist. No science for you!"

3. "We celebrate pride."

Response: "What a strange quality to celebrate. Would it not be better to celebrate humility?"

Well, support us anyway.

---

220 Bite-sized Philosophy, "Jordan Peterson – The idea of cultural appropriation is nonsense," YouTube Post, 4:42, March 18, 2017, https://www.youtube.com/watch?v=NNUcR-eMxaE.

"No. I don't celebrate *anyone's* act of copulating. That would seem to me to be a private matter for sharing between two people, not something to brag or hold a parade about. We think sex is meaningful and important. So much so, we actually believe it is sacred, not for parading about in the streets."

"What's the difference between you and the Alt-Right?"

A great deal. Actually, there are more similarities between the Left and the Alt-Right than there are between conservatives and either of these groups. Both of these groups emphasize group-over-individual. The Left emphasizes "victim" groups. The Alt-Right emphasizes racial groups. Conservatives emphasize individuality and principles, and don't care about race.

For an excellent YouTube video explaining these differences, search "What is the Alt-Right?" by PragerU.[221]

4. *"The government must do something."*

Let us conclude our examples with this one, which is possibly one of the most common, and simultaneously, most invisible beliefs that encourage Leftist politics. It is the assertion that every time anything happens, government should respond. Most of us, including many conservatives, hold this belief without ever really thinking about it. Yet the call for government always to respond logically has one end: it can only result in increased government control. Collectivist tyrannies are the greatest existential threat to our worldview. They become the legalized and deputized will of political correctness. And their track record for both failure, and genocide, is breath-taking.

For excellent explorations of why it is a bad idea to constantly call on governments to "do something," try any book by Dr. Thomas Sowell or pick up *The Tyranny of Experts* by William Easterly, which focuses on how governmental aid and development programs consistently do more harm than good.

---

221 PragerU, "What Is the Alt-Right?," YouTube Post, 4:46, October 26, 2017, https://www.youtube.com/watch?v=MHXLoowY3nY.

THE FINAL ARGUMENT

Proving God

"An honest man, armed with all the knowledge available to us now, could only state that in some sense, the origin of life appears at the moment to be almost a miracle, so many are the conditions which would have had to have been satisfied to get it going."

—Francis Crick OM FRS
British molecular biologist, biophysicist, and neuroscientist

At the beginning of this book, we saw that politically correct arguments have their genesis in atheism. I pointed out that you do not need to be a practicing theist to successfully defend Western values. You can be an atheist and see the value in the Western tradition.

But if you do believe in God, here is an interesting question: Can you successfully argue for His existence? That, after all, is the departure point for all progressive politics: "No God" equals "crisis of meaning," equals "postmodernism," equals "Marxism," equals modern-day progressive "political correctness."

So, what if you could ward off the entire argument by *proving* God? The entire edifice of their strange beliefs implodes if, indeed, these ten words are proven to be true: "In the beginning, God created the heavens and the earth" (Gen. 1:1).

It is not the point of this book to proselytize. If you are atheist and do not wish to enter into discussions of God, and if you feel you are now adequately equipped to argue against political correctness, then by all means, stop here. Thanks for traveling with me.

However, insofar as all of these arguments rest on progressives' certainty that there is no God and, hence, that all morality is arbitrary and socially constructed, it makes sense to end our discussion by demonstrating that neither science nor logic nor the latest evidence from physics in any way supports the progressive claim. If anything, it supports the theist worldview.

The latest developments in astro-physics and the latest insights into DNA do more to *necessitate* the existence of an intelligent Creator than to dismiss one.

Moreover, the arguments leveled against a "flawed and morally arbitrary" Old Testament and the Old Testament God are actually easy to answer. In every case, you will find that the answers indicate that not only is the Judeo-Christian God *not* a capricious and unpredictable Entity, but rather, that His laws, ideas, and moral innovations are universalizable, coherent, and non-contradictory.

Two quick examples:

1. "The principle of an eye for an eye is brutal!"

No, it is not. This new idea was the genesis of our modern, legal notion of *proportionality*. It is supremely important and represented a critical moral revolution for humanity.

Prior to this moral innovation from the Torah, tribes and clans would amplify violence for any and every slight. Retribution was driven by honor at the very least, and rage at the very worst. The biblical injunction mitigated against these problems and limited recourse to proportionate justice only, thereby creating the framework for modern law. "You're welcome!" If you had never thought of it that way, does that not say something interesting about a modern, liberal education?

2. "The creation story is simplistic."

And yet, it created the conditions for the possibility of all science. In ancient, pagan cultures, the sun was almost universally revered as a god. By contrast, in the first words of Genesis, the Hebrew God asserts that the sun and moon are "lamps," to light the day and night. This was revolutionary in religious texts. Not only is this view factually accurate, but it disavowed the Jews of pagan notions of nature-worship.

The sun was a mere thing that performed a particular function. It was not magical, and it was not to be reverenced. Instead, it followed ordered patterns of behavior, set forth by God. Coupled to this idea is the notion that man is made in the image of God. Hence, man can use his reason to discern the patterns and rules underlying God's creation in an ordered and predictable universe. *Et voila*: the necessary conditions for science, from this book and no other.

It is also worth noting: The Bible is the only ancient religious document that posits an absolute beginning for all things, congruent with our understanding of the Big Bang. Fascinatingly, the Big Bang, which we have known about for less than a century, also answers the question: "How could 'light' *precede* the creation of the sun in the biblical account?" For nearly three thousand years, this was a theological problem, until science caught up and solved it, like this: "Let there be light! Bang!" And then later, the sun was formed. This account agrees with the scientific timeline. It is also the *only* creation myth that agrees with the scientific timeline. No other religious document posits a "bright light" followed later on by the creation of stars. It is almost as if this particular God was there when it happened.

In the following chapters, I will briefly summarize the leading scientific arguments for the existence of an intelligent Designer. If you are convinced by these arguments, then the logical next question becomes: *Which* God?

The God of the Judeo-Christian tradition, the prime target of political correctness, is the God on which the entire Western tradition is premised. This God is often dismissed by progressives by the application of modern, politically correct standards to His portrayal in the Bible, particularly in the Old Testament.

I will never forget hearing a person who claimed to be a "progressive Christian" (which I hold to be a contradiction in terms) describing the God of the Old Testament as "just an angry, tribal, village god." (This great intellect had apparently not worked out that in dismissing the God of the Old

Testament, he dismissed this God's predictions of a Messiah-to-come, and thus unraveled his own religion).

So, is the God of the Old Testament dismissible as too petty, too small, too illogical, too biased, too capricious, and too *provincial* to qualify as Almighty God? I will demonstrate that not only do the leading arguments used by politically correct revisionists not adequately dismiss this God as God, but in fact, the instances to which they point actually affirm the perfection of the Old Testament Deity.

No small task. So, with that, let's dive in.

Proving God from Science:

1. THE ARGUMENT FROM THE STARS: THE ANTHROPIC PRINCIPLE

> *"The anthropic principle is the most theistic result ever to come out of science."*
>
> —Robert Jastrow
>
> American astronomer and planetary physicist, NASA scientist
>
> and popular author

The prevailing scientific worldview around the origin of life used to be: "It just happened," or alternatively, "It happened that way because it *had* to happen that way."

But over the past few decades, scientists have begun to understand just how complex and sensitive a nexus of conditions had to occur in order to permit the origins of life on Earth. It turns out that there was no "logical necessity" for life to arise. Instead, given how many things had to happen, just perfectly and just so, the fact that it arose at all defies belief and points to an intelligent Designer.

ReasonableFaith.org puts it this way:

> The universe appears, in fact, to have been incredibly fine-tuned from the moment of its inception for the production of intelligent life on Earth at this point in cosmic history. In the various fields of

physics and astrophysics, classical cosmology, quantum mechanics, and biochemistry, various discoveries have repeatedly disclosed that the existence of intelligent carbon-based life on Earth at this time depends upon a delicate balance of physical and cosmological quantities, such that were any one of these quantities to be slightly altered, the balance would be destroyed and life would not exist.[222]

In other words, life didn't just happen. The chances of life arising would be like winning a lotto in which the odds were trillions and trillions to one, against. And yet, somehow, Life won, and here we are.

When you understand the immense significance of the Anthropic Principle, this very fact—that there is life—beggars credulity. So much so that scientists, atheist or otherwise, even make cautious utterances like this one from Stephen Weinberg, American theoretical physicist and Nobel laureate in physics:

All my experience as a physicist leads me to believe that there is order in the universe. . . . As we have been going to higher and higher energies and as we have studied structures that are smaller and smaller, we have found that the laws, the physical principles, that describe what we learn become simpler and simpler. . . . The rules we have discovered become increasingly coherent and universal. . . . There is a simplicity, a beauty, that we are finding in the rules that govern matter that mirrors something that is built into the logical structure of the universe at a very deep level.

Eugene Wigner, Hungarian-American theoretical physicist and mathematician, and Nobel Prize winner, writes in his essay *The Unreasonable Effectiveness of Mathematics in the Natural Sciences,* "The first point is that the enormous usefulness of mathematics in the natural sciences is something bordering on the mysterious and that there is no rational explanation for it."[223]

---

222 William Lane Craig, "The Teleological Argument and the Anthropic Principle," in *The Logic of Rational Theism,* ed. By Wm. L. Craig and M. McLeod (Lewiston: Edwin Mellen, 1990), https://www.reasonablefaith.org/writings/scholarly-writings/the-existence-of-god/the-teleological-argument-and-the-anthropic-principle.
223 Eugene Wigner, "The Unreasonable Effectiveness of Mathematics in the Natural Sciences," *Communications in Pure and Applied Mathematics,* Volume 13 [1], 1960, maths.ed.ac.uk.

Dinesh D'Souza observers, "The laws that govern the universe seem to be written in the language of mathematics. The greatest scientists have been struck by how strange this is."[224]

Theoretical physicist Richard Feynman adds, "The fact that there are rules at all to be checked [in nature] is kind of a miracle."

There exists no logical necessity for a universe that obeys rules. Yet ours does. And they are standardized, uniform, and interact with one another in harmony. And our universe obeys so *many* rules, all of which have to work together in such precision in order to create the conditions for life, that the implication of a governing Overseer to ensure that all such rules can operate harmoniously and not destroy one another becomes a necessity.

If the basic values and relationships of nature were slightly different, not only would the universe not exist, but neither would we. The universe is so fine-tuned for human habitation that any slight deviation would preclude our chances for appearance.

Paul Davies says, "We have been written into the laws of nature in a deep and, I believe, meaningful way." Davies was referring to what physicists call the "Goldilocks Zone" phenomenon.[225]

Physicist John Wheeler writes: "A life-giving factor lies at the centre [sic] of the whole machinery and design of the world."

Martin Rees, British cosmologist and astrophysicist, explains it in terms laymen can easily follow and easily explain to others. Here is the basic formulation:

- Six numbers underlie the fundamental properties of the universe, and each of these six numbers is exactly calibrated to the necessary conditions for life to exist.[226]

---

224 D'Souza, *What's So Great About Christianity.*
225 Mel Thompson, *Understand Philosophy of Science* (New York: McGraw Hill, 2012).
226 Martin Rees Martin, *Just Six Numbers—The Deep Forces That Shape the Universe* (London: Weidenfeld & Nicolson, 1999).

- If any one of the six, say for example, *the gravitational constant,* were different, even to a fraction of a degree, nothing could exist: no stars, no complex elements, and absolutely no possibility of life.
- It is worth noting: There are actually significantly more than just six such baseline numbers in the Anthropic Principle. But highlighting six is sufficient to display the wonder of it all.

Physicists invite us to picture it this way: Imagine God sitting at a control panel with a set of dials before Him. One dial sets the mass of the proton, another the charge of the electron, another the gravitational constant, and so forth. The number of dials extends out of sight. God then spins the dials. Each dial does not possess, say, six or seven possibilities. It possesses billions. And to enable life on Earth, every single one of every single one of the dials would have to land on the exact correct number, within a factor of billions, all at the same time, the first time, or nothing could exist, including the universe.

What is the probability that a random spin would result in a universe with stars, plants, and even complex life?

It turns out that the answer can be computed. Astronomer Lee Smolin estimates the chances at one chance in ten to the power of 229.[227] That is based on only six dials. There are actually many more.

Stephen Hawking provides us with information that helps to illustrate just one of these "chance" factors (out of Smolin's hypothetical six): "If the rate of expansion one second after the Big Bang had been smaller by even one part in a hundred thousand million million, the universe would have collapsed back into itself before it even reached its present size."[228] That's one dial. It has to land on the correct number to a factor of one part in a thousand million million. The first time. Now, add the next dial. It must do the same. At the same time. The first time. Now, add more dials.

---

227 D'Souza, ibid.
228 Ibid.

One part bigger, Hawking explains, and everything would have dissipated out into space, without coalescing to even form into planets. The chances of this one thing alone being so perfectly calibrated is beyond astonishing. But again, that's only one out of six.[229]

In *Stealing From God,* author Frank Turek offers the following analogy to help us comprehend the precision of just this one metric alone:

> How precise is one in ten to the fortieth power? To get your mind around this degree of precision, imagine a tape measure stretched across the entire known universe. If the gravitational force were represented by a particular mark on that tape measure, we wouldn't exist if the force were set any more than an inch away from where it actually is . . . across a scale as wide as the entire universe. And there are more than a dozen of these precise values.[230]

Let's keep going:

If atomic weight had been stronger, the Big Bang's nuclear burning would have proceeded past helium to iron, making fusion-powered stars impossible. If it had been weaker, we would have had a universe entirely of helium. That's another dial.

Or if silver had been a little greater, all stars would have been red dwarfs, which are too cold to support life-bearing planets. If it had been a little smaller, the universe would have been composed exclusively of blue giants, which burn too briefly for life to develop. According to Davies, changes in either silver or electromagnetism by only one part in 1,040 would have spelled disaster for stars like the sun.[231]

Also, the fact that life can develop on a planet orbiting a star at the right distance depends on the proximity of the spectral temperature of starlight to the molecular binding energy. Were it to exceed this value, living organisms

---

229 Turek, *Stealing From God.*
230 Ibid.
231 Craig, *The Teleological Argument and the Anthropic Principle.*

would be sterilized or destroyed; were it below this value, the photochemical reactions necessary to life would proceed too slowly for life to exist.

And here's another point: Atmospheric composition, upon which life depends, is constrained by planetary mass. But planetary mass is the inevitable consequence of electromagnetic and gravitational interactions.

The conditions go on and on:

> Life depends upon the operation of certain principles in the quantum realm. For example, the Pauli Exclusion Principle, which states that no more than one particle of a particular kind and spin is permitted in a single quantum state, plays a key role in nature. It guarantees the stability of matter and the size of atomic and molecular structures and creates the shell structure of atomic electrons. In a world not governed by this principle, only compact, super dense bodies could exist, providing little scope for complex structures or living organisms.

> Or again, quantization is also essential for the existence and stability of atomic systems. In quantum physics, the atom is not conceived on the model of a tiny solar system with each electron in its orbit around the nucleus. Such a model would be unstable because any orbit could be an arbitrary distance from the nucleus. But in quantum physics, there is only one orbital radius available to an electron, so that, for example, all hydrogen atoms are alike. As a consequence, atomic systems and matter are stable and therefore life-permitting.[232]

And so it continues with a plethora of examples.

An essay on Reasonablefaith.org argues that even the "spinning wheels" analogy is actually too generous because it is predicated only on "correct numbers." It fails to account for "relationships between those correct numbers." As they explain:

> The delicate balance of conditions upon which life depends is characterized by the interweaving of conditions, such that life

---

232 Ibid.

depends for its existence, not merely upon each individual condition's possessing a value within very narrow limits, but also upon ratios or interactions between values and forces which must likewise lie within narrow parameters. The situation is thus not comparable to a roulette wheel in Monte Carlo's yielding a certain winning number; nor even yet to all the roulette wheels (each representing a physical quantity or constant) in Monte Carlo's turning up simultaneously certain numbers within narrowly circumscribed limits (say, wheel 1 must show 72 or 73 while wheel 2 must show 27-29, *etc.*); rather it is like all the roulette wheels in Monte Carlo's yielding simultaneously numbers within narrowly prescribed limits and those numbers bearing certain precise relations among themselves (say, the number of wheel 3 must be one-half the square of the number of wheel 17 and twice the number of wheel 6). It seems clear that worlds not permitting intelligent life are vastly more to be expected than life-permitting worlds.[233]

The Anthropic Principle is so compelling an argument for an organizing Intelligence—for *God*—that Philosopher Anthony Flew, a previously prominent and aggressive atheist, concluded that the fine-tuning of the universe, at every level, is simply too perfect to be the result of chance. In keeping with his lifelong commitment to go where the evidence leads, he now believes in God. He shocked the intellectual world with his 2007 confessional book, *There is a God: How the World's Most Notorious Atheist Changed His Mind.* This is a truly laudable level of intellectual integrity. How few will ever achieve it.

Scientists further observe:

"A common-sense interpretation of the facts suggests that a super-intellect has monkeyed with the laws of physics" (Fred Hoyle FRS, English astronomer).[234]

"The more I examine the universe and study the details of its architecture, the more evidence I find that the universe, in some

---

233 Ibid.
234 "An Astronomer's Take on God," Philosophical Society.com, https://www.philosoph-icalsociety.com/an_astronomer's_take_on_god.htm (accessed January 9, 2020).

sense, must have known we were coming" (Freeman Dyson FRS, American theoretical physicist and mathematician).[235]

Similarly, theoretical physicist Tony Rothman writes, "It's not a big step from the [Anthropic Principle] to the Argument from Design . . . When confronted with the order and beauty of the universe and the strange coincidences of nature, it's very tempting to take the leap of faith from science into religion. I am sure many physicists want to. I only wish they would admit it."[236]

So why not reach their own conclusions? Imagine getting that far intellectually, and not taking the next logical step . . .

Astronomer Owen Gingerich says, "The anthropic principle means accepting that the laws of nature are rigged not only in favor of complexity or just in favor of life, but also in favor of *mind*."[237]

"Okay, everything points to God. Now, how do we make Him go away?"

So, how do atheist scientists "make God go away?" Simple: They posit the existence of multiple universes. In fact, an *infinite* number of universes, each with its own possible arrangements of laws, in order to increase the numbers infinitely. They just add more dials, and they do so in realms beyond view and beyond investigation. They imagine whole casinos.

Infinite universes must imply infinite possibilities for just one universe to hit the exact right numbers, and that is the prevailing atheist argument. I am sorely tempted to add, "among people who claim to be grown-ups."

There are scientific problems with this hypothesis. They are fairly complex and relate to the problems with the genesis and interrelationships of these posited multiple universes. Some such problems are deemed to be insurmountable.

But the more compelling problems are purely logical: There is no evidence for the theory. It is purely speculative. Plus, the theory had to be invented *in*

---

235   J.P. Hannah, *A Skeptic's Investigation Into Jesus* (Eugene: Wipf and Stock Publishers, 2020).
236   Craig, *The Teleological Argument and the Anthropic Principle.*
237   D'Souza, *What's So Great About Christianity?*

order to get rid of the problem of God. This thinking is disingenuous and appears to be ideological ("We cannot possibly have God.") rather than scientific. It is also a blatant refusal, on grounds of emotion and stubbornness, to follow the evidence where it appears to lead.

Stephen Hawking came up with another solution to the Anthropic Principle in order to "make God go away." He invented imaginary time to achieve the same dismissal. When you add imaginary conditions, you must necessarily arrive at imaginary conclusions.

What should we make of all this? At the very least, it rather flies in the face of the atheists' assertion that we are an unimportant species in a backwater of the universe. Instead, it almost looks as though the opposite is the case—that the universe was made with us in mind, even, for our sake and that we exist at the nexus of conditions so incredibly fine-tuned that it almost seems as though a benevolent God designed it all with us in mind.

Not only are we not dislocated and lost in an odd corner of a massive galaxy, but actually, the universe *has to be* just as big as it is and just as old as it is, to support us. As Dinesh D'Souza puts it, "The entire universe with all its laws appears to be a conspiracy to produce, well, us."[238]

The arguments for God from the stars and from the cells, are so strong, that scientists have had to try to find creative ways to get rid of God. This begs the question: "Why would you *want* to?"

Nevertheless, their best solution to date is to try to increase the total amount of probabilistic material by postulating the existence of infinite multiple universes. "Improbable?" the argument goes. "No problem. Just add billions and billions of other universes." Since the existence of such (invisible, un-provable, un-evidenced) universes would increase the probabilistic chances of life occurring in *one* of those universes, they simply argue that we happen to be in that one.

---

238 D'Souza Dinesh, *What's So Great About Christianity?*

Dr. Eugene Koonin of the National Center for Biotechnology Information at the National Institutes of Health, published this theory in an article titled, "The Cosmological Model of Eternal Inflation and the Transition From Chance to Biological Evolution in the History of Life."[239]

He acknowledges that "no compelling scenarios currently exist for the origin of replication and translation, the key processes that together comprise the core of biological systems and the apparent pre-requisite of biological evolution."[240] Translation: our universe couldn't possibly have given birth to spontaneously occurring life. It's too improbable. But maybe if you add billions of universes, then we become the one that hit that improbable number. This is yet another explanation purely on chance, not described by scientific principles. He has only addressed chance and not how.

Revisiting Kant

Do you recall when we discussed the Philosopher Immanuel Kant? He is the character essentially responsible for disconnecting meaning from reality in philosophy. He was even referred to by his contemporaries as "the great all-destroyer." This proposal gave rise to postmodernism and the modern, politically correct idea that no one system of values is superior to any other.

Kant made an interesting mistake. A Christian, he was concerned that science and the positivist ideas of the Enlightenment posed a threat to Christianity. He thus worked hard to divorce the idea of faith (and consequently, all attendant human meaningfulness) from empirical science, famously rejecting reason "to make space for faith."[241]

What followed was two hundred years of descent into meaninglessness. And books like this one, trying to correct his mistake.

---

239 Eugene V. Koonin Eugene, "The cosmological model of eternal inflation and the transition from chance to biological evolution in the history of life," *Biology Direct*, Volume 2 [15], https://www.ncbi.nlm.nih.gov/pmc/articles/PMC1892545.
240 Ibid.
241 Roger Scruton, *Kant: A Very Short Introduction* (Oxford: Oxford University Press, 1982).

Yet Kant should not have bothered. He did more harm than good. His own faith instructs him to seek the truth and to speak the truth. If anything, he should have encouraged science and logical positivism to have at it! Go and find the truth and follow the truth wherever it leads. Two hundred years later, science, at the level of the universe and at the level of the cell, is arguing for the truth of God. What a shame we had to spend two centuries lost in a nihilistic forest of meaninglessness before we got there. And what a shame that, now that we are at this threshold, we find it hard to believe what we are seeing, so trained are we to believe in meaninglessness.

The key learning? *Trust* truth. If it is true, it will be true. You do not need to make excuses for it.

Political correctness, however, can grapple with the problem of proving and excusing its own flawed version of "truth." None of its findings are empirically true; none of its premises are logically true; and its application leads to chaos. It consistently does more harm than good. And it cannot even defend itself with references to truth, insofar as it does not believe in the concept. Today, it's trying to make God go away, against the findings of science.

For our part, we need only seek the truth, speak the truth, and let mistruth implode upon itself. I believe we should also help it along its way by shining a light on its misdeeds, which, again, is the point of this book.

The best books to read on this topic: *What's So Great About Christianity?* by Dinesh D'Souza, *The Reasonable Bible* by Dennis Prager, and *Stealing from God* by Frank Turek.

2. THE ARGUMENT FROM THE CELLS: DNA AND THE LANGUAGE OF LIFE

The Anthropic Principle is extremely compelling. So much so that scientists can't find ways to dismiss it. And now, compound the atheist problem by adding some further impossibilities *on top of* the Anthropic Principle. Above and beyond the extraordinary requirements necessary for the existence of life, we now add an equally daunting set of improbabilities for the *origin* of life.

Remember, we now know that life is not merely a "mechanical" problem. Scientists used to believe that if you could just assemble the right physical parts, you might achieve life. But we now know that this is not so. The problem runs much deeper. In additional to physical parts, life requires complex sets of chemical and linguistic codes.

What does that mean? Well, you can't just have all the right material parts fall into place and get life. No, DNA proves that you need more than that. You need a set of encoded language instructions at the level of the cell. And I repeat, this is *on top of* the necessary conditions of the Anthropic Principle and on top of the mechanical conditions necessary for the organism.

In *The Signature in the Cell—DNA and the Evidence for Intelligent Design*, Stephen C. Meyer takes us on a detailed tour of the history of DNA and the discoveries that point to intelligent design. The book is long and complex but navigable by laypeople with some effort. His core observation is that DNA, which is the necessary foundation of life, does not just contain molecules. It contains "information encoded in a language." This information encoded in a language is necessary for life. For various demonstrable reasons, it could not have developed over time but had to be fully present in the first life, or there would have been no second life.[242]

At the very foundations of life, we see some astonishing things, all of which point to the idea of a mind. We see idea, information, language, and encoding; and we see that all of these things must necessarily precede the first life in order to create the conditions necessary for the first life. If no instructional language was present *in advance* of the first life, even that prototypical example could never develop, let alone the progression of a second-generation. One cannot, therefore, simply allow "millions of years" for generations of life to develop this code.

---

242 Stephen C. Meyer, *Signature in the Cell* (San Francisco: HarperOne, 2009).

Who, then, is the encoder? Who spoke that language prior to the first living being? Who created the instruction manual that had to exist *before* sample number one?

It is notable that this book describes scientists and philosophers staring at this information and converting to believers in God. They could not scientifically deny what they were seeing with their own eyes. Equally fascinating, despite his repeated proofs that everything in his book rigorously follows the scientific method—and that the counterarguments all fall afoul of logical fallacies and anti-science methodologies—and despite his astonishing credentials and decades of first-hand experience in the world of DNA and genetics, some sources nevertheless persist in describing Meyer's findings as "pseudoscience."

It would appear that the social media staff at Google know more about genetic science than Meyer does, even if they do say so themselves. If, by this stage, I have not convinced you that politically correct advocates lie in the interests of their ideology, then I have failed in my mission.

Taken together, the Anthropic Principle, or "the argument from the stars," and the DNA Signature Principle, or "the argument from our cells," discredit the notion that science has "disproven" God. It is utter nonsense and a deceit when proffered.

If anything, science today is fighting tooth and nail to try to find a way around *its own evidence* and to get rid of God. In response to such efforts, we must once more pose the simple but important question: "Why?"

"Fine. So, we haven't disproven God, yet. So where is God, and where did He come from? Who made God? Answer that one!"

To ask this question is to show a pagan understanding of the concept of a deity. In paganism, gods existed *within* the world, *within* the universe, as forces that were subject to nature and who might, to some extent, be able to control nature. It makes sense, in such a context, to pose the questions,

"Where is God, and where did he come from?" In a pagan context, the answer can be: "The god is in that river, or in that mountain, or in this figurine, and he was made by the mating of two gods before him."

However, in the Judeo-Christian context, that question does not make sense. God, in this context, is Creator *of* everything. Therefore, by definition, He is *outside of everything*, including space and time, which are aspects of creation.

Dr. Kent Hovind put it best in a public debate:

> Your question, where did God come from, assumes—or displays that you are thinking of the wrong God. Because the God of the Bible is not affected by Time, Space or Matter. If He's affected by Time, Space or Matter, He's not God.
>
> Time, Space and Matter is what we call a continuum. All of them have to come into existence at the same instant, because if there were matter, but no space, where would you put it? If there were matter and space but no time, *when* would you put it? You cannot have time, space or matter independently. They have to come into existence simultaneously.
>
> The Bible answers that in ten words: "In the beginning (there's "time"), God created the heaven (there's "space") and the earth (there's "matter"). So you have time, space, matter created, a trinity of trinities there: Time has *past, present, future*. Space has *length, width, height*. Matter has *solid, liquid, gas*. You have a trinity of trinities created instantaneously, and the God who created them has to be outside of them.
>
> If He's limited by Time, He's not God. The guy who created this computer is not *in* the computer. He's not running around in there changing the numbers on the screen. The God who created this universe is outside of the universe. He's above it, beyond it, in it, through it. He's unaffected by it.
>
> So the concept that a spiritual force can have any effect on a material body, well then, I guess you'd have to explain to me things like emotions and love and hatred and envy and jealousy

and rationality. I mean, if your brain is just a random collection of chemicals that formed by chance over billions of years, how on earth can you trust your own reasoning processes and the thoughts that you think? So, your question, "Where did God come from?", is assuming a *limited* God, and that's your problem. The God that I worship is not limited by time, space or matter. If I could fit the infinite God in my three-pound brain, He would not be worth worshiping, that's for certain.[243]

The most critical idea here is that God also created *time*, not just place. The idea of an eternal God does not actually mean a God who "goes on forever." In that case, we would ask: Who created Him, and who created *him*, and so on.

Instead, it actually means a God who "stands outside of time." This is different. It is to say God "as the Author of the novel," but not "*in* the novel." The timeline of the novel does not apply to the timeline of the Author.

But we live in a purely material universe

No, that is incorrect. That view has been overturned by the discovery of information encoded into DNA. Life is matter, energy, and *information-that-follows-a-language*. This *information that follows a language* necessarily had to predate life. This, in turn, implies *mind*.

Meyer's book, in audio format, contains over twenty hours of explanation of the science of intelligent design, as observed in cells. Here I will attempt to give my layman's summary of the major points:

- The statistical likelihood of amino acids forming themselves into the correct assemblage necessary for life has been calculated. Scientists have calculated the possibility of this happening, given the entire probabilistic material present since the dawn of the universe. The odds are so great against, that it goes into the tens of trillions (yet another dial). But that's not where the argument ends.

---

243 Ghitamoldovan, "Where did God come from? – Best answer," YouTube Post, 3:25, July 17, 2016, https://www.youtube.com/watch?v=w6AHcv19NIc.

- Even if the correct assemblage somehow happened in spite of it having a one in a billion, billion, billion chance against, it would nevertheless have died instantly and not become a second generation. Why? Because of the presence of ultraviolet light conditions at the time when life is believed to have arisen. So, even if it beat odds that are universe-defyingly against, it would then have been melted.

- Further, it couldn't have taken millions of years and millions of generations or millions of iterations to perfect. Instead, it had to have the full rudimentary language of life on the very first go and then pass that on to the second generation or not at all. Death of the first generation equals death in total. Then you have to spin the dials again. And you don't get to because the odds of the first one were already one to a billion, billion, billion against. Now you are asking for two.

- If the association of amino acids were a completely random event, there would not be enough mass in the entire Earth, even assuming the whole planet was composed exclusively of amino acids, to make even one molecule of every possible sequence of a low molecular weight protein. With arguments of this nature, Meyer dismisses chance as the originator of life.

- Even if all of these impossibilities were defied and the correct structures somehow came into place, they would still not have the animating conditions of life. A human corpse has all the requirements necessary for life, *yet it is not alive*. If chance defied every impossibility and got this encoded language correct the first time and also survived the climactic conditions that would necessarily have destroyed it, *it still wouldn't have been alive*. It would have been a life-resembling assemblage of code. Dead bodies have such code in a high state of development, yet are not alive.

- Communications systems, such as those found in DNA, defy reduction to physical or chemical processes. They are not determined by physical law. They exist in agreement with principles of understanding between an instructor and that which is instructed. There is inherent meaning there that does not arise out of physical or chemical systems.

Living things defy reduction because they contain a system of communications and instructions. As with other systems of communication, the lower level chemical laws cannot account for it, in the same way that the chemicals present in ink cannot account for the meaningfulness of a newspaper headline.

Instead, this is a higher-level code, distinct from chemicals and structures. It actually *requires* a *freedom* from chemical determinism. All possible codes are equally likely. None is chemically or mechanically *more* likely. And under a system of mechanical or chemical inevitability, the necessary freedom to create a code would be precluded. Complex life, based on code, is not possible by chance.

Meyer goes on to dismiss theories such as self-organization and molecular inevitability, using similarly conclusive arguments. His summary findings are that it is not possible for life to have arisen spontaneously. It defies science.[244]

Once again, in order to dismiss these proofs, and in order to claim that Meyer practices pseudoscience, atheists have had to use the same proposals they used against the Anthropic Principle.

And so, we are back to the fiction of alternate universes. First, Meyer points out, there is zero proof for this hypothesis. Secondly, this in no way fixes the problem. In every alternate universe, the same problem would occur, compounded by the Anthropic Principle problem. Positing alternative universes does not solve the problem; it merely transfers it out of sight, where the problem remains unsolvable.[245]

The impossible statistics for life arising spontaneously rest *on top of* the impossible stats of the Anthropic Principle of the universe. So, help yourself

---

244 Meyer, *Signature in the Cell*.
245 Ibid.

to as many parallel universes as you would like. It still doesn't work. Intelligent design, however, easily solves all of these conundrums, without discord.

The biblical account expresses it this way. Psalm 19:1 says, "The heavens declare the glory of God; And the firmament shows His handiwork." Then in Colossians 1:17, we read, "He is before all things, and in Him, all things consist." The term *consist* here is sometimes translated as "hold together," which seems a curious and even conspicuous choice of words for a pre-atom, pre-natural laws observer. And then finally, with reference to the complexity of the human cell, in Psalm 139:14, we see, "I will praise you, for I am fearfully and wonderfully made."

However, though intelligent design perfectly accounts for these astonishing questions, it is politically incorrect, according to a small group of atheist scientists who don't like it and don't want it. Therefore, it is a pseudoscience. So here we are, with all the evidence in the universe, all pointing in one direction with all the bells and whistles and a stubbornly rejected conclusion, as by a child who crosses his arms and says, "Won't!"

Here are responses to some leading arguments against God.

3. PROVING GOD FROM LOGICAL COHERENCE

A capricious, violent, village god, interested only in his own small tribe?

Let us go back to God's very first interactions with us. In the beginning, He makes us in His own image. He then reaches two conclusions. The first occurs when He looks at all of His creation—including us—and decides, "It is good."

He is an approving God. His first thought about us and about everything He created around us was, "It is good."

His second thought about us was fascinating. He concluded that it was not good for man to be alone. That was his first insight into what humans are *like* and into what we need. God cares about loneliness. And He was first to posit the notion that humans need love, friendship, companionship, and camaraderie. Loneliness is bad for us. Psychiatrists and psychologists today posit loneliness and human isolation as arguably the worst thing for mental health. They agree: "It is not good for man to be alone" (Gen. 2:18).

By contrast, search the ancient Babylonian and Sumerian texts for an insight this psychologically sound, this up-to-date, and this fundamentally caring by any other god. The gods of these religions tended to judge people on criteria such as how handsome they were or how brave in battle.

And in response to the idea that God was only interested "in His own small tribe"? Clearly, He chose the Hebrew, or Jewish people, as His "chosen race." But this was not a singling out for privilege. This was a singling out for duty. Specifically, their duty was to represent Him and to spread ethical monotheism throughout the Earth. This is not the arbitrary designation of ethnic privilege. It is a call for one group to share the light. It is actually an obligation. The Jews were not privileged, but "charged." And what was the nature of the obligation? It was to universalize goodness. To teach it to everyone. That is hardly the self-interested act of a racist God Who favors a chosen few. It is the exact reverse.

"The Bible is just one more ancient mythology, and it's riddled with bizarre contradictions and silly rules."

People like to make the Bible's rules seem arbitrary and scatalogical. It is necessary for them to do this if they are to dismiss it as a moral arbiter. It is not dissimilar to the "parallel universes" theory, and it springs from the same compulsion.

They do this because they do not want to be judged by a God for their moral behavior, and so they have a vested interest in aggressively misrepresenting the Bible. Here is one example of how they will do that:

Have you ever seen a Bible-mocking meme about how "mixing cotton socks" is held to be morally equivalent to being gay in the Old Testament? Oh, it *is* there. It's in Leviticus. But one should read the actual verse: "'You shall keep My statutes. You shall not let your livestock breed with another kind. You shall not sow your field with mixed seed. Nor shall a garment of mixed linen and wool come upon you" (Lev. 19:19).

It speaks about cows not mating with non-cows, not mixing seed that shouldn't mix, and not wearing inappropriate mixes. It is a section about genetics and categories for mating. It is not glib fashion advice from a God Who doesn't like cotton socks, and to represent it as such is to intentionally distort the profound intent of the section.

Few people will ever bother to go and read and understand such verses in context. And so, gay rights advocates will simply isolate and freeze this verse, as per Alinsky's techniques, and represent it as bizarre in its disjointed manifestation. They will then share it as a meme, and the public will snort in derision at an outmoded and "silly" Bible.

But let us think about what the Bible is actually saying in these verses. Do you disagree with it?

God created genetics. He created sex. He created procreation. He knows what works, and He knows what shouldn't mix. And here, He gives guidelines. And right beside these guidelines is the verse about men not sleeping with men. Far from being arbitrary, silly and scatalogical—a bizarre, little verse about socks—this whole section is about genetics, mating, and appropriate and inappropriate categories, as designated by the Designer of those categories. One can quickly see why homosexuals would want us to discredit those verses in particular and what their vested interested is in the "cotton socks" representation.

Here is the next problem that gay rights activists face, particularly those who also claim to be Christian (and there are many). Let us say you don't agree. Okay, so you're writing off the rules about homosexuality because God *also* says don't wear bad socks that mix the wrong fabrics. Well, God also says don't murder. Are we going to write that off, too? Will we write that one off on the same grounds as the sock argument, or does that one get to stay? An argument used to dismiss one rule (even a fallacious argument like the one they have used) is also an argument against all of the biblical rules, including injunctions not to steal, commit adultery, hurt a child, and so forth.

"God says it would be better to have a stone tied around your neck and be cast into the sea than to harm a child."

"Well, sure, but He also says we can't mix different cottons, so He's absurd. By all means, hurt the child."

"Fine, but there are other bizarre verses in the Bible. And they were clearly intended for ancient goat-herders, not for us."

For example, there is a verse in the Old Testament forbidding cooking a lamb in its mother's milk. In fact, this injunction appears several times and so was clearly considered important. So, how can a universal God, capable of speaking through all time even to us in the twenty-first century, posit such a stupid and patently rural rule? For goodness' sake: *cooking instructions?* The answer is simple—and actually quite beautiful. God believes in categories, and He is attempting to teach them to us.

He has similar verses about not mixing menstrual fluids with sex. Why? Because in doing so, you are mixing the very essence of life with the symbolic essence of death (a discarded egg).

He enjoined his priests (who were the symbolic representations of life), not to have contact with cadavers (the dead).

He instructed us not to cook a lamb in the milk of its own mother because cooking a lamb is an act of death for the lamb, and to do so within the life-giving milk of its own mother is symbolically perverse. He is teaching us to have *value for life,* and He is teaching us about *conscience.* He is teaching us to be repulsed by that which degrades, and He is teaching us not to mock goodness, not even symbolically.

These ideas are not arbitrary and nonsensical. They are symbolic of the deepest divisions of light from dark, good from evil, day from night. They

410 POLITICAL CORRECTNESS DOES MORE HARM THAN GOOD

create the necessary conditions for justice in teaching us how to discern concepts of righteousness from concepts of evil. Without them, life can be arbitrary and meaningless. Even malicious. Go ahead, kill a thing and cook it right in the carcass of its mother. And feel no moral twinge in doing so. But in the presence of their architecture, we are taught to hold things sacred and to begin to understand values. This verse is not *about* lambs. It is about *us* and our psychology. It is about symbolism that teaches us good-ness over perversity.

"The Bible is sexist! God is identified as a male. And women are held to be less valuable."

Perhaps you are thinking of the Qur'an, which openly states that a fe-male is worth less than a male and that her testimony counts for half of his. But for an in-depth and verse-by-verse explanation of how even the earli-est books of the Old Testament hold women to be every bit as valuable as men, though different in their roles, read Dennis Prager's *The Rational Bible: Genesis*.[246] I defy you to read the book and still come away believing that the Bible is sexist. It simply isn't.

Now, concerning the issue that God is identified as male. This is actually terrifically important, and we would live in a much more violent world were it not so. Remember our multiple discussions about how the absence of a father (as opposed to a mother) leads to more crime than any other societal factor? Fatherlessness is *the* great creator of crime and, especially, of violent crime on the part of men.

Side Note: In the U.S., Asian American families have higher representations of present fathers than any other demographic group. They also commit less crime than any other demo-graphic group.

---

246 Prager, *The Rational Bible: Genesis*.

Men are much more prone to physical violence than women. That is, unless they have a father figure, who teaches them right from wrong. In that case, the propensity for violence all but disappears. It does *not* disappear in the same manner in the presence of a mother figure alone.

Now imagine that dynamic writ large. God *must* be a father figure, if violent males are to be civilized into obeying good societal rules. It matters, and it matters greatly.

Nevertheless, other than clearly identifying Himself as a Father, we do not see any other signs of sexuality in the Hebrew God whatsoever. There is no origin story, no mating story, no sexual desire expressed, in any passage, anywhere, ever.

4. PROVING GOD FROM IDEOLOGICAL IMPACT

Surprising Moral Revolutions of the Old Testament

Over the course of a few examples now, I have merely defended certain misunderstood or misrepresented Bible verses. Now, let us go on the offensive. It is easy to show that the Old Testament created moral innovations that revolutionized human societies for the better. In fact, just about every idea that progressives point to as either arbitrary or oppressive was, in fact, a massive leap forward for our species, thanks to the God of the Old Testament and His laws.

There are enough examples to fill a book by itself (and Dennis Prager's two books on *The Rational Bible* uncover a good many of them). We have already seen a few:

- The Old Testament set the conditions for the abolition of slavery.
- The Old Testament created the conditions for science.
- The Old Testament set the precedent for legal reciprocity as proportionate only.

Here are a few more:

Revisionists love to point to verses in the Old Testament (Deut. 21:18-21) that refer to "killing one's son" and use it as evidence of a barbaric Bible. And once again, the verse *is* there. But it does the precise opposite of what they claim it does. The verse says that if parents want to put a wayward and rebellious son to death, they must bring him before the appointed city council, who will decide his case.

So how is this a moral revolution?

This verse was set forth hundreds of years before Roman civilization. And even in a society as supposedly advanced as that of Rome, fathers had the right of life and death over their family. They could kill a wayward son without question, qualification, or interference.

The Torah, by contrast, made that impossible. A parent who wanted to do that had to take their son before the appointed authorities, who would hear his case objectively. It was a *prevention* of filicide (the killing of a child) and not an encouragement of it. It introduced the strictures of law into this emotional scenario, thus protecting the rights and life of the child. Again—you're welcome.

It is worth noting that there is also no single recorded case of Hebrew communities ever actually putting a son to death under these circumstances. Not one. Clearly, the principle worked.

And how about this innovation, which protects animals from cruelty? The Old and New Testaments make it perfectly clear that humans may eat animals. But the Old Testament has several laws, predating Moses and stretching back to what are called the Noahide laws, which apply not just to Jews, but also to everybody. The laws expressly forbid cruelty to animals, stating, for example, that you may not "tear them limb from limb" but have to provide a quick death.[247]

By contrast, right next door to the early descendants of the Hebrews, the Sumerian practice *was*, in fact, to tear animals limb from limb. There was

---

247 "Eating a Limb from a Live Animal," Aish.com, https://www.aish.com/atr/Eating-a-Limb-from-a-Live-Animal.html (accessed December 3, 2019).

no means of home refrigeration available, and so it was common to tear a limb off of an animal and eat it that night but to leave the animal alive and suffering, so that its meat remained fresh for a few more days. Why did the Assyrian, Babylonian, and Sumerian gods never ban such cruelty? And why *did* the God of the Hebrews do so? This implies conscience (and/or a lack thereof, depending on the god).

Next came literacy among the Jews. In an era when illiteracy was almost universal, it was unheard of among only one people: God's chosen tribe, who were instructed that each man should read the Torah and should teach his children to do so, too. In *Poverty Proof*, I explore how this one dynamic made Jews among the wealthiest and most successful groups in any nation, all through history.[248] It is almost as if being God's chosen people, and doing what He says, works.

Next, we might mention the marriage covenant, as given by God. Radical feminists point to it as an oppressive institution. Far from it, this very institution gave rights to women for the first time in history. A man could not simply take her, have her, and discard her. He was obliged to enter into a relationship with her family, to promise to protect her, to promise to be faithful to her, with consequences to himself if he did not. She, in turn, became entitled to property and to recourse by the law. Moreover, the very socially constructed nature of these arrangements wove communities together, forcing them to negotiate relationships of kin and, thereby, promoting peace.

We have already seen what goes wrong when sex is simply unleashed without boundaries. Its consequences include, but are not limited to, fatherlessness—the greatest violence-generating dynamic we know of—abortion, the use of women as meaningless sexual objects, the spread of diseases, and more.

Finally, let us turn to what I believe is the most misunderstood and misrepresented topic of the Old Testament. Detractors argue that it proves a

---

248 Kruger, *Poverty Proof.*

violent and vengeful God. I argue that if He had not issued the instructions that He gave in these supposedly violent scenarios, He could not possibly *be* God. Here, we are referring to the issue of killing villages and communities in the Old Testament.

Here is the first critical idea: The instructions to kill in the Old Testament were limited in place and time and were given once, to a single individual. For example, it might go something like: "Joshua, go into this village and kill these people." There is no injunction to kill any other people, at any other point in time. The killing is limited to this group only, and it specifies who is to oversee it. This person does not have permission to keep on killing thereafter.

By contrast, the Islamic Qur'an contains "open-ended" exhortations to violence. They are not limited in place, in time, or to a single identified target. Instead, Muslims as a group are encouraged to wage war against all nonbelievers, in perpetuity, until there is no religion but that of Allah. This is extremely different. It is why we do not see Jews blowing up buildings while shouting, "Jehovah is great." They are not allowed to.

So why were the Joshuas of the Bible permitted, even instructed, to kill these particular people? The answer is simple: They practiced child sacrifice. Removed as we are from the ugly realities of history, we do not quite understand the horror of this one. We don't actually get it. In our lifetimes, we have never seen live human babies being thrown into a fire and then burned to death in order to appease a pagan god. I put it to you that if you ever had to witness this mortal horror for yourself, you would arrive at the same conclusion as God did: These people must be utterly destroyed.

I further put it to you that any god who did *not* arrive at this conclusion would have to be flawed at best, and evil at worst. To my mind, the fact that God sent people into these places to wipe out the entire population is *proof* that He is a just and loving God. Anything else would have been an injustice.

In this one idea, perhaps more than any other in this book, we see the difference between the conservative and liberal value systems. Jonathan Haidt pointed out that liberals have great empathy/morality but little to no sense of justice-morality.

Conservatives do not believe that goodness can exist in the absence of justice. Failure to punish such a violating people would not represent kindness or tolerance or progress. Failure to punish such a people would, in itself, constitute a form of immorality. There *must* be consequences for evil.

But there have been thousands of "gods." Why yours?

Comedian and atheist Ricky Gervais expressed the sentiment this way: "There have been nearly 3000 Gods so far but only yours actually exists. The others are silly made up nonsense. But not yours. Yours is real."[249]

Fair point. So, let us set some logical conditions that a "true God" would have to meet. The God of the Bible would have to meet all such conditions, or He could not be God. Also, He would have to be the only Deity who meets all such conditions, or He could not be the *only* God.

Our logical conditions for the only possible God include:

He must be present from the dawn of human history. If a god were introduced as late in history as, say, the period of the Egyptian dynasties, that would already be too late. One might ask: How could a genuine God only enter the scene at the same time as, or after, the Egyptian gods? The Hebrew God passes this test. His devotees were conspicuously present in the very first civilization: Ancient Sumeria.

He must have adherents in an unbroken line from the dawn of history to today. Logically, a "true God" could not undergo periods of disappearance and reappearance. If, for instance, a Norse god like Thor, who was worshipped centuries ago, made a return today, his legitimacy would face some serious questions: Where were you *prior* to the Vikings? Where did you go since the Viking era, and why weren't you present and relevant in the intervening

---

249 Ricky Gervais, Twitter Post, December 29, 2015, 5:33 a.m., https://twitter.com/rick-ygervais/status/681785157808992256.

time? The Jewish Deity uniquely does not suffer these contradictions. He has been present and relevant throughout recorded history, in an unbroken line. No other single deity has this distinction.

His message should be successful and His will known. Logically, if He is God, then He should make His will widely known, and He should be capable of spreading this information successfully. The Bible, as we know, is the bestselling book and the most globally dispersed document in all of human history. No other book of any type or genre can match its penetration into the human community. *The Epic of Gilgamesh*, a Sumerian mythology from the first civilization, fails this test. As does every other mythology and book in history.

His should be the most successfully perpetuated religion. Although numerical representation does not, in itself, confirm truth-value, it would nevertheless be nonsensical for a "true" God to have only the second or third most successful religion on Earth. If His way is true, then it should be successful. It should be pre-eminent, and it should be the most practiced. Christianity is the world's largest and leading religion globally.

His creation account should agree with the science. The Bible does. No other mythology depicts creation beginning with a great light, followed at a later stage by the formation of earth, moon, and stars. The great light is the Big Bang, recorded in God's words, "Let there be light" (Gen. 1:3). The earth, moon, and stars followed only thereafter. This is scientifically correct.

His value system should be fair and universalizable. He cannot favor arbitrary representatives, such as "violent warriors," or "handsome faces," or "tall, Amazonian women" as his criterion for archetypes to emulate. To favor these qualities is to create a fundamentally unfair world, in which violence, or vanity, or one demographic group, must prevail as ultimate arbiters of value. The Hebrew God does not posit capricious values as supreme. He describes Himself as being comprised of goodness and love, and

He demands that people become morally good and that they love one another. He specifically and repeatedly disavows the importance of ethnicity, other than to charge the Jewish race with disseminating his values (to every other ethnicity). This leads to a universalizable system of justice and mercy. If any system is more universalizable than that, humanity has not yet encountered it. By contrast, the atheist position cannot be universalized, and it is dangerous to try.

In his book, *The Moral Landscape*, leading atheist Sam Harris attempted to solve the conundrum of moral values in a vacuum by arguing that "human flourishing" is the standard by which we determine if something is good or bad. Anything that helps humans to flourish is good; and since reason and science can tell us what helps humans to flourish, there is no need for a god to provide us with objective, moral values.[250] Can you see the problem?

Weeding out bad genetics helps humans to flourish as a group. And getting rid of problematic beliefs among a few also helps humans to flourish as a group. And culling the weak and the sick helps humans to flourish as a group.

One might have to neutralize a handful of individuals here or there. But it's okay because doing so would be for the greater collective good. And straight away, we are back to eugenics, Nazism, and communism. Indeed, we are also sowing the seeds of fascism. Were you aware that one of Mussolini's early books, *Man and Divinity*, was a treatise praising atheism as the appropriate way forward for humanity?[251] Sam Harris would surely approve.

This atheist, "good of the species" premise was the precise formula for the creation of eugenics, Nazism, communism, and fascism. This exact conception of morality and its real-world trial were what led to humanity's largest-scale catastrophes—a direct result of placing science, reason, and "human flourishing" at the top of the values pyramid and allowing proselytizing atheists to lead the way forward.

---

250 Sam Harris, *The Moral Landscape* (New York: Free Press, 2010).
251 Benito Mussolini, *Man and Divinity: God does not exist*, Pamphlet, 1904.

It will happen again, every time, if we repeat this failed experiment. And so, contrary to God's system of values, the atheist/scientist system of values is not universalizable.

> **He should permit no interlopers**. Logically, a "true" God should directly and uncompromisingly inform us of the invalidity of other gods and steer us away from entertaining them. The Hebrew God did this explicitly with His very first commandment: "I am the Lord your God . . . You shall have no other gods before me" (Exod. 20:3).

Atheist Richard Dawkins actually turns this into a bizarre charge against God, accusing Him of being "jealous and proud of it." I counter that if He were not so, He could not be a valid God. Furthermore, any failure on His part to dismiss invalid gods would then re-admit all 2,999 other gods, and their misleading ideologies, as valid options. That would be nonsensical.

> **He should disdain magic and superstition.** The Hebrew God is, above all, concerned with ethical conduct. He provides laws and guidelines to these stated ends. He does not provide recipes for magic, or incantations for good luck, or crystals or amulets by which to become rich. A true God should operate within His own systems of universal natural laws, and He should teach His creations to do the same. The biblical God, uniquely, tells His followers to have nothing to do with magic, spells, witchcraft, fortune-telling, necromancy, and every other form of superstitious thinking.

> **People who follow his statutes should be successful.** The Jewish people have been, as a demographic, consistently the best educated and wealthiest people on Earth, regardless of where they have lived. They also account for nearly one quarter of the world's Nobel Prizes, despite representing only 0.2 percent of Earth's population.

As for the Christian West, it is responsible for most of the scientific, medicinal, and cultural breakthroughs (such as human rights and democracy) achieved by humanity over the past two millennia. Indeed, the rationale for this book is to defend against a politically correct backlash, aimed squarely at the preeminence of the West. If the West were not preeminent, there would be no political correctness.

Taken together, we now have one God, Who is conspicuous among all gods. He is distinct in every meaningful metric. There may have been three thousand conceptions of gods throughout our history, in the same way that there are millions of works of fiction pertaining to dragons, fairies, and ghosts.

But there is none like Him. This poses a serious problem for Gervais' "many indistinguishable gods" hypothesis: 2,999 of them fail to meet any of the 'logical, true God' criteria. Only *one* does. And that One meets *every single one* of them. So, your move, Ricky.

And these are just a few quick examples of criteria that only the Hebrew God meets and that no other god has ever met (nor now ever can because it is now too late to go back and meet them). There are many more such criteria. There are also many more rational and scientific arguments that resolve seamlessly in the presence of an intelligent Designer but create irreconcilable contradictions extant God.

The best book on this topic: *Stealing From God: Why Atheists Need God to Make Their Case* by Frank Turek.

So, science argues for the existence of God; the moral revolutions of the Old Testament argue for the validity of God; and logical consistency points to one God only. Maybe, just maybe, there is a God. And if so, the entire liberal-progressive project, from Darwin's "Death of God," through Marxism, communism, and postmodernism, and all the way up to today, is a house of cards—a set of logical errors and fallacies compounding one another over time, an unnecessary and often genocidal departure from simple truth and goodness.

It is time—the house must fall. It is rotten. It is doing more harm than good. It has a body count that is beyond tolerance, and it continues to take its hatchet to good people and excellent institutions. It is ugly, and it must go.

It is time for people to see the cancer behind the mask, and it is time for this idea to die. Because we love truth, justice, goodness, and light, political correctness is an aberration, and we should extend to it just as much tolerance as it extends to us, which is to say, none whatsoever. It is time to stamp it out.

THE WAY FORWARD

Thank you for joining me on this journey. I hope it has been eye-opening for you and that it has helped to address some problems you have faced. I like to picture you being able to articulate concepts that have bothered you for some time, but which you have not up until now been able to put into words. I truly hope that is the case.

Where to go from here? I would like to leave you with a charge: If you are able to articulate arguments well, please teach others. The world needs your insights and your arguments. Truth matters, and its mechanism of dissemination is words. Try to learn and disseminate the stories and fallacies of the major players in this cultural war. If you are raising children, please consider teaching them to reject and be better than the "feelings-driven" culture. By all means, help them to be in touch with their own emotions and to be self-aware. But they should not be *led* by their emotions. They should be led by good decisions instead.

I am going to try to raise my family that way, and I hope that you will try to do the same. As we have seen, the "kindness" narrative—a faulty appeal to emotions—is the inroad to all Leftist ideology. The best book on this topic is *The Coddling of the American Mind* by Greg Lukianoff and Jonathan Haidt. If children themselves understand these concepts, then they will be infinitely better equipped to manage themselves mentally and to become strong.

Next, Western values matter. Teach your kids to admire clever things. To admire success, without envy. To pursue excellence, accountability, and self-determination. Help them not to react to the success of others with bitterness, but with admiration and a willingness to learn.

Do not leave good people hanging out to dry.

When you see Leftist thought-mobs piling on and victimizing someone, for heavens' sake, speak up. Don't leave them to face the hordes alone. In the stories that we have previously considered about victimized professors, each professor, in turn, received loads of support and encouragement, *privately.* Yet they received *none* in public. That is not good enough. The success of bullying always hinges on the weight of public opinion, and bullies are cowards, retreating before united resistance. When we fail to speak up as someone else is attacked, we contribute to the false perception that agreement on this topic is unanimous and settled.

Here is an interesting thought to mull over. In the face of political correctness, *you* carve out the space for others to be free. Or if you don't, they will not be.

Nobel prize-winner Daniel Kahneman points out in his excellent book, *Thinking, Fast and Slow,* that human thought can tend to be lazy and easily swayed.[252] When we see an argument made in isolation and uncontested, it just "seems to be right" to us. If it is an argument from the Left, then those who do not realize that it is ideological will tend to go along with it on those grounds.

Yet if another person comes along and presents a strong counterargument, they may realize their error and change their minds. This is really just a two-and-a-half-thousand-year neurological verification of Solomon's

---

252 Daniel Kahneman, *Thinking, Fast and Slow* (London: Penguin, 2011).

original observation that "the first one to plead his cause seems right, Until his neighbor comes and examines him" (Prov. 18:17).

So, at the very least, please don't let bad Leftist policy go unchallenged. You may see the problem. Others might not. If you don't point out the problem, they may be duped.

A quick case in point: In 2019, a series of social justice articles did the rounds damning Amazon for "paying zero in taxes." This was nonsense on two levels. Every time you purchase an Amazon product, anywhere around the world, tax is automatically added. Secondarily, the entity as a whole had structured itself to be tax-efficient. This means that they had acted in certain ways that governments favor. Governments favor these acts—including such things as spreading education, employing people, building infrastructure, re-investing their money, and more—because they are so positive for society. No government on Earth wants to lose tax money.

Yet in such a case as this, the organization is acting so positively that their government permits them to reduce their own tax burden. To the degree that they do not pay tax, it is because they are a force for good, and not evil. It is not a sign of capitalist corruption; but rather it is a sign of capitalist contribution.[253]

I shared this insight on social media after I had seen a number of social justice warriors use this news piece to point out the "evils of capitalism." I made the comment on every one of their posts, and I made it independently. It was then shared a number of times. This is how we contribute to not permitting bad ideology to flourish.

---

253 Sarah Butler, "Amazon accused of handing over 'diddly-squat' in corporation tax," TheGuardian.com, September 3, 2019, https://www.theguardian.com/technology/2019/sep/03/amazon-accused-of-handing-over-diddly-squat-in-corporation-tax-despite-tripling-payment#:~:text=Amazon%20accused%20of%20handing%20over%20'diddly%2Dsquat'%20in%20corporation%20tax,-This%20article%20is&text=Amazon%20has%20been%20accused%20of,British%20division%20to%20%C2%A314m.

PERSONALITIES TO FOLLOW

I have provided some indications of books to read. In addition, consider following these personalities and commentators on YouTube and social media. They range from the highly academic and deeply intellectual, to the snarky, pithy and amusing. All make valuable contributions to the discussion:

- Thomas Sowell
- Ben Shapiro
- Roger Scruton
- Jonathan Haidt
- Briggite Gabriel
- Jordan Peterson
- Dennis Prager
- Candace Owens
- BlazeTV
- Glenn Beck
- Bill Whittle
- Sargon of Akkad
- Douglas Murray

Are you up for humor, snark and caustic wit? Try:

- Stephen Crowder
- Paul Joseph Watson
- The Hodge Twins
- Katie Hopkins

INTERNATIONAL SOURCES WITH MODERATE-TO-EXTREME LEFT-LEANING BIASES:

- *MSNBC*
- *The Huffington Post*

- *The Rolling Stone*
- *The Daily Show*
- *The Colbert Report*
- *The Guardian*
- Buzzfeed
- *The New York Times*
- The Young Turks
- *The Daily Vox*

MODERATE TO RIGHT-LEANING SOURCES (WHICH I TEND TO FAVOR):

- *Forbes*
- *BBC* (with caution)
- *Fox News*
- *National Review*
- *Sky News* (with caution)
- *Sky News Australia* (which is actively conservative)
- New York Post
- The Daily Wire
- USA Today
- The Wall Street Journal
- The Washington Times

LIGHTING THE BEACONS FOR THE NEXT GENERATION

Your children are precious. They are, simultaneously, the main prey for the liberal Left. Keep them from becoming foot soldiers and fodder. Equip your children with good ideas and defenses. Take the hard-won light from the generations that have come before us; pass it on to them. Civilization is memory. Memory is precious. If our species has such a thing as light, it takes the form of memory. Teach them to be strong, not weak, capable, not safe.

As Van Jones once phrased it at a university address: "I don't *want* you to be safe, ideologically. I don't *want* you to be safe emotionally. I want you to be *strong*. That's different. I'm not going to pave the jungle for you. Put on some boots and learn how to deal with adversity. I'm not gonna take all the weights out of the gym. That's the whole point of the gym."[254]

At the same time, do not batter them into the dust with *our* ideology. I have observed that anything too radical tends to create a swing in the opposite direction in the next generation. Call it the "Minister's Daughter" dynamic.

I grew up in the eighties and nineties and listened to the heavy metal band Iron Maiden. At the time, I remember wandering how much more aggressive or violent pop culture could possibly become. But it didn't go that way. It swung back, way back, to the point where we now observe pop culture informed by fragile students who can't hear a word or see a hat without calling it "violence."

So, do not exasperate your children with these ideas. Explain them and point them out. But let your children come to you and be a reasonable human being who has other interests, who has a sense of humor; be someone whom they can desire to emulate. If you are obsessive and brittle and humorless, you may push them away. If you are amused, humorous, full of life, full of curiosity, open to fun, clearly good, and capable of broad-ranging ideas, then you will not dismiss yourself as a small-minded and, therefore, inimitable

---

254 Lukianoff and Haidt, *The Coddling of the American Mind.*

paranoid. I believe that, above all, a sense of humor shows that a person is reasonable. Counterintuitively, a person without a sense of humor seems unreasonable. There seems to be something missing there.

On that note, please feel free to visit my site, BreakingWoke.com, for a shareable essay on humor versus political correctness.

What's the worst it could come to?

There is a danger in speculating about how bad Leftist tyranny can become. No, it is not the potential for wild conspiracy theories, though that is an issue, too. To my mind, the real danger lies in our postulating a world so bad that we convince ourselves it is not worth fighting the battle to save it. This line of argument leads to fatalistic surrender, which is the worst thing we can do.

Sadly, I must admit that my own Christian demographic sometimes gets this one wrong. We convince ourselves (not without reason) that this is all leading into the One World Order and single government tyranny prophesied in the Book of Revelations.

In doing so, here is what we miss: Leftist tyrannies of this nature have risen and fallen before. They may very well do so again. Alternately, they may attempt to rise again, but be defeated. This depends on how effectively we oppose them.

The Soviet Union really did exist. And then it fell. And since then, other communist regimes have risen and fallen. Venezuela is going through it right now, and it did not have to. There was no moral imperative, nor necessary historical set of predetermined outcomes that made it so. We as humans made it so. We allowed it. We failed to challenge these ideas, failed to fight them tooth and nail; and in that case, we lost.

Could it happen here? Absolutely. The Left is trying very hard to make it happen here and everywhere. It is, conceivably, possible. And then, it might fall again, prior to any final End Times. All of this is to say that your own nation falling to Leftist ideology is not necessarily the same thing as any final outcome. There is no need for us to live through yet another unnecessary, modern Dark Age. We must fight it, and this book is my small contribution toward that end.

Nevertheless, let us indulge the question: How bad *can* it get? We will allow one of the men who designed and originally enforced political correctness and who spoke of peace as he promoted it, to provide us with a roadmap. Here are Lenin's own words:

> The task of the Bolsheviks is to overthrow the Imperialist Government. But this government rests upon the support of the Social Revolutionaries and Mensheviks, who in turn are supported by the trustfulness of the masses of people. We are in the minority. In the circumstances, there can be no talk of violence on our side . . . They have the guns and therefore we are for peace and for reformation through the ballot. When we have the guns then it will be through the bullet.[255]

Lenin was true to his word. He used talk of kindness, of peace. He obtained power. He took the guns—and his party used the bullets, against his own citizens. It can get bad, and that is why we fight.

There is always hope.

Hope is never far away. The Left has been refining its techniques and taking a hatchet to Western civilization for two centuries. But we are catching on; we are calling them out; we are fighting back; and we are getting steadily better at it.

So, what is the antithesis to all this Leftist tyranny into which we have descended and in which we have wallowed together for so many pages? It is something very simple and very beautiful. It is: *freedom.*

Freedom is rare, precious and hard to come by. It is predicated on the sanctity of the individual, and it thrives where people are morally excellent,

---

255 Hedgpeth, *Rules for Radicals.*

negating the need for tyrannical sets of rules. Freedom is perhaps the most beautiful and important thing civilizations ever achieve. It the pre-condition for art; it is the subject of all yearning for the slave and for the captive; it is the dear and treasured goal in whose service men fight wars and die. Freedom is nothing more than an idea. But so important is this complex, basic notion that upon its founding or faltering all else hinges. Freedom is our greatest gift, our most important inheritance, our choicest bequeath to our children. Without freedom, there is death. With it, there is life.

And above all, one thing creates the conditions for freedom. It was expressed this way in Jerusalem, two millennia into our history, by a man who gave us the foundations of our civilization: "You shall know the truth, and the truth shall make you free" (John 8:32).

And when all this is done, and when you can do no more, this much is enough: stand.

—DK

BIBLIOGRAPHY

100Huntley. "The Underlying Questions Behind Faith Based Questions / Ravi Zacharias." YouTube Post. 15:09. January 4, 2016, https://www.youtube.com/watch?v=cGtaTDBznUo.

ABC News. "Outspoken conservative Ben Shapiro says political correctness breeds insanity." YouTube Post. 9:14. October 20, 2017, https://www.youtube.com/watch?v=vj5JXrpwsZs&list=PLYoabUsEB4c2jokT_LQtaoadH1XjWxVEj.

Alinsky, Saul. *Rules for Radicals: A Practical Primer for Realistic Radicals* (New York: Vintage Books, 1971).

"Americans Oppose Cloning Human Embryos for Research." National Right to Life.org. July 26, 2001, https://nrlc.org/uploads/factsheets/FS01AbortionintheUS.pdf.

"An Astronomer's Take on God." Philosophical Society.com. https://www.philosophicalsociety.com/an_astronomer's_take_on_god.htm (accessed January 9, 2020).

Ashtyn&Jon2.0. "Yes, Hitler was a Liberal Socialist Louder With Crowder - REACTION." YouTube Post. 7:43. February 3, 2016, https://www.youtube.com/watch?v=EN1V8onC-Oo.

Ayn Rand Institute. "Yaron Answers: How Can Scandinavian Countries Perform So Well Economically?" YouTube Post. 7:00. July 1, 2013, https://www.youtube.com/watch?v=JTOpBPIoL-g.

"Babies May Start Crying While in the Womb: Crying Behavior Recorded in 3rd Trimester Fetuses." WebMed.com. September 13, 2005, https://www.webmd.com/baby/news/20050913/

babies-may-start-crying-while-in-womb#:~:text=13%2C%202005%20
%2D%2D%20A%20baby's,the%2028th%20week%20of%20pregnancy.

Badcock, Christopher, Ph.D. "It's the Mode for Men to Have More Sex Partners." PsychologyToday.com. March 2, 2017, https://www. psychologytoday.com/us/blog/the-imprinted-brain/201703/ it-s-the-mode-men-have-more-sex-partners.

Banning-Lover, Rachel, "Where are the most difficult places in the world to be gay or transgender?" TheGuardian.com. March 1, 2017, https://www. theguardian.com/global-development-professionals-network/2017/ mar/01/where-are-the-most-difficult-places-in-the-world-to-be-gay-or-transgender-lgbt.

Bell, Kim. "Gender neutral parenting, is this lifestyle for you?" Livingandloving. co. August 14, 2019, https://www.livingandloving.co.za/family/ gender-neutral-parenting-is-this-lifestyle-for-you.

Berrien, Hank. "WATCH: Ben Shapiro Debunks Transgenderism and Pro-Abortion Arguments." DailyWire.com. February 10, 2017, https://www.dailywire.com/news/ ben-shapiro-debunks-transgenderism-and-pro-hank-berrien.

Betz, Bradford. "Dr. Drew Says LA Public Health in 'complete breakdown': 'No city on Earth tolerates this.'" Foxnews.com. May 31, 2019. https://www. foxnews.com/health/dr-drew-says-third-world-countries-would-be-insulted-to-be-compared-with-los-angeles.

Billings, Lee. "Atheism is Inconsistent with the Scientific Method, Prizewinning Physicist Says." Scientific American.com. March 20, 2019, https://www. scientificamerican.com/article/atheism-is-inconsistent-with-the-scientific-method-prizewinning-physicist-says/#:~:text=Atheism%20 Is%20Inconsistent%20with%20the%20Scientific%20Method%2C%20 Prizewinning%20Physicist%20Says,-In%20conversation%2C%20 the&text=Marcelo%20Gleiser%2C%20a%2060%2Dyear,won%20this%20 year's%20Templeton%20Prize.

Bite-sized Philosophy. "Jordan Peterson – The idea of cultural appropriation is nonsense." YouTube Post. 4:42. March 18, 2017, https://www.youtube. com/watch?v=NNUcR-eMxaE.

BlazeTV. Sen. Ted Cruz GRILLS Google Exec on Political Censorship." YouTube Post. 5:18. June 25, 2019, https://www.youtube.com/ watch?v=Dx2wjCz4SyY.

Bomsdorf, Clemens. "Goldfish in a Blender? Marco Evaristti Calls it Art." WSJ.com, August 28, 2013, https://blogs.wsj.com/speakeasy/2013/08/28/ marco-evaristti-and-his-goldfish-are-still-making-waves.

Braun, Eric. *Taking Action for Civil and Political Rights (Who's Changing the World?)* (Minneapolis: Lerner Publishing Group, 2017).

Brodow, Ed. "Open Season on White People—The New Politics of Racism." ClashDaily.com. August 8, 2018, https://clashdaily.com/2018/08/ open-season-on-white-people-the-new-politics-of-racism.

Brookfield, Stephen D. and John D. Holst. *Radicalizing Learning: Adult Education for a Just World* (San Francisco: Jossey-Bass, 2011).

Butler, Judith. *Gender Trouble* (Milton Park: Routledge, 2006).

Butler, Sarah. "Amazon accused of handing over 'diddly-squat' in corporation tax." TheGuardian.com. September 3, 2019. https://www.theguardian. com/technology/2019/sep/03/amazon-accused-of-handing-over-did-dly-squat-in-corporation-tax-despite-tripling-payment#:~:text=Ama-zon%20accused%20of%20handing%20over%20'diddly%2Dsquat'%20 in%20corporation%20tax,-This%20article%20is&text=Amazon%20 has%20been%20accused%20of,British%20division%20to%20 %C2%A314m.

Caldron Pool. Twitter Post. August 22, 2019, https://twitter.com/CaldronPool/ status/1164368247824633856.

Calling an Illegal Alien An Undocumented Immigrant, Digital Image. iGeek. October 18, 2019. http://igeek.com/File:IllegalImmigrantTerms.png.

Card, Orson Scott. *Ender's Game* (New York: Tor Science Fiction, 1994).

Chalabi, Mona. "Gay Britain: what do the statistics say?" TheGuardian. com. October 3, 2013, https://www.theguardian.com/poli-tics/reality-check/2013/oct/03/gay-britain-what-do-statistics-say#:~:text=While%201.5%25%20of%20men%20in,compared%20to%20 3.5%25%20of%20men.

Channel 4 News. "Jordan Peterson debate on the gender pay gap, campus protests and postmodernism." YouTube Post. 29:55. January 16, 2018, https://www.youtube.com/watch?v=aMcjxSThD54.

Channel 4 News. "Jordan Peterson on the gender pay gap, campus protests and postmodernism." YouTube Post. 29:55. January 16, 2018, https://www.youtube.com/watch?v=aMcjxSThD54.

"Christian persecution 'at near genocide levels.'" BBC.com. May 3, 2019, https://www.bbc.com/news/uk-48146305.

CMC Forum, The. "CMCers of Color Lead Protest of Lack of Support from Administration." YouTube Post. 57:06. November 11, 2015, https://www.youtube.com/watch?time_continue=1232&v=OlB7Vy-lZZ8&feature=emb_logo.

Copen, Casey E., et al. "Sexual Behavior, Sexual Attraction, and Sexual Orientation Among Adults Aged 18-44 in the United States: Data From the 2011-2013 National Survey of Family Growth." *National Health Statistics Reports*. Number 88. January 7, 2016, https://www.cdc.gov/nchs/data/nhsr/nhsr088.pdf.

Craig, William Lane. "The Teleological Argument and the Anthropic Principle," in *The Logic of Rational Theism*. Ed. Wm. L. Craig and M. McLeod (Lewiston: Edwin Mellen, 1990), https://www.reasonablefaith.org/writings/scholarly-writings/the-existence-of-god/the-teleological-argument-and-the-anthropic-principle.

Crenshaw, Dan. Twitter Post. 7:48 p.m. August 18, 2019, https://twitter.com/dancrenshawtx/status/1162873906132398081?lang=en.

Crichton, Maddie. "Project Veritas and Politicians Accuse Google of Anti-Trump Bias." Roguerocket.com. June 27, 2019, https://roguerocket.com/2019/06/27/project-veritas-and-politicians-accuse-google-of-anti-trump-bias.

Csaplar Jr., Richard C. "1,400 Years of Christian/Islamic Struggle: An Analysis." CBN.com. https://www1.cbn.com/churchandministry/1400-years-of-christian-islamic-struggle (accessed July 23, 2019).

D'Souza, Dinesh. *Death of a Nation: Plantation Politics and the Making of the Democratic Party.* (New York: St. Martin's Press, 2018).

D'Souza. *The Big Lie: Exposing the Nazi Roots of the American Left* (Avon: Simon & Schuster, 2017).

D'Souza. *What's So Great About Christianity.* (Washington, D.C.: Regnery Publishing, 2008).

Daily Wire, The. "Everyone Reading This is a Bigot." YouTube Post. 6:03. August 30, 2019, https://www.youtube.com/watch?v=Bmd8F_xSWQs&feature=youtu.be.

Darrow, William W., et al. "The Gay Report on Sexually Transmitted Diseases." Volume 71 [9]. AJPH. September 1981.

Davis, Ben. "Lawmakers want to force churches to embrace LGBTQ ideology instead of the Bible." CaldronPool.com. June 20, 2019, https://caldron-pool.com/lawmakers-want-to-force-churches-to-embrace-lgbtq-ideology-instead-of-the-bible.

Day, Vox. *The Irrational Atheist: Dissecting the Unholy Trinity of Dawkins, Harris, And Hitchens* (Dallas: BenBella Books, 2008).

Decetev, Jean, et al. "Retraction Notice to: The Negative Association between Religiousness and Children's Altruism across the World." *Current Biology.* Volume 29 [15]. August 5, 2019,https://www.sciencedirect.com/science/article/pii/S0960982219308759.

Deneen, Patrick. *Why Liberalism Failed (Politics and Culture)* (New Haven: Yale University Press, 2018).

Dieppe, Tim. "Is Islam a religion of peace?" Christian Concern.com. November 7, 2018, https://christianconcern.com/resource/is-islam-a-religion-of-peace.

Doezema, Marie. "France, Where Age of Consent is Up for Debate." The Atlantic.com. March 10, 2018, https://www.theatlantic.com/international/archive/2018/03/frances-existential-crisis-over-sexual-harassment-laws/550700.

Doward, Jamie. "Thomas Piketty's economic data 'came out of thin air.'" The Guardian.com. May 24, 2014, https://www.theguard-ian.com/business/2014/may/24/thomas-picketty-economics-data-errors#:~:text=Only%20a%20few%20days%20ago,the%20world%20at%20his%20feet.&text=Based%20on%20a%20simple%20premise,economists%20and%20business%20leaders%20alike.

"Eating a Limb from a Live Animal," Aish.com, https://www.aish.com/atr/Eating-a-Limb-from-a-Live-Animal.html (accessed December 3, 2019).

Ehlrich, Paul. *The Population Bomb* (San Francisco: Sierra Club/Ballantine Books, 1968).

Ellis, Frank. "Political Correctness and the Ideological Struggle: From Lenin and Mao to Marcuse and Foucault." *The Journal of Social, Political, and Economic Studies.* https://www.questia.com/library/journal/1P3-278437431/polit-ical-correctness-and-the-ideological-struggle (accessed March 2, 2020).

Ellis, Frank. "Political correctness and the ideological struggle: From Lenin and Mao to Marcuse and Foucault." *The Journal of Social, Political, and Economic Studies.* Volume 27 [4]. Winter 2002, https://search.proquest.com/openview/2b06da1bbc242863798d3772bf132cdd/1?pq-origsite=gscholar&cbl=22044.

Fernández-Morera, Darío. *The Myth of the Andalusian Paradise: Muslims, Christians, and Jews Under Islamic Rule in Medieval Spain* (Wilmington: Intercollegiate Studies Institute, 2016).

"Fires in Brazil." Nasa.gov, August 13, 2019, https://earthobservatory.nasa.gov/images/145464/fires-in-brazil.

Fish, Stanley. "When Principles Get in the Way." NYTimes.com. December 26, 1996, https://www.nytimes.com/1996/12/26/opinion/when-principles-get-in-the-way.html.

Fletcher, Martin. "Ingrid Newkirk, the unlikely extremist." NewStatesman.com. June 26, 2019, https://www.newstatesman.com/politics/uk/2019/06/ingrid-newkirk-unlikely-extremist.

Fox News. "Candace Owens: Race has become a business." YouTube Post. 4:21. May 4, 2018, https://www.youtube.com/watch?v=8Am-1IHSGWo&list=LLqP3ZTiYUWbZL3p23LCQg_A&index=849.

Freedman, Andrew. "Climate scientists refute 12-year deadline to curb global warming." Axios.com. January 22, 2019, https://www.axios.com/ climate-change-scientists-comment-ocasio-cortez-12-year-deadline-c4ba1f99-bc76-42ac-8b93-e4eaa926938d.html.

French, David. "Evangelicals Are Supporting Trump Out of Fear Not Faith." Time.com. June 27, 2019, https://time.com/5615617/ why-evangelicals-support-trump.

"Gay and Bisexual Men's Health: Substance Use." CDC.gov. https://www.cdc. gov/msmhealth/substance-abuse.htm (accessed April 18, 2020).

Gervais, Ricky. Twitter Post. 5:33 a.m. December 29, 2015, https://twitter.com/ rickygervais/status/681785157808992256.

Ghitamoldovan. "Where did God come from? – Best answer." YouTube Post. 3:25. July 17, 2016, https://www.youtube.com/watch?v=w6AHcv19NIc.

Giles, Chris. "Piketty Findings Undercut by Errors." FinancialTimes. com. May 23, 2014, https://www.ft.com/content/ e1f343ca-e281-11e3-89fd-00144feabdc0.

Goldberg, Jonah. *Liberal Fascism: The Secret History of the Left, from Mussolini to the Politics of Meaning* (New York: Doubleday, 2007).

Goldberg, Michelle. "Not the Fun Kind of Feminist." NYTimes.com. February 22, 2019, https://www.nytimes.com/2019/02/22/opinion/sunday/trump-feminism-andrea-dworkin.html.

Guardian, The. "Women, face it: marriage can never be feminist – Julie Bindel." YouTube Post. 2:48. May 25, 2016, https://www.youtube.com/watch?v=h RYzl60oxks&feature=share.

Guillermo, Campitelli. "Nonreligious children aren't more generous after all." ResearchGate.net. January 16, 2017, https://www.researchgate.net/blog/ post/nonreligious-children-arent-more-generous-after-all.

Haidt, Jonathan. *The Righteous Mind: Why Good People are Divided by Politics and Religion*. (London: Penguin, 2012).

Hannah, J.P. *A Skeptic's Investigation Into Jesus* (Eugene: Wipf and Stock Publishers, 2020).

"'Harmful' gender stereotypes in adverts banned." BBC.com. June 14, 2019, https://www.bbc.com/news/business-48628678.

Harris, Dan, Ignacio Torres, and Lauren Effron. "Outspoken conservative Ben Shapiro on whether free speech still has a place on college campuses." ABC News.com. October 20, 2017, https://abcnews.go.com/US/outspoken-conservative-ben-shapiro-free-speech-place-college/story?id=50610394.

Harris, Sam. *The End of Faith* (New York: W. W. Norton & Company, 2004).

Harris. *The Moral Landscape* (New York: Free Press, 2010).

Haslam, Nick. "Psychology's Expanding Concepts of Harm and Pathology." *Psychological Inquiry*. Volume 27 [1]. January 2016, https://www.tandfonline.com/doi/full/10.1080/1047840X.2016.1082418.

Hedgpeth, Jeff. *Rules for Radicals Defeated: A Practical Guide for Defeating Obama / Alinsky Tactics* (Scotts Valley: Create Space Independent Publishing Platform, 2012).

Herrera, Jack. "Most Terrorist Victims are Muslim." Pacific Standard Magazine.com. March 18, 2019, https://psmag.com/news/most-terrorist-victims-are-muslim.

Hicks, Stephen. *Explaining Postmodernism: Skepticism and Socialism from Rousseau to Foucault* (Scholargy Publishing, 2004).

Higgins, Heather. "Barack Obama's Poor Understanding of the Constitution." USNews.com. November 3, 2008, https://www.usnews.com/opinion/articles/2008/11/03/barack-obamas-poor-understanding-of-the-constitution.

Holmes, W.C. and G.B. Slap. "Sexual Abuse of Boys: definition, prevalence, correlates, sequelae, and management." Pubmed.gov. 1998. https://pubmed.ncbi.nlm.nih.gov/9846781.

"How Many Couples Are Waiting to Adopt?" AmericanAdoptions.com. https://www.americanadoptions.com/pregnant/waiting_adoptive_families (accessed August 2, 2020).

"I Love How My Male Privilege." Digital image. iFunny. April 13, 2016. https://ifunny.co/picture/r-paul-joseph-watson-if-m-w-i-love-how-dH4M5O2n3.

Ideacity. "Jordan Peterson – Political Correctness and Postmodernism. Youtube Post. 27:51. September 12, 2017, https://www.youtube.com/watch?v=f5rUPatnXSE.

"IKEA sacks employee for quoting the Bible after he was told to participate in pro-LGBTQ event: "I've been hired to sell furniture . . . these aren't my values." CaldronPool.com. July 1, 2019, https://caldronpool.com/ikea-sacks-employee-for-quoting-the-bible-after-he-was-told-to-participate-in-pro-lgbtq-event-ive-been-hired-to-sell-furniture-these-arent-my-values.

Johnson, Paul. *Intellectuals* (London: W&N, 1988).

Kahneman, Daniel. *Thinking, Fast and Slow* (London: Penguin, 2011).

Kalder, Daniel. *Dictator Literature: A History of Bad Books by Terrible People* (New York: Simon & Schuster, 2018).

Kant, Immanuel. *Critique of Pure Reason* (Cambridge: Cambridge University Press, 1781).

Kant. *The Metaphysics of Morals* (Cambridge: Cambridge University Press, 1797).

Kelly, Keith J. "New York Times deletes tweet saying 'airplanes took aim' at towers on 9/11." NYPost.com. September 11, 2019, https://nypost.com/2019/09/11/new-york-times-deletes-tweet-saying-airplanes-took-aim-at-towers-on-9-11.

Kengor, Paul. *The Crusader: Ronald Reagan and the Fall of Communism* (New York: Harper Perennial, 2006).

Klausner, Alexandra. "Health department poured bleach on food meant for the homeless." NYPost.com. November 12, 2018, https://nypost.com/2018/11/12/health-department-poured-bleach-on-food-meant-for-the-homeless.

Koonin, Eugene. "The cosmological model of eternal inflation and the transition from chance to biological evolution in the history of life." *Biology Direct*. Volume 2 [15]. https://www.ncbi.nlm.nih.gov/pmc/articles/PMC1892545.

Kramer, Warren. "How many people have died because of religion?" Quora.com. November 26, 2016, https://www.quora.com/How-many-people-have-died-because-of-religion.

Kruger, Douglas. *Is Your Thinking Keeping You Poor?* (Cape Town, SA: Penguin Random House, 2016).

Kruger. *Poverty Proof* (Cape Town: Penguin Random House SA, 2019).

Kupelian, David. *The Marketing of Evil* (Cave Junction: WND Books, 2005).

LBC. "Jordan Peterson on Why He Refuses to Use Special Pronouns For Transgender People—LBC." YouTube Post. 3:53. May 22, 2018, https://www.youtube.com/watch?v=s_UbmaZQx74.

Legutko, Ryszard. *The Demon in Democracy: Totalitarian Temptations in Free Societies* (New York City: Encounter Books, 2016).

Levin, Mark R. *Unfreedom of the Press* (New York: Simon & Schuster, 2019).

Lukianoff, Gregg and Jonathan Haidt. *The Coddling of the American Mind: How Good Intentions and Bad Ideas Are Setting Up a Generation for Failure* (London: Penguin Books, 2018).

Mac Donald, Heather. "There Is No Epidemic of Racist Police Shootings." NationalReview.com. July 13, 2019, https://www.nationalreview.com/2019/07/white-cops-dont-commit-more-shootings.

Mahdawi, Arwa. "Masculinity is a trap – which is why more men should wear skirts." The Guardian.com. June 19, 2019, https://www.theguardian.com/commentisfree/2019/jun/19/masculinity-trap-why-more-men-should-wear-skirts.

Malkin, Michelle. "Yes, our troops were ordered to ignore Afghan pedophiles." NYPost.com. September 25, 2015, https://nypost.com/2015/09/25/yes-our-troops-were-ordered-to-ignore-afghan-pedophiles.

ManOfAllCreation. "Don't Build Your Own Enemy / Jordan Peterson." YouTube Post. 11:49. November 3, 2017, https://www.youtube.com/watch?v=ErEbqG2DGxU.

McNamee, Roger. *Zucked: Waking Up to the Facebook Catastrophe* (London: Penguin Press, 2019).

"Media Bias: Pretty Much All of Journalism Now Leans Left, Study Shows." Investors.com. November 16, 2018, https://www.investors.com/politics/editorials/media-bias-left-study.

Menzel, Idina. *Frozen.* Walt Disney Records. A5. 2014. CD.

Meyer, Stephen C. *Signature in the Cell* (San Francisco: HarperOne, 2009).

Mikelionis, Lukas. "San Francisco board rebrands 'convicted felon' as 'justice-involved person,' sanitizes other crime lingo." FoxNews.com. August 22, 2019, https://www.foxnews.com/politics/san-francisco-board-adopts-new-language-for-criminals-turning-convicted-felon-into-justice-involved-person.

Minnicino, Michael. *The New Dark Age: The Frankfurt School and Political Correctness.* Volume 1 (Washington, D.C.: Schiller Institute, 1992).

Morin, Kimberly. "Professor Obliterates the idea that Gender is a 'Social Construct.'" YouTube Post. 2:19. May 25, 2017, https://www.youtube.com/watch?v=yASbo5JRmnE.

Murray, Douglas. *The Madness of Crowds* (New York: Bloomsbury Publishing, 2019).

Mussolini, Benito. *Man and Divinity: God does not exist.* Pamphlet, 1904.

Nelson Glick, Sarah, et al. "A comparison of sexual behavior patterns among men who have sex with men and heterosexual men and women." *National Library of Medicine.* May 2012, https://pubmed.ncbi.nlm.nih.gov/22522237.

Old Soul Rebel. "Project Veritas Expose Google." YouTube Post. 25:10. June 25, 2019, https://www.youtube.com/watch?v=TyC5fz2UoAI.

Orwell, George. *Politics and the English Language* (London: Penguin, 1946).

Panahi, Rita. "Christianity is the most persecuted religion in the world." HeraldSun.com. June 24, 2019, https://www.heraldsun.com.au/blogs/rita-panahi/christianity-is-the-most-persecuted-religion-in-the-world/news-story/fccadd1f30733117c2d9dd338a27e7cc.

Parke, Caleb. "Religious freedom expert: Global war on Christians intensifying." FoxNews.com. April 23, 2019, https://www.foxnews.com/faith-values/religious-freedom-christians-sri-lanka.

"Peaceful Demonstration in Sydney." Twitter Post. August 22, 2019. https://twitter.com/messages/87133646-921880207870459904.

Peterson, Jordan B. "Sir Roger Scruton / Dr. Jordan Peterson: Apprehending the Transcendent." YouTube Post. 1:32:35. December 14, 2018, https://www.youtube.com/watch?v=XvbtKAYdcZY.

Piketty, Thomas. *Capital in the Twenty-First Century* (Cambridge: The Belknap Press of Harvard University Press, 2014).

Pinker, Steven. *The Better Angels of Our Nature: Why Violence Has Declined* (London: Penguin Books, 2012).

Prager, Dennis. "Judaism's Sexual Revolution: Why Judaism (and then Christianity) Rejected Homosexuality." Volume 11 [8]. *Crisis Magazine*. September 1993, https://www.crisismagazine.com/2018/judaisms-sexual-revolution-judaism-christianity-rejected-homosexuality.

Prager. *The Rational Bible* (Washington, D.C.: Regnery Publishing, 2018).

PragerU. "Are Some Cultures Better Than Others?" YouTube Post. 5:23. September 18, 2017, https://www.youtube.com/watch?v=m9vBJCMD69w.

PragerU. "Is An Eagle Egg More Valuable Than a Baby?" YouTube Post. 3:21. September 4, 2019, https://www.youtube.com/watch?v=ZR9Ye_Uk-x8.

PragerU. "What Is the Alt-Right?" YouTube Post. 4:46. October 26, 2017, https://www.youtube.com/watch?v=MHXLoowY3nY.

Queen. *Innuendo*. Parlophone. 1. 1991. CD.

Rao, Saira. Twitter Post. 7:58 p.m. August 9, 2019. https://twitter.com/sairasameerarao/status/1159977167847075847.

Rao, Sonia. "Netflix becomes the first major Hollywood studio to speak out against Georgia's abortion law." The Washington Post.com. May 28, 2019, https://www.washingtonpost.com/arts-entertainment/2019/05/28/netflix-becomes-first-major-hollywood-studio-speak-out-against-georgias-abortion-law.

"Research on Children 'Growing Out' of Gender Dysphoria Adds Layer Of Complexity To Transgender Care." Kaiser Health News.org. May 24, 2018, https://khn.org/morning-breakout/research-on-children-growing-out-of-gender-dysphoria-adds-layer-of-complexity-to-transgender-care.

"Reagan Quotes and Speeches." Reaganfoundation.org. October 21 1984. https://www.reaganfoundation.org/ronald-reagan/reagan-quotes-speeches.

ReasonTV. "Yale Professor Attacked Over Halloween Costumes Says We've Evolved to Get Along." YouTube Post. 32:48. April 5, 2019, https://www.youtube.com/watch?v=f56xgHHZQ_A.

Rees, Martin. *Just Six Numbers—The Deep Forces That Shape the Universe* (London: Weidenfeld & Nicolson, 1999).

Reisman, Judith A., Ph.D. "Kinsey: Crimes and Consequences." Dijg.de. https://www.dijg.de/english/reisman-kinsey-crimes-consequences/ (accessed August 20, 2019).

Robinson, Gregory. "Number of people who identify as lesbian, gay or bisexual at UK high." TheGuardian.com. March 6, 2020, https://www.theguardian.com/society/2020/mar/06/number-people-identify-lesbian-gay-bisexual-uk-high.

Ruse, Austin. *Fake Science.: Exposing the Left's Skewed Statistics, Fuzzy Facts, and Dodgy Data* (New York: Simon & Schuster, 2017).

Satter, David. "100 Years of Communism—and 100 Million Dead." WSJ.com. November 6, 2017, https://www.wsj.com/articles/100-years-of-communismand-100-million-dead-1510011810.

Scruton, Roger. *How to Be a Conservative* (New York: Bloomsbury Continuum, 2014).

Scruton. *Kant: A Very Short Introduction* (Oxford: Oxford University Press, 1982).

Shapiro, Ben. "Ben Shapiro DEBUNKS Viral 'Systemic Racism Explained' Video." YouTube Post. 17:49. June 10, 2020, https://www.youtube.com/watch?v=TBDfMQ27Asw.

Shapiro., *Bullies: How the Left's Culture of Fear and Intimidation Silences Americans* (Simon & Schuster, 2013).

Shapiro. "The Myth of the Tiny Radical Muslim Minority (Ben Shapiro)." YouTube Post. 6:17. January 30, 2020, https://www.youtube.com/watch?v=6L2Jilo3qmI.

Shellenberger, Michael. "Why Everything They Say About The Amazon, Including That It's 'The Lungs of The World,' Is Wrong." Forbes.

com. August 26, 2019, https://www.forbes.com/sites/michaelshellen-berger/2019/08/26/why-everything-they-say-about-the-amazon-includ-ing-that-its-the-lungs-of-the-world-is-wrong/#3882e1a05bde.

Smith, Kyle. "Six Ways Thomas Piketty's 'Capital' Isn't Holding Up to Scrutiny." Forbes.com. May 1, 2014, https://www.forbes.com/sites/kyle-smith/2014/05/01/six-ways-thomas-pikettys-capital-isnt-holding-up-to-scrutiny/#3ccb4bcf380d.

Smith, Mark A. *Secular Faith: How Culture Has Trumped Religion in American Politics* (Chicago: University of Chicago Press, 2015).

Sneed, Tierney. "1 in 5? Data and the Debate about Campus Rape." USNews.com. December 16, 2014, https://www.usnews.com/news/articles/2014/12/16/1-in-5-data-and-the-debate-about-campus-rape.

Soave, Robby. "A Year Ago, The Media Mangled The Covington Catholic Story. What Happened Next Was Even Worse." Reason.com. January 21, 2020, https://reason.com/2020/01/21/covington-catholic-media-nick-sandmann-lincoln-memorial.

"Social Media: Is Trump Right About Anti-Conservative Bias? You Bet He is." Investors.com. September 21, 2018, https://www.investors.com/politics/editorials/social-media-trump-conservative-bias.

Somin, Ilya. "Remembering the Biggest Mass Murder in the History of the World." Washington Post.com. August 3, 2016, https://www.washingtonpost.com/news/volokh-conspiracy/wp/2016/08/03/giving-historys-greatest-mass-murderer-his-due.

Sowell, Thomas. *Discrimination and Disparities* (New York: Basic Books, 2018).

Sowell. *Economic Facts and Fallacies* (New York: Basic Books, 2008).

Sowell. *The Thomas Sowell Reader* (New York: Basic Books, 2011).

Taleb Nassim, Nicholas. *Antifragile: Things That Gain from Disorder* (New York: Random House, 2012).

TEDx Talks. "Is Modern Feminism starting to undermine itself? / Jess Butcher / TedxAstonUniversity." YouTube Post. 16:39. September 5, 2018, https://www.youtube.com/watch?v=lgIgytWyo_A.

"The First Amendment Says That the Government May Not 'Establish' Religion. What Does That Mean in a Public School?" FreedomForumInstitute.org. https://www.freedomforuminstitute.org/about/faq/the-first-amendment-says-that-the-government-may-not-establish-religion-what-does-that-mean-in-a-public-school (accessed February 29, 2020).

"The Ongoing Persecution of a Christian Baker." NationalReview. com. June 12, 2019, https://www.nationalreview.com/2019/06/masterpiece-cakeshops-jack-phillips-persecution.

Thinkers. "Jordan Peterson - Gender taught as a social construct in schools: What to do?" YouTube Post. 7:38. October 26, 2018, https://www.youtube.com/watch?v=KGCN7OHeoqk.

Thompson, Mel. *Understand Philosophy of Science* (New York: McGraw Hill, 2012).

Tobin, Jonathan. "What Real Incitement to Murder Looks Like." The Jewish News.com. July 12, 2020, https://thejewishnews.com/2019/08/16/what-real-incitement-to-murder-looks-like.

Tolkien, J.R.R. *The Return of the King* (Sydney: George Allen & Unwin, 1955).

Turek, Frank. *Stealing From God* (Colorado Springs, NavPress Publishing Group, 2015).

Turning Point USA. "Free Market Capitalism Improves People's Lives." YouTube Post. 3:02. July 6, 2020, https://www.youtube.com/watch?v=plm6XqTjbKw.

Unplugged Observer, The. "Jordan Peterson on Differences between Genders as Social Constructs." YouTube Post. 4:19. November 5, 2018, https://www.youtube.com/watch?v=IEq3HorOhfc.

Watson, Paul Joseph. "Los Angeles is a . . . " YouTube Post. 13:15. August 18, 2019, https://www.youtube.com/watch?v=HKCfu4UJQiQ.

White, Debbie. "UNDER ATTACK Christians are the most persecuted religious group on Earth, research reveals." TheSun. co. April 23, 2019, https://www.thesun.co.uk/news/8920568/christians-most-persecuted-religious-group-on-earth-pew-research.

WideWorldOfWisdom. "The Difference Between Liberal and Conservative." YouTube Post. 4:31. March 17, 2010, https://www.youtube.com/watch?v=5KHdhrNhh88.

Wigner, Eugene. "The Unreasonable Effectiveness of Mathematics in the Natural Sciences." *Communications in Pure and Applied Mathematics.* Volume 13 [1]. 1960, maths.ed.ac.uk.

Wing Sue, Derald, et al. "Racial Microaggressions in Everyday Life." *American Psychologist.* May-June 2007.

Wishon, Jennifer. "Global Persecution Report: 'Christians Are the Most Persecuted . . . and It's Accelerating." CBN.com. September 22, 2019, https://www1.cbn.com/cbnnews/politics/2019/april/global-persecution-report-christians-are-the-most-persecuted-and-its-accelerating.

Wolfson, Sam. "Looking for Mr T: the politicization of testosterone." TheGuardian.com. July 28, 2019, https://www.theguardian.com/global/2019/jul/28/looking-for-mr-t-the-politicisation-of-testosterone-and-toxic-masuclinity.

"World Population Review: Rape Statistics by Country 2020." WorldPopulationReview.com. https://worldpopulationreview.com/country-rankings/rape-statistics-by-country (accessed July 22, 2020).

ABOUT THE AUTHOR

Douglas Kruger is an international speaker and author. He has published nine books on issues of entrepreneurship, leadership, culture, wealth, and innovation. He is a member of Mensa—the High IQ Society—and holds a degree in philosophy from UNISA.

As a speaker, Douglas holds the CSP designation (Certified Speaking Professional) from the National Speakers Association, which is their highest earned accolade. In honor of excellence in his craft, his local professional body inducted him into their Speakers Hall of Fame in 2016.

Meet him at www.douglaskruger.com. For his video and article series on how to debunk politically correct ideas, visit www.breakingwoke.com.

SOCIAL JUSTICE

JUSTICE

GOES
TO

CHURCH

THE NEW LEFT IN MODERN
AMERICAN EVANGELICALISM

JON HARRIS

SOCIAL JUSTICE GOES TO CHURCH

In order to understand why so many evangelicals recently support left-leaning political causes, it is important to know a little history. In the 1970s, many campus radicals raised in Christian homes brought neo-Marxist ideas from college back to church with them. At first, figures like Jim Wallis, Ron Sider, and Richard Mouw made great gains for their progressive evangelical cause. But, after the defeat of Jimmy Carter, the religious right stole the headlines.

Today, a new crop of mainstream evangelicals has taken up the cause of the New Left whether they know it or not. As pro-life evangelicals rush to support movements like #BlackLivesMatter and #MeToo, it is important to realize they are walking in footprints already laid down. Their mission may be more successful, but it is not new. To understand where the evangelical social justice movement is heading, it is vital to understand the origins of the movement.

Social Justice Goes to Church: The New Left in Modern American Evangelicalism answers, from a historical perspective, the vital question, "Why are American evangelicals moving Left?"

For more information about

Douglas Kruger

and

Political Correctness Does More Harm Than Good

please visit:

www.douglaskruger.com
www.breakingwoke.com
www.facebook.com/DouglasKruger
@DouglasKruger

For more information about
AMBASSADOR INTERNATIONAL
please visit:

www.ambassador-international.com
@AmbassadorIntl
www.facebook.com/AmbassadorIntl

*If you enjoyed this book, please consider leaving us a review on
Amazon, Goodreads, or our website.*